I0794735

The silent morning

MANCHESTER 1824

Manchester University Press

Cultural History of Modern War

Series editors Ana Carden-Coyne, Peter Gatrell, Max Jones, Penny Summerfield and Bertrand Taithe

Already published

Julie Anderson *War, disability and rehabilitation in Britain: soul of a nation*

Rachel Duffett *The stomach for fighting: food and the soldiers of the First World War*

Christine E. Hallett *Containing trauma: nursing work in the First World War*

Jo Laycock *Imagining Armenia: Orientalism, ambiguity and intervention*

Chris Millington *From victory to Vichy: Veterans in inter-war France*

Juliette Pattinson *Behind enemy lines: gender, passing and the Special Operations Executive in the Second World War*

Chris Pearson *Mobilizing nature: The environmental history of war and militarization in Modern France*

Jeffrey S. Reznick *Healing the nation: soldiers and the culture of caregiving in Britain during the Great War*

Jeffrey S. Reznick *John Galsworthy and disabled soldiers of the Great War: with an illustrated selection of his writings*

Michael Roper *The secret battle: emotional survival in the Great War*

Penny Summerfield and Corinna Peniston-Bird *Contesting home defence: men, women and the Home Guard in the Second World War*

Wendy Ugolini *Experiencing war as the 'enemy other': Italian Scottish experience in World War II*

Colette Wilson *Paris and the Commune, 1871–78: the politics of forgetting*

Laura Ugolini *Civvies: Middle-class men on the English Home Front, 1914–18*

Centre for the Cultural History of War

http://www.arts.manchester.ac.uk/subjectareas/history/research/cchw/

The silent morning

Culture and memory after the Armistice

EDITED BY TRUDI TATE AND KATE KENNEDY

Manchester University Press

Published by Manchester University Press
Altrincham Street, Manchester M1 7JA, UK
www.manchesteruniversitypress.co.uk

British Library Cataloguing-in-Publication Data is available

Library of Congress Cataloging-in-Publication Data is available

ISBN 978 1 7849 9116 6 *paperback*

First published by Manchester University Press in hardback 2013

This edition first published 2015

Printed by Lightning Source

Thanks to John Pegum whose work on *Parade's End* and the Armistice was the original inspiration for this book

For Rosa, Theo and Emilia

Contents

List of illustrations

Notes on contributors

Adrian Barlow was formerly Director of Public Programmes and Lecturer in English at the University of Cambridge Institute of Continuing Education. Now President of the English Association, his publications include *The Great War in British Literature* (2000), *World and Time: Teaching Literature in Context* (2009) and *Extramural: Literature and Lifelong Learning* (2012).

Andrew Frayn teaches at the University of Manchester. He is currently completing a monograph, *Writing Disenchantment: British First World War Prose, 1914–1930*, and has published on Richard Aldington and Ford Madox Ford. He is secretary to the Ford Madox Ford Society and editor of the *New Canterbury Literary Society (Richard Aldington) Newsletter*.

Max Haberich completed his PhD at Clare Hall, University of Cambridge, working in the Department of German on Arthur Schnitzler's and Jakob Wassermann's sense of German-Jewish identity. He has articles on Schnitzler in the journals *Central Europe* (2012) and *Journal of Austrian Studies* (2013).

After a career in literary journalism, publishing and broadcasting, **Alison Hennegan** has returned to the academic world and is a Fellow of Trinity Hall, Cambridge. Recent publications include '"Fit for Heroes": Bliss, Britten and Requiems', *First World War Studies*, 2, 2 (2011) and 'A Sermon for Remembrance Sunday', *Theology* (November 2012).

Klaus Hofmann is a retired professor of English Literature at the Goethe University, Frankfurt. Recent publications include articles on literary aesthetics, Keats, Adorno, Döblin and Malthus.

Kate Kennedy has a PhD from Clare Hall, Cambridge and is a Research Fellow at Girton College, Cambridge. She works on the relationship between music and literature and has published articles on Ivor Gurney, A. E. Housman and Benjamin Britten. She has co-edited special issues of the *Ivor Gurney Journal* (2007) and *First World War Studies* (2011) on music and literature of the First World War. She is currently completing a biography of Ivor Gurney.

John Pegum wrote his PhD thesis at the University of Cambridge on the associations between the geography of the Western Front and the identity of the soldier during and after the First World War. He is now Senior Product Manager for Literature and the Arts at ProQuest where he is responsible for a portfolio of online resources including *Literature Online* (LION).

Jane Potter is Senior Lecturer in Publishing at the Oxford International Centre for Publishing Studies, Oxford Brookes University. Her publications include *Boys in Khaki, Girls in Print: Women's Literary Responses to the Great War 1914–1918* (2005), an edition of the First World War novel *Good Old Anna* by Marie Belloc Lowndes (2011) and *Three Poets of the First World War: Ivor Gurney, Isaac Rosenberg and Wilfred Owen* with Jon Stallworthy (2011). Her current project, with Carol Acton, is on trauma and resilience in medical personnel working in war zones.

Claudia Siebrecht is Lecturer in Modern European History at the University of Sussex. She works on the cultural history of war and her first book is *The Aesthetics of Loss: German Women's Art of the First World War* (2013).

After a career teaching in secondary schools, **George Simmers** wrote a PhD thesis at Oxford Brookes University on the prose literature of the First World War. Since 2006 his blog, *Great War Fiction*, has commented on many aspects of the war and its legacy. He has published papers on Kipling, Bennett, Eliot and others, and a monograph on 'Honeysuckle Cottage', a story by P. G. Wodehouse. He is currently working on *Great War Fictions*, a survey of writing about the First World War from 1914 to the present.

Trudi Tate is a Fellow of Clare Hall and an Affiliated Lecturer in the Faculty of English, Cambridge. Her books include *Modernism, History* *and the First World War* (1998, rpt 2013), *Women's Fiction and the Great War* (1997; edited with Suzanne Raitt), and an edition of Ruby M. Ayres' novel, *Richard Chatterton, V.C.* (2011), as well as essays on the Charge of the Light Brigade and on Australian, American and Vietnamese memoirs of the American/Viet Nam War. She has co-edited special issues of the *Ivor Gurney Journal* (2007) and *First World War Studies* (2011) on music and literature of the First World War.

Peter Tregear is Professor and Head of the Australian National University School of Music in Canberra. He has published widely on music in the Weimar republic and Australian music history, and has conducted numerous first performances and modern revivals of this repertoire. A study of Ernst Krenek's operas from the 1920s (*Ernst Krenek and the Politics of Musical Style*) is forthcoming from Scarecrow Press.

Michael Walsh is Associate Chair (Research) at the School of Art, Design and Media at Nanyang Technological University, Singapore. He has written several books on C. R. W. Nevinson, including *This Cult of Violence* (2002). He has edited several books investigating the relationship between Modernism and the First World War, the most recent being *London, Modernism and 1914* (2010). He is currently working on a monograph of Eric Bogle's songs/poems.

Alexander Watson held a Marie Curie Intra-European Fellowship at Warsaw University, Poland. He completed his doctorate at Oxford University in 2005 and then held Research and British Academy Postdoctoral Fellowships at Clare Hall, University of Cambridge. His first book, *Enduring the Great War: Combat, Morale and Collapse in the German and British Armies, 1914–1918* (2008), was awarded the Institute of Contemporary History and Wiener Library's Fraenkel Prize. He is now a Lecturer in History at Goldsmiths University of London.

Introduction: 'This grave day'

Trudi Tate and Kate Kennedy

> The dead[,] that died for England's honour only,
> Had not been pleased on this grave day to know –
> (Lying in mingled graves or in sombre lonely)
> That crowds would dare stand for honour.[1]

On 11 November 1918, at precisely 11 a.m. British time – 12 noon German time – the infernal noise of the First World War came to an abrupt end. Almost everywhere in the war zones, the machinery of warfare stopped at the agreed moment. Those present found the experience eerie. The greatest war in history ended not with a bang, nor a whimper, but with the most profound sound of all: silence. And after that silence – what?

The essays in this book revisit the end of the First World War to ask how that moment of silence was to echo into the following decades. The Armistice of 1918 brought hopes for a better future, as well as sadness, disappointment and rage. Many people in all the combatant nations asked hard questions about the purpose of the war. In particular, they wondered whether the effort and the suffering had been worth it. These questions are explored in complex and nuanced ways in the literature and art of the period.

This book builds upon the pioneering research of military and social historians such as Hugh Cecil and Peter Liddle, eds, *At the Eleventh Hour*, Adrian Gregory, *The Silence of Memory*, Jason Crouthamel, *The Great War and German Memory*, and Richard Bessel, *Germany after the First World War*, which between them provide detailed accounts of the many ways the Armistice was experienced in Britain and Germany.[2]

We look at the history from a different angle, asking how British and German creative artists addressed, questioned and remembered the Armistice and its silence. Though there are many fine works of cultural history on the First World War,[3] no other book takes quite this kind of comparative look at the cultural effects of the war. This volume offers a genuinely interdisciplinary study, bringing together contributions from scholars in art history, music, literature and military history. It is unique in its comparison of the creative arts of both sides; assessing responses to the war in Britain, Germany and Austria. Together, the different chapters offer a rich diversity of methodological approaches, including archival research, historical analysis, literary and art criticism, musical analysis and memory studies. The chapters reconsider some well-known writers and artists (Virginia Woolf and Käthe Kollwitz, for example) to offer fresh readings of their works. These sit alongside a wealth of lesser-known material, such as the popular fiction of Philip Gibbs and Warwick Deeping and the music of classical composer Arthur Bliss. The wide-ranging discussions encompass such diverse subjects as infant care, sculpture, returned nurses, war cemeteries, Jewish identity, literary journals, soldiers' diaries and many other topics. Together they provide a new depth to our understanding of the cultural effects of the war and the Armistice. Finally, the book has a recuperative impulse, bringing to light rare and neglected materials, such as the letters of ordinary German and British soldiers, Alfred Döblin's Armistice novel, the little-known classical composers uncovered by Kate Kennedy and Peter Tregear, and the strange, anonymous and almost unknown books by a WAAC analysed by Alison Hennegan.

As literary historian Samuel Hynes has argued, the war itself was perceived, discussed and remembered through the creative arts.[4] In Hynes' suggestive phrase, the arts were an important place in which the war was *imagined*. And they are also a place in which a nation imagines itself in time of war. In this book, we ask how Britain and Germany *re-imagined* themselves and the state of peace after 1918. The discussions also range into Vienna, which occupies an important if uneasy place in European culture after 1918.

An armistice is not a declaration of peace, as the *Oxford English Dictionary* reminds us, but is merely a 'cessation from arms; a short truce', from the Latin *arma* and *stitium* – arms and stopping. The exchange of fire stopped on 11 November, but it took many months for the peace treaties to be agreed. The war was suspended; the guns were silent, but that silence did not truly signify peace. Indeed, some historians regard the Armistice of 1918 as merely a ceasefire in what turned out to be another Thirty Years' War, 1914–45.[5] In any case, the ending of the First World War surely shaped events in Europe and the wider world for a further century. Some of the problems of recent decades – in the Balkans and the Middle East, for example – have their deep roots in the First World War and its peace treaties.

For some people, the world after the war was so unsettled that they did not recognise it as being in a state of peace. For Europeans of his parents' generation, writes Eric Hobsbawm (born 1917), '"Peace" meant "before 1914": after that came something that no longer deserved the name'.[6] Similar attitudes can be found among British people of the generation of Virginia and Leonard Woolf (born 1882 and 1880). The world war had ended – or was in a state of suspension – but conflicts continued in Turkey, Greece, Iraq, Russia, Poland, Lithuania, Ireland and elsewhere, some with serious long-term implications.[7]

The Armistice, the silence, and the peace which followed were complex periods in our history which we do not fully understand even now, a century afterwards. At the time, as C. E. Montague remarks in *Disenchantment* (1922), both workers and writers expressed the point 'beyond any doubt that they don't think all is well with the world'.[8] Many people struggled with the problem of understanding how war on this scale had ever come about, and what sort of world was emerging out of it. As peace came, there was a strong sense that too little had been learned from the horror of the war; that the war had produced an inadequate, even perverted, state of peace. British poet Eleanor Farjeon, for example, opens her 1918 poem with Peace declaring: 'I am as awful as my brother War':

> I am awful as my brother War,
> I am the sudden silence after clamour.
> I am the face that shows the seamy scar
> When blood has lost its frenzy and its glamour.[9]

Farjeon imagines peace and war as siblings; strange twins. What does it mean to call them both 'awful'? The term has several quite different meanings. It can mean 'awe-inspiring', 'causing dread' and thus 'terrible, dreadful, appalling'. But it can also mean almost the opposite: 'worthy of, or commanding, profound respect'. An awful thing can be 'solemnly impressive, sublimely majestic' (*OED*). And the person witnessing such an event is also 'awful'; full of awe, and possibly full of terror, too. Farjeon's poem makes use of the entire complex of meanings. The poem is deliberately awkward, uncertain about the peace from the moment it begins.

Silence

Silence is the absence of speech or noise. It can be a general lack of sound, or it can refer to the absence of utterance upon a particular topic: 'muteness, reticence, taciturnity' (*OED*). In his essay 'The Storyteller' (1936), Walter Benjamin comments upon the decline in the human capacity for narrative in the modern world. We have lost the precious ability to 'exchange experiences', he argues. Why? Because experience itself was devalued by the war:

> With the [First] World War a process began to become apparent which has not halted since then. Was it not noticeable at the end of the war that men returned from the battlefield grown silent – not richer, but poorer in communicable experience?

Benjamin argues that the 'flood' of war books which appeared some ten years after the Armistice did not break this silence; on the contrary, they maintained it. The books speak of something other than 'communicable experience'; 'the experience that goes from mouth to mouth'.

> A generation [born in the late nineteenth century] that had gone to school on a horse-drawn street car now stood under the open sky in a countryside in which nothing remained unchanged but the clouds, and beneath these clouds, in a field of force of destructive torrents and explosions, was the tiny, fragile human body.[10]

For Benjamin, the extremity of the war diminishes the participants, negating their sense of their own lived experience and rendering them silent. This effect is still powerfully felt in the mid-1930s – more so than ever.

Like Benjamin, historian Adrian Gregory suggests that individual veterans might have felt silenced by the war, rendered mute by injury or trauma, by resentment or sadness – or simply unable to speak of certain things.[11] The essays in this book trace that sense of being silenced – as well as the opposite, feeling driven to speak out – in the decade or so after the Armistice.

In Britain, the silence of the 1918 Armistice was translated into the silence of Armistice Day (later Remembrance Day). As Adrian Gregory explains in *The Silence of Memory*, the communal silence on

11 November was an invented tradition which was taken up, somewhat unexpectedly but very widely, in 1919. On that first anniversary, the silence was preceded by loud noises: maroons, artillery gunfire or church bells.[12] After such clamour, the silence might seem all the more profound. The BBC, established in 1922, had by the late 1920s the task of conveying that silence to the whole nation, via the wireless. This paradox was referred to as 'Broadcasting the Silence'.[13]

The meanings of the official silence on Armistice Day were much contested in the newspapers of the time. Gregory notes that it was used in some quarters to press for a sense of national unity, to suppress dissent and to legitimise the government of the day. By contrast, the silence was also used to promote pacifist values, and to question the leadership which had taken the nation into war.[14]

In 1928 veteran and writer R. H. Mottram published a collection of essays to mark the first decade after the Armistice. (This is discussed in Jane Potter's chapter in this book.) H. E. Bates provided a preface, in which he noted that veterans had been quite reticent in the years since the war. But that silence has meaning, he argues. 'It has been a significant silence,' he writes, 'like those two brief minutes on Armistice Day, and just as definitely it has meant "never again".'[15] Bates and Mottram felt that something must be learned from the war, and that nations must be firm in resolving 'never again'. This widespread hope of genuinely ending war was, for many people, expressed most powerfully through a complete lack of expression; through silence. Alongside this view, many people spoke out for peace; they felt that the future required political actions: meetings, debates, writings. Silence was not enough. But the *idea* of silence, we suggest, framed cultural thinking about peace throughout the 1920s and 1930s.

Much has been written on the literature of the First World War.[16] Scholars are now paying closer attention to the history of publishing during and after the war, and to the journals in which the literary works were reviewed.[17] In Britain, important debates took place in magazines and journals, such as the *New Statesman*, the *Athenaeum*, the *Nation*, the *Times Literary Supplement*, the *Bookman*, the *Saturday Review*, *Life and Letters*, the *Egoist* and the *Little Review*.[18] Jane Potter's chapter focuses upon two key journals: the *Times Literary Supplement* (founded 1902) and the *Bookman* (founded 1891). She finds a rich vein of discussions about the Armistice, the League of Nations and other political issues, alongside lively debates over writings about the war. Potter shows us how war memoirs, war poetry, pacifist books, military history and other books about the war and the Armistice were received at the time of their publication, and she traces debates over key issues such as the League of Nations through the 1920s and 30s. By 1933, she points out, writers in the journals were asking despondently, 'Peace – for what?'[19]

A few days after the Armistice, on 16 November 1918, the *Economist* magazine's editorial expressed a sense of 'thanksgiving' at the end of the war. It regards the Armistice as 'victory' for the 'cause of liberty and justice'. But the tone of the article is sombre, not celebratory. The 'best men' have been killed, not just from Britain, but from all 'the greatest nations of the earth'.

> That such a war should have been the only means by which they could settle their differences is a sufficient proof that the civilisation under which we lived until 1914 was a mockery. Civilisation in anything like a true sense of the word has to be created.[20]

Many writers at the time felt that the war threw into question the very existence of civilisation. After the war, the task was not just to rebuild, but to create a true civilisation for the first time. The enormity of this task made people despair. Would the vast resources which had gone into the war be as generously provided for the peace? They were not.

This is another meaning of the silence after the war. In *The Waste Land* (1922), T. S. Eliot imagines civilisation in ruins, the rubble inert in a profound, arid silence. History itself seems rendered mute. For Eliot, the great human achievements are reduced to 'stony rubbish'; a 'heap of broken images'; 'empty cisterns and exhausted wells'.[21] More than this: Eliot, like the *Economist*, wonders whether the ruins of lost civilisations are actually the remnants of centuries of barbarism.

If the military fronts fell into an awkward silence on 11 November 1918, the Armistice was marked very differently in civilian zones. In many British cities, for example, the end of the war was greeted with a chaos of noise: guns, sirens, shouting, sometimes music. The public clocks which had been silenced for much of the war were set chiming. Some people made a show of relief or joy, drinking and dancing in the street.[22] Others found this kind of display unseemly, disrespectful towards the dead and the bereaved. For civilians, then, the end of the war was marked with both noisy joy and a quieter sense of sorrow. People felt uncertain how to mark the significance of the peace, and even more uncertain about what that peace would bring.

The Armistice and its afterlife

The uncertainty of Armistice Day is powerfully depicted in Ford Madox Ford's tetralogy *Parade's End* (1924–28). John Pegum's chapter explores how Ford uses representations of noise in his writing about the war experience of his taciturn central character, Tietjens. The noise of a barrage could be so great that the soldier could no longer hear it. But it permeated his whole being. Pegum shows how Ford's intense renderings of noise are played out through the war and into the silence of the peace. Volume 3 of the novel, *A Man Could Stand Up –* (1926), is set in London on 11 November 1918. As Pegum remarks, the moment of peace at 11 a.m. is understood, paradoxically, through 'the physicality and unnerving nature of noise'. Somehow, the central characters, Tietjens and Valentine, find calmness and silence in the midst of chaos. Ford describes how both noise and silence were felt on Armistice Day 1918, and hints at how these were to shape memories of the war in the years to follow.

In Britain, some veterans and civilians campaigned for better rights after the war. Others were more quiescent. Some were perhaps too tired and dispirited to protest or simply wanted a quiet life in the peace. Some people argued for the need for revolution, but it seems this was not a widespread ambition throughout Britain; British governments took what steps they could to dampen down any revolutionary spirit.[23] In Germany, by contrast, the Armistice was closely connected with moves towards revolution. As Klaus Hofmann points out in his chapter, revolts among German troops and workers helped to bring about the Armistice in the first place. Hofmann examines *Bürger und Soldaten 1918* (*Citizens and Soldiers 1918*), part I of Alfred Döblin's *November 1918: A German Revolution*. Döblin was a German army surgeon during the war and a shrewd witness to both the war and the peace. At the time of the Armistice, he was based in Alsace, an area on the border between Germany and France. This exceptional place was truly a 'place of exception' at the time of the Armistice. Döblin's satirical novel traces in close detail the few days of revolution in Alsace in November 1918.

The German revolutions are not much remembered now. People who had suffered in the war attempted to seize control of their own future, hoping to establish a very different kind of German society which would never again take its citizens into war. The revolutions failed, and Germany was soon to move in the opposite direction, into fascism and a second war, even more destructive than the first. Döblin helps us to imagine some of the hopes and the disappointments of the Armistice for

Germans, during a period when many people tried desperately to lay the foundations for a better society out of the ruins of the war.[24]

The Armistice was a time of deep frustration in Germany. Many German people felt that the war had ended prematurely and that the peace settlements were unjust. Civilians in Germany and central Europe suffered considerable hardship during the war, due to serious food shortages. These were caused partly by the war itself, and partly by Britain's economic blockade. The blockade continued for several months after the Armistice and left many civilians starving. Claudia Siebrecht's chapter, 'Sacrifice defeated', examines letters and other writings by German women near the end of the war. These women express courage in the face of hunger and show a willingness to continue to endure suffering for the sake of their homeland. For such women, an unjust peace would make a mockery of the suffering they had endured throughout the war.

After the war, those worst affected by hunger were civilians, especially women and children. Women artists such as Käthe Kollwitz, Martha Schrag, Lotte Prechner and Käte Lassen took up the subject of this hunger, exploring it with a profound sense of sadness. Here we see another kind of silence – the silence of civilian suffering, of children living in deprivation, of human needs crushed under the massive machinery of the war and its aftermath. Where some of the best-known German artists, such as Otto Dix and Georg Grosz, produced angry satiric pictures about the peace, the women artists discussed by Siebrecht express a quiet, intense sorrow.

Two chapters in this book look at another important part of the German-speaking world: Vienna. From 1919 Vienna was no longer the capital of an empire of some 50 million people, but the capital of a new nation-state, Austria (population 7 million). Vienna is well known as a cultural centre after the First World War; with its deep sense of cultural tradition, especially in music, it provided a home for experimental work in all the arts in the early twentieth century. After the First World War, the despondency felt all over Europe was particularly strong in Vienna. It was at once vibrant and gloomy, producing powerful cultural works yet also expressing deep concern, even despair, about the future.

Vienna was home to many intellectuals and artists after the war, including a number of important Jewish writers. Max Haberich's chapter looks at Arthur Schnitzler (1862–1931). In the 1890s Schnitzler was regarded as working at the forefront of the avant-garde, but after the Armistice he was criticised as conservative and accused of failing to engage properly with modernity. Haberich argues that Schnitzler was actually modernist in outlook and practice, yet he never defended himself against his critics. Why? Haberich discusses the rise of prejudice against Jewish people in Vienna in the years immediately after the First World War. He looks anew at this puzzling and much-discussed phenomenon, and maps it upon the complex figure of Schnitzler himself, who identified strongly as being at one and the same time German, Austrian and Jewish.

Like his contemporary Sigmund Freud (1856–1939), Schnitzler felt his work was misunderstood – not because it was difficult, but because there was a tendency towards deliberate, wilful misunderstanding of many works, especially works by Jews, during this period. Drawing upon unpublished letters and other writings, Haberich suggests that Schnitzler was to a great extent silenced by this prejudice, and it hindered his capacity to enter into public debate. When the Nazis came to power, much worse acts of silencing were to follow.

Peter Tregear's chapter takes a different view of Vienna, looking at the composer Ernst Krenek (1900–91). Krenek was too young to be conscripted until the very end of the war, and he did not see frontline service. After the Armistice, he became an avant-garde composer, drawing upon an eclectic range of sources from American jazz to the 12-tone music of Schoenberg. Like Schnitzler, though for different reasons, Krenek was not much appreciated in his native Vienna. In later life, he remarked that his work was so varied and uncertain that people found it confusing, and so ignored it. Tregear suggests that Krenek's ambiguity was a complex comment upon the war and the peace treaties. His work, too, was to some extent silenced, in the sense that it was exploring ideas that could not be heard in Vienna in the years after the Armistice.

If music in the German-speaking world was in a state of radical, unsettling change, music in Britain faced a different set of questions. Music had long been dominated by the great German composers, such as Bach, Mozart, Beethoven, Schubert, Brahms and Wagner. British composers and musicians looked to Germany, and very many went to study there, right up until the First World War.[25] During and after the war, there were moves by some people to promote 'British' (which sometimes seemed to mean 'English') music for British concerts. During the war, concerts were occasionally disrupted by a member of the audience protesting at the inclusion of 'German' music, on the grounds that it was disrespectful towards the British dead.[26] Others took the opposite view: music was international and should not be claimed by any nation, nor should it be put to the service of nationalism or war.[27]

Kate Kennedy's chapter looks at the British composer and veteran

Arthur Bliss, who was less interested in questions of 'national' music than in questions of bereavement and mourning after the war. These were at once deeply personal and widely communal, crossing all national boundaries. In his monumental work, *Morning Heroes* (1930), Bliss draws upon an eclectic range of war writings from different places and historical periods. He seems to make a point of not being narrowly focused upon British experience, but rather uses the experience of 1914–18 to reflect upon the whole history of warfare since ancient times. Kennedy reminds us that ceremonies of remembrance usually included music. Alongside the silence, the sound of voices and instruments brings a further complex of meanings into the communal act of mourning and remembering.

Turning from music to literary responses to the Armistice, Andrew Frayn's chapter looks closely at the post-war writings of C. E. Montague (1867–1928), a journalist who served in the war in his late 40s. Montague's book *Disenchantment* (1922) was one of the first to make explicit the feelings of disappointment and loss which were to be expressed in so many later memoirs about the war. Montague makes use of metaphors of silence in his writings, but, Frayn argues, he refuses to find consolation in silence. For Montague, 'silence is not an appropriate form of commemoration for a brutal and noisy war, writing in a peace which proved to be anything but'. *Disenchantment* helped to break the veterans' silence after the Armistice, though veterans continued to feel that their voices were not properly heard in the years which followed.

Literary historians used to assume that very little was published about the war until the war books 'boom' of the late 1920s and early 1930s. Now, however, we realise that all kinds of war writings appeared in the decade after the Armistice. George Simmers has argued that 'To call the twenties "a decade of literary silence" on the subject [of the war] is the imposition of another kind of silence, by critics who do not want to complicate their own picture of the War.'[28] Simmers' chapter in this book examines three kinds of post-Armistice popular fiction: Philip Gibbs' semi-documentaries, Warwick Deeping's 'heated melodramas' in which the protagonists try to cope with the war's legacies of violence, and the implausibly exciting thrillers of 'Sapper'. All three strands of popular writing are grappling, in their way, with the world after the war; they are both trying to engage with that world and struggling to get away from it. These books find themselves looking back with some nostalgia towards the war; at least then there was a sense of purpose. 'During the war,' Simmers argues, 'both soldiers and civilians had looked forward avidly to the coming of peace. After the Armistice, the future looked considerably less inviting.'

Alison Hennegan's chapter, 'Fighting the peace', turns our attention from popular fiction by (and to some extent, written for) men to consider instead some responses by women writers to the Armistice. Hennegan examines a little-known trilogy by Helen Zenna Smith: *Women of the Aftermath, Shadow Women* and *Luxury Ladies* (1931–33). These novels explore the distress felt by British women who had served as nurses and had seen so much suffering during the war. Smith uses Armistice Day ceremonies in her novels to show how the war generation came to feel excluded and worthless in the peace. Hennegan also looks at two almost completely unknown anonymous works, *W.A.A.C: The Woman's Story of the War* and *W.A.A.C. Demobilized* (both 1930). These are puzzling, fascinating works, published as autobiographies (though there is no way to be certain whether they are genuine). They merge into many other genres, some quite disreputable. Whatever else they might be, Hennegan suggests, these books are part of an effort 'to identify and map emerging, and sometimes contradictory, mythologies of what it might mean to be a young-ish middle-class Englishwoman attempting to make sense of and survive a world irreversibly changed by the First World War'.

Much has been made of gender in the experience of the First World War, but, as Hennegan points out, 'The ties which bind those who served in the war and separate them from those who did not may sometimes transcend gender.' Disillusion, too, is not necessarily gendered. That said, young women who lost a beloved husband or fiancé in the war might never find another partner, or might remarry much later in life. Many such women missed the opportunity to have a family. This loss is rarely spoken, yet, as Hennegan notes, 'the sense of those children who will now never be born to dead men [or their bereaved women] hangs over the period'.

Alongside this almost silent sense of loss was a well-articulated concern about the infants who were born during and shortly after the First World War. Trudi Tate's chapter, 'King Baby', explores the ways in which babies were perceived in Britain in the latter years of the war and into the peace. During the war, existing campaigns to improve infant health were intensified. In fact, higher numbers of babies survived during the war than in previous decades,[29] but infant mortality was still regarded as a serious issue requiring urgent action. Tate traces the practical measures taken to 'Save the Babies' and also looks at the fantasy investments in the tiny new citizens born towards the end of the war. These matters are explored in the writings of Katherine Mansfield, Elizabeth Bowen and Virginia Woolf as well as in the newspapers and medical writings of the day. Tate examines the theories of Truby King, a prominent voice in infant care around the time of the Armistice. King's rigid routines for all aspects of babies' lives could, at worst, leave them silenced,[30] even traumatised, by inadequate feeding and a lack of loving attention.

Turning to British visual art and the Armistice, Michael Walsh explores the ways in which paintings were used to commemorate the war and the peace. He asks, 'What role might art and artists have played in the processes of creating this imagined, yet culturally ingrained, long-term community of mourners?' His chapter explores 'some ethical, theoretical and practical considerations associated with the anticipation, and the creation, of memory in painting at the time of the Armistice in Britain'. He examines some of the debates within official art committees, and the hopes for exhibitions about war and peace. He looks at some of the dilemmas artists faced in trying to memorialise the war. Walsh goes on to think about what the First World War artworks mean today, and how they help us (or not) in our remembering. 'Now, as then,' remarks Walsh drily, 'we appreciate that the boundaries between informing and performing are porous indeed.'

Alexander Watson's chapter takes us from creative works in the public sphere to the private letters and diaries of serving British and German troops. Watson looks at the writings of 40 combatants serving at the time of the Armistice, asking whether they anticipated the end of the war, and, once it came, what thoughts they expressed about it in their private writings. It is a rare privilege to read soldiers' personal writings. Watson looks into this normally silent area of history to see what attitudes were expressed around November 1918. Were the troops on each side surprised by the end of the war? Did they regard the Armistice as a decisive conclusion? The soldiers' writings provide another angle from which we might think about the published works. Each body of writing was almost certainly not aware of the other (and most of the artistic works were created later than the letters and diaries). But read together, they give us a richly layered view of the Armistice, both at the moment it occurred, and in the ways it was remembered afterwards.

Finally, Adrian Barlow's chapter, 'Mixing memory and desire', looks at British and German military cemeteries on the Western Front. Even today, these are places of a particularly eerie kind of silence. During the war, soldiers killed were not usually repatriated, but were buried near their place of death. Many bodies were never identified, but still had to be interred with due respect. Barlow points out that both nations faced the problem of 'how to deal most appropriately with bodies that had no names, and names that had no bodies'. The war cemeteries contain huge numbers of bodies, and to this day have an important function as war memorials. In Langemark cemetery in Belgium, more than 44,000 German soldiers are buried. One mass grave holds nearly 25,000 bodies. 'Like all Great War cemeteries along the Western Front,' writes Barlow, 'it is a site where the desire to acknowledge the past is mixed with the impossibility of conceiving what happened here and what each of the 44,000 individuals interred within this massive enclosure actually endured.' Thousands of visitors still come to these sad places. One German cemetery includes a quotation from Albert Schweitzer: 'The soldiers' graves are the greatest preachers of peace.'

Out of this wealth of material – from the soldiers' private letters and diaries to published literature, visual art, newspapers and classical music – our contributors open out the meanings of the silence of November 1918, and the ways in which it was felt and heard in the decade which followed. Silence, writes Jay Winter, 'like memory and forgetting, has a life history'.[31] The chapters in this book give us a deeper understanding of the 'life history' of the Armistice of 1918, and its afterlife, too, which was to cast its ghostly shadow far into the twentieth century.

Notes

1 Ivor Gurney, 'Armistice Day', unpublished poem, probably composed 1923. There are three versions of this piece in the Gurney archive. These are the first lines of version G.44.193.

2 Hugh Cecil and Peter Liddle, eds, *At the Eleventh Hour: Reflections, Hopes and Anxieties at the Closing of the Great War, 1918* (Barnsley: Leo Cooper, 1998); Adrian Gregory, *The Silence of Memory: Armistice Day, 1919–1946* (Oxford: Berg, 1994); Jason Crouthamel, *The Great War and German Memory: Society, Politics and Psychological Trauma, 1914–1945* (Exeter: University of Exeter Press, 2009); and Richard Bessel, *Germany after the First World War* (Oxford: Clarendon Press, 1993). See further Peter Hart, *1918: A Very British Victory* (London: Weidenfeld and Nicolson, 2008); Bullitt Lowry, *Armistice 1918* (Kent, OH: Kent State University Press, 1996).

3 For example, Samuel Hynes, *A War Imagined: The First World War and English Culture* (London: Bodley Head, 1990); Uwe Schneider and Andreas Schumann, eds, *Krieg der Geister: Erster Weltkrieg und literarische Moderne* (Würzburg: Königshausen and Neumann, 2000); J. M. Winter, *Sites of Memory, Sites of Mourning: The Great War in European Cultural History* (Cambridge: Cambridge University Press, 1995); Glen Watkins, *Proof Through the Night: Music and the Great War* (Berkeley, CA: University of California Press, 2002); Christa Brüstle, Guido Heldt and Eckhard Weber,

eds, *Von Grenzen und Ländern, Zentren und Rändern: Der Erste Weltkrieg und die Verschiebungen in der musikalischen Geographie Europas* (Schliengen: Edition Argus, 2006); Claudia Siebrecht, *The Aesthetics of Loss: German Women's Art of the First World War* (Oxford: Oxford University Press, 2013); Richard Cork, *A Bitter Truth: Avant-Garde Art and the First World War* (New Haven, CT: Yale University Press, 1994); Grace Brockington, *Above the Battlefield: Modernism and the Peace Movement in Britain, 1900–1918* (New Haven, CT: Yale University Press, 2011).

4 Hynes, *A War Imagined.*

5 Eric Hobsbawm, *Age of Extremes: The Short Twentieth Century, 1914–1991* (London: Abacus, 2003 [1994]), 22.

6 Hobsbawm, *Age of Extremes*, 22.

7 Martin Gilbert, *The Routledge Atlas of the First World War*, 2nd edn (London: Routledge, 1994); Adrian Gregory, *The Silence of Memory* (Oxford: Berg, 1994), 12.

8 Workers expressed this feeling by voting for a strike, writers by publishing 'desolatory verses about ashes and dust in the *English Review*'. C. E. Montague, *Disenchantment* (London: Chatto and Windus, 1922), 2. See Andrew Frayn's chapter on Montague in this volume.

9 Eleanor Farjeon, 'Peace', in *Sonnets and Poems* (Oxford: Blackwell, 1918).

10 Walter Benjamin, 'The Storyteller: Reflections on the Works of Nikolai Leskov', in *Illuminations*, trans. Harry Zohn, ed. Hannah Arendt (New York: Schocken Books, 1969), 84. David Ferris, ed., *The Cambridge Companion to Walter Benjamin* (Cambridge: Cambridge University Press, 2004), xiii.

11 Gregory, *Silence*, ch. 2.

12 Gregory, *Silence*, 9–10, 11.

13 Gregory, *Silence*, 133–42; Rachel Cowgill, 'Canonising Remembrance: Music for Armistice Day at the BBC, 1922–27', *First World War Studies*, 2, 1 (2011), special issue, ed. Kate Kennedy and Trudi Tate, 75–107.

14 Gregory, *Silence*, 11–12, citing examples from the *Daily Express* and the *Daily Herald.*

15 H. E. Bates, preface to R. H. Mottram, *Ten Years Ago: Armistice and Other Memories, Forming a Pendant to 'The Spanish Farm Trilogy'* (London: Chatto and Windus, 1928), viii.

16 See, for example, Adrian Barlow, *The Great War in British Literature* (Cambridge: Cambridge University Press, 2000); Santanu Das, *Touch and Intimacy in First World War Literature* (Cambridge: Cambridge University Press, 2008); Dominic Hibberd and John Onions, *The Winter of the World: Poems of the Great War* (London: Constable, 2007); Hynes, *A War Imagined*; Sharon Ouditt, *Fighting Forces, Writing Women: Identity and Ideology in the First World War* (London: Routledge, 1993); George Parfitt, *Fiction of the First World War* (London: Faber and Faber, 1988); Jane Potter, *Boys in Khaki, Girls in Print: Women's Literary Responses to the Great War*

1914–1918 (Oxford: Oxford University Press, 2005); Suzanne Raitt and Trudi Tate, eds, *Women's Fiction and the Great War* (Oxford: Clarendon Press, 1997); Vincent Sherry, ed., *Cambridge Companion to the Literature of the First World War* (Cambridge: Cambridge University Press, 2005); Jon Stallworthy, *Anthem for Doomed Youth* (London: Constable, 2005); Trudi Tate, *Modernism, History and the First World War* (Manchester: Manchester University Press, 1998). The body of war writing which we study continues to grow and change.

17 Mary Hammond and Shafquat Towheed, eds, *Publishing in the First World War: Essays in Book History* (Basingstoke: Palgrave, 2007).

18 Suzanne Churchill and Adam McKible, eds, *Little Magazines and Modernism: New Approaches* (Aldershot: Ashgate, 2007); Peter Brooker and Andrew Thacker, eds, *The Oxford Critical and Cultural History of Modernist Magazines* (Oxford: Oxford University Press, 2009–). See further the Modernist Magazines Project at De Montfort University, directed by Brooker and Thacker.

19 Hugh Ross-Williamson, Leader, *Bookman* (1933), 225.

20 'And Now to Business', Editorial, *Economist* (16 November 1918), 674–5.

21 T. S. Eliot, *The Waste Land* (London: Faber and Faber, 1972 [1922]), lines 20, 22, 384.

22 For a detailed description of these kinds of noisy celebrations, see Stanley Weintraub, *A Stillness Heard Round the World: The End of the Great War, November 1918* (London: Allen and Unwin, 1986).

23 Brock Millman, *Managing Domestic Dissent in First World War Britain* (London: Frank Cass, 2000).

24 See further Klaus Hofmann, 'Revolution and Redemption: Alfred Döblin's *November 1918*', *Modern Language Review*, 103 (April 2008), 471–89.

25 Quite a number of these musicians got stuck in Germany once the war began and were eventually imprisoned, though not mistreated, in Ruhleben Camp near Berlin. See further Lewis Foreman, 'In Ruhleben Camp', *First World War Studies*, 2, 1 (2011), 27–40.

26 For discussions of German music in British concert programmes, see, for example, 'The "Promenades": British and German Music, the Choice of Works', *The Times* (21 August 1915), 9; 'Variety in Music: Promenade Concert Season, British Composers' Works', *The Times* (7 August 1915), 9. *The Times* reports a woman at a concert shouting out against the performance of German music: 'A "Parsifal" Concert: Woman's Protest Against German Music', *The Times* (22 April 1916), 7.

27 See, for example, James Mansell, 'Music and the Borders of Rationality: Discourses of Place in the Work of John Foulds', in Grace Brockington, ed., *Internationalism and the Arts in Britain and Europe at the Fin de Siecle* (Oxford: Peter Lang, 2009).

28 George Simmers, 'A Decade of Literary Silence?', 23 June 2010, *Great War*

Fiction blog. http://greatwarfiction.wordpress.com (accessed 26 February 2013).

29 Jay Winter, 'Aspects of the Impact of the First World War on Infant Mortality in Britain', *Journal of European Economic History*, 11, 3 (Winter 1982), 713–38.

30 If babies' needs are not met for long periods, some will give up hope completely and no longer cry when they are hungry.

31 Jay Winter, 'Thinking about Silence', in Efrat Ben-Ze'ev, Ruth Ginio and Jay Winter, eds, *Shadows of War: A Social History of Silence in the Twentieth Century* (Cambridge: Cambridge University Press, 2010), 5.

1

The parting of the ways: The Armistice, the silence and Ford Madox Ford's *Parade's End*

John Pegum

By 1925 Douglas Haig, Field Marshal and former commander-in-chief of the BEF, was, like the vast majority of those who had fought and survived the First World War, an ex-serviceman. Though his reputation would endure peaks and, mostly, troughs over the next several decades, in the ten years left to him following the end of the conflict he was generally thought of as 'the man who won the war'.[1] He used that reputation, in his unobtrusive way, to champion the causes and concerns of the ex-serviceman community. He established the Haig Fund in 1921, the same year that he retired from the army and also accepted the presidency of the newly formed British Legion.[2] Both the charity and the association were committed to supporting the welfare of the veteran; the former through sales of remembrance poppies (quickly adopted by the mourning British population), the latter by acting as a unified voice for veterans' concerns. Truly, Haig became as synonymous with the remembrance of the war as he had been hitherto with the running of it. And the ceremonies and civilities surrounding that remembrance were fractious indeed. The opposing impulses to celebrate and commemorate, so often represented by ex-servicemen and grieving civilians respectively, struggled for dominance on successive anniversaries of a day which became increasingly incapable of encompassing them both.

Following the raucous and feverish civilian celebrations of 11 November 1918, the tone of the day moved rapidly towards sobriety and reverence. It was unseemly to be festive on the anniversary of the war's end as the full cost, in every sense, was brought home to the nation. Thus the ceremonies and rituals that grew up around the day – the Cenotaph, the Silence, the Exhortation, the Last Post and the poppy – resonate with sentiments that have come to embody the popular feeling of that war: absence, sacrifice, grief, eternal remembrance and unspeakable loss. But many veterans felt forgotten on this day of remembrance when, as Peter Deane remarked in 1930, 'we neglect the survivors as though they didn't exist, and keep our pity for the dead who have no need of it'.[3] Charles Carrington thought of it more personally. He shunned the ceremonies at the Cenotaph, feeling that it was 'too much like attending one's own funeral'. Instead, he went to an annual reunion of army friends for 'no end of a party'.[4] This is just the sort of thing that the editor of the *Saturday Review* would object to. Writing shortly before the Armistice anniversary in 1924, he complains 'what ought to be a day of humble remembrance has been transformed into a day of forgetfulness, a day on which they [the veterans] drown their own selfish cares in the oblivion of rowdy and extravagant frivolity'. He goes on to ask 'Did they give their lives to make the world safe for saxophones?'[5] Forced alliteration aside, the editorial gives vent to a popular feeling. Celebration was an insult to both the sacrifice of the dead and the grief of the bereaved. Ex-servicemen were often in conflict with civilians on Armistice Day anniversaries, sometimes violently so, and the situation could not be permitted to escalate. It was into this climate and with that intention that Douglas Haig wrote to the papers shortly before Armistice Day 1925.

Notionally representing, or being particularly aware of the feelings of, the two groups, Haig believed the day should be made to fit them all. He urged the people of the British Empire to conceive of the anniversary as a 'day of remembrance'. In the morning there should be a thanksgiving service and a parade of veterans to the local war memorial. The afternoon should be filled with 'games suited to the climate' and the evening could be given over to rejoicing 'according to taste'.[6] Haig's proposition that all parties and sentiments could be accommodated on the anniversary seems naive. Indeed, by the following year, the *Scotsman* was reporting on gala dances and balls taking place in Haig's native Edinburgh for the 'Peace Anniversary' on 12 November 1926. This was 'in accordance with the recommendation that the observance of the anniversary on its solemn and festive sides should be separated'.[7] The veterans looking to celebrate were 'out of key with the new age' as the 'Feast-Day became a Fast-Day'.[8] But Haig wasn't alone in troubling over the ex-serviceman's place in the remembrance of the war. Ford Madox Ford, veteran and man of letters, spent much of the decade following the end of the war considering the Armistice, its impact and its opportunities.

Having been invalided from the Western Front in 1917 and then employed as an able administrator in Britain, Ford Madox Ford was at his regimental depot in Redcar, North Yorkshire, when the Armistice was declared. His Armistice Day was somewhat unusual for a soldier fortunate enough to find himself in a land untouched by the ravages of war. Rather than joining enthusiastically in the revels, Ford seems to have organised and catered for them:

> I remember Armistice Day very well because I was kept so busy with military duties that I was on my feet all day until I fell into bed stone sober, at 4 next morning. We barbecued whole regimental pigs for the civilian population in the market-place, we organized mixed banquets, concerts, heaven knows what.[9]

But, apart from being exceptionally tired, he also found himself 'inexpressibly sad'.[10] At the time he attributes that sadness to the 'breaking of [*sic*] after the old strain!' but over the following years he grows to more fully understand the depth of meaning of the day; the moment that a great many possibilities opened up and just as many snapped shut. In *Parade's End*, Ford famously describes the Armistice as a 'crack across the table of History'.[11] In all its seismic imagery it is wholly appropriate and justifiably oft-quoted. Less famously, Ford employs a qualifying phrase immediately before this where he describes the event as 'a parting of the ways' (*PE*, 510). This is gentler and more personal rather than societal but it is just as unalterable. The Armistice was, as we shall see, a moment when two distinct groups parted ways or, at least, were forced to acknowledge the distance that had come between them. The Armistice Day ceremonies of the 1920s paraded that distance and Ford sought to explain it and even redress it.

The four volumes that make up *Parade's End* were written and published in quick succession between 1924 and 1928 – the years running up to the tenth anniversary of the end of the war and preceding what has commonly come to be known as the 'boom' in books by ex-servicemen that sparked with the publication of the novels and memoirs of Remarque, Graves, Aldington, Sassoon, Blunden and dozens of less-literary veterans. The ceremony and sense of the Armistice was still being defined and the spirit of disenchantment, associated with those writers, had not yet become pervasive.[12] *Parade's End* engages with this societal and literary ambiguity and both have their locus in the Armistice Day scenes in the third book in the series, *A Man Could Stand Up* – (1926). The Armistice is, as Saunders points out, 'essential' to the form and structure of not just the third book, but the entire tetralogy.[13] That book, like the others, is as much about relations as it is about retrospection. It is about looking back at the parting of the ways from ten years on, but long before he started work on the series Ford had understood the principal feature of the new peace and found what would become the central theme of his series.

In a poem written shortly after the Armistice, entitled 'Peace', Ford ties together the end of the war with the end of his long-term affair and the freedom that this permits him and his new lover, Stella Bowen:

> The black and nearly noiseless, moving, sea:
> The immobile black houses of the town,
> Pressing us out towards the noiseless sea
> No sounds ...
> And, Thou of the Stars! Beneath the moving stars
> Warm yellow lights upon the moving sea ...
> Moving ...[14]

Bowen clearly offers Ford the warmth and stability that the unfathomable, rudderless relationship with Violet Hunt has hitherto blocked. But that rolling void is more precisely intended to depict the uncertainty thrust on him by the end of the war. The most resonant, threatening aspect of the sea is its noiselessness. Its silence is felt as an uncomfortable, pressing absence which is at odds with the peace and quiet that the title suggests. Ford was not alone in finding the new silence of the Armistice destabilising, but he explores the auditory qualities of the war and the peace and their terrors and freedoms in a more profound and personal way. This chapter will examine Ford's depictions of silences and sensibilities in *Parade's End* and look at how his characters respond to the noise of society and the noise of war. Through Ford's work, I will explore the changes to the experience of silence that were brought about by the Armistice and crafted over ensuing years. How does the Two Minutes' Silence come to be thought so appropriate and does Ford's view of the Armistice anniversary align him more with those wishing to celebrate or commemorate? Before looking at Ford's Armistice Day scenes and that moment when silence is reborn, it is important to understand the noise of war and how it beats the senses of the soldier.

All noise and no noise

From the very outset of the first book, *Some Do Not...* (1924), Christopher Tietjens, Ford's principal character, is defined by his silences. Macmaster, Tietjens' colleague and his opposite in affability and ambition, certainly believes that women in general, and Tietjens' beautiful but ruthless wife Sylvia in particular, are 'alarmed' by his taciturnity (*PE*, 19). The two men, when introduced by Ford, travel in a well-appointed and smooth-running train, a perfect metaphor of pre-war stability, to the country house of the Duchemins where Tietjens will meet Valentine Wannop, another guest, who will challenge his powers of communication. Over breakfast, as the Revd Duchemin rants and Macmaster ingratiates himself with Mrs Duchemin, Valentine and Tietjens take the opportunity of 'gazing at each other' (*PE*, 86). Initially unable to get a word in edgeways in the general conversation at the table, Ford bases their ensuing relationship on the inability of speech to truly communicate. As Calderaro points out, Ford uses the 'breakdown of language' and the disjointedness of his own narrative structure as a symbolic recreation of 'a fading world which had to establish new codes and new means of communication'.[15] The stability of society is clearly going to shatter in the impending war, but even Tietjens' own taciturnity is going to have to be broken down.

That taciturnity and struggle with language is nowhere more clearly seen, or rather heard, than in the episode in which Tietjens escorts Valentine to her home on the evening they spirit Gertie the suffragette away to a safe house in order to escape prosecution for her demonstration at the golf course. The two travel in a dog-cart along the country lanes around the Duchemins' property. A heavy mist has developed and it stands thickly between the hedgerows, entirely obscuring the road and the ditches. Jumping from the cart to navigate a safe route, Valentine 'completely disappeared into the silver' and Tietjens is suddenly alone (*PE*, 124). She calls out from the murk asking him to '"make a noise from time to time"' so that she can get her bearings (*PE*, 125). '"I wish you'd make some noise"' (*PE*, 126). But Tietjens is tongue-tied; asked to say anything, his statistical instinct prevents him. Their journey thus far had been peppered with sporadic conversation – 'about the safeness of the London girl [Gertie] from the police now; about the brickishness of the parson in taking her in' – but mostly they had travelled in silence (*PE*, 130). 'Not absolutely silent of course, but silentish!' (*PE*, 130). After she had leapt from the dog-cart, Tietjens had wanted to call out but it would have 'detracted from his stolidity' (*PE*, 125). He believes that what he considers excessive talk she will find a contravention of their relations. 'He had not known this young woman twenty-four hours, not to speak to, and already the convention existed between them that he must play stiff and cold, she warm and clinging' (*PE*, 129). But Valentine needs sound to orientate herself in the dark and invisible world of the mist. Tietjens finally manages to make noise but not by conversing. He whistles, sings (feeling 'like a fool'), recites German poetry and rattles the whip-stock, alarming the horse which shifts precariously (*PE*, 126). Whereas before, over breakfast, they satisfied themselves with passively gazing at one another, here, reliant wholly upon another sense, they struggle to form new and genuine connections. The relationship between the two is already cast in the convention of silence. In marked contrast to the gossiping and vindictive Mrs Duchemin and Sylvia, they seek the only remaining form of intimate communication. Silence becomes, according to Calderaro, a 'favourable, positive solution' to the noise and prattle of hurtful and dishonest speech.[16] When Tietjens finds himself at the Front, or rather just behind it, Ford is able to place this silent taciturn figure in the face of blasting and forceful noise.

The second book of the series, *No More Parades* (1925), is centred almost entirely in France and on Tietjens. It begins in a reinforcement depot under shell-fire as Tietjens and a fellow officer, the shell-shocked Captain McKechnie, go through the paperwork of a waiting draft. The explosions outside and all around the hut in which they sit reverberate with such force that their effect is not merely auditory but physical.

> An immense tea-tray, august, its voice filling the black circle of the horizon, thundered to the ground. Numerous pieces of sheet-iron said, 'Pack. Pack. Pack.' In a minute the clay floor of the hut shook, the drums of ears were pressed inwards, solid noise showered about the universe, enormous echoes pushed these men – to the right, to the left, or down towards the tables, and crackling like that of flames among vast underwood became the settled condition of the night. (*PE*, 291)

Later, when Tietjens is in temporary command of a battalion in the trenches, the sound of shelling becomes figuratively imagined as the dropping of 'an immense collection of fire-irons: all the fire-irons in the world' (*PE*, 610). At another time, the sound is like 'the rushing up of innumerable noises determined not to be late' (*PE*, 556). The sound seems to be the insane music of a lunatic orchestra. 'The performers threw about biscuit tins filled with horse-shoes; they emptied sacks of coal on cracked gongs, they threw down forty-storey iron houses' (*PE*, 559). But always, despite his varied attempts to describe the sound of explosions, Ford insists on the physical impact of those sounds. The reverberations, running through a trench, like 'black angels gone mad', are like solid noise which 'swept you off your feet … Swept your brain off its feet' (*PE*, 557). Silence was employed by Tietjens and Valentine as an appropriate means of overcoming the intolerable prattle and meaningless noise of society. But the sounds, the solid noise, of explosions cannot be defeated so passively.

Tietjens and McKechnie argue in the hut during the bombardment, yelling 'sharp, injurious, inaudible words' in an attempt to drown out the engulfing noise (*PE*, 293). Comfort comes, not from ignoring the crescendo of noise, but from attempting to defeat it by creating more noise. The extravagant display of power that the shelling represents leaves the two in an intolerably frail position. But by trying to 'out-shout the row you were safe … That was not sensible, but you got ease that way!' (*PE*, 305). When the shelling stops the ensuing silence is also felt physically. The sudden absence of noise leaves a vacuum which silence floods to fill. After being braced against the noise, the stillness is 'painful to ears in which the blood audibly coursed' (*PE*, 293). For Ford, absolute silence and absolute noise are eerily similar in experience and effect.

Shell-fire could be intense when an attack was being made or repulsed, but bizarrely it could be too intense to be heard. Sassoon's George Sherston learns of this odd effect of war from a wounded comrade in 1916. Durley, who has been wounded in the throat, which forces him to speak in a 'strained whisper', has the war 'very much on his mind'.[17] The vividness of his account of the battalion's engagement at Delville Wood, from which Sherston was absent, and his own muted voice reveal the inaudibility of the shelling. Waiting to go over the top, Durley remembers that the shells of the preliminary bombardment were 'screeching overhead'. But he does not recall the sound of the shells impacting, only their effect: 'the earth going up in front of the Wood, and twigs falling on my tin hat' (389). As the moment for the attack approached, the shelling intensified, but this too has a visual rather than an auditory impact. 'When it got near zero, the earth was going up continuously' (389). The intensity of the sound had dulled his senses and the explosions are not heard but felt. 'You couldn't hear the shells coming – simply felt the earth quake when they arrived' (389). It was, he says, a strangely cinematic effect of 'all noise and no noise' (390). Richard Blaker, too, in his novel *Medal Without Bar* (1930), dramatises this inaudibility of intense gunfire. His hero, the artillery officer Cartwright, stands in an observation post directing his battery's fire upon a village during the battle of the Somme. Though the shells pour into the shattered village, he can hear 'no distinguishable sound' from the place. The noise is so intense and uniform that it 'cancelled itself out into something not unlike silence'.[18]

It was an effect that Ford had experienced for himself. Writing shortly after the battle of the Somme had commenced, he noted that 'the noise of the bombardment is continuous – so continuous that one gets used to it, as one gets used to the noise in a train and [the] ear picks out the singing of the innumerable larks'.[19] That strikes one as slight bravado in light of his later insistence on the physical and psychological discomforts of the noise. But it does show the root of the similarities Ford forms between silence and noise, a most important connection to draw on later in *Parade's End* and depicted most obviously in Tietjens' recollection of a young shell-shocked soldier at the Front.

> The boy had lain, his face to the light of the lamp, on his pile of rugs – army blankets, that is to say … A very blond boy's face, contorted in the strong light, shrieking – positively shrieking obscenities at the flame. But with his eyes shut. And two minutes after that *strafe* had begun you could see his lips move, that was all. (*PE*, 557)

Like Tietjens and McKechnie, the soldier tries but fails in his attempt to out-shout the mad clamour of the barrage. The noise of war drowns all that can be thrown at it and, as is seen here, even itself.

Where does this leave Tietjens? Taciturn by nature, silently stung by the cruel vindictiveness of his wife, he had thought he had found a form and a companion in silence in Valentine who could bring comfort. But against the brute force of the war, he is all at sea, that strangely noiseless sea that could so easily be war as peace. In search of a safe harbour, a new means of finding a fixed point in the swirl of senses caused by war, Tietjens' mind alights on a word: 'Bemerton' (*PE*, 567). The trench in which he sat, in the silence before the storm of a German advance, had been filled incongruously by an air of the seventeenth century. A bugler, a cornet player in fact, auditioning for a part in the Divisional concert that he might not live to see, had sounded the 'exact, quiet' tune a little way down the Line (*PE*, 564). The German barrage, as Brigade has informed him, would commence in under a quarter of an hour and it is only in this liminal state, in the silence of anxious expectation of torrential noise, that Tietjens is able to discover the solution to his predicament.

'Bemerton, Bemerton, Bemerton' (*PE*, 567). The name of the parsonage held by George Herbert, the seventeenth-century poet, comes to Tietjens in a wave of remembrance and significant associations. Herbert being one of the few figures, living or dead, that Tietjens truly admires, he finds himself going one step further and actually puts himself in Herbert's place. 'He imagined himself standing up on a little hill, a lean contemplative parson, looking at the land sloping down to Salisbury spire' (*PE*, 567).

The vision, like the cornet's air, seems so out of place, particularly in light of the impending barrage, that Tietjens finds it almost preposterous. 'Imagine standing up on a hill! It was the unthinkable thing there!' (*PE*, 567). Unthinkable because, of course, in the denuded landscape of the Western Front, where opposing sides burrowed deep into the ground for protection and concealment, such a simple act as standing on a hill would prove lethal. Unaware that he has uttered this preposterous notion aloud, Tietjens finds that his idea has resonated deeply for his attentive and admiring sergeant. They have both felt that the condition of trench warfare has dislocated an aspect of their former or potential freedom. The vision of Herbert on a hill has reminded them of a way of being that they never knew they had longed for. '"You really mean to say, sir, that you think a man will be able to stand up on a bleedin' 'ill ..."' (*PE*, 570). For the sergeant from Lincolnshire, where hills are scarce, deliverance from the confinements of the Western Front comes through realising the promise of Herbert's elevated position. For Tietjens, it is a mystical hill as much as a material one. The sergeant's simple and heartfelt observation also helps Tietjens to realise what his own form of deliverance would be. 'He thought he suddenly understood. For the Lincolnshire sergeant-major the word Peace meant that a man could stand up on a hill. For him it meant someone to talk to' (*PE*, 607). The sergeant's hill is not just the opposite of the subterranean trenches but also of his pre-war native fen county. Tietjens similarly finds in the desire for talk a solution to the bombardment of war and the pre-war.

The noise of war was constant. It was never all quiet on the Western Front; not in incident and certainly not in terms of artillery, aerial or small-arms fire. By November 1918 the guns had rumbled on for over four years, reaching a crescendo at Ypres, on the Somme and at Verdun for months at a time. The preliminary bombardment for the battle of the Somme in 1916, and the blowing of the mines on the Messines Ridge in 1917, were of such magnitude that they could be heard, and even felt, in southern England. But the long months between campaigns saw only a slackening, not a cessation, of the continual artillery activity. Dawn and dusk in the Ypres salient were heralded by the routine half-hour German and Allied artillery strafes of the opposing lines. As techniques were developed, artillery and machine-guns could be targeted on roads and villages known to be used at night, ensuring that even in darkness there was no cover and certainly no quiet. The ever-presence of the guns made many combatants, like Robert Graves, conceive of the end of the war in terms of their silencing. 'We always thought of the end of the war as "when the guns stop".'[20] Then, on the morning of 11 November, in a second, the guns did stop. Before looking at how Ford writes that seismic moment of peace, I want to look at the moments that immediately preceded and succeeded the Armistice.

The world reborn

Days before the Armistice was actually announced, it was evident to many combatants that the war was nearing its end. A British machine-gun battalion at Aulnoye on the evening of 9 November held a 'one-franc sweepstakes about the exact time of the armistice'.[21] The nature of this new phase of open warfare, the antithesis of all those years of static trench fighting, was such that units were dispersed and their precise location hard to pinpoint. Nevertheless, news of the approaching cease-fire spread rapidly on the morning of the 11th, reaching most units before the appointed hour. Despite the prospect of peace, there was no slackening of the British advance, and hostilities continued right up to the appointed moment. Perhaps the most famous incident of this kind was Brigadier-General Freyburg's attack on the German-held village of Lessines. Later he wrote to Winston Churchill, reporting that his cavalry

> rushed [the German] outpost lines at the gallop at 5 minutes to eleven and charged into the village only 9 strong shooting up the streets with revolvers and chasing bosche round blocks of buildings. We captured a bridge head at 2 minutes to eleven and mopped up the village to the tune of 4 officers 102 other ranks and several machine guns.[22]

It was, in Freyburg's opinion, 'the most wonderful finish to my war'.[23] Private Orin Fye, an American gunner, recalls his officer reminding the unit that 'an 11:00 cease-fire meant that they were to fire until 11:00'.[24] For the artillery, who were left behind in the wake of the rapidly advancing infantry and cavalry, the moment of the Armistice could be marked in only one way.

The guns could not be permitted to peter out. Peace should not be allowed to spread slowly, but should be heralded by the crash of artillery fire. The significance of the guns falling silent was not lost on the artillerymen, and batteries, according to Frank Sibley, acted out a ceremony of noise in anticipation of the stillness. 'In one battery each man took a shell and waited in line for his turn to fire the gun.'[25] The officers of another battery all took hold of the firing lanyard of a single gun and fired the unit's last shot. Yet another battery, with a desire to include as many men as possible in that momentous event, attached long ropes to its guns' lanyards. 'Some two hundred men got hands on each rope, and one man, with a watch, went out forward.' On the stroke of 11 o'clock, the man dropped a handkerchief and the guns sounded in unison for the final time. 'Eight hundred men could claim to have fired that "last shot".'[26] What followed was silence. The Western Front was suddenly, not progressively, at peace. An American Signals unit, conscious that peace would not be seen but heard, made a recording of the moment of Armistice. The read-out from their six microphones makes that silence visible. The jagged lines clearly show that all guns are firing before 11 o'clock. After the hour, the lines are at rest and flat, but for two small depressions picked up by one microphone due to the exuberance of a soldier firing his pistol in celebration. Apart from the occasional excited American, the Western Front was silent. It was a silence that many found unnerving. Captain Evans of the Royal Welch Fusiliers recalls that 'the most remarkable feature of that day and night was the uncanny silence that prevailed'.[27] It is when he hears 'no rumbling of guns, no staccato of machine-guns' that the reality of this new peace is borne in upon him.[28] For the soldier on the Western Front, then, silence was the most startling aspect of the peace. By contrast, for the civilian in Britain, and for Ford's Valentine Wannop, the moment of peace meant jarring and confusing noise.

The third book in Ford's tetralogy, *A Man Could Stand Up* – (1926), whose London Armistice Day scenes act as the displaced centre, starts at the girls' school where Valentine is employed as a physical instructress. At the precise moment of the Armistice she has been called to the school telephone, drawn away from the playground where she had been holding the schoolgirls 'only just within the margin of control' (*PE*, 503). Shortly after she puts the receiver to her ear, plunging immediately into its incomprehensible chatter, the sound of the peace explodes. 'It [the telephone] was drowned then, for a long period in a sea of shrill girls' voices from the playground, in an ocean of factory-hooters' ululations, amongst innumerable explosions that trod upon one another's heels' (*PE*, 504). Ford's insistence on the physicality and unnerving nature of noise forms the base for this entire episode.

Valentine is bounded on one side by the 'voluminously echoing playground' and on the other by the 'long, tinny, nightjar's calls' of the telephone (*PE*, 503, 528). They are all 'intolerable noises', though they mean quite different things (*PE*, 503). The playground, where Valentine had left the girls standing 'electrically' in a 'moment of considerable suspense', was now riotous with the sounds of celebration (*PE*, 503). The telephone, vehicle of 'inscrutable Destiny', is, for Valentine, an instrument of sensory torture (*PE*, 503). It is 'incomprehensible', 'spitting vehemence', 'hissing' and 'bitter' (*PE*, 504). At length Valentine deciphers the disjointed and distorted voice on the end of the line as Mrs Duchemin, now Lady Macmaster, who has rung to inform her that Tietjens is returned from the Front and is in London, possibly mad, certainly abandoned. In a fit of unusual impetuosity, Valentine tears the receiver from the phone 'with incidental satisfaction', and thus severs the connection with pre-war prattle and, as the sounds from the playground dissipate also, with the raucousness of the peace celebrations. She is left alone in silence. 'She had missed the sound for which the ears of the world had waited for years, for a generation' (*PE*, 505). Thus Valentine's silent reception of the Armistice is carefully contrived to be so, in accordance with that of the troops at the Front. By locating Tietjens and Valentine, and their long-awaited reunion, in London but also removing them from the swirl of celebrations, Ford examines this moment of progression from war to peace and presents the possibilities he hopes will come from it.

Peace meant relief but, for Valentine's schoolgirls as for millions of others, it also meant release; a chance to throw off the oppressive burden of wartime sternness and self-restraint. The threat of bombers had caused the street lamps to be extinguished in the capital for the duration of the war, and so the peace was greeted with illumination as well as noise. The celebrating crowds could best be described as well-meaning rioters as they 'blew horns, waved flags, sang and danced'.[29] Some overturned trams, set fire to them and even chased those they thought to be conscientious objectors.[30] Troops of many nationalities mingled and were feted by the civilians. It was, as Ford writes, a sort of 'puerperal fever: the world was being reborn'.[31] As Saunders points out, the Armistice is 'an ending which is also a new beginning'.[32] Ford uses this historic moment knowing that it is the only phenomenon that would enable Tietjens and, indeed, Valentine to shake off their taciturnity and reserve.

Entering the square in which Tietjens' rooms are situated is, for Valentine, 'like being suddenly dead' (*PE*, 645). The square is like a backwater which the flowing tide of celebrating and cheering humanity ignore. The house itself is dark and silent and empty. Meixner suggests that the barrenness of the house mirrors post-war England, stripped, as it is, of its 'treasure, human and otherwise'.[33] Hynes believes it reflects Tietjens' emptied and bare state of mind.[34] I would argue, however, that Ford is forging a stronger relationship between this little corner of cloistered London and the barren and scarred battlefields of France than with the surging and celebrating crowd outside. The shouting of the crowd through which Valentine had jostled had become a 'solid and unvarying thing' (*PE*, 645). It becomes 'like life' and thus the house, which is by contrast 'so silent and so still', assumes the aspect of death (*PE*, 645). But in this new world, where meaning is shifting and realigning on new paths, the house and its owner will challenge that association. Valentine nearly collides with the bounding Tietjens as he hurries out of the house, but he ushers her in. It is nearly empty; in a great room upstairs, Valentine discovers Tietjens' field equipment: camp-bed, chair, table, washing-basin. All service-issue army equipment and set up incongruously 'as if set down in a field' in the middle of the room looking 'frugal' and 'glorious' (*PE*, 650–1). It is a further tug towards the Western Front and one that allows Ford to make Valentine take the final leap towards a new way of being and communicating.

Valentine follows a carefully constructed train of thought that shows that 'her mind so marches with' Tietjens' (*PE*, 651). On seeing the camp-bed and associated equipment, a perfectly formed tableau of life on the Western Front, she has already thought that 'all along that immense line men could stand up!' (*PE*, 651). So she has been brought into alignment with Tietjens and the fen-country sergeant major marvelling now at the new realities of the peacetime world. She then sees a stack of books, obviously brought back by Tietjens from the Front, and examines them in the hope that learning his recent reading habits might help her understand his present state of mind. They are a 'job lot', running 'along against the wall like an ill-arranged range of hills' (upon which a man can now stand), and Valentine expects that one of them, 'the tall one', will be a collection of George Herbert's poems (*PE*, 651). That expectation, and ensuing thought that '*he* [Tietjens] ought to be a Country Parson' though he 'never would be now' as they have chosen each other, brings Valentine and Tietjens together (*PE*, 651). But understanding what they have lost causes Valentine to recognise what they have gained and, most importantly, what she wants. 'Why did she take it that they were going to live together? She had no official knowledge that he wanted to. But *they* wanted to TALK. You can't talk unless you live together' (*PE*, 651). Just as Tietjens before in the trenches, Valentine has connected peace with dropping a burden and unstooping. The burden was that taciturnity they assumed as a defence from prattling chatter and its solution is talk. As if to confirm the prophecy that their minds 'so march' in union, Valentine then spies the handwritten phrase of the sergeant-major that started this whole sequence. '*A man could stand up on a bleedin' 'ill!*' (*PE*, 652). The line, and what could be considered heavy contrivance, causes Valentine's heart to jump in shock. To add even more gravitas to the phrase, it is written on the document informing Tietjens that his wife will not divorce him. But all that aside, Ford is clearly bringing the reader to a point; the importance of the Armistice lies not in its military victory, but in its personal freedom.

When Tietjens returns to the house he encounters Valentine on the staircase from the room in which she has just experienced this significant awakening. It was important that Tietjens was absent from his home in order for her to reach the same conclusion and when they meet again they slip into their familiar pattern, albeit with a subtle but significant change. 'They looked at each other for a long time. What had happened to their eyes? It was as if they had been bathed in soothing fluid: they could look the one at the other. It was no longer the one looking and the other averting the eyes, in alternation' (*PE*, 669). Silence again, simply drinking each other in, as they did at their first meeting, but now there is a greater understanding as a result of their shared but individual revelation. Again, like on the dog-cart in the mist, they find themselves in liminal space – between two floors, between one way of being and another. But now Valentine does not need to wish that Tietjens would call out and make some noise. She hears what is unsaid. 'She knew that he desired to say "I hold you in my arms. My lips are on your forehead. Your breasts are being hurt by my chest!"' (*PE*, 670). They have both found a new way of being, for themselves and each other, but initially, on Armistice night, they are still silent though now sure of each other.

When they ascend, back to the camp-room, it is soon filled with a small band of joyous soldiers, friends who had served with Tietjens and bring something of the spirit of jubilant London into this quiet backwater. McKechnie too has turned up, still shell-shocked and irascible, but the wartime strain between him and Tietjens has been dropped also. Surrounded even more by the spirit of the Front, Tietjens absents himself briefly to return in uniform. Ford brings both his protagonists back to the point at which they realised they wished to be together; Tietjens as soldier and surrounded by comrades from the trenches and Valentine back in the room in which she had joined her thinking with his only moments before. It's a thought felt by their companions too:

> An officer, yelling like an enraged Redskin, dealt him an immense blow behind the shoulder blades. He staggered, smiling into the centre of the

> room. An officer gently pushed her into the centre of the room. She was against him. Khaki encircled them. (*PE*, 673)

The Armistice has brought Tietjens' comrades to his house in the same way it has brought Valentine. Now these comrades will be the final catalyst, literally shoving the two together, that will confirm their union. 'The whole world round them was yelling and prancing round. They were the centre of unending roaring circles' (*PE*, 674). The two are surrounded by sound, not just of those raucous officers encircling them but of the wider circle of London. The world is in tumult, in the act of being reborn, and Valentine and Tietjens are in the eye, indeed *are* the eye of that storm. At the heart of Ford's Armistice scene is a stillness and a silence. Valentine and Tietjens embrace, 'frightened' and 'amazed'; they cling to each other as they set out on their post-war existence (*PE*, 674). But their silence, and Ford's statement on silence, is at odds with what the Armistice ceremony became. Valentine and Tietjens are sober but not mournful. They are hopeful, purposeful and intent on their future. For them, the Armistice is not the parting of the ways but a convergence.

The great silence

Exactly one year on from the Armistice, at 11 o'clock on 11 November 1919, the guns, maroons and sirens sounded momentarily throughout Britain. What followed was two minutes of complete and engulfing silence. King George V had requested this national pause as a fitting and suitable form of remembrance and communal commemoration. The notion was quickly seized upon and advertised through the press. The *Daily Express* announced four days before the anniversary of Armistice Day that all would 'gladly interrupt our business and pleasure, whatever it may be and unite in this simple service of Silence and Remembrance'.[35] The impact of 'The Silence', as it soon came to be called, was, as Gregory argues, 'enormous'. The public had 'universally responded' and many believed that it should become a 'regular act of commemoration, occurring annually'.[36] Gregory has attributed the success of the Silence to its multi-layered symbolic meaning. It is clearly reverent and spiritual, forming a silent prayer from the living to the lost, but it is more than that. Its particular resonance with the grieving nation came about due to its inherent contradiction. The Silence is both a communal and a personal ceremony. It enforces a 'public unity of action' demanding that all observe the cessation of activity and embrace in a moment of national unspoken prayer.[37] But it is also an intensely private event. Each individual is marooned in their own personal silence and with their own thoughts.

This is precisely where Ford places Valentine and Tietjens on that first Armistice night – in a moment of calmness in the centre of the wild, noisy celebration. They become the Two Minutes' Silence, not just in their abstraction from everyday life but also in the opportunity that it allows them to find newness. Ford writes that he 'never fail[s] to be deeply moved by the two minutes' silence of this day wherever I meet it'.[38] He too acknowledges that its particular profundity comes from its ability to isolate and unite. 'For once action is suspended universally so thought must come into play.'[39] Ford believes that the Two Minutes' Silence gives the opportunity for communal thought. But, as we have seen, many ex-servicemen found that the post-war Armistice services were out of step with their emotions on the day and the Silence, as keystone of the ritual of commemoration, was particularly contentious in their eyes.

If the national form of commemoration comes as a silence, and the general feeling is that 'nothing can be said that is sufficient to the subject', then any objection or testimony put forward by the ex-servicemen can be deemed as unpatriotic and insensitive.[40] The 'regrettable scene' in Liverpool on Armistice Day 1921 was reported in just these tones.[41] About 200 ex-servicemen, 'purporting to represent the unemployed of the city', forced their way through the crowd that was gathered for the Two Minutes' Silence at 11 o'clock and proceeded to 'demonstrat[e] their grievances'. The 'scandalous procedure lasted for nearly a minute', as the men shouted 'Anyone want a medal?' and 'What we need is food not prayers.' The crowd remained 'silently still' as mounted police 'compelled' the demonstrators to 'remain standing for the remainder of the two minutes'.[42] The original silence of the Armistice was manufactured by the troops at the Front who ushered in peace with a crescendo of noise. But the post-war Silence, though borrowing the ceremony, has supplanted the military meaning with an entirely civil one. This silence is not about martial or personal victory. It is about individual and communal loss.

But Ford hoped for much more from the Silence, and his depiction of it for Valentine and Tietjens reveals that. They are brought together by the Armistice, the soldier and the civilian, rather than being distanced by it. More than that, though, they have found the means by which they can ensure their future together. They have learned the necessity of talk. Up to this point talk meant chaotic noise, but at this moment when all meanings and symbols are in flux, or at least going through a process of redefinition, it has come to mean, for them, freedom from their former selves. Their silence, at the centre of the prancing and yelling, is a preparatory pause before their talk can begin, not an absence brought about by the futility of speech. In the context of the civilian and veterans' discord over the appropriate timbre of the Armistice anniversaries, Ford is showing a third way. The ceremony need not, as Haig also implied, be overly mournful or shamefully celebratory. For Ford, it can and should be as Valentine and Tietjens are: forward-looking and peaceful. The end of the war is, in Ford's words, 'the ending of our determination to kill', and so each anniversary must be seen as an opportunity to renew that vow to live in peace personally and nationally.[43]

This was the parting of the ways that Ford was referring to; a realisation that the war had been fought to defeat 'not Germans or even Germany [...] [but] an atrocious ideal'.[44] Tietjens and Valentine overcome their own atrocities and retire peacefully to the countryside and even slip from the main focus of the last book in the tetralogy. But the Two Minutes' Silence on Armistice Day was not based on such measured principles. Its strength is also its weakness. It is an inaudible memorial heard differently by every ear. Ford solves the dilemma of the Armistice and its meaning for Tietjens and Valentine alone. But it was a continuing conundrum for the nation until a second war overtook it and loaded it with even more misery and meaning.

Notes

1 Gordon Corrigan, *Mud, Blood and Poppycock* (London: Cassell, 2003), 204.
2 Adrian Gregory, *The Silence of Memory: Armistice Day 1919–1946* (Oxford: Berg, 1994), 71–2.
3 Peter Deane, 'The Tragedy of the Survivors', *Nation and Athenaeum*, 48 (1930), 103.
4 Charles Carrington, *Soldier from the Wars Returning* (London: Hutchinson, 1965), 258.
5 'Cenotaphs and Cabarets', *Saturday Review* (8 November 1924), 465.
6 Earl Haig, 'Message from Earl Haig', *Daily Express* (6 November 1925), 1.
7 'Armistice Festivities', *The Scotsman* (13 November 1926), 11.
8 Carrington, *Soldier*, 258.
9 Ford Madox Ford, 'Preparedness', in *War Prose*, ed. Max Saunders (Manchester: Carcanet, 1999), 72.
10 Max Saunders, *Ford Madox Ford: A Dual Life*, 2 vols (Oxford: Oxford University Press, 1996), vol. 2, 54.
11 Ford Madox Ford, *Parade's End* (Harmondsworth: Penguin, 1982

[1924–28]), 510. Subsequent references to this work are to this edition and are given in parentheses in the body of the text.

12 See further Andrew Frayn's chapter in this volume.

13 Saunders, *Ford*, vol. 2, 228.

14 Saunders, *Ford*, vol. 2, 54.

15 Michael A. Calderaro, *A Silent New World: Ford Madox Ford's Parade's End* (Bologna: Cooperativa Libraria Universitaria Editrice Bologna, 1993), 73–4.

16 Calderaro, *Silent New World*, 81.

17 Siegfried Sassoon, *The Complete Memoirs of George Sherston* (London: Faber and Faber, 1972 [1937]), 388. Subsequent references to this work are to this edition and are given in parentheses in the body of the text.

18 Richard Blaker, *Medal Without Bar* (London: Hodder and Stoughton, 1930), 179.

19 Ford Madox Ford, *Letters of Ford Madox Ford*, ed. Richard M. Ludwig (Princeton, NJ: Princeton University Press, 1965).

20 Robert Graves, *Goodbye to All That* (Harmondsworth: Penguin, 1960 [1929]), 210.

21 Stanley Weintraub, *A Stillness Heard Round the World: The End of the Great War, November 1918* (London: Allen and Unwin, 1986), 77.

22 Martin S. Gilbert, *Winston S. Churchill*, vol. 4, Companion Part I (London: Heinemann, 1977), 416–17.

23 Gilbert, *Churchill*, vol. 4, 416.

24 Weintraub, *Stillness*, 202.

25 Weintraub, *Stillness*, 202.

26 Weintraub, *Stillness*, 170.

27 Captain J. C. Dunn, *The War the Infantry Knew, 1914–1919: A Chronicle of Service in France and Belgium with the Second Battalion His Majesty's Twenty-Third Foot, The Royal Welch Fusiliers, Founded on Personal Records, Recollections and Reflections, Assembled, Edited and Partly Written by One of their Medical Officers* (London: Abacus, 1997 [1938]), 568.

28 Dunn, *War the Infantry Knew*, 568.

29 'Delight of Light: Radiant Joy at Night', *Daily Mail* (12 November 1918), 3.

30 A group of Australian soldiers reportedly overturned an omnibus and, taking the wooden floorboards from it, set fire to them at the base of Nelson's Column in Trafalgar Square.

31 Ford, 'Preparedness', *War Prose*, 72.

32 Saunders, *Ford*, vol. 2, 215.

33 John A. Meixner, *Ford Madox Ford's Novels: A Critical Study* (Minneapolis: University of Minnesota Press, 1962), 216.

34 Samuel Hynes, *A War Imagined: The First World War and English Culture* (London: Bodley Head, 1990), 433.

35 Editorial, *Daily Express* (7 November 1919), 1.

36 Gregory, *Silence*, 17.

37 Gregory, *Silence*, 18.
38 Ford, 'Preparedness', *War Prose*, 72.
39 Ford, 'Preparedness', *War Prose*, 72.
40 R. H. Mottram, *Through the Menin Gate* (London: Chatto and Windus, 1932), 204.
41 *Liverpool Weekly Post* (12 November 1921), 10.
42 All quotations here from *Liverpool Weekly Post* (12 November 1921), 10.
43 Ford, 'Preparedness', *War Prose*, 72.
44 Ford, Preparedness', *War Prose*, 72.

2

Alfred Döblin's *November 1918*: The Alsatian prelude

Klaus Hofmann

> 'That there has been war is not yet over.'
> 'Daß Krieg gewesen ist, ist nicht zu Ende.'[1]

In Germany and for Germans, the Armistice of 1918 is ineluctably tied to a failed revolution. On 24 October, with the end of the war and German defeat in sight, the German navy command issued a secret order for a suicidal engagement with the British fleet. On 29/30 October sailors of the German fleet anchored outside Wilhelmshaven refused to obey orders. The subsequent arrest of the sailors involved in the mutiny led to a solidarity action demanding their release, which turned into a sailors' revolt, spreading from Kiel to other ports in the Baltic and the North Sea. This quickly developed into a revolutionary movement in support of a *Räterepublik*, engendering *Arbeiter- und Soldatenräte* – workers' and soldiers' councils – all over Germany. The movement did not succeed. The prospect of a German soviet republic waned in the course of a brutal internal conflict. The Armistice in its turn did not end the war, but rather suspended and adjourned it. As a pause in an unsettled and unfinished conflict, it overruled the formal closure of the war at Versailles and persisted until September 1939, when it gave way to the last phase of what Eric Hobsbawm calls a thirty years' war.[2]

The most elaborate literary presentation of the interweaving of armistice and revolution is Alfred Döblin's *November 1918, eine deutsche Revolution*, a novel about the 1918 Armistice and, as the title indicates, 'a German revolution', which, as Döblin is at pains to point out, failed to be '*the* German Revolution'.[3] The novel, written before and during the Second World War, is motivated by the question of 'how it had all come about'[4] and takes a broad view on the Armistice leading up to a new war.[5]

Alfred Döblin was born on 10 August 1878 in Stettin, Pomerania, modern-day Szczecin in Poland. His parents, of Polish-Jewish origin, had migrated to Germany. His father, Max Döblin, ran a small tailoring business. When Alfred Döblin was ten years old, his father abandoned the family, eloping to New York with a young employee. His mother moved with her five children to Berlin, reduced to dependency on her well-to-do brother. Döblin managed to attend the *Gymnasium* and subsequently studied medicine in Berlin and Freiburg/Breisgau, his doctoral thesis being published as *Gedächtnisstörungen bei der Korsakoffschen Psychose (Memory Disorder in Korsakoff's Psychosis)*.[6] After internships in various hospitals, among them the mental institution Buch near Berlin, he practised, with wartime interruption, from 1911 to 1933 in the less affluent quarters of Berlin's east as a general practitioner specialising in neurological and internal diseases. During the First World War he served as an army surgeon in Lorraine and Alsace. In 1933, on the day after the Berlin Reichstag was set on fire,[7] he fled to Switzerland and a year later moved to France. He became a French citizen in 1936. At the beginning of the Second World War he worked for the propaganda branch of the French information ministry under Jean Giraudoux. After the German invasion in July 1940 he fled to Portugal, then moved to the United States, where he passed the war years in Los Angeles in economically precarious circumstances. A job in the 'story department' of MGM ended after one year. In Los Angeles he converted to Roman Catholicism. In 1945 he returned to France and then to Germany as the chief of the French military government's *Bureau des Lettres* in Baden-Baden and, after 1949, in Mainz. In 1947 he revisited Berlin. In 1953 he again moved to Paris but had to return, for health reasons, to Germany, where he died on 26 June 1957 in a sanatorium at Emmendingen near Freiburg.

Döblin started his literary career early in the century when he was in contact with Herwarth Walden's journal *Der Sturm*, in which an early novel, *Der Schwarze Vorhang* (*The Black Curtain*), was serialised in 1912. His first book, *Die Ermordung einer Butterblume und andere Erzählungen* (*The Murder of a Buttercup and other Stories*), appeared in 1913. His first published novel, *Die drei Sprünge des Wang-Lun. Chinesischer Roman* (*The Three Leaps of Wang-Lun. A Chinese Novel*), came out in 1916, though dated 1915. During and after the First World War he worked on *Wallenstein* (1920), a novel about the Thirty Years'

War. *Berlin Alexanderplatz. Die Geschichte von Franz Biberkopf* (*Berlin Alexanderplatz: The Story of Franz Biberkopf*) (1929) was Döblin's breakthrough to literary success. *Pardon wird nicht gegeben* (*Men without Mercy*), written in exile in France, came out in 1935. His last novel, *Hamlet oder Die lange Nacht nimmt ein Ende* (*Tales of a Long Night*), was published in 1956.

Late in 1937, with the twentieth anniversary of the 1918 Armistice approaching, Alfred Döblin, then living in exile in France, started to work on the novel that was eventually published much later, in 1991 by Walter Verlag, under the title *November 1918, eine deutsche Revolution. Erzählwerk in drei Teilen* (*November 1918. A German Revolution. A Narrative Work in Three Parts*).[8] The publication of the novel was complicated by war and post-war conditions. Part I, *Bürger und Soldaten 1918. Roman* (*Citizens and Soldiers 1918. A Novel*), came out in November 1939.[9] What was planned to be the first complete edition, *November 1918/Eine deutsche Revolution/Erzählwerk*,[10] had, for reasons of French military censorship, to be published without part I, which was reduced to a 'Vorspiel' to the first volume of part II, *Verratenes Volk* (1948). The second volume of part II, *Heimkehr der Fronttruppen*, appeared in 1949. Part III, *Karl und Rosa*, was published in 1950.

While viewing the 1918 Armistice and its concomitants in the wide context of a thirty years' war, Döblin focuses on the brief period between November 1918 and January 1919, the weeks during which a revolution seemed to be under way, while, in fact, politics in Germany were set on their fateful course, with the military reasserting itself in an unrevolutionised society. For that brief period, the Armistice seems to be a historical moment of promise, the promise of peace and of a new society, nationally and internationally. In these equivocal weeks the Armistice figures as an interstice, a standstill not just of arms, but of history itself, which may take a new direction, never to return to war. It is, in Hannah Arendt's words, 'the legendary hiatus between end and beginning, between a no-longer and a not-yet'.[11] The notion of the 'hiatus' corresponds to Walter Benjamin's concept of 'messianische Stillstellung' as propounded at the time of Döblin's writing in the seventeenth thesis of 'Über den Begriff der Geschichte':[12]

> The historical materialist approaches a historical object only where it confronts him as a monad. In this structure he recognises the sign of a messianic arrest of happening, or (to put it differently) a revolutionary chance in the fight for the oppressed past. He takes cognisance of it in order to blast a specific era out of the homogeneous course of history [...][13]

> Der historische Materialist geht an einen geschichtlichen Gegenstand einzig und allein da heran, wo er ihm als Monade entgegentritt. In dieser Struktur erkennt er das Zeichen einer messianischen Stillstellung des Geschehens, anders gesagt, einer revolutionären Chance im Kampfe für die unterdrückte Vergangenheit. Er nimmt sie wahr, um eine bestimmte Epoche aus dem homogenen Verlauf der Geschichte herauszusprengen [...][14]

'Messianische Stillstellung', the 'messianic arrest of happening', which disrupts 'the homogeneous course of history', is proximate to the concept of the *Ausnahmezustand*, to which Benjamin's eighth thesis alludes as 'the real state of emergency'. This concept was introduced into modern political theory by Carl Schmitt[15] and has gained a renewed topicality with Giorgio Agamben's *State of Exception.*[16] Agamben draws our attention to the Latin term *iustitium*, denoting the suspension of the law. *Armistitium/interstitium/iustitium*: this triad establishes a relationship between Döblin's novel and the discourse marked by the names of Schmitt, Benjamin and Agamben,[17] a relationship defined, however, by difference. The state of exception induced by the Armistice stands in contrast to the constitutional category central to that discourse. It is not brought about by the act of the sovereign, as Schmitt stipulates in the opening sentence of his *Political Theology*,[18] but by the breakdown of sovereignty. On the day after the Armistice the mayor of a little garrison town near Strassburg feels thrown back into the state of nature:

> 'We are on our own, the wire does not function, Strassburg, Berlin are silent. Paris is not yet connected. We live in the primal state. [...] What I mean is disorder.'
>
> 'Man ist allein, der Draht funktioniert nicht, Strassburg, Berlin schweigen, Paris ist noch nicht da. Wir leben im Urzustand. [...] Gemeint ist Unordnung.' (I, 37)

The apparent recurrence of the state of nature harbours the possibility of a revolutionary entry into a new social contract, establishing sovereignty on a new basis. *Arbeiter- und Soldatenräte* are constituted with this in mind. Rudiments of the old order, on the other hand, survive. In between an incipient and a residual authority there opens a space in which tyranny and licence are equally possible and liberties can be taken for as well as against liberty.

A compact version of this peculiar state of exception, which unfolds as a state of uncertainty wavering between revolution and restoration, is presented in the novel's first part, *Bürger und Soldaten 1918*. It focuses on the short period between 10 and 22 November, during which Alsace, Germany's contested western province – soon to be ceded to France – runs the full course from the breakdown of authority to the assertion of a new regime. For about ten days, until the French regiments make their entry and close the window of revolutionary opportunity, Alsace experiences a state of exception, of which that region is itself the spatial correspondent.[19]

Precariously situated between France and Germany, Alsace is an exceptional territory. Though entangled in conflicting nationalisms, it attempts to elude their demands. The Alsatians profess their Germanness by speaking German, a German dialect, that is, and thereby assert a non-French identity. At the same time they are averse to political affiliation with, let alone integration into, the German state. They try to avoid identification with either nation, yet hardly aspire to the sovereignty of a nation-state of their own, notwithstanding the brief existence of a 'Republic of Alsace-Lorraine' between 11 and 22 November 1918.[20] Their existence 'beyond' is suggested by their name: Alsatians are those who 'sit beyond', Alemannians or Swabians settling beyond the Rhine, that is, beyond what is thereby defined as the proper region of Alemannians or Swabians. The self-denying manoeuvre inherent in the region's and its people's name is supplemented by the Alsatians' habit of setting aside their ethnic name, Swabians, *Schwobe*, as a disparaging term for those on the other side of the Rhine, in fact for all Germans. Conferring their own name on those from whom they distance themselves, they are left without their ethnic name, merely defined as Alsatians, 'else sitters', assuming the existence of Rumpelstiltskin, who feels safe as long as nobody knows his name.[21]

Alsace had been part of the German kingdom and, as such, of the Holy Roman Empire ever since these entities were set up in the Middle Ages. After the Thirty Years' War (1618–48), however, victorious France usurped Austria's role of administering the greater part of Alsace. The Westphalian Peace Treaty (1648) established French sovereignty over most of Alsace. The annexation of Strassburg in 1681 completed the appropriation, which was legalised at the Peace of Rijswijk (1697). At the time of the French Revolution Alsatians widely identified as *citoyens* of the new Republic. Rouget de Lisle, an officer with the republican troops, presented his 'Chant de guerre pour l'armée du Rhin', known as the Marseillaise, on 26 April 1792 to Strassburg's mayor, Friedrich von Dietrich. Döblin's novel reminds us that 'Strassburg […] has given France her national anthem' (I, 333). The Alsatians' attachment to the new Republic was temporarily damaged by a frenzied policy of francisation during the *terreur*, when measures of ethnic cleansing, even the reduction of the German-speaking population by a quarter through the guillotine, were given serious consideration.[22] When Alsace was reclaimed in 1871 after the Franco-Prussian War, the new *Reich* conspicuously failed to achieve a genuine attachment. Alsace was not included as another sovereign German state into the federation of the *Reich* but was kept, together with parts of Lorraine, like a Prussian colony. It was only belatedly endowed with the status and constitution of a *Reichsland* in 1911. The rule of martial law during the war added to the Alsatians' disaffection, which could not be mended by last-minute constitutional changes towards full autonomy.[23] Döblin's novel takes the reader's knowledge of the historical background for granted and makes only scant reference to it. A chapter on Louis XIV's annexation of Strassburg in 1681 was cancelled by Döblin, who had reason to feel that it would endanger publication under French military censorship.[24]

Its peculiarity makes Alsace a unique site for the state of exception brought about by the Armistice. Here, the conflicting nationalisms of France and Germany may fold and vanish in a no-man's land, or, rather, in a land whose inhabitants evade an identification with either nation and show little desire, nor see a viable chance, to develop their local patriotism into an aspiration to a nation-state of their own.[25] The Alsatian revolutionaries' slogan, 'Not German, not French, not neutral. The red flag is the victor!',[26] points beyond the historical phase of nationalism which has run its course to the catastrophe of a world war and may now give way to a new era.

In a kaleidoscope of episodes, some of which will turn out to be the incipient phases of the novel's various plots, *Bürger und Soldaten 1918* presents, in a provincial setting, the diverging and conflicting possibilities and options offered by the Armistice, ranging from the creation of a new social and political order to the acceptance of, even a longing for, the takeover by the French. Döblin draws on personal experience. He spent the last year of the war – and the first week of the Armistice – as a doctor at the military hospital in Hagenau, a provincial town north of Strassburg. Many of the incidents and observations in *Bürger und Soldaten 1918* can be found in an early memoir, 'Revolutionstage im Elsaß'.[27]

The novel opens intriguingly on the day between the proclamation of the republic in Berlin on 9 November and the Armistice of 11 November, avoiding the historical significance of either date.[28] At dawn on 10 November, Frau Hegen, charwoman at the military hospital of an unnamed Alsatian garrison town, sets out on her daily round to collect horse manure for her vegetable garden before turning to her side-job of making breakfast for a blind colonel at his apartment and then proceeding to her work at the hospital – a routine which unobtrusively exhibits the military character of the place, horse droppings being its inconspicuous manifestation. Her attention is drawn to shouting in the schoolhouse which serves as the soldiers' quarters, a noise which the reader rather than the woman will take as an indication of an irregular insubordination. This first hint is supplemented by her employer's, the colonel's, decision to pack and leave and by the disorderly departure of soldiers, waving red bands, to the nearby airfield. Frau Hegen's husband, an invalid, spends the early morning by the kitchen table, saying to himself 'Well, it is 10 November', while reading the newspaper of 8 November for classified ads and grocery prices.

The novel then turns to an airman dying at the hospital and on this occasion the reader overhears the news that 'they are here, the sailors'.[29] In the adjacent room, in a conversation between two patients, Oberleutnant Becker and Leutnant Maus, a sudden, disconnected question gives another hint: 'You have been out and made enquiries. What about this revolt?' (I, 12). Bit by bit irregularities seep into the routine of the garrison town, its hospital, its private homes. The novel avoids looking directly at what is going on within the military in order to create an atmosphere of surmise and uncertainty. The *Oberstabsarzt*, the hospital's director, hears his wife complain that the orderly delegated as her errand boy has absconded with the shopping money. Telephone lines are blocked or calls not answered. Young soldiers with red armbands turn up at the hospital, presenting themselves to staff and patients: 'This is the garrison's soldiers' council. Anything to report?' In their exchange with Ziweck, a deserter and malingerer under observation at the hospital, they make the decisive pronouncement: 'Look. It is revolution. The war is over.'[30] It is the day before the Armistice.

The violence of the soldiers' revolt is brought home by the appearance of Leutnant von Heiberg at his girlfriend's parents' villa. He is on the run, having killed two soldiers who assaulted and killed their colonel. The incident exhibits the split within the military, the antagonism between regular soldiers and officers, which delineates the opposition of revolution and reaction. For the time being, the revolutionaries prevail. The common soldier Bottrowski, who will later turn up among the Spartacists in Berlin, gives von Heiberg, his former superior, unaware of the latter's predicament, a piece of his mind:

> 'But now the war is over and you have lost the game. You, Heiberg. For you are part of them, like my daughter is part of me, and now we can do differently, and now it will be different.'
>
> 'Aber nu ist der Krieg aus und ihr habt verspielt. Ihr, Heiberg. Denn du gehörst dazu, wie meine Tochter zu mir gehört, und jetzt können wir anders, und jetzt wird es anders.' (I, 30)

Equally audible are the forebodings of the reactionaries' eventual revenge. Two senior officers, pressed into cooperation with the garrison's soldiers' council, are among the novel's early examples of what will become a murderous roll-back. One of them, a major, confides to the other, a general: 'We'll tear their heads off in return.'[31] Later in the novel, the two will, along with Leutnant von Heiberg, show up in Berlin, the general taking to a more placid occupation in the film industry,[32] while the major will be active in organising demoted officers.[33] Von Heiberg will end up with a *Freikorps* fighting against the Soviets in the Baltic.

Under chapter headings giving the date of each day between 10 and 13 November the novel moves through the first days of the Armistice. A carnivalesque surge of liberation traverses Alsace, its capital, Strassburg, as well as the little garrison town.[34] In vain do old and new authorities, the police and the soldiers' councils, attempt to stop the insubordination spreading among the military as well as the civilians. Bottrowski, for instance, sees himself in the position of a sovereign when he participates in the liberation of the local prison:

> 'I was there with my gun, on three sites. The wardens said, there are common criminals among them, thieves, assault and battery. I said: now it's amnesty. Every king has a right on his birthday to release inmates. We have as much of a right. Told them to shut up. Not a mouse stayed inside.'
>
> 'Ich war mit meiner Knarre an drei Stellen dabei. Die Gefängniswärter haben gesagt, es gibt gemeine Verbrecher dazwischen, Diebe, schwere Körperverletzung. Da hab' ich gesagt: jetzt ist Amnestie. Jeder König hat an seinem Geburtstag das Recht, Leute frei zu lassen. Soviel Recht haben wir auch. Und sie sollen das Maul halten. Ist keine Maus drin geblieben.' (I, 29)

A peculiar mass solidarity of everyone looking after themselves rules the day. Fräulein Köpp, a hat-maker, who in the turmoil has lost track of the father of the child she is carrying, sees a chance to find a better, namely richer, candidate for the role (I, 46–8). Herr Jund, a local plumber and fitter, is eager to take advantage of the situation and persuades his mistress, whose husband fought on the French side and is not yet back, to acquire a café cheaply from the expelled owner (I, 55–6). Walter Ziweck, the inmate of the hospital's arrest cell, gets hold of two guns and stages his personal version of a socialist revolution (I, 69–74). He forces his way into the house of his former employer, the local ironmonger, declares it confiscated and occupies it along with Barbara, the maidservant, whose solidarity and amorous attachment he quickly wins. He resolutely defends his expropriated property against the old order, the police, as well as against the new powers, the soldiers' council. However, he succumbs to the power of alcohol and is eventually returned to his cell in the hospital. Later on, at the evacuation of the hospital, he will be liberated, if not confiscated, at the instigation of Barbara, his new girlfriend, who wants to keep him as her spoil and to prevent his eviction to Germany: 'She was aggressive and insisted on the rights of revolution' (I, 93). He sustains his revolutionary posture: 'At night Ziweck climbed on the roof and raised the red flag.'[35]

Ziweck's assault on private property is the exception. Widespread, however, is the appropriating of public property, the looting of public, especially military, stores, linked to the *Reich*. In Strassburg the registrar of the *Intendantur* and his assistant, both Alsatians serving in the German army, decide to help themselves to pieces of furniture from their office, a table, a chair, an iron box, a stove, along with shovel and coal-scuttle (I, 113–14). People's common property, which the state held in trust, reverts to the people whose body disintegrates into so many private bodies. In the garrison town soldiers declare the magazines soldiers' property and decide to redistribute them among the population in order to prevent any resumption of military action. They throw the large stock of clothing and military gear out of their barracks' windows.

> With what relief did they throw down the stuff. For they knew what it was that figured here as underwear, spades, boots: material, gear for a new winter campaign. There sidled the shovels for the trenches and for the opening of their own graves. These coats were supposed to clothe new regiments to be shredded in them. Death, blood, roaring from all cannons. They flung them far away, out of the window, down to the greedy civilians. There they were in good hands. From there they would never come back.

> Mit welchem Erlösungsgefühl schütteten sie die Sachen herab. Denn sie wussten, was das war, was sich hier als Unterwäsche, Spaten, Stiefel ausgab: Material, Ausrüstung für einen neuen Winterfeldzug. Da flogen die Schaufeln, für die Schützengräben und um ihnen selbst das Grab zu öffnen. Mit diesen Mänteln sollten neue Regimenter eingekleidet werden.

> In ihnen sollten sie zerschossen werden. Tod, Blut, Kanonenkrachen aus allen Stücken. Sie schleuderten sie weit weg, von sich zum Fenster hinaus, herunter auf die gierigen Zivilisten. Da war es gut aufgehoben. Von da würde es nie wiederkommen. (I, 78)

Peasants from the countryside and the urban population crowd in front of the barracks to snatch what they can. Similarly, the hospital is gutted of everything useful, including the marble slabs from the operating theatre. Frau Hegen and many of the hospital's personnel help themselves to the hospital's large supplies of linen, towels, napkins, crockery, and food:

> She who, for a whole decade took punctual good care of the blind colonel and diligently collected horse manure in the street, sensitive to any disturbance of her personal order – what had happened to her! What a change at such a great age, a revolution in miniature.

> Sie, die pünktlich ein Jahrzehnt den blinden Hauptmann betreute und sorgsam auf der Straße Pferdemist sammelte, empfindlich gegen jede Störung ihrer Ordnung – was war mit ihr geschehen! Welche Verwandlung in so hohem Alter, eine Revolution im kleinen. (I, 133)

While she is out on the rampage, her husband at home is poring over old lists specifying copper and brass household items which, in 1915, were to be handed over to the authorities to support the war effort. Requisitioning of private property then corresponds nicely with the free dispensing of public property now (I, 88).

The revolution in Alsace exhausts itself in the old society divulging its ugly truth of being an agglomeration of egoisms, which were kept at bay by suppression and are now liberated into a brief spell of anarchy. This liberation accounts for the carnivalesque air which is avidly noted by Bakhtinian critics.[36] The disintegration of that society seems to result in a particularisation into self-seeking individuals, yet, in fact, it produces a disorder of conflicting forces and groups. The volume's title, *Bürger und Soldaten*, denotes two separate entities, which might translate into 'Alsatians and Germans' were it not for the fact that both the civilian population and the military split up into Alsatians and non-Alsatians. A large segment of the citizens of Alsace are *Reichsdeutsche* or *Altdeutsche*, 'Old Germans' – not so old, in fact. Most of them moved into Alsace after 1871, often as civil servants. Against them rather than a class enemy the Alsatians direct their wrath, as Bottrowski, the red activist, reports:

> 'Last Thursday they let go in town. Revolution, you may think. Not at all. Against us! Against the Germans. […] They did not dare touch us, but

they did attack civilians and businesses. Now a soldiers' council has been established over in Kehl and since the ninth we've got one here. Ever since, the Alsatians have been on their bums.'

> 'Da haben sie am vorigen Donnerstag in der Stadt losgelegt. Du denkst, Revolution? Nicht in die Tüte. Gegen uns! Gegen die Deutschen. [...] An uns haben sie sich nicht rangetraut, aber an Zivil und Geschäfte. Da hat sich denn nu drüben in Kehl ein Soldatenrat gebildet, und am Neunten hatten wir ihn auch. Da waren die Elsässer Neese.' (I, 28)

Repulsion and expulsion are the Old Germans' dire lot, though they may be reluctant to leave, like Heinz, the nephew of one of the garrison's departing officers (I, 120). He has sent his family over the Rhine, but stays, encouraged by his wife, hoping to keep or regain his living as a forester. Near the end of *Bürger und Soldaten* he writes a long letter to his wife, through which we learn about the entry of the French troops into Strassburg on Friday 22 November, and about his disgust at the sudden hostility of friends and neighbours.[37]

> The older boys sat on the smokestacks and the snotnoses, who had attended our schools and for whose education we had to contribute so and so much every year, clung to the bridge's railing, crowing: 'Vive la France! Sock it to the *Schwob*!' So great, Rike, is the perfidy of the people and we have to gather our hearts with all our might so that they don't break.

> Auf die Schornsteine setzten sich die großen Jungs, und diese Rotznasen, die in unsere Schulen gegangen waren und für deren Unterricht wir Jahr um Jahr soundso viel zuzahlen mußten, hingen an dem Brückengeländer und krähten: 'Vive la France! Gebbs dem Schwob!' So groß, Rike, ist die Untreue der Menschen, und wir müssen unser Herz gewaltig zusammenpacken, auf dass es nicht zerbricht. (I, 305)

Likewise the Protestant minister of the garrison town is bitter and disappointed at what he sees as the disloyalty of his former fold:

> Since early morning he had been wandering up and down the room. All morning the town had been in agitation, the dear old town, in which he had lived for fourteen years, preached, baptised, wedded, buried. His wife was in Stuttgart, his son in the east, and what will it be like now in the east, the Bolsheviks will be advancing and flooding our fatherland. O my poor Germany.

> Seit dem frühen Morgen wanderte er im Zimmer hin und her. Seit dem Morgen wogte es in der Stadt, in der lieben alten Stadt, in der er ganze fünfzehn Jahre gelebt, gepredigt, getauft, getraut, eingesegnet hatte. Seine Frau

> war in Stuttgart, der Sohn im Osten, und wie wird es jetzt im Osten sein, die Bolschewisten werden vordringen und unser Vaterland überschwemmen. O mein armes Deutschland. (I, 44)

In the novel – as in historical fact – the number of Alsatians professing their Germanness at this moment is insignificant, though it is respectfully represented by a central character, Hilde, the nurse who will follow the protagonist, Friedrich Becker, to Berlin; and, closer to home, by her father, the architectural supervisor of Strassburg cathedral, working for the *Dombauamt*. He is apprehensive of the French takeover:

> 'You know French, father.' 'To speak, yes, Hilde. But to think, no. And I don't have to think it. What I think and have thought is good. [...] I won't betray my life. There is no reason for it.'

> 'Du kannst Französisch, Vater.' 'Sprechen, Hilde. Aber denken, nein. Ich habe auch nicht nötig, es zu denken. Was ich denke und gedacht habe, ist gut. [...] Ich verrate mein Leben nicht. Ich habe keinen Grund dazu.' (I, 127)

In Anton Erbe, owner of a small hotel in Strassburg, we meet a victim of Prussian rule in the Alsace. He has recently been liberated from prison where he had been detained without sentence since 1917, under suspicion of treason, because his wife, a Lotharingian from Nancy, had returned to her family over the border and kept up a correspondence with her husband (I, 116–19). The widow Anny Scharrel, an enigmatic lady of the cultivated upper class, is happy to be rid of the stultifying German dominance.[38] A *Justizrat*, an Alsatian in the German civil service, welcomes his son, who had defected to the French side and is now returning with the French troops. The mass of the population is depicted with humour and cynicism as a self-seeking, unprincipled rabble of opportunists ready to change colours. The ladies of the 'Patriotic Women's Association', the *vaterländische Frauenverein*, which had been founded in allegiance to the German *Vaterland*, are busy sewing tricolour flags and banners in preparation for the new, French era (I, 81). Here as elsewhere in the novel, Döblin's portrait of the Alsatians is satiric, even disparaging.

In the military, the tension between Alsatians and non-Alsatians takes a back seat to the antagonism between ranks and officers, which unites the common soldiers of both ethnic groups against their superiors. Since Alsatians stand out among the revolutionary activists, particularly after the arrival in Strassburg of 180 sailors from Wilhelmshaven claiming to represent the 16,000 Alsatians in the German navy,[39] the revolutionary front seems to be very much between Alsatian ranks and non-Alsatian officers; yet it is, in fact, as much a confrontation between Alsatian military personnel, mostly sailors, and Alsatian civilians. The latter, represented by Strassburg's social democrat mayor Jacques Peirotes,[40] keep their distance from the revolutionaries, even disowning their Alsatian compatriots who are suspected of being bought and sent by the Germans. Peirotes assesses the situation correctly when he warns Thomas, an Alsatian from Weißenburg and speaker for the sailors' council:

> 'Should you, friend Thomas, still go to the Kleberplatz and proclaim the Republic Alsace-Lorraine, then I can predict something [...] When you are in the square, there won't be a single socialist nor one Alsatian. Not a soul. Those present will be *Altdeutsche*. The Old Germans. Wilhelm's patriots. And the Alsatians will speak out aloud what they now say under their breath: That you are German envoys, that they sent you here with German money, from Berlin, so that they can go on keeping us under their whip.'

> 'Und wenn du etwa doch auf den Kleberplatz gehst, Freund Thomas, und da die elsaß-lothringische Republik ausrufst, so sage ich dir etwas voraus. [...] Wenn du auf dem Platz bist, kein Sozialist ist da und kein Elsässer! Nicht eine einzige Seele. Wer da ist, sind alles – Altdeutsche. Die Altdeutschen. Die Patrioten von Wilhelm. Und die Elsässer werden laut sagen, was sie schon jetzt munkeln: Ihr seid deutsche Abgesandte, man hat euch mit deutschem Geld hergeschickt, von Berlin, damit sie uns weiter unter ihrer Knute haben.' (I, 155)

Indeed, politically the confrontation between citizens and soldiers is very much one between Alsatian citizens and Alsatian sailors, deflecting attention from the opposition of German and Alsatian. Thomas, the prominent figure among the Alsatian sailors from Wilhelmshaven, and Bottrowski, the Prussian soldier from Berlin, are allied in their revolutionary cause and, eventually, in their disappointment at the failure of their revolutionary mission.[41] In the eyes of the civilian population the revolutionaries, Alsatian or not, are members of the German army and navy and as such representatives or instruments of the oppressors. The Alsatian soldiers and sailors call upon their fellow countrymen to recognise their oppressors along the lines of class struggle instead of national allegiance and to join the German revolution against the oppressor rather than identify that very revolution with German oppression, blind to the class enemy in French uniform. Proletarian solidarity is meant to win the day against nationalist antagonism, which plays into the hands of those who will send workers to the trenches in order to keep them from the barricades. A new Germany will supersede imperialism and nationalism and will encompass Alsace in a spirit of internationalism. The Alsatians, however, are aware that such encompassing internationalism will be a national embrace after all, Alsace ending up as an 'international republic within the national framework of Germany', as Maurice Barrès, chauvinist advocate of the French case, quips (I, 335). The revolutionaries' endeavour to tear Alsace away from French capitalism to German socialism is, in Alsatian eyes, indistinguishable from a German attempt to tear Alsace away from France. 'They wanted to save Alsace from the French.'[42] Indeed, the futility of the promise of a new Germany is palpable early on, when, on 11 November, the chairman of the newly constituted soldiers' council in Strassburg, Sergeant Rebholz, receives from Berlin the message that the new government under Ebert has asked the German supreme command to retain its function in the new republic. Rebholz shrewdly remarks: 'So, everything stays as it was, everything shall stay as it was.'[43] Under these circumstances even the Alsatian socialists, not to mention the non-socialists, see no reason to resist what is beyond their power anyway: the French takeover, implemented by the entry of French troops on 22 November. Thomas, the sailor, reports that Mayor Peirotes laughed at him: 'Our revolution ... consists in chasing away the Prussians, and this the French are taking care of.'[44] Bottrowski sums up:

> 'Without the French it would have worked out, I swear. But socialism can't compete with them, for a bourgeois. They want their flags and uniforms and officers and medals. Patriotism, "*Heil Dir im Siegerkranz*" or the Marseillaise. The capitalists are on top and are rubbing their hands.'
>
> 'Ohne die Franzosen wär's gegangen. Darauf schwör' ich. Aber mit denen kann der Sozialismus nicht konkurrieren, für einen Bürger. Die wollen doch ihre Fahnen und Uniformen und Offiziere und Orden. Patriotismus, "Heil dir im Siegerkranz" oder die Marseillaise. Die Kapitalisten sind obenauf und reiben sich die Hände.' (I, 215)

As far as the tension between civilians and the soldiers' councils loosens it is to the disadvantage and disgrace of the revolutionaries, who give in to the demands of law and order and soon find themselves reduced to policing the streets in collusion with bourgeois forces.

> And so they sat and lingered in the grand and gloomy court house, patrolled the street, together with others, as vigilantes, yes, the heroes of Wilhelmshaven turned vigilantes.

> Und so saßen und lungerten sie in dem großen düstern Landgerichtsgebäude herum, gingen Patrouille auf der Straße, gemeinsam mit andern, als Bürgerwehr, ja, die Helden von Wilhelmshaven als Bürgerwehr. (I, 210)

Alongside this collusion, which betrays the revolutionary mission of the soldiers' councils, civilians continue to mistrust the military in German uniforms, no matter how much both sides may profess socialism.[45] One episode provides a graphic illustration of this: In the garrison town, a local committee is constituted on the upper floor of the central café while in the square outside, from an improvised platform, the soldiers' council announces the deposition of the house of Hohenzollern, declares its good will for peace, offering liberty and fraternity to the Alsatian people.

> On the first floor of the café the windows have been opened, the mayor appears, two soldiers on the speakers' platform give a military salute, he bows.

> Im ersten Stock des Cafés haben sie die Fenster geöffnet, der Bürgermeister zeigt sich, auf dem Rednertisch stehen zwei Soldaten und grüßen militärisch herüber, er verneigt sich. (I, 39)

In both directions the response is reticent. Only the local chemist, carried away by a feeling of self-importance since he has found himself the focus of public attention as the sole owner of newspapers from Strassburg on the morning of the 11th, unwisely ventures into fraternising gestures towards the military socialists, though as a regional patriot rather than a socialist. He addresses the soldiers' council:

> 'Nobody dare lay hands upon us! The Alsatian people needs its freedom like any other people. We extend a brother's hand to you.'

> 'Möge sich keiner an uns vergreifen! Das elsässische Volk braucht seine Freiheit wie jedes andere Volk. Wir reichen euch die Brüderhand.' (I, 39)

He will have to pay for this. Denounced as a revolutionary, he will be beaten up in his shop soon after the German troops have left (II, 81).

Collusion between local initiatives and soldiers' councils is by no means the rule. Local militia vie with the military in bloody skirmishes for public authority:

> The first wounded soldiers arrived at the barracks and were immediately transferred to the hospital. […] These brawls flared up under very dispiriting circumstances, namely in dispute with the so-called militia, of which the soldiers complained bitterly.

> Da fuhren aber schon an der Kaserne vor, und wurden sogleich weiter ins Lazarett geleitet, die ersten verwundeten Soldaten. [...] Entstanden waren diese Schlägereien unter sehr entmutigenden Umständen, nämlich in Debatten mit der sogenannten Bürgerwehr, über die sich die Soldaten bitter beklagten. (I, 76)

A reluctance to commit themselves to a German revolution creeps into the soldiers' councils. When on 11 November the Strassburg soldiers' council is informed of a telegram from Ebert's new government in Berlin[46] saying that the imminent military occupation by the French will not prejudice the final status of Alsace-Lorraine but will leave open whether Alsace will be French, neutral or German, the message meets with a different reception from Alsatian and non-Alsatian soldiers. The chairman, Rebholz, would like the assembly to take a stand on the matter. An Alsatian urges that they proceed with the agenda; a German insists that 'Alsace is German and stays German.' To cover up the embarrassment the assembly resorts to shouting 'Es lebe die Weltrevolution' and regains a tenuous unity by chanting, in German, the *Internationale*, the socialist hymn that originated in the Paris Commune of 1871: 'Wacht auf, Verdammte dieser Erde' (I, 42). Alsatian disposition against revolution, particularly a German revolution, quickly saps the revolutionary vigour even of the Wilhelmshaven sailors.[47] By the Strassburg soldiers' council's last session the division between Alsatians and non-Alsatians has become conspicuous. Sergeant Rebholz, *altdeutsch* himself, presides over, or rather confronts, a taciturn, predominantly Alsatian assembly, and is ostracised in and by the court-room which has been the council's meeting-place:

> He looked in his own way, soliciting an answer, almost imploringly into the wide, previously crowded, now bleak chamber, which was changing back into a court-room with all its might and was pronouncing the verdict on Rebholz: that he who would have so much loved to stay had to wander.

> Er blickte auf seine Art lange und Antwort heischend, beinahe bittend in den großen, ehemals von Getümmel erfüllten, jetzt öden Saal, der sich schon kräftig wieder in einen Schwurgerichtssaal zurückverwandelte und auch das Urteil über Rebholz sprach: nämlich er, der so gerne bleiben wollte, müsste wandern. (I, 277–8)

The hope for international socialist solidarity, which maintains the sailors' morale and indeed corresponds to apprehensions on the side of the allies that the revolutionary sparks may spring over to French and British troops and civilians,[48] is treated in the novel with both sympathy and mockery. Rumours that the French soldiers, too, are in revolt and that the British navy are following the German sailors' example are echoed in the novel with sarcasm:

> Some soldiers shouted 'hurrah' and did not stop. […] The universal conciliation of nations could not fail to happen. And there it was. […] At last the crews in the British navy have seized power. […] They have hoisted the red flag.
>
> Hurra schrien einige Soldaten und hörten nicht auf […] die allgemeine Völkerversöhnung konnte nicht mehr lange ausbleiben, und da war sie schon. […] Endlich in der englischen Flotte haben die Mannschaften bereits die Macht an sich gerissen. […] Sie haben die rote Flagge gesetzt. (I, 67–8)

Similarly, the prospect of a revolutionary solidarity between the nations is satirised by the novel quoting the awkward prose of a newspaper article:

> 'At last, after a long, brutish labour […] the red flag reinstalls humanity as the universal watchword. Why should it not find resonance with the French soldier? Prussian militarism has vanished! The German nation has emerged from its chrysalis, it is the same fledgling bug of freedom as the French nation. In socialism we find the well of eternal youth. A new age has begun.'
>
> 'In der roten Fahne kommt nach langen tierischen Wehen […] endlich die Losung auf Menschlichkeit wieder zum Vorschein. Warum sollte sie beim französischen Soldaten keinen Anklang finden? Der preußische Militarismus ist versunken! Das deutsche Volk ist aus der Puppe geschlüpft, es ist derselbe flügge Freiheitskäfer wie das französische Volk. Im Sozialismus liegt der Born ewiger Jugend. Eine neue Zeit ist angebrochen.' (I, 66)[49]

The tone is different when Louis, Frau Scharrel's cousin, who lost his sight in the war, expresses his hope for a socialist internationalism:

> 'In spite of four and a half years' military rule there is still socialism in France. I hope that the German working class will execute the revolution and then – ' The blind man swung his fist.
>
> '[T]rotz vier ein halb Jahr Militärherrschaft gibt es noch Sozialismus in Frankreich. Ich hoffe, die deutsche Arbeiterklasse wird die Revolution durchführen und dann – ' Der Blinde schwang die Faust.[50]

Though the novel respects the young Frenchman's serious pathos, it cannot help exposing the futility of his hope. Against the *fata morgana* of a socialist world revolution it depicts an internationalism of a different kind. A chapter is devoted to a group of defectors of various nationalities living literally underground in a forest near Douai under joint British-German command, all of them well catered for by one Scarpini, an excellent French cook, and his two German kitchen boys, Hans and Friedrich. They are a segment of the vast number of 'Frenchmen, Russians, Germans, soldiers and civilians [who] squatted together defending themselves – against the war.'[51]

Revolutionary internationalism, forebodings of a world revolution, do not find an echo, much less a matrix, in Alsace, no matter what expectations the region's peculiar disposition and situation may have raised. Döblin does not envisage the prospect of the transnationalism which would, ten years after the publication of *Bürger und Soldaten*, reactivate the political potential of the middle region between France and Germany as the centre of a European union. For the post-Second World War European movement, the strip of land straddling the faultline between France and Germany, a zone palimpsestically circumscribed by the short-lived middle realm of the Carolingian Emperor Lothar I in the ninth century, has the role of a heartland, with Strassburg, Luxemburg and Brussels dominating the political topography. This non-socialist development is certainly not what the Strassburg soldiers' council diffidently proposes at its last meeting: 'to make Alsace the bridge between France and Germany on which the international revolution may march' (I, 278).

In *Bürger und Soldaten 1918* the historical and cultural disposition of Alsace to grasp the opportunity of the Armistice in order to transcend or subvert the nationalism that has plunged the world into a disastrous war disappoints the expectations it raised. The only transcending power emanating from Alsace will eventually be the spiritual influence and tutelage which the fourteenth-century Alsatian mystic, Johannes Tauler, exerts upon Friedrich Becker, one of the main characters in *November 1918*. In so far as Becker in various crises, eventually in his death, achieves salvation by entrusting himself to Tauler's guidance, he abides by Tauler's initial call heard in a dream vision on the train taking the inmates of the military hospital out of Alsace: 'Oh, stay here. [...] Look around you. [...] Keep looking. You are a godly man. Do stay. [...] Come. Do not forsake me. Do not forget my country. One day I shall send you a sign, a helpful sign.'[52] In this appeal Alsace stands for a spiritual condition, a refuge from political as well as moral disaster, which will stay accessible wherever Becker may wander. This shift in the meaning of the denomination

'Alsace' is, however, a late addition to *Bürger und Soldaten*, introducing a spiritual and metaphysical dimension to *November 1918* which will evolve in the subsequent volumes.[53]

Alsace as a topographical, cultural, social and political entity, the main setting and subject matter of *Bürger und Soldaten 1918*, does not transcend the conditions of the historical process which has ground to a halt with the Armistice. The revolutionary effort in Alsace collapses. There is no Alsatian revolution. For all its protestations of internationalism, revolutionary socialism is suspected of being a national, possibly nationalist, concern after all. Rather than becoming immersed in a German revolution the Alsatians settle for the accustomed social order under French administration. The German revolution, for its part, will run its course to a failure to which the Alsatian revolutionary episode will have been both prefiguration and epitome. The bulk of *November 1918. A German Revolution* is set in Berlin. With the entry into Strassburg of French troops on 22 November the state of exception ends for Alsace. For the short period of ten days history seemed to offer a chance for radical change. Anarchy harboured prospects of both revolution and restoration. But what might have been the moment of a new order emerging turns out to be the comedy of an order breaking down and being re-established under changed colours, a comedy very much in the vein of that great Alsatian satire of the late fifteenth century, Sebastian Brant's *Ship of Fools*.

Notes

1 Alfred Döblin, *November 1918. Eine deutsche Revolution. Erzählwerk in drei Teilen*, ed. Werner Stauffacher (Olten/Freiburg i. Br.: Walter, 1991), I, 233. Subsequent references to this work are to this edition and are given in parentheses in the body of the text. Unless otherwise indicated, the English translations of Döblin's texts are mine.

2 Eric Hobsbawm, *Age of Extremes: The Short Twentieth Century 1914–1991* (London: Michael Joseph, 1994).

3 For a review of German novels on the November Revolution, see Ulrich Kittstein and Regine Zeller, eds, *'Friede, Freiheit, Brot!' Romane zur deutschen Novemberrevolution* (Amsterdam: Rodopi, 2009).

4 'And after I had indulged my thirst for adventure in the South America book I turned to the shores of home. I thought of Berlin, the far-away city, and examined, similar to 1934 in *Men without Mercy*, how it had all come about.' ('Und nachdem ich im Südamerikabuch meine Abenteuerlust befriedigt hatte, wandte ich mich den heimischen Gestaden zu. Ich dachte an Berlin, an die

ferne Stadt, und prüfte nun im Geist, ähnlich wie 1934 in 'Pardon wird nicht gegeben', wodurch alles gekommen war.') 'Epilog', in *Autobiographische Schriften und letzte Aufzeichnungen*, ed. Edgar Pässler (Olten: Walter, 1980), 437–51 (448). First published in Paul E. H. Lüth, ed., *Alfred Döblin zum 70. Geburtstag* (Wiesbaden: Limes, 1948).

5 'Well, the whole looks like the *Hornberger Schießen* and it is a German revolution. All the same, 20,000 workers will be shot subsequently, there will be the Kapp-Putsch and then even World War II will materialise. It takes twenty years, but then it is there, and the dailies provide the sequel to the report.' ('Nun, das Ganze sieht nach dem Hornberger Schießen aus, und es ist eine deutsche Revolution. Immerhin werden im Anschluß daran 20 000 Arbeiter erschossen, der Kapputsch kommt, und dann stellt sich sogar Weltkrieg Nummer 2 ein. Es dauert 20 Jahre, aber dann ist er da, und die Tageszeitungen liefern die Fortsetzung des Berichts.') 'In Summa', being the final section of 'Überblick', written for a prospective American publisher of Part II in 1942/43 (III, 793–99 [799]). In 1934 Döblin wrote: 'May no one rail against Hitler; he is the man, along with Göring, etc., to suit Germany, he is the straight sequel to Noske. With Hitler the vanquished army of 1918 returns to Germany, something Wilhelm did not want to happen; he strikes the backstabbers from the rear [...] and the war, which was only interrupted in 1918, is being resumed.' ('Schimpfe niemand auf Hitler, er ist der Mann, einschließlich Göring etc., der für Deutschland passt, er ist die glatte Fortsetzung von Noske, mit Hitler kehrt die 1918 geschlagene Armee nach Deutschland zurück, was Wilhelm ja nicht wollte, und schlägt die Männer vom Dolchstoß von hinten nieder ... und der 1918 nur abgebrochene Krieg wird fortgesetzt'.) Letter of 12 January 1934 to Gottfried Bermann, in Alfred Döblin, *Briefe*, ed. Heinz Graber (Olten: Walter, 1970), 185.

6 Berlin: Klett, 1905.

7 'Als ich Abschied nahm ...' in *Autobiographische Schriften und letzte Aufzeichnungen*, 429–31.

8 The current edition of the novel is *November 1918. Eine deutsche Revolution. Erzählwerk in drei Teilen* (Frankfurt a.M.: S. Fischer, 2008), a re-edition of the 1991 edition by Werner Stauffacher at Walter Verlag. There is an abbreviated English translation, in two volumes, *A People Betrayed. November 1918: A German Revolution* and *Karl and Rosa. November 1918. A German Revolution*, trans. John E. Woods (New York: Fromm International, 1983). This translation does not include *Bürger und Soldaten*.

9 *Bürger und Soldaten 1918. Roman* (Stockholm: Bermann-Fischer/ Amsterdam: Querido, 1939).

10 *November 1918/Eine deutsche Revolution/Erzählwerk* (Munich: Alber, 1948–50).

11 Hannah Arendt, *On Revolution* (New York: Viking Press, 1963), 206.

12 In 1940 Hannah Arendt was in close contact with Benjamin, who, shortly

before his death, entrusted her with a manuscript of his 'Theses on the Philosophy of History'. See Detlev Schöttker and Erdmut Wizisla, eds, *Arendt und Benjamin: Texte, Briefe, Dokumente* (Frankfurt a.M.: Suhrkamp, 2006). Arendt made the theses, translated from the version published by Adorno in 1955 and titled 'On the Concept of History', available to readers of English in Walter Benjamin, *Illuminations: Essays and Reflections*, trans. Harry Zohn, ed. Hannah Arendt (New York: Harcourt, Brace and World, 1968).

13 Walter Benjamin, 'On the Concept of History', in *Selected Writings 4 (1938–40)*, trans. Edmund Jephcott et al., ed. Howard Eiland and Michael W. Jennings (Cambridge, MA: The Belknap Press of Harvard University Press, 2003), 396.

14 'Über den Begriff der Geschichte', in *Gesammelte Schriften* I/2, ed. R. Tiedemann and H. Schweppenhäuser (Frankfurt a.M.: Suhrkamp, 1974), 703.

15 Carl Schmitt, *Politische Theologie: Vier Kapitel zur Lehre von der Souveränität* (Berlin: Duncker und Humblot, 1922); *Political Theology. Four Chapters on the Concept of Sovereignty* (Chicago: University of Chicago Press, 2005).

16 Giorgio Agamben, *State of Exception* (Chicago: University of Chicago Press, 2005 [2003]).

17 For a recent examination of the trio, see David Pan, 'Against Biopolitics. Walter Benjamin, Carl Schmitt, and Giorgio Agamben on Political Sovereignty and Symbolic Order', *The German Quarterly*, 82, 1 (2009), 42–62.

18 'Souverän ist, wer über den Ausnahmezustand entscheidet.' / 'Sovereign is he who decides on the state of exception.'

19 In 'November 1918: Topographie of a Revolution', in Steffan Davies and Ernest Schonfield, eds, *Alfred Döblin, Paradigms of Modernism* (Berlin: De Gruyter, 2009), 276–95, Ernest Schonfield writes about the 'symbolic function' of the region and of Strassburg in particular (282–4).

20 On 10 November the Executive Committee of the *Arbeiter- und Soldatenräte*, with Joseph Rebholz as president, was formed. It proclaimed the socialist *Republik Elsass-Lothringen*. On the 11th the *Landtag* of Elsass-Lothringen reconstituted itself as *Nationalrat* and formed a government (*Verwaltungsausschuss*). It was recognised by the revolutionaries. It was meant to negotiate as a sovereign government with the French yet was soon dominated by those who demanded unconditional unification with France. See Pierri Zind, *Elsass-Lothringen/Alsace Lorraine, une nation interdite, 1870–1940* (Paris: Copernic, 1979), chapter V, 'Le Désarroi d'Elsass-Lothringen'; also Robert Heitz, 'La "Revolution" Strasbourgeoise de 1918, Temoignage vécu', in *L'Alsace contemporaine. Études politiques, économiques, sociales* (Strasbourg and Paris: Éditions F.-X. Le Roux, 1950), 373–82. Döblin's novel emphasises the failure of the more radical plans of the Wilhelmshaven sailors to proclaim a socialist republic.

21 An affinity with Alsatian neutrality is evident in Döblin's statement 'Aber

ich war kein Deutscher und werde auch kein Franzose.' Letter to Elvira and Arthur Rosin, 23 March 1934, in Döblin, *Briefe*, 191.

22 Susanne Lachenicht, *Information und Propaganda: Die Presse deutscher Jakobiner im Elsaß (1791–1800)* (Munich: Oldenbourg, 2004), p. 54, referring to Hellmut G. Haasis, *Gebt der Freiheit Flügel. Die Zeit der deutschen Jakobiner 1789–1805* (Reinbek: Rowohlt, 1988) and F. C. Heitz, *Les societés politiques de Strasbourg pendant les années 1790 à 1795* (Strasbourg, 1863).

23 The novel fleetingly touches upon the attempts at constitutional change of October 1918 on pages 268 and 334.

24 The chapter 'It grew colder towards evening' ('Gegen abend nahm die Kälte zu'), II, 126–34, was initially entitled 'Marshall Pétain enters Strassburg' ('Marschall Pétain zieht in Straßburg ein') and included the subsection 'How Strassburg fell to Louis XIV' ('Wie Straßburg an Louis XIV. fiel'). This and other subsections, one on the miserable entry of Alsatian refugees expelled from Germany and one on the entry of Pétain and the grand parade in his honour, were suppressed by Döblin. They are printed in II, 520–2.

25 The main initiatives of the Alsatians concentrated on the struggle for autonomy within the German and, after 1918, the French state. For a recent study of Alsatian regionalism, see Christopher J. Fischer, *Alsace to the Alsatians? Visions and Divisions of Alsatian Regionalism, 1870–1939* (Oxford: Berghahn Books, 2010); also Karl Heinz Rothenberger, *Die elsass-lothringische Heimat- und Autonomiebewegung zwischen den beiden Weltkriegen* (Bern: Peter Lang, 1975).

26 'Ni Allemands, ni Francais, ni neutres. C'est le drapeau rouge qui est le vainqueur.' R. Heitz, 'La "Revolution" Strasbourgeoise', 377.

27 'Revolutionstage im Elsaß', in *Schriften zur Politik und Gesellschaft* (Olten: Walter, 1972), 59–71; first published in *Neue Rundschau*, February 1919. A present-day supplement to Döblin's memories is provided by Pascale Hugues in her family history, *Marthe und Mathilde. Eine Familie zwischen Frankreich und Deutschland* (Hamburg: Rowohlt, 2008), the more so as her book shows affinities with Döblin's in including her great-aunt Georgette, Alsace-born schoolteacher in Berlin, Spartacist and comrade-in-arms of Rosa Luxemburg.

28 Michel Vanoosthuyse (*Le Roman historique: Mann, Brecht, Döblin* [Paris: Presses Universitaires de France, 1996], 288) draws attention to the peculiar opening of the novel and adduces Benjamin's reference to the topos of a revolutionary calendar in the fifteenth of his theses in 'On the Concept of History'. This book's chapter on Döblin, 'Le roman "délibératif"', is reproduced in a condensed version in Michel Vanoosthuyse, *Alfred Döblin. Théorie et pratique de l'"oeuvre epique'* (Paris: Belin, 2005), 146–81.

29 As mentioned in 'Revolutionstage im Elsaß', there were sailors agitating in Alsace before the main contingent arrived on 14 November, as recounted in 'Die Wilhelmshavener Matrosen' (I, 150–7).

30 'Siehste. Es ist Revolution. Der Krieg ist aus' (I, 20).

31 'Dafür werden wir ihnen die Köpfe abreißen' (I, 61).

32 See 'In der Apotheke und im Filmatelier', subsection 'Ein General unter Filmstatisten' (II, 344–50).

33 See 'Schmeißfliegen und Leichenfledderer' (I, 247–60).

34 'The faces of those Alsatians as if it were a fancy-dress party and they the lookers-on … Windows and balconies of the houses by the market crowded with civilians. The lark, one single beaming, Schadenfreude, disdain, mischievous amusement of onlookers.' ('Die Gesichter dieser Elsässer, als wenn es ein Maskenball wäre und sie Zuschauer … Fenster und Balkone der Markthäuser voll Zivil. Das Gaudi, ein einziges Strahlen, Schadenfreude, Geringschätzung, übermütiges Zuschaueramüsement.') Döblin, 'Revolutionstage im Elsaß', 60.

35 'In der Nacht kletterte Ziweck auf das Dach und hißte die rote Fahne' (I, 136).

36 Michel Vanoosthuyse (*Le Roman historique*, 291–2) emphasises this aspect, but he misses the point of the specific nature of 'a revolution in Alsace' by homogenising the whole novel under the Bakhtinian formula of the *roman délibératif* and indiscriminately subsuming the events in Alsace under the label of 'a German revolution'.

37 'Der Forstmeister sieht die Franzosen einziehen' (I, 301–8).

38 'Frau Anny Scharrel' (I, 314–27); also 'Reception at Frau Scharrel's' ('Empfang bei Frau Scharrel'), II, 126–34.

39 Cf. 'Die Wilhelmshavener Matrosen' (I, 150–7). Sailors from Wilhelmshaven arrived in Strassburg on 14 November. A note to p. 153 (I, 365) quotes a report in the Strassburg *Freie Presse* of 16 November: 'Then delegates from Wilhelmshaven entered, 180 Alsatian sailors, empowered by the 16,000 Alsatian-Lotharingian sailors at Wilhelmshaven to greet the dear old home country and to further the case of the International so that our countrymen can participate in the new age of golden liberty and people-uniting peace. This avant garde of the revolution was greeted with lively satisfaction.' ('Dann traten Abgesandte aus Wilhelmshaven herein, 180 elsässische Matrosen, die von 16 000 elsaß-lothringischen Matrosen aus Wilhelmshaven bevollmächtigt sind, die alte liebe Heimat herzlich zu grüßen und im Sinne der Internationale da zu werben, damit auch die Landsleute der neuen Zeit goldener Freiheit und des völkerversöhnenden Friedens teilhaftig werden. Man begrüßte diese Vorkämpfer der Umwälzung mit lebhafter Genugtuung.') The considerable number of Alsatians and Lotharingians in the German navy has been explained as the effect of a policy that tried to avoid the risk of troops being deployed in their home region. Cf. I, 209.

40 Jacques Peirotes (1869–1935), social democratic politician and journalist, from 1900 editor of the Alsatian party paper *Freie Presse*, from 1911 member for Strassburg in the Alsace-Lorraine parliament, from 1912 member for Colmar in the German Reichstag, from 10 November 1918 mayor of Strassburg.

41 Cf. 'Matrose Thomas' (I, 208–15).

42 'Sie wollten das Elsaß vor den Franzosen retten' (I, 150).

43 'Also bleibt alles beim alten, es soll alles beim alten bleiben'(I, 43).
44 'Unsere Revolution [...] besteht darin, die Preußen zu verjagen, und das besorgen für uns die Franzosen' (I, 280).
45 The uneasy to tense relation between the German military and the Alsatians is a prominent topic in 'Revolutionstage im Elsaß'.
46 The editor's footnote (I, 354, n.41) establishes that Döblin transplants to the 11th a telegram of 17 November sent by the Berlin government to the Strassburg workers' and soldiers' council: 'Contrary to erroneous opinion we state: The occupation of Alsace–Lorraine by the Entente does not prejudice the solution of the Alsace–Lorraine question at a peace conference. Alsace–Lorraine will, in accordance with the right of self-determination of nations, have to decide its fate. Ebert, Haase.' ('Gegenüber irrigen Annahmen stellen wir fest: Die Besetzung Elsaß-Lothringens durch die Entente präjudiziert nicht die Lösung der elsaß-lothringischen Frage durch die Friedenskonferenz. Elsaß-Lothringen wird nach dem Selbstbestimmungsrecht der Völker über seine Schicksale selbst zu entscheiden haben. Ebert, Haase').
47 Cf. 'Die Wilhelmshavener Matrosen' (I, 150–7) and 'Matrose Thomas' (I, 208–15).
48 Siegfried Bünger points out, with reference to Public Record Office, Cab. 23/14. WC 500 A, that Lloyd George cautioned against sending troops into Germany where they would - like the German troops in Russia - be infected with the 'bolshevik virus'. 'Die regierenden Kreise Großbritanniens und die revolutionären Ereignisse in Deutschland 1918/1919', in *November 1918. Revolution - Reform - Parlamentarismus* (Sachsen: Rosa-Luxemburg-Stiftung, 1999), 111–19 (113).
49 According to a footnote (I, 367), Döblin quotes from an article by Joseph Rebholz, chairman of the Strassburg soldiers' council, in the Strassburg *Freie Presse*: 'The Red Flag on Strassburg Cathedral' / 'Die rote Fahne auf dem Münster in Straßburg'.
50 From 'A French veteran who lost his eye-sight hopes for the world revolution' ('Ein französischer Kriegsblinder hofft auf die Weltrevolution'), suppressed subsection of the chapter 'Paris, Fears and Sins' ('Paris, Ängste und Sünden'), II/1, 537–9 (539).
51 'Franzosen, Russen, Deutsche, Soldaten und Zivilisten hockten beieinander und verteidigten sich gemeinsam - gegen den Krieg' (I, 216).
52 'Ach, bleibe hier. [...] Blicke dich um. [...] Blicke mehr. Du bist fromm und gut. Bleibe. [...] Komm. Verlaß mich nicht. Vergiß meines Landes nicht. Ich werde dir eines Tages ein Zeichen schicken, ein hilfreiches' (I, 139–40).
53 This is explored further in my article 'Revolution and Redemption: Alfred Döblin's *November 1918*', *Modern Language Review*, 103 (2008), 471–89. The passages involving Johannes Tauler are absent from the manuscript of *Bürger und Soldaten 1918* and from the 15 chapters published in the journal *Die Zukunft* between March and July 1939.

3

'A strange mood': British popular fiction and post-war uncertainties

George Simmers

The response of British writers of popular fiction to the Armistice was mixed. John Buchan would later write of 'that curious summer of 1919 when everyone was feverishly trying to forget the war',[1] and many did indeed turn away with relief from stern patriotism and uplift, towards South Seas escapism or light comedy; others directed their gaze towards the actual post-Armistice world, and they were often disturbed by what they saw. Rarely did writers of the time suggest that the end of hostilities had ushered in an era that was likely to be untroubled; Philip Gibbs expressed the uncertainties of 1919 very forcibly at the beginning of his 1920 novel, *Back to Life*:

> Many of the men who came back were in a strange mood – restless, morbid, neurotic. Their own people did not understand them. They could not understand themselves. They hated war, most of them, but this peace seemed flat and unprofitable to their souls. [...] Wives complained that their husbands had 'changed'. Their characters were hardened and their tempers were frayed, so that they were strangely irritable and given to storms of rage about nothing at all. It was frightening ... There was an epidemic of violence and of horrible sensual crimes with women victims, ending often with suicide. There were mob riots by demobilised soldiers or soldiers still waiting in camps for demobilisation. Police stations were stormed and wrecked and policemen killed by bodies of men who had been heroes in the war and now fought like savages against their fellow-citizens. Some of them pleaded guilty in court and made queer statements about an utter ignorance of their own actions after the disorder had begun. It seemed as though they had returned to the psychology of that war when men, doped with rum, or drunk with excitement, had leapt over the parapet and remembered nothing more of a battle until they found themselves panting

> in an enemy trench or lying wounded on a stretcher. It was a dangerous kind of psychology in civil life.[2]

During wartime it had been possible (and many had thought it imperative) to sustain a myth of national cohesion and common purpose. The problems and disharmonies of the pre-war years (around class, gender and Ireland, for example) had mostly been set aside for the duration. Middle-class readers had been able to reassure themselves by reading books such as Ian Hay's *The First Hundred Thousand* (1915), an account of military training in which rebellious Glasgow trades unionists are efficiently transformed into loyal soldiers. The Pankhursts' *Suffragette* magazine changed itself into *Britannia* soon after war began, and concentrated its animus against those men who were not doing enough for the war effort. The Irish, despite the 1916 Easter Rising, provided a supply of brave volunteers; they were also used as comic relief in British war stories.

After the Armistice, it was clear that the social problems of the Edwardian age had not been swept away. Women's war work had strengthened the case for the female vote, so the militant suffragism of the Edwardian period was no longer necessary, but the position of women in the post-war world would need to be renegotiated. In novels ranging from bestsellers like A. S. M. Hutchinson's *If Winter Comes* (1921) to *Parade's End* (1924–28) by Ford Madox Ford, the soldier is represented as a force for decency who is undermined by women on the home front. The Russian Revolution had made the middle classes more aware of a threat from the proletariat; the early months of peace saw soldiers on strike because of delays in demobilisation, and industrial conflict broke out as industry settled to a post-war world. In Ireland, Sinn Féin asserted itself, and was met by the ex-soldiers of the Black and Tans. The war to end war had finished in a peace that seemed far from stable.

This chapter will consider three contrasting responses to post-war uncertainties from writers of popular fiction. The novels of Philip Gibbs (1877–1962) are semi-documentaries, disturbing readers with reports from a troubled Britain and war-ravaged Europe; Warwick Deeping (1877–1950) wrote heated melodramas whose heroes were trying to cope with the violent legacies of the war; while for 'Sapper' and other thriller writers, the conflicted world of the 1920s demanded as tough-minded a response as that which had brought victory in wartime.

Philip Gibbs

Philip Gibbs was one of the first novelists to attempt a comprehensive picture of the post-war world. Before the war he had been a reporter who had begun to produce state-of-the-nation novels, such as *Intellectual Mansions, S.W.* (1910) and *Master of Life* (1913). Titus Harsnett, the hero of the latter novel, inherits a fortune and a huge industrial empire in Yorkshire, and the book tells the story of his attempt to run it decently, negotiating a middle way between the extremisms of his fellow owners and the socialists. During the war Gibbs became one of the most valued of war correspondents, noted for his intelligent concern for the fighting troops. Afterwards, he left journalism in protest at his newspaper's support for the Black and Tans in Ireland, and in the immediate post-war years he produced two novels, *Back to Life* and *The Middle of the Road,* as well as the best-selling non-fiction *Realities of War* (1920), which rewrote his war reporting with the greater freedom available after the Armistice.

Gibbs, appalled by the 'slaughter of boys and the suicide of nations',[3] gives in this book a graphic account of the war's horrors, going beyond what could have been said during the conflict, and laying blame on those he considered not to have done enough to bring the war to a speedy close. As wartime commentators might have done, he blames the 'jazzing, card-playing, theatre-going' civilians of London who 'were not much interested in the life of the trenches; anyhow they could not understand'. He blames

> the 'fug committees' (it was Lord Kitchener's phrase) at the War Office, the Board of Trade, the Foreign Office, the Home Office, the Ministry of Munitions, the Ministry of Information, where officials on enormous salaries smoked cigars of costly brands and decided how to spend vast sums of public money on 'organisation', which made no difference to the man stifling his cough below the parapet in a wet fog of Flanders, staring across No Man's Land for the beginning of a German attack.[4]

His most telling criticisms, however, and the ones that he would not have published before the end of the war, were those of the General Staff. He makes a deliberate display of fairness, describing Haig's good qualities before analysing his 'lack of real genius';[5] of generals as a whole he writes:

> I met many other generals who were men of ability, energy, high sense of duty, and strong personality. I found them intellectually, with few exceptions, narrowly moulded to the same type, strangely limited in their range of ideas and qualities of character.

> 'One has to leave many gaps in one's conversation with generals', said a friend of mine, after lunching with an Army Commander.[6]

His post-war novels show a similar willingness to make unfashionable judgements. *Back to Life* is hardly a novel at all. Its narrator is a war correspondent who has previously written novels, including one called *Intellectual Mansions*. A plot gradually emerges, about a doomed love affair between an Englishman and a German woman, but much of the book is straight reportage about the state of post-war Europe.

The narrator travels with the advancing British army of 1918 through the parts of France and Belgium that had been occupied by the enemy. He hears stories of brutal German atrocities against civilians, but the novel is determined to make it clear that cruelty is not practised only by Germans; it shows how violence breeds retaliation. In the *Grand Place* of a French town the narrator hears 'women's shrieks – shriek after shriek, most blood-curdling, and then becoming faint'. He is at the scene of the *tonte*, the forcible shaving of 'those who were too complaisant with German officers'.[7]

When the victorious British army crosses the Rhine, Gibbs explains that 'many of our officers had a secret dread of this advance into German territory, not because they were afraid of their own skins, but because they had a greater fear of being called upon to do "dirty work" in the event of civilians sniping and any sign of the *franc-tireur*'. The situation of the British army at the end of the war is compared explicitly with that of the Germans at the start:

> 'Our turn for atrocities!' whispered young cavalry officers, remembering Louvain and Alost, and they hated the idea. We were in the state of mind which led to some of the black business in Belgium when the Germans first advanced – nervous, ready to believe any rumour of treacherous attack, more afraid of civilian hostility than of armed troops. A single shot fired by some drunken fool in a German village, a single man of ours killed in a brawl, or murdered by a German out of vengeance, might lead to bloody tragedy.[8]

In the event, the German civilians prove friendly, and the occupying British meet no sign of hatred, a situation which contrasts tellingly with what happens when a friend of the narrator takes a German bride home to London; His family treat her 'with a studied unkindness that had broken her nerve and spirit'.[9] They persecute her, asking questions like 'Why the Germans boiled down their dead?' and 'Why they crucified Canadian prisoners?';[10] a relationship which had offered hope of reconciliation is destroyed by British insularity.

The resentments and hatreds of post-Armistice Britain are more centrally the theme of *The Middle of the Road* (1923), Gibbs's next novel. Its main character is Bertram Pollard, an ex-soldier awkwardly back home and feeling the distance between himself and his upper-class wife. Her friends speak approvingly of Mussolini's *fascisti* in Italy, and of the ruthless tactics used by the paramilitary Black and Tans against Irish dissidents. Meanwhile, resentment grows among the unemployed, who are tempted by 'Bolshevism – that strange foreign growth, so alien to English ideas'.[11] Beggars hand supposed good-luck charms in the shape of a slipper to members of the idle rich. Rumours spread that these 'silver slippers' are reminders of the coming revolution, and of the retaliation due to their recipients. Gibbs, usually a very definite writer, leaves it unclear whether these are actually sinister, or just lucky charms.

Bertram, like the heroes of most of Gibbs's novels, is usually a passive observer, hearing everyone's point of view, however extreme, and feeling distressed by the apparent lack of any common ground between political opponents. He maintains a position in 'the middle of the road', but finds it a lonely place to be, because the novel is so structured that most of the views he comes across are extreme, and those who hold them are impervious to argument. Post-war England is represented as divided and potentially violent.

Gibbs conveys the fears of those, on either side of the class divide, who cannot see their imagined opponents as fully human, but only as stereotypes. Interestingly, this first half of the book becomes a debate about who has the right to call themselves ex-soldiers. The upper classes want to maintain their officer status in peacetime, while the unemployed other ranks feel that their war service gives them a moral right to better treatment. Gibbs's spokesman Bertram is forced to choose where he stands when he is offered a job helping to organise a defensive militia in case of a general strike (the implication is that this force would use methods like those of the Black and Tans in Ireland). When he refuses, his wife brands him a class traitor.

In this novel, life is entirely about big political problems; wherever Bertram goes, he is confronted by the headline issues of the day, and by people talking, voicing entrenched attitudes but never convincing anyone else, or being convinced by the arguments of others. If a good novel is about subtly drawn characters and the nuances of their interaction, then Gibbs's are not good novels; the characters are types, and their interactions do not reveal depth or subtlety. But he is an excellent reporter, and half way through the book his hero becomes a newspaper correspondent too. We follow him through Europe and see some extraordinary scenes. There is a particularly vivid description of a dawn outside Mountjoy prison on the morning that a Sinn Féin militant is to be hanged:

> All round the prison were strong forces of troops. Several armoured cars were drawn up, and a searchlight was turned on a dense black crowd of people waiting there through the night, for the coming of dawn. They were mostly women and young girls, with shawls over their heads [...]
>
> Between each prayer there rose another sound, the strangest, most terrible sound of a human kind that Bertram had ever heard beyond a battlefield. It was like the cry of the Banshee, as he had imagined it in childhood. It rose and fell in rhythmic anguish, from all those shawl-covered women, kneeling with bowed heads, or raising their heads and hands like a Greek chorus to the heavens above.[12]

Bertram progresses through the horrors of post-war Europe. He is first in France, where reconstruction is slow, and where there is hatred of the British because Lloyd George will not endorse the demand for full reparations from Germany. Then to economically crippled Germany, where inflation is unstoppable and political resentment is fuelled by the belief that the German army was never defeated in the field. (Gibbs in 1923 gives a very clear picture of the social factors that will encourage Nazism.) Finally he reaches post-revolution Russia, chaotic, violent and starving. Gibbs himself had been there in 1921, at the invitation of the Imperial Famine Relief Fund, at a time when the *Daily Mail* was claiming there was no famine in Russia – reports to the contrary, according to the *Mail*, were just Red propaganda to obtain economic aid. Bertram's journey in the novel is closely based on Gibbs's own journey, described in his autobiography *The Pageant of the Years* (1946). The horrors are not stinted; he sees starvation, typhus, degradation, cruelty.

The Middle of the Road was a bestseller. By the end of its first year of publication it was in its fifteenth edition, having sold 36,000 copies. The contemporary success of Gibbs's work is intriguing, in that he offers nothing like the standard recipe for attracting high sales figures – passion, fantasy and a satisfying closure. On the other hand, his fifty novels do not have the qualities that might attract serious students of literature. In the words of Stuart Laing, one of the few writers to give scholarly attention to Gibbs's novels, 'in terms of standard literary history his work has vanished without trace – indeed it has never been acknowledged'.[13] The success of this book shows the existence of a public demanding a serious account of the post-war world, and perhaps also one attracted to Gibbs's brand of liberal despair, and to the self-dramatisation of his hero as a lonely figure caught between extremes.

Warwick Deeping

While Gibbs's serious documentaries found an appreciative audience, there were readers who demanded more from their fiction than political arguments and a passive hero agonising over the state of the world. A more emotional and dramatic response to the legacy of the war can be found in the novels of Warwick Deeping (1877–1950), whose politics and attitudes were very different from Gibbs's. Deeping had trained as a doctor, but, as Mary Grover explains, 'He practised medicine for one year in Sussex, and then, on the success of his first novel, *Uther and Ingraine* in 1903, gave up medicine for writing and only practised again in the First World War.'[14] He volunteered for the RAMC, and went as a medical officer to Gallipoli, Belgium and Egypt (though Grover has deduced that his duties were more administrative than medical). He saw the violence of war at first hand, and his most characteristic novels from now on would be about men coping in one way or another with the legacy of that violence in an unstable post-war world that was very likely to disappoint their ideals and their ambitions.

His 1921 novel *The House of Adventure* belongs to a not uncommon post-war genre, the novel of rebirth. Brent, a British soldier, swaps his own identity disc with that of a dead man and rejects his own unsatisfactory pre-war existence. He attempts to remake his life after the war by helping to rebuild a damaged and deserted French village. Brent represents all that is positive about the war. He 'had been trained to a disciplined and orderly way of killing Germans', while the enemy, for their part, had treated him decently when he became a prisoner. The war has not left him embittered, only keen to make the most of the new world of opportunities. He makes an enemy of a French ex-soldier called Louis Blanc, however. Deeping's imagination works through bold melodramatic contrasts, and the difference between the two soldiers is extreme. Brent is brave, undemonstrative, positive and capable of deep emotion; Blanc is swaggering, cowardly and flashily sexual. The two of them battle for a woman (whom Brent comes slowly to love, and whom Blanc tries to rape) and for the future of the village. Brent wants to reconstruct it, much as before the war, for the sake of its original inhabitants; Blanc wants to make money out of battlefield tourism, leaving the village ruined as a wonder for others to gawp at.

The novel asks questions about the attitudes necessary for the remaking of Europe, but also about the war's legacy of violence. Blanc is the personification of ruthless wartime violence, uncontrolled by morality. Brent has to answer his violence with violence, and the book describes a series of vicious fights, in the course of which Louis Blanc is blinded and crippled. Brent wins because he displays the quality that many of the British thought had helped them to win the war – a dogged steadfastness in a cause that is righteous.

Violence, whether physical or suppressed, is a constant presence in Deeping's novels, and has sometimes been underestimated by critics. Samuel Hynes, for example, surmises that Deeping's bestseller *Sorrell and Son* (1925), which he describes as an 'unremarkable plodding novel', was popular because Deeping gave answers to post-war social issues conservatively and reassuringly.[15] Yet there is little that is reassuring in the savagery of Sorrell's fantasies of violence against Buck, the bad soldier of that novel – 'Buck had one of those round flat heads with the pink skin showing at the crown, and a great broad neck that bulged slightly over his collar. An axe, a hammer, – and one smashing blow on that pink, bald patch –!'[16] The book's drama lies in Sorrell's struggle to repress this violence.

The difficulty of repressing anger is the central subject of Deeping's 1923 novel, *The Secret Sanctuary, or The Saving of John Stretton.* Stretton had been an officer in the trenches, under difficult conditions – 'Bursts of savage shelling, counter-attacks to repel, the ground like chaos, everything difficult – water, rations – getting the wounded away!' One night he led some men on a difficult and dangerous mission, in the course of which several were killed. Returning, he met a brigade-major, nicknamed 'Slaughterhouse', of whom a fellow officer would later write: 'I think he was about the stupidest man I have ever met; his neck was as thick as his head, and he had eyes like blue marbles. He hardly ever gave you a word of praise, and he was a bully.' 'Slaughterhouse' engages the exhausted officer in a fruitless dispute; Stretton's nerve snaps, 'and in twenty seconds he had said things to Slaughterhouse which half the brigade would like to have said. And then that shell came. It covered us all with dirt. The brigade-major was killed, and Stretton knocked unconscious, but if he hadn't been knocked out that morning he would have been up for a court-martial, sure as fate –'.[17]

Invalided home, Stretton has the symptoms that Deeping, as a military doctor, would have classified as mild shell-shock – 'Slight tremor of the hands. Some sleeplessness. No mental clouding but a slight hesitancy in speech.' On occasion, however, he attacks people. A hospital orderly, a platform attendant, a selfish and bullying man elbowing a girl in a bus queue. All these seem to be the same physical type as 'Slaughterhouse', and all are aggressive and officious. The third victim suffers a fractured skull, and Stretton is jailed for two months.

The rest of the novel describes Stretton's cure, which, predictably for the period, involves a rugged country life and the love of a good woman. Less conventional is the representation of Stretton's post-traumatic violence. It takes him over and is something over which he has no control. We are told that 'it had belonged to some sinister underworld in him'; Rollin Beal, who is a doctor, explains it thus:

> 'Imagine a sort of leak in the brain, imagine our most primitive and savage impulses able to rush through this leak and produce sudden acts of uncontrollable violence.'[18]

The wartime origins of the impulses, however, suggest that this violence is the violence of war itself, returning to punish the post-war age; the attacks seem to be the uncontrollable expression of a moral instinct repelled by the types of person of whom Stretton (like Warwick Deeping) disapproves. His remarks to 'Slaughterhouse' were what 'half the brigade would like to have said' but could not express. Now Stretton's unconscious expresses itself, but in ways that cannot be permitted in civil society. Later in the novel, he has another fit of violence, against Isobel Cropredy, a girl who has taunted him. (A reviewer in 1923 accurately called Isobel 'a creature of depravity scarcely credible'.)[19] The description of their conflict has urgently sexual undertones. Stretton has spurned her, so she lies in wait for him with a riding whip. While he struggles to take the whip off her, 'he felt her strong young teeth in his shoulder'. There is one of those asterisks that novelists use as euphemisms for a scene that cannot be described. Then:

> It was dark when she came out of the wood on to the stretch of heath below the cottage. She was weeping with rage and pain and the disillusionment of a balked desire; her hair was down; her stockings hung about her ankles. A little behind her walked the man, a figure of humiliation and self-horror; one sleeve of his shirt had been torn off, and there was blood on his face and the marks left by her fingernails.[20]

The reader might be tantalised by hints of sexual violence while being able to feel morally absolved, because it is the woman's fault. Similarly, we are allowed to collude emotionally in Stretton's violent attacks on bad people, while officially, as it were, we side with the wise doctors who see the outbursts as things to be controlled. This duality, very like that of the Sunday newspapers that describe sexual misdemeanours in detail while expressing abhorrence at them, is undoubtedly part of Deeping's appeal. His work is very unlike the socially cohesive fiction of Philip Gibbs, which follows Galsworthy's model of finding merits and faults on both sides of a conflict. *The Secret Sanctuary* is conservative in its political attitudes, but it is only partially reassuring, and does not demonstrate what Rosa Maria Bracco in her study of post-war fiction calls 'the perceptual balance which is characteristic of so many middlebrow novels'.[21] Nor does it offer a completely trouble-free closure: at the end of the novel, another objectionable person appears. Stretton is tempted to violence once again, and is only restrained by the firm words of the girl who loves him. However, the possibility of future outbreaks of violence remains.

Throughout Deeping's novels and stories of the immediate post-war period, he is working towards the creation of a genre that would bring him immense popular success. Mary Grover has analysed how Deeping's own social, personal and literary insecurities found expression in his novels and suggests that 'Deeping's over-riding preoccupation was from the outset, autonomy', the search for independence and self-respect in a hostile and unstable world.[22] The ex-soldier is the ideal personification of this theme; at a loss in a post-war society that does not value him, he struggles to maintain his integrity and to repress his own potential for violence. The repression is made difficult because the 'good' ex-soldier's opponents have no qualms about using violence. Where the Deeping hero has internalised the moral idealism that justified the war, the typical Deeping villain has embraced the spirit of amoral *realpolitik* that must also be part of any war. The struggle between the two always takes place in a post-war world that seems structured to give an advantage to the man unhampered by morality.

'Sapper'

Considerably less troubled by the ethics of engagement with the post-war world were the heroes of a more extraverted genre, the thriller. 'Sapper' (Cyril Herman McNeile, MC) had achieved fame during the war years with his tough-minded stories of combat. His first post-war novel was *Mufti* (1919), an attempt at a state-of-England novel considerably less sophisticated than Gibbs's, but equally irresolute about the future.

When the first of the Bulldog Drummond stories began serialisation in *Hutchinson's Story Magazine* in September 1919, however, 'Sapper' created a hero who could confront the problems of the troubled peace with gusto and, cheerfully lacking the scruples of Gibbs's protagonist, could put to use the methods and attitudes learned in war.

Captain Hugh Drummond shows none of the symptoms of post-war distress that trouble many other fictional ex-officers. He was not horrified or demoralised by the war; on the contrary, he thoroughly relished it:

> The ordinary joys of the infantry subaltern's life – such as going over the top, and carrying out raids – had not proved sufficient for his appetite. He had specialised in peculiar stunts of his own: stunts over which he was singularly reticent; stunts over which his men formed their own conclusions, and worshipped him accordingly.[23]

After four punishing years of war, Drummond still displays the same boisterous enthusiasm with which Julian Grenfell, writing home in October 1914, had greeted the beginning:

> it's all the best fun one ever dreamed of, and up to now it has only wanted a few shells and a little noise to supply the necessary level of excitement. The uncertainty of it is so good, like a picnic when you don't know where you're going to.[24]

Fifty years later Philip Larkin would look at a photographs of men queuing to enlist in August 1914 and write, 'Never such innocence again';[25] yet enthusiastic innocence was precisely what Drummond offered his readers in the early 1920s. He faced the post-war world, not tired and disillusioned, but full of bright cheerfulness and a simple sense of right and wrong. He is one of the least conflicted characters in literature; his relationship with his wife Phyllis is utterly uncomplicated. (The only problem that ever threatens their marriage is the frequency with which she is kidnapped – for which she always blames the villains, and not her husband.)

The one thing that bothers Drummond in peacetime is boredom, which he alleviates by putting a notice in *The Times*:

> Demobilised officer, finding peace incredibly tedious, would welcome diversion. Legitimate if possible; but crime, if of a comparatively humorous description, no objection. Excitement essential. Would be prepared to consider permanent job if suitably impressed by applicant for services. Reply at once Box X10.[26]

Advertising in this way is presented as an amiably eccentric act, but not only does Drummond almost immediately find a task worthy of his efforts, he also finds a group of friends of the same mind, willing and eager to help him, and to take his orders.

Opposed to this team is a disparate array of villains. Many thrillers of the 1920s contain a scene in which anti-social elements gather for a meeting and offer the reader a cross-section of the enemies of society. *Bulldog Drummond* starts with such a conference, which happens, significantly, 'on the very day that a British Cavalry Division marched into Cologne, with flags flying and bands playing as the conquerors of a beaten nation'.[27] The exact composition of the group sitting round the table will vary from book to book, but it will usually include a foreign capitalist (often American, sometimes Jewish), some socialist agitators (with 'a greedy, hungry look, a shifty untrustworthy look – the look of those who are jealous of everyone better placed than themselves'),[28] a Russian or other foreigner who is manipulating the deluded socialists, and some ordinary criminals such as (often supposedly Jewish) 'white-slavers'. In *Bulldog Drummond*, this group is joined by the intellectual aesthete, Lakington.

The presence of the socialists and Russians in these imagined conspiracies shows the level to which middle-class anxiety had risen, following the Russian Revolution and the reports of soldiers' strikes and protests in Britain itself at the end of the war.[29] Myths of Bolshevist conspiracies and the duping of otherwise decent men by paid propagandists allowed readers to reconcile their wartime belief that Tommies were essentially decent (if not always bright) with the fact of the current unrest. Typically such conspiracies have a chain of duping going on, with trades unionists duping the workers, revolutionaries duping the trades unionists, and a master criminal at the top. As Agatha Christie puts it in *The Secret Adversary* (1922; written before she had established her characteristic format, and owing a great deal to *Bulldog Drummond*): 'The Bolshevists are behind the labour unrest – but this man is behind the Bolshevists.'[30]

Anti-Semitism easily found its place within this fantasy. While it is true that some 'white-slavers' were East European Jews, popular fiction of the day greatly over-emphasises Jewish involvement in people-trafficking.[31] Typically, popular fiction shifted the responsibility for prostitution away from the purchaser and on to the woman or the trafficker; to scapegoat Jews shifted the responsibility even more comfortably. The thriller writers developed existing myths and prejudices by representing the various perceived enemies of society as linked together, a fantasy that has its roots in wartime rumours about the subversive 'Hidden Hand'. The most notorious public eruption of these conspiracy theories occurred when Noel Pemberton-Billing, MP, won the 1918 libel action arising from his claim that the audience for Maud Allan's performance of Wilde's *Salome* would be composed of perverts and traitors of the type included in a secret list of 47,000 German agents who had infiltrated the British political elite.[32] For thriller writers, as for Pemberton-Billing, the excitable logic of the conspiracy theorist linked sexual subversion with political subversion.

In the second Drummond novel, *The Black Gang* (1922), Drummond and his associates become proactive, seizing and punishing the enemies of society before they have the chance to commit worse offences. The punishments approximately fit the crime; for white-slavers the sentence is 'Flog them to within an inch of their lives … It is the punishment for their method of livelihood';[33] socialist agitators, on the other hand, are taken away to an island where they are subjected to a regime that imitates Russian communism in its severity and arbitrariness.[34] In order to carry out this retribution, Drummond and his friends become 'the Black Gang', masked and hooded, and covered from head to toe in black silk. Contemporary readers must have been reminded of Mussolini's Blackshirts, and perhaps too of the Black and Tans. There may even have been echoes of the epic film success of the war years, D. W. Griffith's *Birth of a Nation* (1915), in which the American South is saved from the corruptions of the Reconstruction era by the heroic hooded figures of the Ku Klux Klan.

The Drummond of *The Black Gang* stepped temporarily over the borderline of legality while conducting his vigilante operations. Another hero of the immediate post-war period, A. M. Burrage's Captain Dorry, established himself firmly on the wrong side of the law. In *The Strange Career of Captain Dorry*, a series of stories in *Lloyds Magazine* for 1921, Dorry is an unemployed ex-officer (with MC) who meets an engaging and mysterious man called Fewgin, receiver of stolen goods and reader of minds. By observing Dorry, Fewgin astutely realises that he is a candidate for recruitment to his select band of ex-army thieves – who steal only from 'certain vampires who made money out of the war, and, by keeping up prices, are continuing to make money out of the peace'.[35] Drummond in *The Black Gang* punished the enemies of England in ways impossible for the police – but his motives were disinterested. When Dorry and Fewgin commit outright crime, they usually profit from it, at the expense of profiteers, corrupt socialists and fake mediums.

While such stories of vigilante enterprise are signs of the times, there are indications that their appeal may have been limited when the heroes became too determined on punishing the wrongdoers. Captain Dorry never made it out of the fiction magazines into hard covers, and after *The Black Gang*, Drummond became more reactive than proactive in his conflicts with wrongdoers. Tired of war, readers seem to have been less impressed by heroes who went looking for trouble than by those who could deal with it firmly when it chanced to arrive.

The Drummond of the first book, setting the pattern for the typical hero of the post-war thriller, is dogged, uncomplicated, patriotic and amateur; he often presents himself as stupid,[36] and he is lucky. These characteristics reflect the modest self-image of many British soldiers, who had defeated a German army which at the beginning of the war had been manifestly superior in weaponry, manpower and strategy. British resilience and improvisation had won the day. Humourless cleverness is reserved for villains; Carl Peterson is a 'genius', and Lakington, the aesthetic secondary villain, is 'one of the most brilliant scientists who have ever been up at Oxford'. He is also a distinguished art connoisseur, who has now deliberately chosen 'to turn his brain to crime. Not vulgar common sorts of crime – but the big things, calling for a master criminal.'

By Drummond and his imitators, stupidity was borne almost as a badge of honour, and stupidly facetious language could even be used as a weapon – 'this particular form of baiting invariably infuriated Peterson' we are told.[37] When *Bulldog Drummond* was adapted for the West End stage in 1921, with Gerald du Maurier in the title role, the theatrical newspaper *The Era* reported on the event:

> 'We've given you the sex play,' said Mr Gerald du Maurier at the fall of a 'tremendous' curtain on Tuesday night, 'and we've given you the "high-brow" play. Now we want to give you a change, – and here's what "Sapper" and I think is best described as a "thick-ear" play!' And the audience cheered lustily, evidently quite pleased with said change.[38]

Unlike the villains, the theatrical audience was in on the joke about stupidity, as were hundreds of thousands who read the novels.[39] The thriller is a boisterous literary game, whose playful nature is signalled by the gusto of its excesses and the extravagance of its coincidences. *The Era*'s reporter went on to remark that 'There are thousands of Captain Hugh Drummonds about in real life' (and indeed there were 200,000 demobilised ex-officers in Britain) and to claim that the play 'has an extra usefulness':

> It shows the real Drummonds what may happen if they advertise in the same way as the fictitious one did. It shows them that they'll as likely as not get a 'thick ear,' though they may, to their consolation, quite possibly manage, before getting it, to do some good in some direction or other. On the other hand they may not. They certainly will not if they are denied the absolutely amazing luck that is not denied to the fictitious one.

The reviewer marks a distinction between the thriller and real life that the work itself makes evident. Readers and audiences who took the hint could realise that thrillers offered a great deal of latitude in the seriousness with which they should be taken. Many who did not subscribe to the prejudices expressed were still able to find enjoyment in the works, which, although there is much in them that does not appeal to twenty-first-century tastes, are more likely to have acted as outlets for exasperations and anxieties than as blueprints for political action. The novels of Gibbs and Deeping, on the other hand, demand to be taken very seriously or not at all. This flexibility of interpretative possibility must have been an important factor in keeping *Bulldog Drummond*, alone of the texts discussed in this chapter, in print for most of the past ninety years.

The different kinds of writing considered in this chapter share a certain nostalgia for the loss of wartime cohesion, and an uncertainty about the present. 'War's hell, of course. But there's something about it,' a nurse tells Bertram in *The Middle of the Road*. He replies, 'It's the impulse that's gone. There doesn't seem to be any purpose.' These post-war novels document the confusion and loss of impulse, but offer no guide to rediscovering a sense of purpose, except by looking back to the best values of wartime. During the war, both soldiers and civilians had looked forward avidly to the coming of peace. After the Armistice, the future looked considerably less inviting.

Notes

1 John Buchan, *The Dancing Floor* (1926), collected in *The Adventures of Edward Leithen* (London: Hodder and Stoughton, 1939), 202.
2 Philip Gibbs, *Back to Life* (London: Heinemann, 1920), 221–2.
3 Philip Gibbs, *Realities of War* (London: Heinemann, 1920), 426.
4 Gibbs, *Realities of War*, 437.
5 Gibbs, *Realities of War*, 43.
6 Gibbs, *Realities of War*, 46.
7 Gibbs, *Back to Life*, 75. Later, a nun puts the punishment into a historical context for him: 'I remember – 1870. They cut the hair of women who had

disgraced themselves – and France – by their behaviour with German soldiers. We thought then that it was a light punishment … we think so now, monsieur!' (80)

8 Gibbs, *Back to Life*, 141.
9 Gibbs, *Back to Life*, 274.
10 Gibbs, *Back to Life*, 275. For discussions of these kinds of atrocity stories, see Peter Buitenhuis, *The Great War of Words* (London: Batsford, 1989); Trudi Tate, *Modernism, History and the First World War* (Manchester: Manchester University Press, 1998), ch. 2.
11 Philip Gibbs, *The Middle of the Road* (London: Hutchinson, 1923), 87.
12 Gibbs, *The Middle of the Road*, 171–2.
13 Stuart Laing, 'Philip Gibbs and the Newsreel Novel', in Peter Humm, Paul Stigant and Peter Widdowson, eds, *Popular Fictions: Essays in Literature and History* (London: Methuen, 1986), 128.
14 Mary Grover, *The Ordeal of Warwick Deeping: Middlebrow Authorship and Cultural Embarrassment* (Madison, WI: Farleigh Dickinson University Press, 2009), 77.
15 Samuel Hynes, *A War Imagined: The First World War in English Culture* (New York: Atheneum, 1991), 350.
16 Warwick Deeping, *Sorrell and Son* (London: Cassell, 1925), 90.
17 Warwick Deeping, *The Secret Sanctuary* (London: Cassell, 1923), 20.
18 Deeping, *The Secret Sanctuary*, 24.
19 *Times Literary Supplement* (18 January 1923), 46.
20 Deeping, *The Secret Sanctuary*, 134.
21 Rosa Maria Bracco, *Merchants of Hope: British Middlebrow Writers and the First World War, 1919–1939* (Providence, RI: Berg, 1993), 12.
22 Grover, *The Ordeal of Warwick Deeping*, 93.
23 'Sapper', *Bulldog Drummond: The Carl Peterson Quartet* (London: Wordsworth Editions, 2007), 65. All references to *Bulldog Drummond* and *The Black Gang* are to this edition.
24 Letter to his mother, 11 October 1914. Quoted in Nicholas Mosley, *Julian Grenfell: His Life and the Times of his Death 1888–1915* (London: Persephone Books, 1999), 353.
25 Larkin, 'MCMXIV', *The Whitsun Weddings* (London: Faber and Faber, 1964), 28.
26 'Sapper', *Bulldog Drummond*, 14–15.
27 'Sapper', *Bulldog Drummond*, 3.
28 'Sapper', *Bulldog Drummond*, 209.
29 During the actual war, the British army was less affected by protest or mutiny than were the armies of the other major combatant powers. The soldiers' strikes of 1919 were mainly caused by delays in the process of demobilisation, though there was also disquiet at the possibility that British troops might be sent in large numbers to fight in Russia.

30 Agatha Christie, *The Secret Adversary* (1922), collected in Agatha Christie, *1920s Omnibus* (London: HarperCollins, 2006), 31.

31 Edward Bristow quotes statistics for people convicted of people-trafficking in London, Hamburg and Berlin in 1908, which show that 214 out of 578 (37%) could be identified as East European Jews, mostly from Russia or Russian Poland. Edward Bristow, *Prostitution and Prejudice: The Jewish Fight against White Slavery* (Oxford: Oxford University Press, 1982). Bristow suggests that the preponderance of Jewish people arrested for this crime may partly be due to Jews having been sought and prosecuted more strenuously. Bristow makes it clear that to link the Jews of the Russian Revolution with the Jews of the white slave trade was objectively absurd. In Poland, for example, Jewish gangsters and pimps were employed to break strikes; they did not foment them.

32 A full account of the case can be found in Philip Hoare, *Oscar Wilde's Last Stand: Decadence, Conspiracy, and the Most Outrageous Trial of the Century* (London: Duckworth, 1997). It was revealed at the trial that the list of supposed traitors included the name of Asquith and his wife, and Haldane, the former Minister for War. See also Jodie Medd, '"The Cult of the Clitoris": Anatomy of a National Scandal', *Modernism/Modernity*, 9, 1 (2002), 21–49.

33 'Sapper', *Bulldog Drummond*, 214.

34 During the 1920s there were some real-life imitations of the Black Gang's tactics. In 1925, for example, a group of British fascists kidnapped the communist leader, Harry Pollitt, and took him to South Wales for a weekend of re-education.

35 A. M. Burrage, 'The Strange Career of Captain Dorry: I. Second in the Field', *Lloyd's Magazine*, March 1921, 381.

36 Epithets such as 'simple' and 'stolid' are constantly applied to the dogged ex-soldier hero of Agatha Christie's *The Secret Adversary* (1922). In Buchan's *The Three Hostages* (1924), even Richard Hannay refers to himself as 'stupid'. On the other hand, we are occasionally reminded that Bulldog Drummond is not actually as stupid as he looks.

37 'Sapper', *Bulldog Drummond*, 148.

38 'Bulldog Drummond', *The Era*, London (30 March 1921), 5.

39 For a full analysis of the astonishing sales figures achieved by the Drummond novels, see Jessica Meyer, 'The Tuition of Manhood: Sapper's War Stories and the Literature of War', in Mary Hammond and Shafquat Towheed, eds, *Publishing in the First World War: Essays in Book History* (Basingstoke: Palgrave, 2007). By 1939 *Bulldog Drummond* had accumulated sales of 396,302 copies, and *The Black Gang* 277,383.

4

Fighting the peace: Two women's accounts of the post-war years

Alison Hennegan

Quite early on in the novel *Women of the Aftermath* (1931) by Helen Zenna Smith (Evadne Price) there is an evocation of the crowds in and around Piccadilly Circus on the first Armistice Day, 11 November 1918.[1] The description is an often savage piece of writing, punctuated by the italicised and increasingly ironic refrain, '*We've won the War!*' The narration is torn between disgust, understanding, empathy and rejection of the drunkenness, the crudity and the desperate desire for oblivion in those for whom the sense of loss is stronger than that of relief and rejoicing. Gender and class hostilities are never far below the surface (Nell Smith, the middle-class narrator, is viciously accused of being stuck up when she doesn't respond in kind to a drunken Tommy's clumsy advances in the crowd [*WA*, 37]). It's as though the 'social glue' which, for some people, made them feel that 'we're all in it together' during the war itself is already coming unstuck, as people revert to older, deeper loyalties and antipathies.

Only a few days later, on 15 November, Virginia Woolf noted in her diary:

> Peace is rapidly dissolving into the light of common day. You can go to London without meeting more than two drunk soldiers; only an occasional crowd blocks the street. But mentally the change is marked too. Instead of feeling that the whole people, willing or not, were concentrated on a single point, one feels now that the whole bunch has burst asunder and flown off with the utmost vigour in different directions. We are once more a nation of individuals.[2]

In Nell's account there is a suggestion that, for those participating, the first Armistice Day is time suspended in time, that in some sense what they do now 'won't count', will have no consequences. An old flower seller throws her day's flowers (her livelihood) into the air and tells everyone to take what they like (*WA*, 31); decorum is thrown to the wind, just for today; the prevailing mood is poised between the 'ecstatic' and the lost – the 'abandoned', in no benign sense.

Nell, the narrator, has her own female version of the idea we're told was so strong among the men, that 'the best have gone, we who are left are the lesser', and she feels it especially in relation to Tosh, a close woman friend killed by a shrapnel fragment while driving her ambulance 'somewhere in France', as described in Helen Zenna Smith's earlier work, *Not So Quiet ...: Stepdaughters of War* (1930).[3] Tosh was always an interestingly ambiguous figure, poised between conventional notions of masculinity and femininity. In her flouting of smaller conventions and meannesses she might have seemed to offer another way of doing 'being a woman'; but she did not survive into the peace, so was never able to test her ideas and herself against post-war conventions, nor yet help to change them.

The second chapter of Smith's later novel *Luxury Ladies* (1933) also contains a description of an Armistice Day, but this one is more than a decade later. This, too, is an often savage piece, and once again punctuated with italicised, choric repetitions and near-repetitions, all linked by the word 'silence', as in '*The Silence of a society that has learned little and has already forgotten too much*' or '*Silence, silence, a dead world of thick, horrible silence ...*'[4] Among those who have forgotten, in one sense, is Nell herself, who becomes aware as she waits for and observes the Two Minutes' Silence how little she has thought of many who were once so important to her during the war years, although she thinks of them now. At one level this could simply be seen as a useful narrative device which enables Smith to provide information or reminders about characters in her earlier work, *Not So Quiet...* But at another it chimes with a recurring theme of Smith's post-war trilogy, which is that life has been 'suspended' if not actually ended for many of the women who served in and survived the war. As Nell stands in silence, she remembers the letter in which her first husband broke the news of the extent of his wounds:

> 'I've been blinded. I expect Mother told you, but there's something she doesn't know – there'll never be any perambulator on that lawn of ours, Nell. Understand?' I understand. But it doesn't matter, nothing matters except war, War, WAR. We war-women have had the feeling knocked out of our make-ups – nothing matters – nothing. We're dead women; dead for the duration of the war and God alone knows how long after, and we don't want children ... Dead women don't want children ... (*LL*, 40)

Nell may be unusual in her vehement assertion that she does not want a child, but the sense of those children who will now never be born to dead men hangs over the period. Each of the three stanzas of Vera Brittain's 1919 poem 'The Superfluous Woman', for example, ends with a different italicised line, the last of which is '*But who will give me my children?*'[5]

To Nell the Last Post as played in the years during and immediately after the war and the one played now, years later, to mark the end of the Two Minutes' Silence, are two very different things. This year, those who had managed to refrain from talking through the silence now clearly hear the Last Post as a welcome indication that they're free to talk again. Nell thinks wearily and angrily of other, wartime Last Posts she heard so often:

> The 'Last Post' … a square, undecorated military cemetery with its muddy earth-mounds and rows of plain crosses lying at the foot of 'The Hill of the Witches' Hand' – a swift place to hide men who have died violently and dreadfully. Ambulance following ambulance down the slope to the cemetery with its load of flag-covered coffins … 'Pass the word along, Smithy; don't go in too near the gates or you'll stick in the mud – it's three feet deep today.' … A record day for burial; countless young lives ending prematurely as numbers in a row of muddy earth-mounds in a bare military cemetery … the droning of the padre … a nod from the bugler to his mate … 'Ready?' … The 'Last Post' filling the valley and the notes caught up and flung back by the hills …
>
> A different 'Last Post' today – as different from the old familiar one as chalk from cheese, or have I forgotten already? Somehow today's does not carry the haunting sadness and terrible finality of the old version … This 'Last Post' belongs to another generation.
>
> I shall not come again to the Cenotaph ceremony. I am too old. I am out of place here.
>
> '*Oh God, our help in ages past*' … (*LL*, 41–2)

A little later Nell by chance encounters in the crowd a member of her old ambulance unit, Skinny, whom she has not seen for more than a decade. Skinny has been equally distressed, and angered by the crowd's response:

> 'It's a farce. In a few more years there won't be any of our generation left to make a protest. A few more years after that, and they'll have to make a preliminary speech … Can't you hear the B.B.C. Announcer: "This is London Regional calling. We are about to take you over to the ceremony of the Armistice at the Cenotaph. For the benefit of those who have not read this week's *Listener* …" A few years after and it'll be dropped. Like "Good Queen Victoria's Birthday Celebrations". "Who was Good Queen Victoria,

> Mummy, and why must we celebrate the twenty-fourth of May?" I remember asking that myself as a kid. And yesterday I heard a kid say: "Mummy, what is the Armistice, and why must we have two minutes' silence?" God, Smithy, that gave me a funny feeling inside; made me feel like a bit of ancient history …' (*LL*, 48).

For today's readers, most of whom, it's probably fair to say, would also need to ask 'why must we celebrate the twenty-fourth of May?', this may well be an uneasy passage. How much longer, we might also ask, will Armistice Day have widespread meaning? We might, however, go on to consider that only a few years ago the Two Minutes' Silence, as something to be observed at 11.00 a.m. on 11 November rather than on the nearest Sunday, itself seemed a dead observance, yet it has recently been revived. Ways of memorialising can, it seems, be rediscovered as well as lost.

Skinny describes to Nell her rage at having heard some mindless young woman prattling her way through the Two Minutes' Silence:

> 'She looked pained and surprised when, at the end of the "Last Post", I leaned over and whispered: "You hell-fired bitch! I'd like to wring your scraggy neck and see if that would quieten you!", and walked out of her life, leaving her gasping like a codfish …' (*LL*, 48)

Skinny goes on to say to Nell, in words and sentiments that might remind us of poems such as Philip Johnstone's angry 1918 'High Wood' which foresees the coming of battlefield tourism:[6]

> 'I've got too much imagination; I can hear the Guide at the Unknown Warrior's Tomb explaining through a megaphone to the next generation the lovely gesture that tore our hearts with agony when it happened in our time: "This tomb was placed here after the Great War, 1914–1918. The unidentified body of a soldier was buried beneath this tablet that all citizens with a 'Missing' relative could gain comfort in believing he was buried among the heroes of Westminster Abbey" … Yes, I can hear that – and some brainless bitch in the crowd saying: "Well, ain't that too cute? …"' (*LL*, 49)

This fictional account of two women's angry and despairing responses to what feels to them like a universal obliviousness is echoed in contemporary factual writing. Vera Brittain, for example, wrote a number of Armistice Day pieces during the late 1920s and early 1930s. Here, in a 1930 *Manchester Guardian* article, she writes of her initial anger at having heard her children's nursemaid tell them 'that soon it would be

November 11th and they would both be able to wear a lovely red poppy on their clothes':

> Did this young woman, my outraged memories demanded, so utterly lack imagination that she really proposed to attach that symbol of grim death to that frill of yellow muslin which shielded my baby daughter's innocent head from the colder winds of Heaven?[7]

But a moment's thought reminds Brittain that her nursemaid was only eight when the war ended, and that in the twelve years that have passed since then she has 'bridged the gulf between childhood and adulthood'. Why then should Brittain 'so resent the fact that she sees in the sale of Flanders poppies merely a rather superior Flag Day'? Armistice Day is for her nursemaid as far distant as Trafalgar and Waterloo or Mafeking: 'it is associated in her mind with ancient songs and long-ago conversations emerging from the dim shadows of early childhood'.[8]

Even in the closing stages of the war and the months immediately following the Armistice, fighting poets had feared and foreseen a universal forgetting; so, for example, as early as March 1919 Sassoon's 'Aftermath', which vividly recalls some of the most horrific sights, sounds and smells of the trenches, ends with the italicised lines:

> *Have you forgotten yet? ...*
> *Look up, and swear by the green of the spring that you'll never forget.*[9]

By the time the Menin Gate, Lutyens's great memorial monument, was completed in 1927, Sassoon's sonnet marking the occasion began:

> Who will remember, passing through this Gate,
> The unheroic dead who fed the guns?[10]

By November 1932 Brittain writes that 'the usual protests' against the perpetuation of Armistice Day ceremonies are finding their way into the press. Noting that a Derbyshire clergyman has refused to hold a special service in his church, Brittain, like Skinny, fears that 'Armistice Day is a dying institution'. She links this willingness to forget with a refusal to acknowledge what is already happening in Europe – the rise of fascist dictatorship and apathy in the face of it.[11]

It's true that we might do well to remind ourselves that even the very first Armistice Day in 1918 was not universally marked with sombre mourning and grave reflection on the meaning and cost of the war. Ivor Gurney's poem 'The Bugle', for example, written in January or February 1919 and describing London on 11 November 1918, speaks of how

> [...] in the gray street women void of grace
> Chatter of trifles,
> Hurry to barter, wander aimlessly
> The heedless town,
> Men lose their souls in care of business,
> As men had not been mown
> Like corn swathes East of Ypres or the Somme
> Never again home
> Or beauty most beloved to see, for that
> London Town might still be busy at
> Its sordid cares
> Traffic of wares.

Little wonder that:

> In soldiers' faces one might see the fear
> That once again they should be called to bear
> Arms, and to save England from her own.[12]

For Nell, the unthinking behaviour that so distresses her at the Cenotaph in the late 1920s is less a form of denial, a refusal to face present facts and looming menace in Europe, and more a matter of a generation gap which can only intensify as the years proceed, leaving her and her peers isolated, irrelevant remnants and unwanted survivors of a time now best forgotten. Their plight is intensified by the tendency of the day's popular journalism to conflate two very different groups of women: those who were already adult during the war, and the young women of the mid-to-late 1920s who were children then. The increasing use of the word 'girl' to describe any female from the age of four to fifty adds a further layer of confusion. In her 1928 novel *Keeping Up Appearances*, Rose Macaulay has exuberant satirical fun with the tabloids' endless fascination with 'the post-war woman' and, more often, 'the post-war girl'. Through the deliberations of Daisy, who writes little paragraphs and book reviews for a daily paper, and who muses discontentedly on the sort of articles male editors endlessly ask her to write, we get a taste of contemporary debates. But there's one topic she knows she will never be asked to debate:

> Is one Post-War Girl different in any respect from any other? No, that wouldn't do; the press knew she wasn't; it would regard even the question as heresy. You might admire or blame the Post-War Girl but you must not deny her existence as a separate entity ... Daisy wrote and read of her daily, and knew her simple characteristics by heart, even as she knew those of the girl of an earlier generation, who took no exercise, who fainted, or, alternatively, did embroidery, all day, and always obeyed her elders.[13]

Nell frequently expresses resentment at the ignorance of younger women who take for granted freedoms secured for them by Nell's generation but who show very little, if any, understanding of the cost at which such freedoms were won. Later when she has been reduced to begging on the streets, singing popular songs, with a cardboard placard round her neck which says 'EX-WAAC. ALL I ASK IS A STEADY JOB. WON'T ANYBODY HELP?',[14] Nell will discover that there is little point in supplicating the predominantly female office workers thronging Ludgate Circus and the Strand:

> sheer waste of energy appealing to their sympathy with 'Little Grey Home in the West' when all they are worrying about is the little grey office in the E.C. district ... as for an ex-Waac, fifty per cent of them are too young to know what an ex-Waac is. (*SW*, 127)

Remnants or revenants, the women who actually served during the war have themselves become 'grey ghosts', in the words May Wedderburn Cannan used in 1919 when writing of the war's dead:

> Now must we go again, back to the world
> Full of grey ghosts and voices of men dying,
> And in the rain the sounding of Last Posts ...[15]

Nell and her kind are the new 'grey ghosts' or 'shadow women', as Smith calls the 1932 middle volume of her trilogy. In the post-war world, ex-servicewomen are as much an inconvenience as the demobilised servicemen; both are very often, it appears, 'surplus to requirements' for the post-war nation.

Nell Smith, or 'Smithy' as she is known to her friends, might indeed be deemed doubly a ghost and a shadow, given that the four books of her 'autobiography' are fictions created by a writer; one moreover who, in choosing to write as Helen Zenna Smith, has created for herself a name that appears to be a formal version of Smithy's own – a form of double bluff. *Not So Quiet...: The Step-Daughters of War*, in which Nell was first introduced to readers, remains one of the most familiar and widely discussed of that outpouring of books that began to appear in increasing numbers from 1928 into the 1930s and that were particularly concerned with female experiences of the war. Of recent years *Not So Quiet...* has been praised by many, and censured by others for inaccuracy and inauthenticity. Helen Zenna Smith never herself served in France, although she was able to draw upon the diaries of Winifred Young, who did.[16] Nevertheless the book seems to have a secure place in the canon of women's writings of the First World War. However, the three novels that succeeded it – *Women of the Aftermath*, *Shadow Women* and *Luxury Ladies*, published from 1931 to 1933 – are much less well known. Critical comment on the novels is often dismissive, and not always, one suspects, based on complete readings. The books are seen as potboilers, as melodramatic hack work. But all of them are far more interesting than that, and deserve better at the hands of critics.

In many ways their subject matter is familiar enough to readers of novels and memoirs of the period: the movement from female middle-class security and certainty, through harsh immersion in the violent, terrifying and horrifying world of war work in France, and the emergence into a post-war world rendered unrecognisable and barely inhabitable in the face of loss and suffering. For Nell, hard-won happiness proves short-lived or delusory: *Women of the Aftermath* ends in disaster; *Shadow Women* appears, after considerable suffering and much despair, to end happily, with the promise of marriage to an admirable man; but *Luxury Ladies* begins with his death from cancer, after a mere eighteen months of supremely happy married life. *Luxury Ladies*' own apparently 'happy ending' does not necessarily reassure its readers, who have learned by now to take nothing for granted.

The narrative arc of the trilogy begins just a few days before the announcement of the Armistice. It describes Nell's wretched first marriage to Roy, a 'second-choice' husband whom she has married because she believes – wrongly, it transpires – that the man she really loves has been killed in action. Her husband has been desperately wounded: he is blind, has lost a leg, has been castrated and his nerves are shot to hell. He bitterly resents the sergeant 'who earned his V.C. out of me' (*WA*, 39) by bringing him in from no-man's land. Although he had offered to release Nell from her engagement she, in a female version of chivalry, had refused to let him. Once back in England, he has set about making life hell for everyone in the vicinity: for his wife, for the household servants and for his admittedly extremely unpleasant mother, who had rejoiced in 'giving' her son to the war, and rejoices still in having a blinded, bemedalled hero to tend and display as she wheels him round Wimbledon Common. She is blithely unaware (although her daughter-in-law and the reader quickly realise it) that more than a little sadism and sexual confusion underlie her pleasure and pride in her wrecked, infantilised son's dependency.

When Robin, the man Nell had believed to be dead, resurfaces from his prisoner of war camp, she initially resists her desire for him, but eventually she acts upon it. Her wretched (but mainly enraged) husband kills himself, which might secure for him our sympathy were it not for the fact that he leaves a masterly suicide note of pretended self-sacrifice and abnegation but one actually heavy with venomous reproach – a letter which, when read out in court, earns Nell the censure of the Coroner, the freely expressed loathing of the eager audience, public shaming in the press and ostracism by her family.

From this point on everything changes for Nell, and the three novels chart a specifically female odyssey through the post-war world. She journeys through a short-lived affair with Robin and enters an unstable and unsustaining world, characterised by frenetic parties and a restless swapping of sexual partners by people simultaneously seeking and terrified of personal commitment to others, impatient of pre-war conventions and lacking the emotional energy or moral conviction to find new workable codes or values. Jettisoned by Robin, who goes back to his wife, Nell begins to make a precarious way through the very limited range of possibilities that face an uneducated, untrained, middle-class woman who has forfeited both the material and emotional support of her family. Only the shadier aspects of 'entertainment' – back row of the chorus, one-line walk-on parts, dance hostess – seem possible. Temporarily she is rescued from her frighteningly rapid descent by becoming mistress to Giles, a callow, mother-dominated, wealthy young pup too inexperienced to realise that Nell is no virginal young thing, but ten years his senior and much battered by life. Only her chance re-encounter with Soupy, an RFC pilot whom she knew in France, saves her. He ignites in her a passion for aviation and teaches her to fly. *Women of the Aftermath* ends with Nell crashing the light aircraft which she has cajoled Giles into giving her for a birthday present, and *Shadow Women* begins with her in hospital, badly injured and with a face severely and seemingly irretrievably disfigured by the flames that engulfed her in her burning aeroplane.

For a skill-less, moneyless, no longer young woman, Nell's facial disfigurement immediately rules out a whole host of possibilities; it also makes it most unlikely that Giles will continue to want to keep her as a mistress. Nell, once discharged from hospital, begins the pitiless struggle for survival. The £50 that Giles encloses in the letter ending their relationship is soon exhausted, partly because Nell's lack of any sort of training in household economics means that even when she is trying to be sensible with money, she doesn't know how to. She is easily duped into thinking things are 'investments' when they are in fact extravagances, and, desperate about her ravaged face, she lets herself believe the ludicrous claims of a quack doctor and parts with a whole £25 for a pointless 'cure'. The supposed virtue of 'optimism', her 'something will turn up' mentality, easily confused with a pluckily courageous spirit, also proves to be a vice for someone placed as she is. A vacuous hopefulness pre-empts a realistic appraisal of her situation, and stops her from thinking strategically about her options until a harsher reality presents itself.

> If I had carefully conserved my capital [the £50 Giles sent her as 'severance pay'] the Embankment would have been delayed for a few months, but it is the inevitable end for such as I. I am so utterly useless. I cannot cook, housework is an unsolved mystery to me, I have no trade or profession – and if I had, how many skilled women are there unable to get work? I can drive a car and pilot an aeroplane, but without influence it is hopeless trying to earn a living in these lines … [W]omen chauffeurs are not wanted unless they are also gardeners – 'Wanted a lady gardener-chauffeur' – no use to me, no use, I am a drug on the woman market. (*SW*, 53–4)

Nell's descent, already begun in *Women of the Aftermath*, continues here via the Thames Embankment, sleeping on benches, washing in horse troughs to the mingled amusement and indifference of passers-by, joining the community of vagrants whom the police are legally constrained to 'move on', even if the odd kindly officer occasionally turns a blind eye. Nell's downward spiral takes us into cheap lodging houses (ninepence a night for lousy bedding, outdoor WCs, sleeping in your clothes as the necessary safeguard against their theft) and the exhausting and pointless quartering of London, on foot, in quest of jobs suggested by the Labour exchange, which she will never get because she now looks so disreputable with her ravaged face, shabby clothes and broken shoes. It is a steadily downward progress which anticipates that of Orwell's Dorothy Hare in *A Clergyman's Daughter* (1935).

Although Smith's trilogy is particularly concerned with women's post-war world, it is far from oblivious or indifferent to the suffering of ex-soldiers. At many points in the books, Nell draws men's and women's experiences together. So, for example, her description of the terror and pain of being trapped in her burning, plummetting aircraft at the end of *Women of the Aftermath* has unmistakable echoes of RFC pilots being shot down (*WA*, 27); as she struggles to come to terms with her desperately ruined face, she simultaneously regrets the revulsion she had sometimes felt for wounded men with facial injuries, and foresees clearly how others will now react to her. Later, her own experience of spiralling into poverty and eventual destitution, as described in *Shadow Women*, is mirrored by that of male acquaintances and friends, including Jim, whom she marries. The experiences that bind those who served in the war and separate them from those who did not may sometimes transcend gender.

Appearances, Nell realises, are all, and most people can judge others by nothing else. And those whose appearance is sufficiently off-putting will not really be seen at all. *Shadow Women*'s title comes from Nell's sense, as she exhausts herself walking around London in the quest for work, that she holds little sense of reality for most of the people she passes:

> Walking, walking, walking, head throbbing, limbs like lead … Round you the passers-by merge into a sort of grey blur. You are a shadow woman in a shadowy world. Reality goes. All sense of time fades – half an hour, an hour, what does it matter when you are walking the pavements in search of work at ninepence an hour that will never materialize? … 'Tea', 'dinner', 'breakfast', 'supper' – all dreamwords meaning food. Forget them, you will never require them in your vocabulary again, shadow woman of the pavement. (*SW*, 64)

That final phrase, 'shadow woman of the pavement', more than hints at a theme which runs through the trilogy: a constant implicit – and sometimes explicit – questioning of any neat and tidy distinctions between what does and does not constitute prostitution. Nell's worlds are peopled by a very diverse array of women: 'society women', 'respectable' middle-class women whose lives are suddenly overturned, aspiring actresses, struggling chorus girls, women sliding down the social ladder into poverty and sometimes actual destitution. But whether heterosexual or lesbian (like Skinny, equivocally attached to a much older, very wealthy woman who is as much would-be saviour as exploiter), for almost all of them genteel and not so genteel forms of prostitution are never far distant. The lines are increasingly blurred between being 'a mistress' (almost respectable) or being passed around from one man to another in a group of male friends (merely raffish and the sign of a free spirit), to being straightforwardly available to any man – and sometimes woman – who is prepared to buy meals, give gifts and make the odd 'present' (a euphemism for cash).

Again, we are in familiar territory: Katherine Mansfield's Miss Ada Moss, the protagonist of 'Pictures' (1922),[17] had once been an aspiring singer. But now she is tired of hoofing it round the theatrical agents who offer her fewer and fewer parts in silent films. The story ends with her on the verge of deciding whether or not to be 'kind' to the northern businessman who has bought her drinks in a hotel lounge where she had gone for one last, defiant taste of the luxury of an afternoon tea she couldn't afford. It is also the world of some of the female characters in Norah Hoult's 1928 collection, *Poor Women*, and, several years later, of Storm Jameson's nameless middle-aged protagonist in her 1933 novella, *A Day Off*.[18] And, if we cross the Channel and go to Paris, it is also the world of many of Jean Rhys's female characters.

In some respects this is all part of the period's battle over the sexual double standard. Christabel Pankhurst's solution to the problem, and her battle cry during her campaign for her own sexual and political revolution, may have been 'Votes for Women, Chastity for Men', but there were of course other views, arguing for equal sexual 'freedom' for both sexes. What 'sexual freedom' might look like, however, was the difficult question. Throughout the four novels devoted to her progress Nell wrestles with the shifting meanings and value of female 'virtue' and purity. Tosh, her close friend and fellow ambulance driver, had expressed herself with characteristic pungency on the subject, when their unit was in the throes of one of the periodic purity purges instituted by their unsympathetic female commandant:

> 'As if morality matters two hoots when it comes to convoying wounded men. Personally, if I were choosing women to drive heavy ambulances their morals wouldn't worry me. It would be "Are you a first-class driver", not "Are you a first-class virgin?" The biggest harlot or the biggest saint ... what the hell does it matter as long as they put up a decent performance behind the steering wheel and can keep their engines clean?' (*NSQ*, 126)

Even Tosh's open-mindedness had its limitations, however. When, years later, Nell once more encounters Skinny at the Cenotaph, her primary reaction is not one of delight:

> Ordinarily I might not respond so enthusiastically to Skinny's presence. In France she was the one I liked least in the whole convoy, possibly because Tosh detested her – a queer thing, personal dislike. I had no reason to dislike Skinny, but Tosh was my friend, and I followed her in most things ... And there were ugly rumours – more than rumours. Nineteen-fifteen. The years have broadened my outlook – people's private lives are their own affair ... and I'm lonely, devastatingly lonely. (*LL*, 46)

It is not unreasonable to speculate whether Tosh's intense antipathy to Skinny sprang in part from her own personal uncertainties about sex and gender. Tosh's personal appearance, often commented upon, seems to be a mixture of the ambiguously matronly, a younger version of Britannia (traditionally, in the hands of political cartoonists, a curiously androgynous female archetype, with her sexless profile and coal-heaver shoulders) and the prepubescent. It is something she is rather touchy about, as when Skinny comments on her newly shorn hair, cut to discourage the head lice that infest it:

> 'You look like a Shakespearean page, Tosh, or Rosalind,' continues Skinny.
> Tosh goes on stirring the Bovril.
> 'Something fascinatingly boyish,' says Skinny.
> Tosh swings round, 'Boyish my bottom,' she snaps, 'Take your Bovril and shut up. I hate being lousy; I don't care a curse what I look like.'
> There is silence. (*NSQ*, 22)

Later in the chapter, after a witch hunt ruthlessly conducted by the commandant, Skinny and another member of the unit are sent home on grounds that permit the real reasons for their departure to remain opaque. 'The next news in the mess [is] that Skinny and another girl were leaving immediately for England, sacked for refusing to obey orders …' (*NSQ*, 127). Not that it fools anyone; later, in *Luxury Ladies*, Nell recalls the male drivers' response: '"I *don't* think!" winked the drivers' (*LL*, 45).

The accounts of Skinny's ill-advised comments about Tosh's 'boyishness' and Skinny's own downfall are separated in the chapter by detailed descriptions of the work which the women undertake in the interim, ferrying coffins to the makeshift military cemetery. Nell's account includes a passionate denunciation of the waste of lives, especially young ones; the intolerable contrast of the muddy, barren, wrecked landscape with the lush peacefulness of the Sussex Downs, just across the Channel; the mixture of terror and boredom that makes up most days. At the centre of the chapter, then, are the most fundamental realities of the war – destruction, devastation, the death of the body, and the death of hope and faith for those who survive. Wrapped round it, and played out in the women's cubicle and commandant's office, is a lesser drama of small female cruelties and petty tyrannies enacted in the name of 'morality' and 'purity', words which, increasingly, have little meaning in the context of the war's infinitely greater horrors whose consequences these women ambulance drivers witness every day.

Nell may feel that her post-war capacity to view Skinny's sexuality more tolerantly than she did in France is a consequence of the years that separate 1915 from 1930. And it is true that those years witnessed an increasing awareness of the possibilities of sexual love between women, even if much of that awareness was hostile, as reactions to *The Well of Loneliness* and the trial of its publisher on the grounds of obscenity in 1928 indicate (although the commandant of the ambulance unit described in that novel behaves with more understanding, though no less awareness, of the love between Stephen Gordon and Mary Llewellyn).[19] But it is also possible that Nell, like Tosh, is not entirely in love with heterosexuality. Almost all her sexual relationships with men are badly flawed and invariably compromised by her material dependency. One of the exceptions is her close friendship with Soupy, the ex-RFC pilot, who eventually dies in a peacetime air crash, and with whom Nell's relationship, and short-lived marriage, is one of passionate comradeship. Cicely Hamilton's 1909 book *Marriage as a Trade*[20] was only one in a long line of nineteenth- and early twentieth-century works making the case for more conventional types of marriage as a form of licensed prostitution, and certainly it is hard to find anywhere in Smith's trilogy a decent heterosexual relationship: almost all of them are tainted by the women's financial and social dependency on the men. Even Nell's splendid stepfather, who enters her life at a desperate point and does all he can to help her, comes to realise that in marrying Nell's mother he has united himself with a fool and a mean-minded bigot. The one admittedly very important exception to Nell's catalogue of failed relationships with men is her marriage to Jim, an ex-officer who, like Nell, is already falling fast down the ladder of destitution when she encounters him. But within months of marrying Nell, Jim develops terminal cancer and dies, so we do not know whether the marriage's early promise would have held.

The rest of *Luxury Ladies* offers us a dismaying litany of the many failed relationships Nell observes around her as, via Skinny's introductions, she enters a world made up not of 'Bright Young Things' but of 'Bored' ones. This is a world of heavy drinking, drugs, obsessive partying and physical recklessness, a mixture of sexual promiscuity and deep sexual disillusionment: total 'freedom' and little satisfaction. As such, it is easily dismissable by a hostile reader as a collection of the period's narrative clichés, Waugh-and-water perhaps. A more sympathetic reading, however, would see the book as a form of Vanity Fair, an exhibition of those who fail in their effort to make and maintain truthful and honourable unions, and an exhibition through which Nell moves, reaching eventually the person with whom she believes she can make a lasting, loving relationship. Berry is a woman young enough to be the daughter Nell has always declared she never wanted, although describing her feelings for the young woman as 'maternal' removes otherwise disquieting problems of sexual definition and identity.

Love of Berry also helps to heal some of the biggest causes of Nell's post-war bitterness: her resentment of a younger generation of women, her violent internal rages against the harsh inequities of her post-war world, her distress at the many cruelties women practise against other women. The cruelty is not confined to the young who lack Nell's own raw experience of the war. It can also be found in women of her own generation and earlier, women who lived through the war yet seem either to have been untouched by it or to fail to understand the way in which it has shaped their post-war world – her own mother and mother-in-law, for example. *Not So Quiet…*, *Women of the Aftermath* and *Shadow Women* all offer frequent examples of women behaving tyrannously to each other. To Nell it seems that:

> The strain of cruelty in all women is never so noticeable as when they are in authority over their poorer circumstanced sisters. The antagonism between the sexes is as nothing to the antagonism of woman to woman. […]
>
> Generally speaking, women are too young in governing to govern cleverly. They lack a nice discrimination. They are natural bullies, they bully their husbands, children, relations, trades-people, shop assistants, animals and anyone else who dare not or cannot answer back. But of all bullies the average housewife employer of a casual charwoman is the most revolting. (*SW*, 106)

The rage Nell feels towards them is very great, and some passages in the books are shocking in their levels of verbal violence, as, for example, when Nell has been insolently rejected by a prospective employer:

> A little adversity might teach you kindness, forbearance, pity, humanity …
>
> It might.
>
> But in case it did not, I would like to work for you one day, and when you began your repertoire of catty tortures as I knelt subserviently on your cold oilcloth, I would joy supremely in swiping you across your smug jaw with a cold, wet, dirty floor-cloth – swish! just like that, and follow up my offensive with the scrubbing bucket of ice water over your astounded head. That, I think, would be a far more effective method of ramming home an object lesson you badly need. (*SW*, 109)

Such passages are not uncommon in the trilogy and in *Not So Quiet…*, and it can take a reader some time to notice that they are almost always heard only as Nell's inner thoughts; the people who arouse the anger rarely hear it voiced. Outwardly, for them, Nell's demeanour remains within the 'proper' bounds of female decorum, but the reader witnesses something raw, fierce and sometimes murderous. The constraints of middle-class femininity remain in place in most of her interactions, but the reader is made privy to the cost at which this is achieved. This tension between the voiced and unvoiced is relevant to discussions of these books' 'melodrama', a charge often levelled against them critically, and is more generally connected with other aspects of the books' style and structure. George Simmers, for example, has described Smith as 'an accomplished pasticheuse'[21] and goes on to describe her 'Just Jane' books (which certainly brightened my childhood) as 'a perfect-pitch adaptation of Richmal Crompton's "William" series with not much changed except the gender'. Which rather raises the question of how much you think is changed by gender. Jane Marcus, in her Afterword to a modern edition of *Not So Quiet…*, has described Smith's style there as a 'new form of cinematic, dialogic and dramatic interior monologue'.[22] The trilogy, however, is generically and stylistically more diverse than that.

Indeed, what we see in Smith's trilogy is something we might call 'vernacular modernism'. Her prose makes constant use of rapid and fluid movement between Nell's narration, her own internal monologues and those of other characters for whom she is ventriloquising. It is characterised by frequent use of ellipses and by *leitmotifs*. It would be easy to maintain that this is flagrant poaching or pastiche: she takes her ellipses, perhaps, from Woolf's *The Waves*; her use of Big Ben to punctuate an important section of *Shadow Women* (55–8) and its brief return in *Luxury Ladies* comes from *Mrs Dalloway*. Nell's Big Ben, however, is no reassuring presence, even though Nell used 'to sentimentalize' over it:

> But Big Ben is not friendly. He is a hardened old cynic who has no time for failures. All very well to hear him striking midnight on the wireless when exiled in a foreign land, tears in your eyes, a lump in your throat and forgetfulness of rain, slush and fog in your mind – but at three a.m. on a raw morning Big Ben is quite a different proposition. Fat, well-washed, smug, swollen-headed old humbug. (*SW*, 56)

The paragraph continues with an increasingly vicious and violent Big Ben pouring contempt on Nell and any other 'luckless down-and-out huddled in his shadow on a hard bench' (56), all of it framed in terms of the danger such people and their destitution represent to the state, the insult their very existence constitutes to a great nation:

> 'Look at me, I'm useful, but you, you're merely a social problem to which there is no solution, except perhaps the lethal chamber. That's the answer to the riddle of you down-and-outs – kill you off like vermin. You're no good alive, you submerged has-beens and never-wassers. Once down, how many of you get up again? How many of you have the guts to strike out and force

> yourselves out of the rut? Tell me that?' demands Big Ben, striking the half contemptuously. (*SW*, 57)

(The reference to the lethal chamber as the best solution to social problems has its own obvious menace in the context of coming events and those future possibilities which Vera Brittain believed most people wished to ignore.) A critic might maintain that the old woman Nell encounters, who has clearly fallen on hard times and is of somewhat sibylline aspect, fleetingly reminds us of Woolf's old woman singing outside the tube station; but Smith's old woman is not viewed from above, but by another down-and-out sitting on the Embankment bench next to her.

Despite the mass of realistic quotidian detail in the novels – places, prices, meals, clothes, interiors – Smith's trilogy rejects generic unity and instead moves constantly between vivid little vignettes, personal meditation, observation, social analysis, polemic, recollection and elegy. Often she seems to have relinquished all pretence of realism or realist novelistic practice. So, for example, a character will frequently launch into a monologue too long for credibility, which seems sometimes to be little more than a not very well disguised article or 'think piece' on a contemporary ill or preoccupation. It seems to be happening, for example, in the disgruntled diatribe issuing from the elderly male diner in Lyons Corner House one Sunday evening and overheard by Nell as she nurses a solitary cup of coffee in *Shadow Women* (240–4). His target is the BBC's programming policy, which he wrongly claims makes use of 'ratepayers' money' to produce broadcasts of opera, scientific talks and religious services, none of them, he argues, wanted by listeners. Listeners, according to the speaker, are switching off in their droves, which isn't good news for those who would like to sell them wirelesses. The speech is long and might appear to be simply a newspaper article *manqué*, lightly dramatised and attributed to a quickly characterised speaker. True, Smith has made some gestures towards justifying the monologic voice; in this case the speaker is an elderly man, with a hungry young woman in tow who has hopes of him, and will put up with the ceaseless flow if it's the price she has to pay for supper. She does not lack spirit, however, and, as he finally pauses for breath, the vignette ends with her deflating one-liner: '"You, being in the wireless business, would notice it", says the young woman politely' (244). Nevertheless, even with Smith's gestures towards narrative, four pages of a single speaker's unbroken speech is a lot.

Yet despite what might be argued to be faults of novelistic construction, such monologues invariably prove to be part of some larger scheme; in this instance, the chapter opens out into a broader consideration of the function of popular and popularised classical music in public places such as Lyons Corner Houses with their live bands. The narrative goes on to describe the social aspects of the work performed by the orchestra, and especially its leader, then makes a sudden move from the larger, busy, bustling but anonymous world of the diners to focus on a single, female figure: 'And [the band-leader's] keenest fans are the lonely women who sit drinking coffee – making the same cup last for hours on end …' (*SW*, 247) Suddenly we are in the world of Katherine Mansfield's or Dorothy Richardson's women customers at the ABC café, or Miss Moss in 'Pictures', or the women in Jean Rhys's short stories or Nora Hoult's. And from there we go, via an *excursus* on the gentle art of 'getting off',[23] to what is in effect a five-page essay on the essential loneliness of the ill-paid, unattached white-collar woman worker in the period and the desert of isolation and *ennui* which a Sabbath-observing nation imposes on so many. Lyons Corner House offers 'a veritable palace of light and laughter' to 'women who have nothing to do and no one to speak with from the time the office closes on Saturday until it opens on Monday' (250).

The 'dreariness and loneliness of an English Sunday to the friendless worker' which 'must be experienced to be believed' (*SW*, 251) is powerfully described with telling detail in a voice that alternates between third and first person, complete with the recounting of an extravagant, cinema-influenced, happy-ever-after fantasy spun by Nell as she muses (254–5), in which she saves a child from dangerous traffic, earns the undying gratitude of his loving family and is introduced to their celebrated friends:

> I have lived in a world of dreams where these things happened over and over again in a swiftly moving kaleidoscope …
>
> But no one has spoken to me. (255)

The band has played the National Anthem and departed, and most of the diners have gone.

In the middle of 1932 Virginia Woolf was embarking upon an effort to create a new form, the 'novel-essay', but *The Pargiters* could not be made to work to her satisfaction. The essays went, and what remained became *The Years* (1937). I am not, of course, seeking to claim that Price's trilogy is the equal of any of Woolf's *oeuvre* but an impartial reading of these books will discover that there are many ways in which 'quality writing' and 'pot-boiling' may, in their treatment of women's lives in the post-war years, draw closer than we might expect.

***

The problems of genre and authenticity posed by Helen Zenna Smith's novels seem insignificant when considered in relation to two other contemporary, and now hardly known, accounts of women's experience of the war and its aftermath. In March 1930 T. Werner Laurie published *W.A.A.C: The Woman's Story of the War.* In July, when *W.A.A.C.* had already gone through five impressions, he published *W.A.A.C. Demobilized.* On the verso of the title page a boxed announcement for its predecessor, *W.A.A.C.*, says 'five large editions'. The text continues:

> **W** A A C
> **A** woman's story of the War
> **A**nonymous
> **C**ompelled to cloak her identity. 7/6

The advertisement goes on:

> We have had many a war novel written from the man's point of view. Here is one in which a woman tells an intimate story of her adventures and impressions and love affairs during the War. It is a frank and realistic narrative which thrills and amazes the reader.

This is a rather curious description, oscillating between the sober and the titillating. 'Frank' is always a slightly questionable word in the publisher's lexicon, and we note that this is, apparently, a 'realistic' narrative but not necessarily a 'true' one.

W.A.A.C. Demobilized is prefaced by a selection of reviews of its predecessor, introduced by a note from 'the Author', and printed in two parallel columns, the 'pros' and the 'antis'. For example:

> *W.A.A.C.* 'is a remarkably well-written book'. – *Western Mail*
> 'There is no hint of literary merit in her story.'– *Birmingham Gazette*
> 'We congratulate the writer on her sincere exposition of the women's fine work on the Western Front.' – *Yorkshire Herald*
> 'The story is a crudely coarse farrago of filth.' – *Sunday Graphic*
> 'It is in the fitness of things that the splendid part which women played in the War should be set forth, and this has been done very effectively in this anonymous recital, which is absorbingly interesting.' – *East Anglian Daily Times*
> '"Connie" casts unfounded aspersions upon a group of splendid women.' – Letter in *The Daily Express.*

T. Werner Laurie's was an interesting imprint with a slightly uneven reputation. His list included some standard authors, among them some eminent foreign ones – Guy de Maupassant, Upton Sinclair (who became a personal friend and shared a house with Laurie's family for a number of years), Catulle Mendès, Pierre Loti and Arthur Schnitzler. But he also had a reputation for books that sailed close to the wind (as, indeed, did many of those by the authors listed above). The section of his catalogue that follows *W.A.A.C.* includes a long list of 'sex education' books, many by the quite well-regarded Jersey author, Walter M. Gallichan, and contains a full-page advertisement for *The Story of a Terrible Life* by Basil Tozer. Here again doubtlessly titillating material (the 'terrible life' which Tozer recounts was led by 'a notorious female trafficker with whom the author … was at one time compelled to associate') is apparently balanced by social responsibility (the publication of the book 'has led already to the drafting of a Parliamentary Bill which will render "the obtaining of women by conspiracy, fraud or intimidation … punishable with penal servitude for seven years, and in its worst forms for ten years"'). Although *W.A.A.C.*'s descents into dubiously erotic material were clearly among the things that aroused the greatest hostility in some reviewers, they are in fact very few and far between, and are almost entirely confined to the narrator's feelings for the Intelligence Officer, Rupert C––, the only man she claims to have loved. *W.A.A.C. Demobilized*, however, has many episodes whose titillation value seems at least as important as their place in an unfolding narrative of exploration and the search for self-determination.

W.A.A.C. Demobilized is generically difficult to place. It sometimes feels like the work of a different author from its predecessor. *W.A.A.C.*, first published in March 1930, went through three more impressions in April, and reached 4,000 sales. *W.A.A.C. Demobilized* was first published in July 1930, and advance sales must have been good because, if we can trust the publisher's claim, it went into a second impression before publication.[24] *W.A.A.C.* is generally written in a spare, sometimes bald prose, with just occasional lurches into the purple in passages dealing with the narrator's desire for and love-making with Rupert C––. (However, it boasts a thoroughly misleading photographic frontispiece, which shows a woman standing, in three-quarter profile, with her face largely obscured, and holding a young child who looks over her shoulder at the viewer. At no point does anything in the book that follows explain this image, although a prospective purchaser might assume the book was to be a tale of a woman 'betrayed'.) *W.A.A.C. Demobilized* is sometimes quite badly written, partly because it is much more dependent than its predecessor on large swathes of badly handled dialogue.

That *W.A.A.C.* might have been a truthful account is not difficult to believe. It is true that it is easy enough to mention real people in an effort to establish verisimilitude – included, for example, are Major Hawker, the RFC flying ace, who was eventually killed in a dog-fight with Baron von Richthofen; and 'Mlle Moreau', Emillienne Moreau, the 18-year-old heroine dubbed 'The Lady of Loos' because of her insistence on going repeatedly, under fire, to help wounded civilians while the town was being bombarded. At one point 'Connie', the WAAC, recounts a conversation in which an upper-class Irish woman asks her if she, too, is a friend of Christabel Ellis, who was celebrated for driving ambulances in Serbia and Russia and eventually became the Commander of the Women's Legion. Nevertheless, even if a sprinkling of real names does nothing to guarantee factual truth, the narrative of the earlier book often has the sort of inconsequence and randomness that strikes true as the recollections of one who, as she tells us, 'kept no diary or notes during the war, unfortunately, so what I write is only what I can remember – incidents which crowd in upon me in quick succession' (*W.A.A.C.*, 52). Precise dates and sequences of events may therefore credibly remain elusive. Even a lack of certain sorts of circumstantial detail can be presented as a virtue:

> It is not my intention to disgust readers by piling on the agony, labouring the horrors of battle and of what one saw in hospitals. That has been done by other writers – overdone in my opinion. I have read war books whose authors appear to think their readers must be devoid of imagination, if not half imbecile. Or is it that they delight in wallowing in anatomical and gruesome portrayals of war victims in hospitals and in the trenches, and gloat over the bloodshed? I wonder if they saw what they describe, or draw on their imagination? (*W.A.A.C.*, 101–2)

It is harder to feel confident about the veracity of *W.A.A.C. Demobilized*. The book often feels unconvincingly melodramatic and it is dependent on a level of coincidence which strains belief. Quite late in the book the author offers what might appear to be a defensive comment that anyone who has travelled as widely as she has will know how very often one encounters again people first met in very different parts of the world (*WD*, 118–19). Much of *W.A.A.C. Demobilized* is a sort of travel writing, the post-war odyssey of a woman unexpectedly rich, the primary heir of Rupert C–– (the man she loved and who died before they could marry), and with nothing to keep her in post-war England:

her father dead, a beloved brother killed in the war and a mother who had rejected her utterly because of the scandal of her liaison with Rupert. For some five years, the narrator tells us, she travelled in South America, the United States, Hawaii, Japan, Australia, China, Fiji, Canada and back to Europe. In each place she compares people, places, customs and institutions with those of England, not always to the latter's advantage. Her experiences provide cues for constant mini-meditations on subjects of social and political concern: the sexual double standard, for example; British colonial rule and the obligations which being part of an imperial power impose on British women abroad (219); Britain's cavalier treatment of colonial soldiers whom it abandoned after the war (201–3). She expresses scepticism about tales of wartime atrocities committed by the Axis powers, and about the virtues of British manhood (98–9). She emphasises the outstanding qualities – loyalty, integrity, courage – often shown by the men of supposedly 'lesser breeds' whom she encounters on her travels beyond Europe, and asserts the greater civilisedness of ancient people, such as the Chinese. Such sentiments do not, however, overcome her anxieties about miscegenation (98–9), and she sometimes expresses some of the same prejudices against Jews and black people that occasionally disfigure Nell Smith's narrative (for example, *WD*, 214–17; *LL*, 154–60).

And just as the fictional Nell and a host of real-life people watch with foreboding the rise of fascism first in Italy, then Germany and Spain, so, too, Connie casts a cold and apprehensive eye on the Italian *fascisti*:

> Self-opinionated, arrogant, boastful, a little army of juvenile potential Don Quixotes. Or jumped-up jacks-in-office … I had talks with lots of them, and they seemed all to be the same – one mind, one opinion, one idea. And of course they want to fight, in spite of their declaration to the contrary … Most of them were babies when the European War began. Well, some day they may go to war, and when they do they will realize its damned absurdity and stupidity – at least the survivors will. They will step in where angels will eventually be wise enough (let us hope) not to tread. (*WD*, 231–2)

Such laudable sentiments are, however, undercut by a nasty little episode when some rich Americans and the narrator decide to steal some ancient church gates from an Italian village (235–8); they succeed, with absolutely no sense of shame, and no sense of what it is they are stealing and why the villagers are so enraged and feel so violated.

Running through the book's unsettling mixture of liberalism, imperialism, conservative attitudes and radical impulses is a constant near-pornographic thread of erotic extravaganzas, including sexualised torture, which sits awkwardly with the earlier book's repudiation of gratuitous descriptions of wounding, mutilation and physical suffering. The sexual theme is introduced very early in *W.A.A.C. Demobilized.* During her stay in Buenos Aires Connie describes a narrow escape from more than one would-be 'white slaver', or sexual trafficker of women. The white slave trade was, of course, one of the recurring subjects of 1920s popular fiction and film, but it was also a reality. With the contemporary rise of sexual trafficking, we are perhaps less patronisingly amused than we used to be by what sometimes appears to be a huge urban myth in earlier decades. Connie's narrow escapes from white-slaving in Buenos Aires leave her compulsively fascinated by all nations' 'arrangements' for making women sexually available to men, and her near-obsession takes her frequently to red-light districts and to dubious restaurants or hotels. It is not always easy to decide whether this is yet another T. Werner Laurie author providing the house speciality, or whether something more serious, less titillating, is going on. One of the recurring themes of *W.A.A.C.* is the change which the war wrought in many women's emotional and sexual lives: 'passion' versus love; desire for sex *per se*, rather than in the context of 'love'; the difficulty of distinguishing one from the other; all the perplexities of determining what constituted virtue or decent ethics in this turbulently transformed world. So here, for example, the unmarried Connie wrestles with her desire for Rupert:

> The weeks which followed after [Rupert] was gone were terrible. So often I had felt contempt – all women do who have retained their virginity – for girls who let men get them in their power. Yet with me it had been worse. Rupert had tried to restrain me. He had kept himself in check. I it had been who had forced him to give way at last; I who had more than surrendered myself. What must he think of me now that it was all over? Since that night I had not seen him again. (*W.A.A.C.*, 61)

When Gwen, a fellow nurse and still a virgin, confides her own feelings of desire, Connie is appalled:

> [She] put her arms round my neck, kissed me, and then whispered in my ear: 'Connie, I want a man most frightfully.' Though I no longer called myself a moral woman, a 'respectable woman' as they would have said at home, I was horrified. Gwen had seemed to me to be so different from other girls I had been meeting, and so clean-minded. She had high ideals, too, and was the last girl I should have expected to say a think like that – or feel like that. So the war atmosphere – that atmosphere which destroyed the souls

> of many of us, as it destroyed the bodies of others – had engulfed her too. (*W.A.A.C.*, 127)

The struggle going on in the narrator about whether female sexual freedom is natural or shameful continues in *W.A.A.C. Demobilized.* The representation of the struggle makes possible the description of her various 'falls', reassuringly accompanied by anxious self-questionings and recrimination afterwards, and these are the familiar techniques of certain sorts of erotic writing. In this sequel, we see constantly mixed attitudes about sex: wanting to argue for the utter normality of strong sexual passions in women (and the abnormality of their lack), while also retaining idealised notions of sexual love. There is no innate contradiction here, obviously, but there seems to be one for the narrator. Purity *and* passion, or purity *versus* passion? Some passages in the book may seem clearly gratuitous – this for instance:

> On some women the sight of a snake has a most curious effect. A middle-aged woman whom I know intimately has confided to me that she experiences a pleasurable vibration when her pet snake glides over her nude body, which she allows it to do. (*WD*, 130)

But others might as easily be placed in the context of the many efforts being made in the 1920s and 1930s to find ways of writing honestly and without false shame about sexual matters. So, for example, the author describes her confusion and distress at discovering that 'I had thought and fully believed during the War that when the War was over, what is called "respectability" would return to me of its own accord. It had not done so' (122–3). The sexual desires which she had thought a product of the extremity of war's upheaval remain.

The author's peregrinations bring her a steadily increasing self-confidence and self-reliance, and on her eventual return to England she becomes a successful entrepreneur, taking especial pleasure in her ability to employ other women. She has become the 'career woman' whom Smith's narrator both fears and aspires to be. For much of Smith's trilogy, the qualities inculcated in Nell by her war experiences have made her bitter, harsh, cynical, distrustful, inefficiently ruthless, full of wasteful or harmfully discharged energies and morally rudderless. *Not So Quiet...* ends with a description of Nell as one who is in effect already dead:

> Her soul died under a radiant silver moon in the spring of 1918 on the side of a blood-spattered trench. Around her lay the mangled dead and the dying. Her body was untouched, her heart beat calmly, the blood coursed

> as ever through her veins. But looking deep into those emotionless eyes one wondered if they had suffered much before the soul had left them. Her face held an expression of resignation, as though she had ceased to hope that the end might come. (239)

In some senses, however, the end never does come for Nell, because the war itself has not ended; there are too many 'grey ghosts'. Moreover, like many women, in life and fiction, she finds there is a 'war after the war' to be fought, one which will continue to test her and to demand similar courage and endurance.

Even women who had *not* been much tested during the war found they might be during the peace. Mrs Lancing, the tellingly named middle-aged protagonist of 'The Casualty List', a 1932 short story by Winifred Holtby, had had an 'easy' war. She lost no sons and always felt awkward in the face of women who had. When a friend's son is killed, Mrs Lancing feels a guilty envy: 'Her sin had always been to covet honour.'[25] Her post-war life remains materially comfortable. But the sense, and fact, of mortality are increasingly pressing, and the obituary columns of her elders and contemporaries have, she realises, become *her* 'casualty lists'; and although she heard no cries of 'Stretcher bearer! Stretcher bearer!' at the Front, she realises that her future will increasingly hold stretchers and nurses and death. The story ends with an agitated maid bursting into the room to tell her that her husband has had 'a fainting fit or something' and, as she calmly gives orders for the doctor to be called and goes to her husband, the narrator tells us 'She was not out of it this time. This was her war, and she had learned how to behave.'[26]

Unlike Nell and Mrs Lancing, the narrator of *W.A.A.C. Demobilized* seems to have found a way to escape the war after the war and instead makes her energies and passions work for her to help her shape a satisfyingly independent and productive life. What correlation there is between such a triumphant narrative and 'real-life' lives is a different matter, although Virginia Nicholson's *Singled Out* would seem to provide many examples of such women.[27] Many aspects of works by other middle-class women writers of the period, however, echo the rage, despair and fear that Nell Smith so often expresses. The two WAAC books may or may not be autobiographies; Helen Zenna Smith's works clearly are not. Becoming unduly preoccupied with whether such works are 'true', in the sense of being soundly based on autobiographical record and recollection, is a red herring. So, too, I suggest is the effort to determine their proper rung on the literary critical ladder. Sensationalist hack work? Middlebrow fiction with aspirations above its station? Failed modernism? What books such as these may exemplify, instead, is an effort to identify and map emerging, and sometimes contradictory, mythologies of what it might mean to be a young-ish middle-class Englishwoman attempting to make sense of and survive a world irreversibly changed by the First World War.

Notes

1 Helen Zenna Smith (pseud. of Evadne Price), *Women of the Aftermath* (London: John Long, n.d. [1931]). Subsequent references to this work are to this edition and are given in parentheses in the body of the text.

2 *The Diary of Virginia Woolf*, vol. 1, ed. Anne Olivier Bell (Harmondsworth: Penguin, 1979 [1977]), 217.

3 Helen Zenna Smith, *Not So Quiet…: Stepdaughters of War* (London: Albert E. Marriott, 1930). Subsequent references to this work are to this edition and are given in parentheses in the body of the text.

4 Helen Zenna Smith, *Luxury Ladies* (London: John Long, n.d. [1933]), 37, 40. Subsequent references to this work are to this edition and are given in parentheses in the body of the text.

5 Vera Brittain, 'The Superfluous Woman' (written July 1919; published in *Poems of the War and After*, 1934), in Dominic Hibberd and John Onions, eds, *The Winter of the World: Poems of the First World War* (London: Constable, 2007), 291.

6 'High Wood' (1918), in Brian Gardner, ed., *Up The Line to Death: The War Poets, 1914–18* (London: Methuen, 1964), 157.

7 Vera Brittain, *Because You Died: Poetry and Prose of the First World War and After*, ed. Mark Bostridge (London: Virago, 2008), 134.

8 Brittain, *Because You Died*, 134.

9 Siegfried Sassoon, 'Aftermath' (1919), in Gardner, ed., *Up the Line to Death*, 154.

10 Siegfried Sassoon, 'On Passing the New Menin Gate' (1928), in David Roberts, ed., *Minds At War: Essential Poetry of the First World War in Context* (Burgess Hill: Saxon Books, 1996), 352

11 Brittain, *Because You Died*, 143–4.

12 Ivor Gurney, 'The Bugle' (1919), *The Guardian*, 13 November 2010.

13 Rose Macaulay, *Keeping Up Appearances* (London, Methuen, 1986 [1928]), 20–1.

14 Helen Zenna Smith, *Shadow Women* (London: John Long, n.d. [1932]), 77. Subsequent references to this work are to this edition and are given in parentheses in the body of the text.

15 May Wedderburn Cannan, 'Women Demobilized: July 1919', *The Splendid Days* (1919), in Hibbert and Onions, eds, *The Winter of the World*, 286.

16 Jane Marcus, 'Afterword', *Not So Quiet…: Stepdaughters of War* (New York, The Feminist Press, 1989), 266.

17 Katherine Mansfield, 'Pictures' (1922), in *The Collected Stories of Katherine Mansfield* (London: Penguin, 2007).

18 Norah Hoult, *Poor Women* (London: Jonathan Cape, 1928); Storm Jameson, *A Day Off* (London: Nicholson and Watson, 1933).

19 Radclyffe Hall, *The Well of Loneliness* (1928), introduced by Alison Hennegan (London: Virago, 1982).

20 Cicely Hamilton, *Marriage as a Trade* (London: Chapman and Hall, 1909).

21 http://greatwarfiction.wordpress.com/2007/05/21/my-dustjackets (accessed 1 March 2013).

22 Marcus, Afterword to *Not So Quiet*, 265.

23 That is, getting picked up by a man.

24 Publication details on the reverse of the title page.

25 *Remember, Remember! The Selected Stories of Winifred Holtby*, ed. Paul Berry and Marion Shaw (London: Virago, 1999), 86.

26 *Remember, Remember!*, 90.

27 Virginia Nicholson, *Singled Out: How Two Million Women Survived Without Men after the First World War* (London: Viking, 2007). The historian Martin Pugh has argued that the notion of a post-war world of spinsters, created by the loss of a generation of fighting men, is a potent but dishonest myth. He maintains that the number of spinsters in England just before war began was at least as high, or slightly higher, than in the post-war period; and that the number of marriages actually rose during the inter-war years. He wonders that Virginia Nicholson 'managed to write a whole book' based on the 'misconception' of the 'lost husbands'. Martin Pugh, *We Danced All Night: A Social History of Britain Between the Wars* (London: Bodley Head, 2009). We should, however, remember that the proportion of officers' deaths was very much higher than those of other ranks; those women who might have expected to marry men of their own class were, in that sense at least, in a worse situation than working-class women whose chances of marriage remained higher.

5

King Baby: Infant care into the peace

Trudi Tate

In 1920 the *International Journal of Psycho-analysis* quoted a brief but telling sentence from a Hungarian pacifist pamphlet: 'War,' wrote the pacifists, 'is to be overcome, if anywhere, in the nursery.'[1] Is war ever to be overcome? Can the ways in which we care for babies and children make any difference? These were pressing questions during and after the Armistice in many of the combatant nations. They led to progressive ideas about childcare and the education of young children from, for example, Rudolf Steiner in Germany and Maria Montessori in Italy. Montessori lectured in Britain in the early 1920s, and her ideas were received with considerable interest by British educators.[2]

Furthermore, as has been well documented by scholars, the First World War affected the reception of psychoanalysis in Britain. Freud's ideas gained in influence during the war and especially in the 1920s, partly because they were found helpful in the treatment of war trauma in soldiers.[3] In this same period, Melanie Klein formulated new ideas about the experiences and fantasies of infancy and early childhood.[4] These are two separate issues – war trauma in adults and the study of infant development – yet they sit in some kind of relationship at the end of the First World War. This chapter explores that relationship and the ways in which it is articulated in literature after the Armistice.

The importance of psychoanalysis in the history and literature of the First World War is well known. Here I will address a less well-known movement which was probably much more influential than psychoanalysis at the time, and which we might describe as the *opposite* of psychoanalysis, for reasons which I hope will become clear later. And I will focus not upon soldiers, but upon babies: the generation who would be called upon to serve in the next great war. How were babies perceived during and after the First World War and why is this important? These questions are registered in powerful yet subtle ways by writers of the period.

Armistice day: Virginia Woolf

Like many people, Virginia Woolf waited anxiously and sceptically through the autumn of 1918 for peace to be declared. On 12 October she writes in her diary that news of an armistice is expected soon. Despite her scepticism, she cannot help feeling excited: 'Whatever we have done this week has had this extraordinary back ground of hope; a tremendously enlarged version of the feeling *I can remember as a child* as Christmas approached.'[5]

When the Armistice finally comes, Woolf welcomes the fact of peace, but views the public celebrations with suspicion and resentment. She is somewhat ashamed of feeling so grumpy, and worries at the issue, trying to understand precisely what bothers her. Both she and Leonard feel restless and find themselves going up to London, perhaps just to be with other people to mark the event.[6] (Sassoon similarly recalls feeling it was 'imperative' to 'rush up to London' to observe – but not to share – the celebrations.[7]) Woolf is soon disillusioned, even a little disgusted, by the behaviour of the revellers: 'everyone seemed half drunk [...] every wounded soldier was kissed, by women [...] crowds drifted up and down the pavements waving flags and jumping into omnibuses'.[8] For Woolf, this is a lazy and mindless form of patriotism, 'sordid and depressing'.[9] Woolf knew she could be a snob, and this perhaps colours her response here. But she is also noticing something important. She observes that many people, like themselves, are just roaming around aimlessly: 'nobody had any notion where to go or what to do'.[10] Everyone seems to feel a 'restlessness & inability to settle down, & yet discontent with whatever it was possible to do'. 'Taxicabs were crowded with whole families, grandmothers & babies, showing off; & yet there was no centre, no form for this wandering emotion to take.'[11] This is precisely the problem; people feel 'no centre, no form'. To borrow a term from psychoanalyst Wilfred Bion, at the end of the war there is no 'container' for individuals or groups; no place to put their uncertain yet powerful emotions.[12] The momentous event feels trivial and empty, like, says Woolf, 'a mixture of Bank Holiday and Sunday'.[13]

As the war comes to an end, Woolf thinks about the next generation; what will the peace bring for them? This is particularly on her mind because her sister Vanessa Bell, to whom she is very close, is soon to give birth to her third child.[14] On the morning of the Armistice, Woolf writes in her diary of the sound of guns and sirens 'announcing peace'. At 11.30 a.m. she writes a letter to Vanessa. 'The guns have been going off for half an hour, and the sirens whistling; so I suppose we are at peace, and I cant help being glad that your precious imp will be born into a moderately reasonable world.'[15] Of course she is pleased that the child will come into a world no longer at war, but what sort of world is it? The same day, she notes in her diary, 'The crowds [celebrating the Armistice] had nowhere to go; nothing to do; they were in the *state of children* with too long a holiday.'[16]

The sense that citizens are being treated like children, behave like children, or feel vulnerable like children can be found in many of the writings about the war and the peace which followed. Freud, for example, complained that the political climate during the First World War infantilised whole nations. In his essay 'Thoughts for the Time on War and Death' (1915), Freud worries that civilised states are relinquishing long-established moral values. They lie to their populations; coerce people into military service; censor the true conditions of the war; suppress political dissent; and control the newspapers, the main sources of information (and lies) about the war. For Freud, the state behaves like a bullying parent towards its citizens.

> The state exacts the utmost degree of obedience and sacrifice from its citizens, but at the same time it treats them like children by an excess of secrecy and a censorship of news and expressions of opinion [...] This in turn leaves people vulnerable to all kinds of rumour and falsehood, since the official information is so unreliable. States openly express their 'rapacity and lust for power', which the individual citizen is under great obligation to sanction and support, in the name of patriotism.[17]

Many British writers of the time expressed similar views. On the one hand, the war required considerable self-sacrifice and discipline from people. Citizens were required to be responsible, self-sacrificing adults, with the promise, or at least the hope, that adult rewards would follow. On the other hand, people were treated as recalcitrant children, cajoled and coerced, conscripted and imprisoned, spied upon and threatened, but also treated to astonishing and imaginative entertainments – tanks in city streets, public amusements, song and dance; awful bread, but plenty of circuses – instead of disinterested political responsibility and discussion.

The democracy that emerges from the First World War in Britain is quite precarious. It is both real and a fiction. The franchise is genuinely extended in 1918; new groups have real access to parliament. But the democratic processes are compromised. How are people to make rational decisions if they do not have trustworthy information from reliable sources? How do we know if the newspapers or the government are lying to us? How can we be responsible participants in democracy if we cannot trust what we are told about what is going on; if we are manipulated and told a mixture of fact and fantasy; reality and fiction – and we cannot always tell the difference? These are precisely the questions faced by children when families manipulate them, mix lies and truth, and exploit children's emotional dependency. It strikes me as significant that the insights of psychoanalysis – which help to expose the lies at work within the intimacy of the home – became more influential at a time when whole states were behaving like powerful but dysfunctional families.

Even if one accepted the need for propaganda, manipulation and lying during the war – for the greater good of winning the conflict – many observers were dismayed to find these techniques continuing into the peace. I think this is what Woolf is trying to describe. She worries about the political structures of the war persisting into the peace; that out of all the suffering, we have learned – nothing.

Some months after the Armistice another celebration was held to mark Peace Day, on 19 July 1919, following the signing of the Versailles Treaty. There were processions, choirs, fireworks.[18] The weather was awful, with constant rain. Woolf was sceptical of the celebrations, and of herself, too. 'I'm desolate, dusty, & disillusioned,' she writes in her diary. She half hates the event, half hates herself for being detached. She notes that the servants are able to participate, and they seem to enjoy it thoroughly. She envies the servants' capacity to join in even as she disdains what she sees as their gullibility. Again, there is an element of snobbery here, but Woolf is also struggling to find political clarity; to understand the event and its cultural significance.

'I dont know,' she writes gloomily. 'It seems to me a servants festival; something got up to pacify & placate "the people" – & now the rain's spoiling it, & perhaps some extra treat will have to be devised for them.'[19] Now she is getting to the thing that bothers her. 'Thats the reason of my disillusionment I think. There's something calculated & politic & insincere about these peace rejoicings.' This still doesn't satisfy her, and she worries at the topic a few lines later. 'I can't deny that I feel a little mean at writing so lugubriously; since we're all supposed to keep up the belief that we're glad & enjoying ourselves.'

'So on a birthday,' she continues, 'when for some reason things have gone wrong, it was a point of honour in the nursery to pretend. Years later one could confess what a horrid fraud it seemed.'[20] Again we find Woolf turning to thoughts of childhood as she contemplates the end of the war. What do they mean here? Does Woolf diminish the importance of events, and disparage the participants, by drawing such parallels? Perhaps, but I want to make the opposite case. For Woolf, what happens in the nursery, to babies and little children, is tremendously important, both for the children themselves and for the whole society.

Elizabeth Bowen: 'Tears, Idle Tears'

I turn now to Woolf's contemporary, Elizabeth Bowen. Born in 1899 and a teenager during the First World War, Bowen served as a volunteer in a hospital for shell-shocked soldiers in 1918. Her husband, whom she married in 1923, had served in the war and had been gassed.[21] Alongside her knowledge of war-affected veterans, Bowen was deeply interested in the ways in which adult lies and secrecy affect the lives of children. This interest emerges powerfully in her stories reflecting upon the period after the Armistice.

In Bowen's story 'Tears, Idle Tears' (1941),[22] a little boy named Frederick Dickinson frequently bursts out crying for no apparent reason. His mother finds it unbearable. The story begins with Frederick weeping loudly in Regent's Park. His mother tells him off. 'Frederick, knees trembling, butted towards his mother a crimson, convulsed face, as though he had the idea of burying himself in her.' The mother is mortified. 'He was too big to cry; the whole scene was disgraceful.' She finds his crying a 'shame of which she could speak to no one; no offensive weakness of the body could have upset her more'.[23]

Mrs Dickinson is a widow. Her husband Toppy was an RAF pilot, who died after a 'ghastly crash' (483), when Frederick was two, some five years earlier. The exact time of the story is not specified. It was published in 1941, but seems to be set in the 1930s or possibly late 1920s. Toppy is killed in a peacetime military accident. Now Frederick is seven. He often cries, without knowing why. It just swells up inside him and forces its way out. He feels terrible. His mother makes him feel worse. 'She looked a mother of sons, but not of a son of this kind' – 'a great blubbering boy' (481).

Mrs Dickinson is elegant, poised, courageous. She has a genius for making her child feel bad. 'She was one of those women who have an unfailing sense of what not to say, and say it' (482). The only blot on her ordered if lonely existence is her son's crying; it makes him abject, an outcast; people are repelled. He even repels himself: 'the hot, gummy rush of tears, the convulsion of his features, the terrible square grin he felt his mouth take all made him his own shameful and squalid enemy' (482).

After the plane crash, Frederick's father was unconscious in hospital. He took two days to die. Mrs Dickinson sat by the bedside, behaving with complete decorum, never weeping, in case he recovered consciousness. When death came, she remained poised. A kindly friend 'had put the unflinching widow into a taxi and driven back with her to the Dickinsons' bungalow' (483). She urges Mrs Dickinson to have a good weep, but she cannot. She is like a machine. The friend thinks her reaction is unhealthy. Eventually Mrs Dickinson goes to check on baby Frederick, asleep in his cot. He looks so much like his dead father that she now breaks down and weeps. She clutches the baby's blanket to her face (the baby is underneath); she cries over him, her body shaking the cot. The baby is silent. The mother falls asleep, her arm around the baby. The mother's friend and another woman, a servant, come to find her.

> Under his mother's arm, as still as an image, Frederick lay awake, not making a sound. In conjunction with a certain look in his eyes, the baby's silence gave the two women the horrors. The servant said to the friend: 'You would think he knew.' (484)

What does the baby know? At some level, he knows of his father's death. He knows all of his mother's grief; the immensity of the loss to them both. But more than this. He absorbs his mother's feelings, and will carry them inside himself for years afterwards. In crying on him, into him, the mother unconsciously passes her grief to the child. In so doing, she frees herself of painful feelings. She can be the gallant, brave widow and enjoy the admiration of their friends. Her son cries her tears for her. She rejects him when he weeps. In disowning him, she also disowns her own feelings of loss.

Banished to a distance in the park (in the present of the story), Frederick eventually finishes crying. A young woman looks at him curiously, and tells him of a man called George she once knew. George used to cry, too, for no reason that anyone could understand. '"He doesn't know why he does it", she said, "but he's got to. It's as if he saw something. [...] It's as if he knew about something he'd better not."' The young woman has some sympathy for the weepers. 'The eyes of George and Frederick seemed to her to be wounds, in the world's surface, through which its inner, terrible, unassuageable, necessary sorrow constantly bled away and as constantly welled up' (486). To put it another way; some people feel the suffering of the world, so that others don't have to. Some people carry the emotions of others. These sufferers are then rejected for being too unseemly, too unhappy – for expressing, visibly, the feelings that others have managed to banish.

Two things emerge from this story which are important for understanding literature after the Armistice. First, Bowen has a nuanced perception of trauma. She explores the complex ways in which trauma can be unconsciously passed on to someone else. Babies and young children are especially vulnerable to absorbing the emotions of others. This was a problem for many families after the First World War. Many of the men who had been traumatised by the war received no diagnosis or help afterwards.[24] Within the family, some of these men (and, in some cases, women) were violent, unreasonable; some were withdrawn. Trauma can inhibit or even destroy the capacity to love. All of these problems could have a serious effect upon the children of the family. Some children suffered neglect or violence from traumatised parents. And some unconsciously absorbed the sufferings, the unbearable emotions, of the adults around them. This can happen within families at any time in history, but it is more pronounced in times of war.

Secondly, Bowen identifies a matter which was a topic of considerable interest during the First World War and into the following decades. That is, do babies have an interior life; a psyche; a developing character? Or are babies just bodies that need to be fed and cared for, with the internal world, the mind and spirit, developing later, perhaps around the time that language emerges? Bowen clearly takes the view that babies do have internal worlds; vulnerable yet complex, and capable of absorbing and carrying the feelings of others. It is noticeable in the story that there is no scope within the family for Frederick to feel his own grief for the loss of his father. This is perhaps the greatest tragedy of carrying someone else's sorrows; you are never able to fully experience, or to heal, your own pain.

Both Bowen and Woolf identify important issues which emerged in Britain at the end of the First World War: the problem of trauma being passed from adults to children; the sense that adults were being infantilised by the state; the lack of a 'container' when the war was over. And both writers are worried about the kind of world bequeathed to children born after the Armistice. These were widespread concerns.

People wondered what was to be done about the loss of life, and about the next generation of citizens. How could the nation be rebuilt in both numbers and strength? And how should we raise our children to avoid war in the future, or, conversely, how could we raise children to be fitter and stronger to cope with future wars?

In its editorial of 2 July 1917, *The Times* reiterated its belief that the war was being fought for 'the fruits of [...] freedom' for the next generation. But, it asks: 'What steps are we taking to see that our successors have the health and strength to make the best of them? Are we so watering the tree of life and digging it about that its leaves may be [...] "for the healing of the nations"?'[25] The answer was not necessarily to produce more babies. Some commentators argued for this,[26] but there was an equally strong movement to care better for the babies already born.

Baby Week

'His Majesty King Baby reigns this week,' announced the *Daily Telegraph* on 2 July 1917, adding that, 'The Queen will be the first to acknowledge his sovereignty.'[27] For the *Daily Express*, it was 'KING BABY – HIS WEEK [...] [For] the next seven days King Baby will receive as much attention as any monarch in these democratic days can expect':

> The capital of Baby's kingdom this week will be in the Central Hall, Westminster, where there will be a National Baby Week Exhibition. Here a congress of mothers will discuss the rearing of the perfect baby and the best methods of ensuring that every baby, rich or poor, shall have a good physical start in life.[28]

Triplets and twins were presented to the queen in a 'Baby Guard of Honour'. 'It is babies this time, not bayonets.' 'Eighteen triplets were held in arms of proud women. Their six mothers could not hold them all.'[29] This was the beginning of the first Baby Week, a publicity event which was pioneered in the United States in 1914, and taken up in Britain with considerable enthusiasm during the First World War. Baby Week had strong institutional backing. The National Council for Baby Week had the queen as patron and the prime minister as its president. Lord Rhondda, a senior politician, was chairman.[30] Eighty-two welfare associations were represented on the Council. Baby Week also received strong support from the churches, the medical profession and other social institutions. A serious effort was made across social groups to 'save the babies'. It is striking that this movement became so active during the First World War. As the Countess of Warwick remarked drily in an article in the *Daily Express*, 'the collective conscience is suddenly aware that you cannot waste babies and adults at the same time', what J. Cossar Ewart called 'the burning of the candle at both ends'.[31]

The *Daily Express* reported that 'Lord Rhondda, speaking at a meeting held at the Guildhall yesterday in support of the National Baby Week campaign, said that the lives of 2,000 children under the age of one year and 3,000 under the age of five were lost every week. Of these at least 1,000 could be saved.'[32] This was a commonly expressed view. More than half a million children under the age of five had died in the years 1911 to 1914. This meant that 25 per cent of all deaths were of young children.[33] These figures were reported in a supplement by senior civil servant Arthur Newsholme to the 1916 *Report of the Local Government Board* (published 1917) and much discussed in the press and medical journals in 1917.[34] At least half of these infant deaths were seen as avoidable. Douglas Sladen in the *Contemporary Review* argued that 'The figures of infant mortality are terrifying.' A baby died every five minutes. 'In 1915,' he writes, 'in war-time, death carried off more British babies than British soldiers.'[35] The bishop of London made the point even more strongly in a speech for Baby Week:

> 100,000 babies died during the first twelve months from their birth. This was an appalling thing from a national point of view. While nine soldiers died every hour in 1915 twelve babies died each hour, so that it was more dangerous to be a baby than a soldier.[36]

What was to be done? The problem was not the number of births. 'With the falling birth-rate we have no concern at present. But how are we to save countless babies not only from death but from incapacitation?' wrote one commentator.[37] And as *The Times* leader-writer remarked in 1919, 'Birth control is a vexed and difficult question, but there can be no two opinions about the necessity for death control.'[38]

Some eugenicists of this period saw infant mortality as a good thing, or at least a natural process which supposedly weeded out the weak individuals, leaving a stronger, healthier population. But the evidence suggests that this was not the prevailing view among government or local authorities, nor in the medical profession.[39] Some, such as Newsholme, argued vigorously against the eugenicist view, not least because it was obviously false, even on its own terms. The areas of Britain in which most babies died did not benefit thereafter from a healthy population of young children. Rather, the conditions which had led to the babies' deaths also weakened and even killed off older children.[40]

Efforts to reduce child mortality had been made throughout the nineteenth century, with some success. The infant mortality rate continued to fall in the first thirty years of the twentieth century. Somewhat surprisingly, as historian J. M. Winter has pointed out, the greatest improvements in fact took place during the First World War.[41] At the time, however, there was great concern at the numbers of babies dying in their first year of life. It was seen as a crisis, requiring urgent action.

Social reformers knew very well that the bad housing and low wages of industrialisation were among the main causes of infant mortality. Reformers and health professionals also argued that families' care for babies could be improved. Mothers, especially, would benefit from education in nutrition, hygiene and other matters to keep their babies healthy. But parental skills were not enough if the home environment was unsafe. According to many commentators, the fundamental problem was bad housing, especially in industrial areas. Too many landlords and employers provided dirty, damp housing, without such basic amenities as running water, food cupboards or working drains. Arthur Newsholme published five influential government reports in the years 1910 to 1916, documenting the rates of infant mortality in different areas of Britain, and trying to ascertain the precise causes.[42] It was a complex issue. Housing was a serious problem in some areas (such as the 'deplorably bad' housing owned by collieries in county Durham). The worst problem Newsholme described was that of sanitation – domestic waste and human excrement. In much of the industrial north, he wrote, sanitary conditions were close to 'barbarism'. These areas had the highest rates of infant mortality.[43] As Eyler points out, conditions in some places had hardly improved since the 1840s: 'household refuse was often stored in fixed pits in back yards, from which it had to be carried through the house for removal'. Worst of all were the 'midden privies', often uncovered and leaking, shared by several households. In his 1910 Report, Newsholme quoted a report from a Durham County Medical Officer of Health, noting that many privies were 'greatly dilapidated and without proper doors, so their contents escape onto the surface of the streets'. Excrement was thrown in the street for collection, or even carried through the houses in baskets, 'to be emptied into the [waste] cart in the street'. 'Under these circumstances,' writes the Medical Officer in despair, 'the ground of the streets and back streets and in many instances also the interiors of the dwelling become fouled with excremental filth.'[44]

As Eyler notes, people living in such conditions could not avoid bringing particles of waste and bacteria into the house on their feet or clothing. Flies brought in more. 'Infants and young children ingested the filth in contaminated food or inhaled it as airborne dust. Infants who were artificially fed were especially vulnerable. In the poorest households there were often no places to prepare or store safely a baby's food.'[45] Babies were most at risk after they were weaned, as it was almost impossible to keep their food from spoiling or being contaminated. Infant mortality in the second six months of life was particularly high in poor areas.

It was also well known that babies and children of all classes were at risk from contaminated milk. No government had managed to compel suppliers to provide safe milk to consumers. This too was a serious issue around the period of the First World War. As C. W. Saleeby commented in 1919, 'If milk, instead of being opaque, were a transparent fluid, no one in this country would drink it. The filth which it invariably contains under present conditions would be altogether too disgusting.'[46] Along with the dirt was contamination with dangerous bacteria, to the point that milk was referred to as 'white poison',[47] the '"white plague" of civilization'.[48] The problem was not ignorance; the risks of contaminated milk had been known since the nineteenth century.[49] But there was a continuing failure to keep milk clean at all stages of production and delivery, and, in poorer households, a lack of any safe, clean place to keep milk away from flies and bacteria.

The First World War brought these old issues into new focus. Some of the millions of men who served must have wondered why they were risking their lives for a society which allowed the rest of their family to live in poverty, and their babies and young children to die of preventable illnesses (particularly diarrhoea). 'In the wealthier suburbs one baby in twenty dies in infancy,' wrote Dorothea Irving in *Nash's and Pall Mall Magazine* in July 1918. 'In the congested parts of great cities one baby dies in every five. Whose fault is it?' Irving does not blame the parents. The real problem is the environment in poor neighbourhoods. 'How can people be clean with one tap of water for four families, and when every drop used has to be carried up and down three flights of stairs?'[50] Furthermore, poor people felt exploited by food profiteers. The *Daily Telegraph* reports a canon preaching in Baby Week 1917, who cites a letter he has received from a 'working woman'. She complains that: 'While our husbands are being murdered in France, we are being starved.'[51]

Politicians and social reformers were conscious of this discontent, and acknowledged that many working-class people had good reason to complain about their living conditions. Some commentators worried about the likelihood of revolution after the war; this was a factor in the introduction of 'Homes fit for Heroes' schemes in the 1920s.[52] Others had different priorities, arguing that it was important to build up the numbers and strength of the population to preserve the Empire after the war[53] and to maintain a strong position in relation to Germany, whose population was slightly larger. We see these matters discussed in great detail in the newspapers during the war. One way of addressing both these questions was through infant welfare, to keep more babies alive, and in better health.

Among the reformers, we can see two conflicting strands of thinking. One argument was that infant health could be improved only if the problems of poverty and bad housing were addressed. Widespread reforms were urgently needed to get poorer families into better living conditions – housing, food, wages, medical care. This would include reforms at government level, including a single Ministry of Health to coordinate health matters. This ministry was finally established in June 1919.[54] From this point of view, Baby Week and its associated campaigns were seen by some as not merely a waste of time, but a positive nuisance because they took attention and effort away from real reforms. One letter writer to *The Times* in 1917 likened Baby Week to the Charge of the Light Brigade, 'futile' and 'so much wasted energy'.[55]

The other way of thinking sought to reduce infant mortality by educating mothers through campaigns such as Baby Week, which offered a wealth of advice and information. Underlying the education campaigns was the view that mothers could not always be relied upon to look after babies competently. 'When will men realise that women do not know by instinct how to look after babies; that maternal instinct does not confer skill?'[56] Even when educated, mothers were not to be left to care for their children unsupervised. Mothering was transformed into a scientific endeavour, to be undertaken under the guidance of experts.

Baby Week tried to educate mothers of all classes in the best methods of feeding and hygiene. For middle-class people, there was also advice about the best way to set up a nursery in the home, the best prams and many other items. In the press, much of the Baby Week education is intertwined with advertising by manufacturers, often presented as if it were factual information. For example, the front page of the *Daily News and Leader* on 5 July 1917 has advertisements for Dunkley prams and for Ingram's 'Agrippa' teat. The *Daily Telegraph* on 3 July 1917 has a long advertisement for Glaxo infant milk, presented in the style of a news article, and advertisements for Woodward's Gripe Water which claim that mothers of 'prize-winning babies' use this product. On the same page is an advertisement for Nestlé's milk, headed 'An Urgent Call to Save the Babies!' Nestlé had a special Baby Week offer of a free book, 'Heroes All – a magnificent Album of Portraits of over 200 Soldiers and Sailors who were reared entirely on Nestlés Milk.'

As I have suggested, none of this addressed the underlying problems of poor housing or sanitation. Nonetheless, Baby Week was seen by many commentators as providing much useful education and support to mothers. It continued for more than a decade,[57] and brought a number of self-proclaimed baby 'experts' into public prominence.[58]

Truby King

One of the most influential voices in this period was a New Zealander named Frederic Truby King (1858–1938). He was invited to Britain in 1917 to contribute to the campaigns to improve infant health. In 1918 he established a mothercraft training centre in London for the Babies of the Empire Society, and was involved in the activities of Baby Week 1918.[59] After he left Britain, King's work was continued by supporters such as Matron Mabel Liddiard (1882–1962).[60]

King started his work in New Zealand some years before the First World War. He had a large range of interests. He was a farmer and rose expert, and studied medicine in Edinburgh (1880–86). Back in New Zealand he became the superintendent of a lunatic asylum in 1889; he held this post for about thirty years. He suffered from poor health, but was an energetic and it seems persuasive man. As a farmer, he tried to improve the survival rate among his calves. Among other things, he believed that feeding at regular intervals seemed to help. He then offered his thoughts on the best ways of caring for human infants, to reduce the mortality rate.[61]

Truby King had two main ideas about babies. First, he promoted breastfeeding for the first nine months of the baby's life.[62] He was by no means the only campaigner on this issue, but he was no doubt an important influence. After nine months, cow's milk was permitted in a modified form that King called 'humanised', so that it was supposedly more digestible by human babies.[63] And if breastfeeding were really impossible, King allowed humanised cow's milk from birth, but with an immensely complicated formula which changed every few weeks as the baby grew. Whether King's recipes for artificial milk were better or worse than others available at the time has not really been established.[64] The *Lancet* was somewhat sceptical in 1918 as to whether 'the human infant should be standardised'[65] with King's highly complicated formulas. King also had a successful business producing artificial milk. This potential conflict of interests – making good profits from artificial milk while promoting breastfeeding – was not much commented upon at the time. Later, however, his artificial milk and his formulas for artificial feeding were criticised as much too complicated. As one doctor complained in the *Lancet* in 1940, medical students were being taught 'to approach infant care as [they] would a difficult mathematical problem'.[66] Or as another asked in 1937, 'what is humanised milk; and are Truby King nurses always right?'[67]

Secondly, King argued that all aspects of baby care should be done to a strict, even rigid, routine, for all babies, large or small, with very few exceptions. Babies should be fed by the clock, four-hourly, with no night feeds.[68] This schedule should begin at birth. The baby should feed for a set amount of time (with no allowance for differences in babies' capacity to suck, or mothers' breasts, or the baby's size).[69] Between feeds, the baby should sleep.

Even the baby's bowel movements were supposed to be regulated. From a few days old, the mother or nurse should hold the baby over a potty after the 10 a.m. feed. The baby should get into the habit of using the potty. If it didn't, the mother should intervene, first with gentle methods such as prune juice. If these didn't work, then she was advised give an enema, even to a young baby, to force the bowels to empty at the prescribed time. (Whether many mothers followed this piece of advice is another question.)

King discouraged mothers from playing with babies. It was good to cuddle during the feeding time (brief as that was), but for the rest of the time the baby should be left alone to sleep. No playing, no cuddling, no conversation, because these would over-stimulate babies. 'Never nurse, rock or pat baby to sleep.'[70] Mothers were encouraged to put the baby in a pram between feeds, at the far end of the garden, in all weathers.[71] This gave the baby plenty of fresh air. But it also kept adults at a distance, in case they were tempted to talk or play with the baby. And, if the garden was big enough, the mother or nurse would not be troubled by the baby screaming with hunger. King did not acknowledge the possibility that babies were left hungry by his system. He warned that babies wanting to be picked up, even just for comfort, must not be 'spoilt'; they must be left to 'cry it out'.[72] Historian Philippa Mein Smith describes King's system as 'active puritanism'.[73]

A new generation of unsentimental nurses was trained in the Truby King method. Known as 'Plunket nurses', after King's patrons, Lord and Lady Plunket, they helped mothers to breastfeed successfully and guided them through their babies' early development.[74] Plunket nurses were undoubtedly much appreciated, especially in New Zealand, for what was often friendly support to new mothers. But they also put mothers under pressure to withstand their babies' cries. Middle-class mothers who could afford to employ a Plunket nurse could absent themselves and avoid hearing the baby cry. Of course, there is a long history of wealthier people employing servants to care for their children. What is different here is the attempt to turn childcare into a kind of factory production line, working to a strict time schedule. Or, as psychoanalyst John Bowlby commented some decades later, the supposed efficiencies of the institution (the state orphanage, for example) were brought into private homes. But institutions are never good places for babies or young children, as Bowlby and others point out.[75]

As Bowlby argued, the most important thing the individual family can offer to a baby is attachment. For Bowlby, good mental health requires 'that the infant and young child should experience a warm, intimate, and continuous relationship with his mother (or mother-substitute), in which both find satisfaction and enjoyment'.[76] Truby King's methods disrupt attachment at its very source.

Katherine Mansfield: 'Bliss'

In Katherine Mansfield's story 'Bliss' (1918), a middle-class, flighty woman named Bertha employs a full-time nanny, recognisably in the Plunket mould, to look after her baby.[77] Although she is home all day, Bertha hardly sees her daughter. Nanny takes the baby to the park, bathes and feeds her. The story is set on a particular evening, when Bertha and her husband are putting on a dinner party for their fashionable, arty friends (much mocked by Mansfield). As she waits eagerly for the guests to arrive, Bertha is seized with moments of 'bliss' – 'as though [she had] suddenly swallowed a bright piece of that late afternoon sun' (91). As the feeling increases, she fears she is becoming hysterical (93). Her response is to go to the nursery to visit her baby.

Nanny is not pleased to see her. She sets her lips 'in a way that Bertha knew, and that meant she had come into the nursery at another wrong moment' (93). The baby is delighted. She looks at her mother and begins to jump; she stares and smiles 'charmingly'. Bertha watches Nanny and child, 'her hands by her side, like the poor little girl in front of the rich little girl with the doll' (93). She is seized by a sudden desire to look after her own baby:

> 'Oh, Nanny, do let me finish giving her her supper while you put the bath things away.'
>
> 'Well, M'm, she oughtn't to be changed hands while she's eating', said Nanny, still whispering. 'It unsettles her; it's very likely to upset her.' (94)

For the nanny, what the baby needs above all is routine, repetition, predictability. Nanny regards feeding as a mechanical exercise, not an emotional experience; indeed, emotion – nurture – is seen as potentially damaging to babies. For all her flightiness, Bertha is sensitive enough to see that her baby is being subjected to a loveless regime. She senses that the baby's inherent sense of 'bliss' is being destroyed. She recognises that this is a tragedy for the baby and for herself. She misses the joy of a living relationship with her baby, leaving them both emotionally deprived. All of this is unspoken, denied at the very moment of recognition. This is a brief moment in Mansfield's story, which mainly focuses upon the precarious quality of Bertha's marriage, and the suspicion that her husband is having an affair. (The husband, for his part, boasts about his neglect of their child: 'My dear Mrs. Knight, don't ask me about my baby. I never see her. I shan't feel the slightest interest in her until she has a lover' [102].) But the *emotional* centre of the story is not the marriage, which Mansfield treats with considerable satire, but the lost potential of the relationship between mother and baby. Mansfield takes that relationship seriously. Many of her stories of modern life are miniature tragedies, rooted, in many cases, in the unwitting neglect of children.[78]

Published in 1918, 'Bliss' engages with precisely the questions of childcare and emotional neglect which come into new focus towards the end of the First World War. A curious paradox emerges towards the end of the First World War, through the Armistice, and into the peace. As soldiers are being demobilised, de-institutionalised, something strange is going on in the domestic sphere. Babies are being institutionalised, subjected to regimes eerily like those of the army. Babies and their mothers are told this regimentation will make them happy. Where does this lead us? As I have suggested, adults were in certain respects infantilised during the First World War. At the same time there was a drive to treat children as objects. While a certain amount of routine suits many babies and children very well, the strictness of Truby King's method would work universally only if babies really were objects, with no internal world.

King sees the baby as a kind of machine which needs mechanical attention. The baby's response – in many cases, screaming with hunger because four hours is too long for most babies to wait for a feed – is disregarded. For King, the baby has no point of view. The expert knows what is best; the mother or nurse implements that knowledge. If the baby isn't happy, then this is because the routine is not enforced rigidly enough. This system worked perfectly well for some infants, whose bodily rhythms happened to match King's prescriptions. And it no doubt suited some adults; it might be a relief to think that the baby didn't have a point of view, that one didn't have to take notice of crying. And if the parents were able to put the baby out of earshot, they didn't even have to bear the noise of its distress. But of course many mothers did hear the distress, and were profoundly distressed by it. If they were convinced by King's arguments, they believed they would seriously harm the baby by feeding it when it seemed hungry. So with great effort, mothers waited by the clock, trying to believe that this was best for the baby. Even some medical professionals complained about the experience of witnessing babies left hungry by this regime. In an article in the *British Medical Journal* in 1919, Dr G. D. Laing argued that to specify 'the exact amount to be given at each feed' was 'absurd'. Babies' appetites vary over time and one baby differs from the next in size, growth rate, strength of suckling and many other factors which will affect how they feed.[79] Laing concluded his long and carefully argued article with a rather startling fantasy of revenge upon those who promote regimented feeding: 'A fitting judgement on those who condemn infants to be fed at such long intervals on such small quantities would be for them to live the rest of their lives in a small house with a succession of such babies and listen to their pitiful cries by day and by night.' He evidently felt this point strongly, returning to it in a letter to the *BMJ* a month later: 'It is babies fed on this plan to whose pitiful cries I referred, for I have lived in the same house with them, and suffered much in consequence.'[80]

Like a number of commentators at the time, Laing found it unbearable that adults should choose to treat babies in a way which causes distress. He suggests that the new method is perhaps a reaction to the practice of over-feeding babies on inappropriate food in the past: 'About twenty or twenty-five years ago a great deal was written and said about infant feeding, and it was pointed out that babies were grossly overfed; this was quite true in many instances, for they were given milk and very thick barley water and much sugar and cream, and the food was more or less forced down their throats.' However, 'now we have gone to the other extreme and in consequence a great many infants are underfed and some nearly starved'.[81]

Later research on babies raised in institutions, informed by the work of psychoanalysts such as Bowlby, Winnicott and Bion, has shown that Truby King's system was disastrous for many babies. (Many mothers could have told us that, too.) If babies' needs are not met at the right time, they will eventually fall into despair. Truby King believed that the baby giving up hope was a good thing; the baby had learned to fit into the adult schedule.[82] But if you leave a baby hungry for too long, she will become traumatised. The baby does not simply feel hunger; she feels hunger pangs as if they were an attack on her body. She needs the mother for food, and also to stave off the fantasies of attack.

As Winnicott argues, babies can keep an image of the mother in their minds for a period. They can survive her temporary absence, because she is alive in the baby's psychic reality. But only for a while. (The precise time would vary from one baby to the next.) 'The feeling of the mother's existence lasts x minutes,' writes Winnicott.

> If the mother is away more than x minutes, then the imago fades, and along with this the baby's capacity to use the symbol of the union ceases. The baby is distressed, but this distress is soon mended because the mother returns in $x + y$ minutes. In $x + y$ minutes the baby has not become altered. But in $x + y + z$ minutes the baby has become *traumatized*. In $x + y + z$ minutes the mother's return does not mend the baby's altered state.

He continues: 'Trauma implies that the baby has experienced a break in life's continuity, so that primitive defences now become organized to defend against a repetition of "unthinkable anxiety" [...]' Most babies, says Winnicott, never suffer x + y + z quantity of deprivation. So, 'the majority of children do not carry around with them for life the knowledge from experience of having been mad'.[83] Those babies whose mothers did steel themselves to resist their cries, every day, for months, may well have been traumatised, and knew what it felt like to be mad.

As the silence of the Armistice marked the shift from war to uneasy peace, King hoped for a new kind of silence in the nursery. Babies make a lot of noise if they are hungry and left to wait too long. This is a healthy reaction to an unhealthy situation. But over time, if their needs continue to be unmet, babies will give up hope and lapse into silence.[84] This lack of crying can be a sign of trauma. King welcomed such silence as a sign that his strict regime was working.

Truby King's supporters punned on the familiar terms 'King Baby' and 'His Majesty the Baby' to promote the idea of the 'Truby King Baby', who was supposedly the best-nurtured infant in the world. Despite the benefits of breastfeeding, nothing could be less like a king than the baby raised by these methods. Truby King babies were denied the most basic autonomy of body and mind. They were not supposed to feel hunger in their own natural rhythms, nor even to excrete according to their own needs. They were not allowed to self-comfort by sucking a finger or thumb – King devised mittens and splints to prevent oral gratification. And babies' minds were denied much of the stimulus they need – human voices, physical contact, stories, songs, things to look at and learn from.[85]

Creating a container

The First World War was often described as a kind of satanic machine or as a battle of men against machines, which the machines always won.[86] The men themselves sometimes felt they needed to be machines to survive (as we see in the war art of Wyndham Lewis, for example), which might have been a factor in war trauma. Surely one of the lessons of the war was the recognition that to treat soldiers as mechanical objects was both cruel and counter-productive. In this context, it is curious to find a movement towards the idea of what Daniel Beekman calls the 'mechanical baby' at this particular historical moment. What does it mean? I suggest it has its roots in the feelings discussed earlier in the diary and letters of Virginia Woolf of there being no adequate 'container' at the end of the war. The Armistice and the early days of the peace feel uncertain, nebulous, even frightening. Trust in social and political institutions, such as the government and the press, is compromised. Many people wonder whether state authorities are really trustworthy; and if not, how is the nation being led? Where are we going in the peace; can we trust our leaders not to take us back into war? Evelyn Waugh bases his satire in *Vile Bodies* (1930) on precisely these anxieties. In this novel, post-war Britain is run by dishonest fools; the civilians are ignorant and complacent; nothing has been learned from the experience of the war.

Babies born after the Armistice come into what seems a formless, unpredictable world. In the many families which take up the Truby King method, babies' tiny lives are vigorously regulated, thus providing a comforting illusion of structure – a 'container' which at least makes the adults feel more secure. Alongside this, Truby King's ideas might also be working as a means of repudiating knowledge too painful to face – knowledge of the terrible death toll, the thousands of men left mentally or physically disabled by the war, the effects of trauma and, perhaps above all, the suspicion among many people (though by no means all) that the sacrifice has not been worth it. The fantasy of a 'mechanised' baby which has no feelings, and which requires simply mechanical care, perhaps deflects the anxieties about adult trauma. To put it another way: we repudiate the idea of trauma by convincing ourselves that the most vulnerable members of our community – babies – are like objects or machines, and function best in a sterile, regulated, unemotional, non-tactile environment. If babies are not soft and vulnerable, and if they have no internal world, no feelings to be disturbed, then perhaps we adults are not so troubled by the war after all.

These ideas are lurking, I suggest, in the writings of Woolf, Bowen and Mansfield discussed earlier. They are present in a different form in Siegfried Sassoon's poem, 'Survivors', written in Craiglockhart in 1917:

> No doubt they'll soon get well; the shock and strain
> Have caused their stammering, disconnected talk.
> Of course they're 'longing to go out again' –
> These boys with old, scared faces,[87] learning to walk.
> They'll soon forget their haunted nights; their cowed
> Subjection to the ghosts of friends who died, –
> Their dreams that drip with murder; and they'll be proud
> Of glorious war that shatter'd all their pride ...
> Men who went out to battle, grim and glad;
> Children, with eyes that hate you, broken and mad.[88]

For Sassoon, the suffering of soldiers turns them into infants, 'learning to walk'. And they are like traumatised children, 'broken and mad'. In the poem, this second infancy is a debilitated, helpless state, out of which one grows into a forgetful, frightened old age. Similarly, in Edgell Rickword's poem 'War and Peace', the pain of injury makes 'with child's voices, strong men howl or bleat'.[89] For both Sassoon and Rickword, the war destroys such men's chances of a normal adult life. Those who have children risk passing on their trauma to the next generation. At the same time, civilians complain about being infantilised by the structures of lying, secrecy and propaganda during the war, some of which continue into the peace. And finally, new ways of caring for babies during this period risk driving them into a kind of madness when their needs are systematically not met.

The legacy persists, in ghostly forms, to the present day.[90] One of the babies born in 1919, around whom so much hope and anxiety circulated, was to become the writer Doris Lessing. Both her parents had served in the war. Her father had been a soldier and was badly wounded, losing a leg and suffering life-long effects of trauma. Her mother was a professional nurse who never recovered from the distress of caring for war-wounded men, many of whom died or were permanently damaged. Lessing's memoir *Alfred and Emily* (2008) reflects upon the long-term influences of the war, and how it blighted her childhood. Writing nearly ninety years after the Armistice, she still feels the disappointments of the peace. Like the child in Bowen's story 'Tears, Idle Tears', Lessing feels she has carried her parents' traumatic memories of the First World War throughout her life. 'Do children feel their parents' emotions?' she wonders in her old age. 'Yes, we do, and it is a legacy I could have done without. What is the use of it? It is as if that old war is in my own memory, my own consciousness.'[91] 'That war, the Great War, the war that would end all war, squatted over my childhood,' she writes. 'And here I still am, trying to get out from under that monstrous legacy, trying to get free.'[92]

Notes

1 Geza Szilagyi, 'Psycho-Analytic Literature in Hungarian', *International Journal of Psycho-analysis*, 1, 4 (1920), 469.

2 Austrian Rudolf Steiner contributed to the pioneering Waldorf School movement in Germany, which started in Stuttgart in 1919. He visited Britain several times. His lectures given in Torquay in 1924 were published as *The Kingdom of Childhood*. On the reception of Montessori in Britain, see, for example, the journal *Child Study*, to which she contributed an essay in July 1920.

3 Suzanne Raitt, 'Early British Psychoanalysis and the Medico-Psychological Clinic', *History Workshop Journal*, 58 (2004); Mark Micale and Roy Porter, eds, *Discovering the History of Psychoanalysis* (Oxford: Oxford University Press, 1994); Mark Micale and Paul Lerner, *Traumatic Pasts: History, Psychiatry, and Trauma in the Modern Age, 1870–1930* (Cambridge: Cambridge University Press, 2001); Peter Leese, *Shell Shock: Traumatic Neurosis and the British Soldiers of the First World War* (Basingstoke: Palgrave, 2002).

4 Melanie Klein, *Love, Guilt and Reparation and Other Works 1921–1945* (London: Virago, 1988 [1975]); Klein, *Envy and Gratitude and Other Works 1946–1963* (London: Vintage, 1997 [1975]); Jacqueline Rose, *Why War? Psychoanalysis, Politics and the Return to Melanie Klein* (Oxford: Blackwell,

1993); Lyndsey Stonebridge and John Phillips, eds, *Reading Melanie Klein* (London: Routledge, 1998); Mary Jacobus, *The Poetics of Psychoanalysis: In the Wake of Klein* (Oxford: Oxford University Press, 2005).

5 Virginia Woolf, *The Diary of Virginia Woolf*, vol. 1, ed. Anne Olivier Bell (Harmondsworth: Penguin, 1979 [1977]), 200 (12 October 1918), emphasis added.

6 Woolf, *Diary*, 1, 216 (12 November 1918).

7 Siegfried Sassoon, *Siegfried's Journey 1916–1920* (London: White Lion Publishers, 1973 [1946]), 97.

8 Virginia Woolf, *The Letters of Virginia Woolf*, vol. 2, ed. Nigel Nicolson and Joanne Trautmann (London: Chatto and Windus, 1976), 293.

9 Woolf, *Letters*, 2, 292.

10 Woolf, *Letters*, 2, 293.

11 Woolf, *Diary*, 1, 217 (12 November 1918).

12 W. R. Bion, *Attention and Interpretation: A Scientific Approach to Insight in Psycho-Analysis and Groups* (London: Tavistock, 1970); W. R. Bion, 'A Theory of Thinking' (1962), in *Second Thoughts* (London: Karnac Books, 1984), 110–19. See also R. D. Hinshelwood, *A Dictionary of Kleinian Thought*, rev. edn (London: Free Association Books, 1991), 246–53. '[C]ontainment is a process, not a static structure,' write Karl Figlio and Barry Richards, 'The Containing Matrix of the Social', *American Imago*, 60, 4 (2003), 408. See also Peter Carnochan, 'Containers without Lids', *Psychoanalytic Dialogues*, 16 (2006), 341–62.

13 Woolf, *Letters*, 2, 293.

14 The baby, Angelica Bell, was born on Christmas Day 1918. Frances Spalding, *Vanessa Bell* (London: Weidenfeld and Nicolson, 1983).

15 Woolf, letter to Vanessa Bell, 11 November 1918, *Letters*, 2, 290.

16 Woolf, *Diary*, 1, 217 (12 November 1918), emphasis added.

17 Sigmund Freud, 'Thoughts for the Time on War and Death' (1915), in *Civilization, Society and Religion*, Penguin Freud Library, 12 (Harmondsworth: Penguin, 1985), 66.

18 See, for example, 'Peace Day in London: Song and Dance for each Borough', *The Times* (15 April 1919), 9; 'Peace Day: Full Text of the Treaty', *The Times* (28 June 1919), 12; 'How London Kept Peace Day', *The Times* (30 June 1919), 14; 'Peace Day Marketing: Housewives Busy Shopping Ahead', *The Times* (19 July 1919), 11; 'Peace Day: Allied Tribute to the Fallen', *The Times* (19 July 1919), 15; 'Peace Day: A March of Victory', *The Times* (31 July 1919), 13.

19 Woolf is aware that servants are habitually treated like this, not just in times of war. Many servants took up the opportunities provided by the war to get out of service and into better-paid work. See further Alison Light, *Mrs Woolf and the Servants* (Harmondsworth: Penguin, 2008).

20 Woolf, *Diary*, 1, 292–3 (19 July 1919).

21 Maud Ellmann, *Elizabeth Bowen: The Shadow Across the Page* (Edinburgh:

Edinburgh University Press, 2003), 29–30, 56–7. Deirdre Toomey, 'Bowen, Elizabeth Dorothea Cole (1899–1973)', *ODNB*.

22 Bowen's title is taken from a poem within Tennyson's *The Princess* (1847). For a discussion of Bowen's use of Tennyson, see Martin Bidney, 'Nostalgic Narcissism in Comic and Tragic Perspectives: Elizabeth Bowen's Two Fictional Reworkings of a Tennyson Lyric', *Studies in Short Fiction*, 33 (1996), 59–68. Bidney reads this story as a comic critique of narcissism. In my view this reading neglects Bowen's serious engagement with the problems of neglect and loss suffered by the child in the story.

23 Elizabeth Bowen, 'Tears, Idle Tears' (1941), in *Collected Stories* (London: Jonathan Cape, 1980), 481. Subsequent references are to this edition and are given in parentheses in the body of the text.

24 Peter Barham, *Forgotten Lunatics of the Great War* (New Haven, CT: Yale University Press, 2004); Ben Shephard, *A War of Nerves* (London: Jonathan Cape, 2000).

25 'The Next Generation', *The Times* (2 July 1917), 9.

26 For example, Father Vaughan, preaching at the Brompton Oratory during Baby Week, urged families to have more babies to compensate for the loss of life in the war. 'Fill the Cradles', *Daily Telegraph* (2 July 1917), 7. There are many such examples, but it is important to recognise that this was not the only, nor always the dominant, point of view. See further Richard Soloway, 'Eugenics and Pronatalism in Wartime Britain', in Richard Wall and J. M. Winter, eds, *The Upheaval of War: Family, Work and Welfare in Europe, 1914–1918* (Cambridge: Cambridge University Press, 1988); Susan Pederson, *Family, Dependence, and the Origins of the Welfare State: Britain and France 1914–1945* (Cambridge: Cambridge University Press, 1993), ch. 2.

27 'Baby Week: The Cradle and the Empire', *Daily Telegraph* (2 July 1917), 7.

28 'King Baby – His Week: Campaign to Improve the Race', *Daily Express* (2 July 1917), 3.

29 'Baby Guard of Honour: Triplets and Twins Presented to the Queen', *Daily Express* (3 July 1917), 3.

30 During the war, Lord Rhondda was president of the Local Government Board, then, from June 1917, minister of food control. John Williams, 'Thomas, David Alfred, first Viscount Rhondda (1856–1918)', *ODNB*.

31 'The Children's Mesopotamia: How Peace is as Bad for Them as War', *Daily Express* (6 July 1917), 2; J. Cossar Ewart, 'The Saving of Child Life', *Nineteenth Century and After* (July 1917), 118.

32 'Save the Babies!', *Daily Express* (3 July 1917), 3.

33 'Child Mortality', *British Medical Journal* (14 April 1917), 490.

34 For example, 'Child Mortality', *British Medical Journal* (14 April 1917) discusses Newsholme's report. See also 'A Healthy People', *The Times* (11 April 1917), 3, and 'Lessons from Baby Week', *Lancet* (6 July 1918), 18–19. Newsholme was medical officer of the Local Government Board 1908–19. He

was awarded a KCB in 1917, as reported in *The Times* (13 February 1917), 6. John M. Eyler, 'Newsholme, Sir Arthur (1857–1943)', *ODNB*. See further Eilidh Garrett, Chris Galley, Nicola Shelton and Robert Woods, eds, *Infant Mortality: A Continuing Social Problem* (Aldershot: Ashgate, 2006); Enid Fox, 'Powers of Life and Death: Aspects of Maternal Welfare in England and Wales Between the Wars', *Medical History*, 35 (1991), 328–52. Reports on mother and child health were also published by the Carnegie UK Trust in 1917: J. M. Winter, *The Great War and the British People* (Basingstoke: Macmillan, 1985), 149.

35 Douglas Sladen, 'The National Baby Week', *Contemporary Review* (July 1917), 98.

36 *Daily Telegraph* (2 July 1917), 7. For E. S. Stevens, the nation was wasting its 'most valuable asset – its future wealth of citizens'. 'National Baby Week: A Plea', *Nash's and Pall Mall Magazine*, 59 (July 1917), 373.

37 Stevens, 'National Baby Week: A Plea', 373.

38 'Child Welfare' (editorial), *The Times* (2 July 1919), 13.

39 John Eyler, *Sir Arthur Newsholme and State Medicine 1885–1935* (Cambridge: Cambridge University Press, 1997), 305.

40 See the debates between Newsholme and eugenicist Karl Pearson on this subject, discussed in Eyler, *Newsholme*, 299–305.

41 J. M. Winter, 'Aspects of the Impact of the First World War on Infant Mortality in Britain', *Journal of European Economic History*, 11, 3 (Winter 1982), 718. For a critique of some of Winter's arguments, see Linda Bryder, 'Healthy or Hungry? The First World War', *History Workshop Journal*, 24, 1 (1987), 141–57.

42 Eyler, *Newsholme*, ch. 11; John M. Eyler, 'Newsholme, Sir Arthur (1857–1943)', *ODNB*.

43 Eyler, *Newsholme*, 308.

44 Eyler, *Newsholme*, 309.

45 Eyler, *Newsholme*, 309.

46 C. W. Saleeby, 'A Clean Milk Supply', *The Whole Armour of Man: Preventative Essays for Victory in the Great Campaigns of Peace to Come* (London: Grant Richards, 1919), 112. This chapter was revised from an article in *The Daily Telegraph* (3 February 1919).

47 P. J. Atkins, 'White Poison? The Social Consequences of Milk Consumption, 1850–1930', *Social History of Medicine* (1992), 207–27; see also 'Enemies of Baby: London Milk "The Worst in the World"', *Daily News and Leader* (4 July 1917), 3.

48 Saleeby, 'A Clean Milk Supply', 112. Historian Linda Bryder suggests that the shortage of fresh cow's milk during the First World War might be one reason that more babies survived. Bryder, 'The First World War: Healthy or Hungry?', 150.

49 Saleeby, 'A Clean Milk Supply', 113.

50 Dorothea Irving, 'National Baby Week Past and Present', *Nash's and Pall Mall Magazine*, 61 (July 1918), 310.
51 'A Mother's Appeal', *Daily Telegraph* (2 July 1917), 7.
52 Mark Swenarton, *Homes Fit for Heroes: The Politics and Architecture of Early State Housing in Britain* (London: Heinemann, 1981).
53 See, for example, Anna Davin, 'Imperialism and Motherhood', *History Workshop*, 5 (Spring 1978), 9–65.
54 Eyler, *Newsholme*, 333–6. Also important was the Maternity and Child Welfare Act of 1918; Winter, *The Great War and the British People*, 176, 195.
55 J. C. Barker, 'Infant Mortality' (letter), *The Times* (4 July 1917), 10. That said, Lord Rhondda, who first brought the matter of a Ministry of Health to Cabinet, and campaigned tirelessly for its formation, was also chair of the Baby Week Council; for some people, at least, the two matters – political reform and popular education – were not incompatible. Eyler, *Newsholme*, 333. A single Ministry of Health was one of Lord Rhondda's greatest causes, but he died a few months before it was officially established. Williams, 'Thomas, David Alfred, first Viscount Rhondda (1856–1918)', *ODNB*.
56 Sladen, 'National Baby Week', 100.
57 See, for example, *The Times* editorials on Baby Week (4 July 1925), 15; (4 July 1928), 17.
58 On the history of babycare experts, see Christina Hardyment, *Dream Babies: Child Care from Locke to Spock* (London: Jonathan Cape, 1983); Daniel Beekman, *The Mechanical Baby: A Popular History of the Theory and Practice of Child Raising* (London: Dobson, 1979 [1977]); Deborah Dwork, *War is Good for Babies and Other Young Children: A History of the Infant and Child Welfare Movement in England 1898–1918* (London: Tavistock, 1987); also Linda Bryder, 'Breastfeeding and Health Professionals in Britain, New Zealand and the United States, 1900–1970', *Medical History*, 49 (2005), 179–96.
59 Information on Truby King is drawn from Lloyd Chapman, *In a Strange Garden: The Life and Times of Truby King* (Auckland: Penguin, 2003); Philippa Mein Smith, *Mothers and King Baby: Infant Survival and Welfare in an Imperial World: Australia 1880–1950* (Basingstoke: Macmillan, 1997); Philippa Mein Smith, 'King, Sir (Frederic) Truby (1858–1938)', *ODNB*; Linda Bryder, *A Voice for Mothers: The Plunket Society and Infant Welfare 1907–2000* (Auckland: Auckland University Press, 2003).
60 Mein Smith, 'King, Sir (Frederic) Truby', *ODNB*. Liddiard was matron (1918–36) and later nursing director (1936–45) of the Mothercraft Training Society, and published *The Mothercraft Manual* (London, 1924) which was reprinted many times. Liddiard's dates are taken from *The Times*' brief obituary (3 April 1962), 17.
61 In 1907 King and his supporters established the Royal New Zealand Society

for the Health of Women and Children, known as the Plunket Society after its patron, Lady Plunket. Mein Smith, 'King, Sir (Frederic) Truby', *ODNB*.

62 Frederic Truby King, *Feeding and Care of Baby* (London: Macmillan, 1913 [1908]); *The Expectant Mother and Baby's First Month*, rev. edn (London: Macmillan, 1924), 25; Mary Truby King, *Mothercraft*, 2nd edn (London: Simpkin, Marshall, 1934), 3–4.

63 *Mothercraft*, 3.

64 Chapman opens his biography of King with an account of a middle-aged man who believed his digestion had been ruined by King's milk formula. This was not an unusual view.

65 *Lancet* (13 April 1918), 542–3. King rejected this accusation in a letter to the *Lancet* (4 May 1918), 655.

66 'The Truby King Tradition', *Lancet* (3 August 1940), 140, referring to a letter in *Lancet* (6 July 1940), 22.

67 'Milk Curd and Infant Feeding', *Lancet* (21 August 1937), 458.

68 Truby King, *Expectant Mother*, 32–7; Mary Truby King, *Mothercraft*, 64.

69 *Mothercraft*, 61. King recommended no more than 10 minutes' feeding per breast.

70 *Mothercraft*, 41. Similarly, Charis Barnett claims that babies need all their energy for digestion and growth; their brains cannot cope with the stimulation of conversation, interesting sights, etc. She argues in favour of 'wholesome neglect'. *Common Sense in the Nursery* (London: Christophers, 1922), 152.

71 *Mothercraft*, 45.

72 *Mothercraft*, 168.

73 Mein Smith, 'King, Sir (Frederic) Truby', *ODNB*.

74 The *Lancet* in 1922 praised King's Mothercraft Training Society for its success in helping mothers to sustain (or restart) breastfeeding. 'Breast-Feeding After Weaning', *Lancet* (8 July 1922), 88.

75 John Bowlby, *Child Care and the Growth of Love* (1953), 2nd edn, ed. Margery Fry (Harmondsworth: Penguin, 1965), 159–60. Christina Hardyment remarks that in the early twentieth century, 'the sad fact was that [hospital routine] became a model for family life'; 'normal feeding practice was to be borrowed from orphanage discipline'. Hardyment, *Perfect Parents: Baby-care Advice Past and Present* (Oxford: Oxford University Press, 1995), 127.

76 Bowlby, *Child Care and the Growth of Love*, 77.

77 Katherine Mansfield, 'Bliss' (1918), in *The Collected Stories of Katherine Mansfield* (Harmondsworth: Penguin, 2007 [1945]). Subsequent references are to this edition and are given in parentheses in the body of the text.

78 For example, in 'Sun and Moon', 'The Doll's House', 'The Garden Party', 'Prelude' and 'At the Bay'. The husband in 'A Married Man's Story' admits, without embarrassment, that he feels no love at all towards his baby, and suspects that his wife feels the same (*Collected Stories*, 424). In 'The Stranger',

the parents take very little interest in their children, even when the mother has been away from them for many months.

79 G. D. Laing, 'A Criticism of Some Modern Methods of Infant Feeding', *British Medical Journal* (8 February 1919), 150–1.

80 G. D. Laing, 'Methods of Infant Feeding', *British Medical Journal* (15 March 1919), 326. Here Laing is responding to G. H. Hickling, 'Methods of Infant Feeding', Letter, *British Medical Journal* (22 February 1919), 231–2.

81 Laing, 'A Criticism', 150.

82 Truby King, *Expectant Mother*, 73; Hardyment, *Perfect Parents*, 181.

83 D. W. Winnicott, 'The Location of Cultural Experience', *Playing and Reality* (London: Routledge, 1991 [1971]), 97–8.

84 This unnatural silence has been observed in recent years among babies living long term in state institutions, in China or Romania, for example.

85 The lack of mental stimulation in the Truby King system was commented upon at the time. See, for example, Mrs L. Allen Harker, who argued that babies need company, cuddling and the sound of the human voice. 'The Happy Infant: A Lesson for Baby Week', *Daily News and Leader* (3 July 1917), 2.

86 Trudi Tate, *Modernism, History and the First World War* (Manchester: Manchester University Press, 1998), 135; Daniel Pick, *War Machine: The Rationalisation of Slaughter in the Modern Age* (New Haven, CT: Yale University Press, 1996).

87 The manuscript version of the poem in the *Oxford Digital Archive of First World War Poetry* has the phrase 'scared faces', which appears in most published versions of the poem. However, the *Oxford Digital Archive* also includes a page proof of the poem which prints 'scarred faces'. The proofs are said to have been corrected by Sassoon and Edward Marsh. There are no visible corrections on the digitised version of this page, the original of which is held in the Harry Ransom Research Center, University of Texas.

88 Siegfried Sassoon, 'Survivors', in *Counter-Attack and Other Poems* (London: Heinemann, 1918); rpt in *Collected Poems 1908–56* (London: Faber and Faber, 2002), 83.

89 Edgell Rickword, 'War and Peace', in *Collected Poems*, ed. Charles Hobday (Manchester: Carcanet, 1991), 17.

90 For example, two midwives wrote to the *Lancet* in 1981 that some hospitals still used Truby King's rule of strictly timed, short feeds for newborn babies. They describe an experiment which showed that breastfeeding was more likely to succeed if times were not prescribed. Sylvia Slaven and David Harvey, 'Unlimited Suckling Time Improves Breast Feeding', *Lancet* (14 February 1981), 392–3. In the 1990s the contentious babycare books of Gina Ford revived a highly regulated Truby King approach, especially to matters of sleep and feeding.

91 Doris Lessing, *Alfred and Emily* (London: Fourth Estate, 2008), 258.

92 Lessing, *Alfred and Emily*, viii.

6

'What a victory it might have been': C. E. Montague and the First World War

Andrew Frayn

Disenchantment has long been associated with writing about the First World War, building on the war books boom of 1928 to 1930, solidified by the histories written by Leon Wolff and Alan Clark in the wake of the Second World War, and by film interpretations such as Richard Attenborough's version of Joan Littlewood's *Oh! What a Lovely War* (1963; film 1969), inspired by Clark, and Kubrick's *Paths of Glory* (1957). C. E. Montague was one of the earliest authors to write in this mood following the war, and certainly the first to address it boldly on the cover of a volume, when he published *Disenchantment* in 1922. It was not yet accepted that disenchantment would be the dominant memory of the war, and Montague was instrumental in breaking the perceived silence of literature which detailed the 'realities of war', to use the title of Philip Gibbs's 1920 war memoir. Michael North goes so far as to describe *Disenchantment* as 'the first instance of what was to become a new genre, the postwar reassessment', and Janet Watson calls it 'a forerunner of the soldier's story'.[1] *Disenchantment* reassesses the experience of the war, national values and also the appropriate literary form in which to remember the war. It is a volume neither explicitly factual nor fictional (though often described as memoir), and roughly chronological but without an obvious protagonist or plot. The form betrays its origins, expanded and revised from leader articles written for the *Manchester Guardian*; it was marketed by Chatto and Windus as 'belle-lettrist'.

In this chapter I discuss the importance of silence for the First World War and the Armistice, and argue that in Montague's post-war writings silence does not offer consolation. Rather, it manifests itself negatively in a number of ways: as an eerie, uncanny absence of sound; as the pyrrhic victory won with the Compiègne Armistice and the subsequent peace; and as the unspoken or unutterable, the taboo during and after the war. I draw on Montague's post-war works which deal most directly with the conflict: *Disenchantment*, his war novel *Rough Justice* (1926) and his collection of short stories *Fiery Particles* (1923).

Silence and the First World War

To understand the dynamics of silence and sound in Montague's writings about the First World War, we need first to note that silence is not merely an absence of sound. Nicky Losseff and Jenny Doctor note that 'Dictionary definitions of silence privilege its negative qualities', and Maria-Luisa Achino-Loeb notes that 'because silence is experienced as absence, it is interpreted as non-existence and tied to negativity'.[2] John Cage describes the conviction that 'sound has, as its clearly defined opposite, silence' as ignorant, and his *4'33"* famously asks its audience to appreciate its own ambient noise.[3] Silences in music, of course, are known as 'rests', periods waiting for the music to return, and William O. Beeman argues that they are essential to create a performable piece.[4] Silence is itself communicative, asking for anticipation and engagement; Adam Jaworski sees silence as 'a metaphor for communication'.[5] A better definition of auditory silence, then, is an environment in which there are no foregrounded sounds. The early twentieth century was replete with background and ambient noise, particularly in the industrial cities which had developed over the course of the previous century. Adrian Gregory comments that:

> Silence was something that many of the inhabitants of urban Britain may barely have known. By the early twentieth century there existed the continuous background noise of a modern society; the constant sound of people talking and moving in densely populated areas and the sounds of traffic, motorised and horsedrawn, would have been ever present, varying only in intensity.[6]

Aldous Huxley later put it more bluntly: 'The twentieth century is, among other things, the Age of Noise.'[7] That said, the noise of the modern city was far exceeded on the Western Front, and many of the great novels, memoirs and autobiographies are made all the more vivid by their punctuation with onomatopoeic blasts of sound; Montague describes, for example, 'the usual changes of sounds in battles [...] the first continuous barking of many guns slackened off irregularly into isolated barks and groups of barks'.[8] The magnitude of the noise experienced on a day-to-day basis by the troops is suggested by the large-scale recreations of trenches in films such as *All Quiet on the Western Front* (1930), and Pierre Sorlin argues that 'Violent, unrestrained, the soundtrack transformed the movie theatre into a battlefield; spectators were overwhelmed by the gunshots, the rattling of machine-guns and the whistling of bullets.'[9] Silence might have been hard to find in the modern industrial world, but it was even rarer on the Western Front.

Silence and the Armistice are intimately linked: the literal silencing of the artillery and personnel of the Western Front led eventually to peace. Furthermore, the enduring form of commemoration of the First World War and its Armistice is the Two Minutes' Silence at 11 a.m. on Remembrance Sunday, the nearest to 11 November. The First World War was the first war for which this form of remembrance was considered appropriate. The burial of the Unknown Soldier on Armistice Day 1920 further deepened the meaning of the Silence. Silence draws on 'a religious sense of "silent prayer" and communion between the living and the dead' and has a 'double nature as public and private commemoration. The Silence enforced public unity of action; everyone had to stop and silently pay their respects at the eleventh hour. The solidarity of the community was enforced by the fear of shame.'[10] The Silence was about public performance, and was policed in the same way as the initial wave of volunteering; to dissent from honouring those who served in the war was to make oneself the object of potential ostracism or antagonism. It was also contemplative, a silence in which thoughts were able to rest upon the object of commemoration. Jay Winter comments that 'every decision to commemorate is a decision to simplify and clarify a message by leaving out substantial parts of the story surrounding it';[11] similarly, James V. Wertsch comments that commemorative performances have a 'tendency to eschew ambiguity and to present the past from a single committed perspective'.[12] The officially sanctioned solemnity of Armistice commemorations meant that alternative vibrant and boisterous celebrations were restricted, seen as unofficial and dissenting – even if many of those who wanted to remember the war as a victory were those who had worked hard to win it.

The marginalisation of combatants, combined with the process of reintegration and reinterpretation of wartime experience, meant that discontent was likely, but was also subject to censure. Disenchantment was subject to what Zerubavel describes as a 'conspiracy of silence', in which 'breaking the silence actually violates not only some individuals' personal sense of comfort, but a collectively sacred social taboo, thereby evoking a heightened sense of fear'.[13] Montague certainly challenges existing discourses about the war, although the only apparent fear in *Disenchantment* is that lessons will not be learned. He speaks to civilian fears about the reintegration of former servicemen, and the social and political conflicts of the 1920s, described as 'that new lie-infested and infected world of peace' (*D*, 127). Gregory states that 'The vast majority were reintegrated into civil society surprisingly well', but a significant minority were left with worse conditions, all the more galling for the sacrifices made in the service of the nation:

> in the immediate post-war period 'unemployed man' and 'unemployed ex-serviceman' were close to synonymous. Only approximately one in nine ex-servicemen were unemployed, but in early 1922 approximately 600,000 of the 1,000,000 registered unemployed were ex-servicemen, representing over two-thirds of the male unemployed.[14]

These figures became an awkward issue which veterans believed that civilians were unwilling to address. A letter to *The Times* of 4 February 1920, signed 'Ex-Battery Commander', offered a biting assessment:

> On leave from the Front we were welcome and honoured guests – especially as we gained promotion: 'My Cousin the Major.' [...] [When] at last we came home, were demobilized and doffed our uniforms, we realized how much our welcome had depended on the glamour of our clothes, with all that they implied. In mufti we were no longer heroes, we were simply 'unemployed', an unpleasant problem.[15]

This problem led to dissatisfaction with representations of the war in the dominant heroic mode as veterans began to reinterpret it through the lens of post-war disenchantments. Samuel Hynes suggests that 'Disenchantment is a condition of loss, and that was the way the war extended its presence into English culture after the Armistice – as forms of loss.'[16] Hynes notes that these are physical ruins of body and land, as well as the metaphorical ruins of the pre-war world. He does not, however, note the loss of the war experience itself – the move back into a civilian environment was as traumatic for many as the Armistice was a relief. Combatants often claimed that their experience was inexpressible because it was incomprehensible to those who had not fought. Montague's work was important in facilitating this shift in understanding: Niall Ferguson describes *Disenchantment* as 'surely the most influential of all post-war titles'.[17]

C. E. Montague

Charles Edward Montague (1867–1928) was instrumental in breaking the perceived 'silence' about the war, and in stimulating an interest in revisionings of the war. He was a respected journalist before the war, writing primarily about current affairs and the theatre. Montague's prose style is prolix but clear and never laboured. He was a published novelist before the war, and *A Hind Let Loose* (1910), his first novel, is a satire on some of the less politic actions of journalism. His experience of the war is foregrounded in his subsequent writings, and he had a wide range of military roles during the conflict. Hynes asserts that 'Montague came to his task with a special set of qualifications';[18] he served in the front line, and was then an Intelligence Officer behind the lines, in which role he conducted tours for distinguished visitors and wrote official war articles. These experiences allowed him to see enchantment and disenchantment from a variety of perspectives.

C. E. Montague's birth, upbringing and formative experiences established him as a questioning, educated Liberal. Although born in Ealing, the third of four sons, Montague's parents were Irish and he considered himself an Irishman, championing Home Rule enthusiastically. He studied at the City of London School, and then went to Balliol College, Oxford, on a classical scholarship.[19] It was at Oxford that a parody of Thucydides brought him to the attention of C. P. Scott, then the editor of the *Manchester Guardian*, later its owner, and also later Montague's father-in-law.

Montague believed in the value of physical endeavour and, for the most part, was at odds with the official line of the *Manchester Guardian* on the First World War. The paper maintained the liberal intellectual tradition of questioning warmongering, which can have come as no surprise to its readership only a decade after its notable and largely unpopular opposition to the Boer War. Montague initially fell in with this viewpoint. He wrote in his leader of 4 August 1914, the day on which Britain declared war with Germany:

> What causes misgivings is the unmistakeable evidence in the House of Commons of the war-feverish condition in which Parliaments sometimes abdicate all their own most imperative duties and valuable rights and agree off hand to anything that is proposed to them with a portentous air of urgency too deep for words – even a few words of businesslike explanation.[20]

Montague did not support the declaration of war and showed no impulse to enlist. As Adrian Gregory argues, enthusiasm for the war was not as widespread as is commonly believed.[21] In the following week, Montague posited that 'there has never been a war in which the non-combatant could contribute so largely to our success as the war which is now beginning'.[22] However, once it became clear that the war would have to be pursued and would require significant resources of manpower, Montague felt it was important to support the conflict in the interests of a speedy resolution. His leaders from late August into September 1914 reflected this shift, and he showed his pride at the flood of young men from Manchester and its environs who joined the growing number of volunteer battalions.[23] Montague decided that he wanted to enlist too, although he was placed at a disadvantage by his shock of white hair; H. W. Nevinson would later write that 'Montague is the only man I know whose white hair in a single night turned dark through courage'.[24] The vigorous, physical nature of the army training was appealing to the active Montague. He found himself at odds with the rest of the editorial staff, and C. P. Scott wrote to L. T. Hobhouse, *Guardian* correspondent and professor of sociology at the University of London, about the 'impossibility of getting any harmony between what I could write and what Montague had written and was writing'.[25] Montague was from this point out of step with Scott and the paper's general line. Keith Grieves notes that 'the outbreak of war highlighted a philosophical gulf between [Scott and Montague] which was never satisfactorily closed'.[26] After the war, he wrote fewer long leaders for the *Guardian*. Although he remained on the staff until 1925, Montague was a solitary and sometimes contrary figure on the newspaper.

Disenchantment

Implicit in *Disenchantment* is the enchantment which is being negated, derived from a highly idealistic view of war and the values which were being defended. George Mosse argues that decisions to enlist were motivated by 'patriotism, the search for a purpose in life, love of adventure, and ideals of masculinity'.[27] Even the most disenchanted authors continued to see value in the camaraderie of the training camp and the endurance of strong homosocial bonds. Richard Holmes suggests that *Disenchantment* 'is often very telling (and surprisingly romantic) in its assessment of infantry soldiers'.[28] Those bonds of togetherness draw on the public school ethos which promoted teamwork through sport, advocating physical action and 'sporting', chivalric conduct. In *Disenchantment* Montague describes the initial period after joining up as leisure, almost a return to childhood: 'To have for his work these raptures of play was the joy of the new recruit who had common health and good-humour' (*D*, 6). Even the iniquities of war are understood through the metaphor of sport. In the chapter 'The Duty of Lying' Montague writes:

> In war your licence to lead the other fellow astray is yet more ample [than in sport]. For war, though it may be good sport to some men, is not a mere sport. In sport you are not 'out to win' except on certain terms of courtesy and handsomeness. Who would take pride in a race won by a fluke? (*D*, 104)

War would ideally, for Montague, be fought by the same codes of behaviour as sport, but he acknowledges that there are fundamental differences between the two: 'the prize of victory in war is no symbol; it is the thing itself, the real end and aim of all that you do and endure' (*D*, 105). He sees the relationships between the sporting ethos and war, that the former is a preparation for unified action, building loyalty and obedience to authority in the shape of form, house, school and then monarch, who stands for church, army and nation. Mark Connelly demonstrates in his discussion of war memorials in schools that 'the dead had done their duty to God, King, Country and institution. The obligation to be ready to emulate that example if called upon to do so was placed upon their successors.'[29] The idea of sportsmanship endures even into 'The Old Age of the War', as Montague describes 'the first hours of that ultimate winding-up of the old, long-decaying estate of hopes and illusions' (*D*, 181). These values endure past the Somme and Passchendaele, and even past the end of the war, and the importance of national values and their promotion of unity remains: 'Sober or drunk, the men were contumaciously sportsmen, incorrigibly English' (*D*, 182). Sporting behaviour endures in those who have fought, but implicit in that statement is the lack of those qualities elsewhere.

Montague suggests that the decline in chivalry comes from a lack of warfare. Political weakness ensues from a lack of physicality in promoting national unity and purging empty rhetorical gestures. This is a stance more usually associated with Thomas Mann and Germany, but Montague wants to purge from the top down.[30] In ''Ware Politicians' Montague asserts that 'an immense tolerance of political rubbish had grown up. On decade after decade of indulgence the man of booming phrases and grandiosely noble professions had swelled into a marvel of inflation' (*D*, 90). The seduction of people away from Christian values leads to superficiality. Empty rhetoric is decried, prefiguring Hemingway's denunciation in *A Farewell to Arms* of the 'abstract words such as glory, honor, courage, or hallow'.[31] That hollowness is manifested in the 'bear movement in Newbolts and Burkes, and, corresponding to this, a bull movement in stocks of the Little Flanigan group' (*D*, 154). The values promulgated by works such as Newbolt's *Vitaï Lampada* – famous for its refrain 'Play Up! Play Up! And play the game!'[32] – are still upheld by Montague, although they are usually seen today as symptomatic of the values rejected by disenchanted authors. The latter allusion is to Goldsmith's *The Good-Natured Man*, in which Mr Flanigan is 'a true English officer [...] not contented with beating the French, but he will scold them too'.[33] This triumphalism is abhorrent to Montague:

> Some Allied non-combatants did almost unthinkable things in the first ecstacy of the triumph that others had won. One worthy drove into Cologne in a car plastered over with Union Jacks, like a minor bookie going to Epsom. It passed the wit of man to make him understand that one does not do these things to defeated peoples. (*D*, 184)

These non-combatants claim to represent Britain by the flags they display, but flag-waving is set apart from the conscientious, sympathetic band of soldiers who fought in the front line. The irony of the undignified dignitaries is bitter, and is emphasised by the radically different emotions in victory. Fighting troops are relieved, not wishing to celebrate the defeat of opposing combatants subjected to the same discipline and hardships and relieved, in the main, at no longer being in danger. Those who have not fought are seen both as being responsible for the start of the war in the first place, and for the scenes which followed.

Silence in wartime

Silence during wartime is an uncanny, haunting quality for Montague. It is no longer a known quantity, contrasted with the repetive, almost omnipresent thunder of artillery. In 'A Trade Report Only' Montague describes a location known as The Garden, 'the Holy Terror, as some men used to call it', which is 'under some sort of taboo' compared with the rest of the Western Front.[34] Eden is a parallel, in the tranquillity of the location and also the fear of imminent danger. The taboo takes two forms in the story: firstly, the openness of the territory contrasted with the enclosure of the trenches. The narrator asks:

> Did nobody fire just because in that place it was so easy for anybody to kill? No trench could be dug; it would have filled in an hour with water filtering through from the full stream flanking The Garden. Sentries stood out among the fruit trees, behind little breastworks of sods, like the things you use to shoot grouse. These screens were merely a form; they would scarcely have slowed down a bullet. They were not defences, only symbols of things that were real elsewhere. Everything else in the place was on queer terms with reality; so were they. ('TRO', 214)

The sporting metaphor is continued, and soldiers are envisaged as game birds, there only for the purpose of being picked off in organised shooting. Meaningful defence is impossible in The Garden, implicitly more so than on the rest of the Western Front. Secondly, the 'queer terms with reality' manifest themselves also in the silence of the open territory. The noise and danger of the Western Front have become normalised, and combatants who have to endure the opposite conditions feel in immediate danger. The narrator tells us that 'I happened to notice the sleepy old grumble of guns from the rest of the front, and I envied those places. Sane, normal places; happy all who were there; only their earthworks were crumbling, not the last few certainties that we men think we have got hold of' ('TRO', 225). The piercing of the silence begins the second section of the story significantly – 'Our first event was the shriek' ('TRO', 214) – before returning to silence. Silence in spaces where noise is expected is troubling, even feared. Silence is the focus of Montague's story; this foregrounding of what usually exists in the background gives it an uncanny quality. Silence is recognised, but it is not in its usual position. In talking about silence as a lack of intentional speech, Zerubavel suggests that 'Part of the reason we resent silence breakers is that by defying the conventional figure-ground configurations that most of us take for granted, they disturb our cognitive tranquillity.'[35] In Montague's story, the reversal of the usual figure-ground configuration is unsettling, but it has also become normalised; cognitive tranquillity is already continually disturbed, paradoxically by tranquillity itself, and to disturb that further is the cause of acute anxiety. The cure is the apparent physical presence of an enemy, manifested in 'the crack of a dead branch heavily trodden upon [...] Better an audible enemy, one with a body, one that could trample on twigs, than that vague infestation of life with impalpable sinisterness' ('TRO', 224).

In wartime the idea of peace is unthinkable, even undesirable. The peace offered by The Garden is a 'mephitic mock-peace' and, the narrator concludes, 'no one can paint a miasma' ('TRO', 233). Peace is cast, bizarrely, as a foul-smelling fog. This perhaps also alludes to the presence of decaying bodies in the trenches, and suggests another reason for the fear of silence: the gas attack was a dangerous form of air as miasma, which hung over the combatants from its first use in the spring of 1915.[36] In the latter stages of the war peace was, in many quarters, a taboo subject. The army was famously planning for the war to carry on into 1919,[37] and even at the German request for an Armistice in October 1918, following the cessation of hostilities with the Bulgarians and Turks, there was little expectation that this would necessarily lead to peace terms. Bullitt Lowry observes that 'the Allied leaders [...] saw the First German Note as a good sign, indeed an excellent one, but in their eyes, it by no means assured an early German surrender'.[38] For Montague, silence while the war endures is pernicious, and a subtly mocking reminder of the distant possibility of a peace which would end the conflict.

Rough Justice, silence and desertion

Montague's novel *Rough Justice* brings together many of the themes discussed above, and is his only full-length treatment of the war. It is a *bildungsroman* about Auberon Garth, a young, energetic man who bears a striking resemblance to the young Montague. Auberon is the embodiment of muscular Christianity, and he embraces the positive values of the public school spirit while failing to learn in an academic sense. His friend Victor Nevin embodies opposing values, similar to those against which Montague cautions in ''Ware Politicians'. An intellectual *par excellence*, Victor is blessed with the gift of rhetoric, but not of action; he is 'enlivened by saying fine things'.[39] Victor's aim in his sophistry is 'to tie [the war] cannily down into harmlessness', but in doing so 'he poetised the smash till Auberon could scarcely regret it any longer'. This speech is a silence in the novel. We hear from Victor's mouth only the first words: '"Young England," he murmured, "greets Armageddon"' (*RJ*, 193). This is far from an incitement to fight, but the rest of the speech is unheard, appearing only in brief quotations recounted by Auberon. Auberon, inspired by Victor's grand words, tells his father that they, along with the cricket pro Fulford and the gardener Bert, with their varying levels of education, fitness and adaptability, will all enlist together as privates: 'Victor is for the plain thing. We've both always cut O.T.C.-ing. And Bert's coming with us, if you'll let him off' (*RJ*, 221). Montague's naming of Victor is ironic: he lives up to his lofty name until the start of the war, blessed with intelligence, wit, the legal career which uses his rhetorical skill and the woman, Molly, who is desired by all the other men. The outbreak of war means that action is suddenly valued more than wit. Victor's fine words are silenced in the novel as Auberon's action, fortitude and resilience come to the fore, recalling Montague's own eventual decision in the summer of 1914.

Victor is effectively silenced in wartime, unable to interact with the officer class to whose company he is more suited and accustomed. In France as a private, he is unable to communicate with Regimental Sergeant-Major Lloyd, to whom he pointedly offers champagne 'in that raffish, unnatural voice' as he plays up to the more senior man: 'Lloyd made no answer. He took two pennies out of his right trouser-pocket and laid them down beside the glass of beer that the barman had now brought him. Then he walked straight out of the place' (*RJ*, 242). The lack of answer highlights Victor's alienation in the army, and he attracts further resentment as Captain Black recommends him on Fulford's suggestion:

> 'Here's the man you're wanting to help at that billeting job, [...] a Sahib; talks French like a Froggy; rising light of the Bar; Oxford degree; a bit of a flyer, all round.'
>
> 'Not me – he'd know a lot too much for me,' the middle-aged Adjutant replied. An old N.C.O. of the Regular Army, he dreaded the touch of quick civilian brains. They might be inquisitive, critical, dangerous to a man's peace. (*RJ*, 252–3)

The NCO is content with a relatively safe position behind the line. The Regular Army is tacitly criticised for its inability to make use of Victor's verbal facility in both French and English, and of civilian expertise more generally. This failure to adapt is shown as symptomatic of the lassitude which prolonged the war needlessly, and makes Victor 'lifeless', 'a battered mind in a quelled body' (*RJ*, 272, 271). The repeated strafe of his superiors pushes Victor to the limits of his endurance. He would be a fine leader in the manner of Colin March and Claude Barbason, the two extravagantly decorated staff officers who we see both in this novel and in the story 'Honours Easy' in *Fiery Particles*, a biting satire on the undeserving allocation of decorations, but he is a poor private.

Victor is equally unable to interact effectively with the other privates, although they endeavour to help him as much as possible out of camaraderie. He cannot embrace the strength in national unity which Auberon advocates so passionately: 'The one thing that I feel to be more worth doing just now than anything else in the world is for every soul in this island to stick tight together until we can pull through this beast of a war' (*RJ*, 217–18). It is Victor's inability to communicate that leads to his desertion, which is not a conscious decision but a series of circumstances in which he makes bad choices. He is concussed following the nearby explosion of a shell, and sees himself as a deserter even before he deserts, wondering from his shell-hole if the marching feet he hears are 'A Provost-Sergeant's party? – out gleaning deserters? The very thought threw him into a mad panic' (*RJ*, 280). He is unnerved by his fatigue and when the party, which, it transpires, consists of members of his section, passes he doubts their reaction to finding him:

> He was not sure of them. Would they say they had found him skulking about in the rear of the line, just when his Company had gone in? You see, he did not know them – had never really fraternised with his fellows – not even enough to know that all privates are tacitly leagued together to avert from any one of themselves the major severities of the law – no more than he knew how courts-martial, for all their grim looks, will struggle until the going down of the sun to find some excuse for the poor brother-in-arms who has failed. (*RJ*, 281)

Victor is placed in a social no-man's land, unable to socialise with his superiors and unable to communicate with the other privates due to his suspicion of those suited to physical work. The final statement reflects the small number of convictions achieved at courts-martial, but is in this case bitterly ironic.[40] Victor's decision not to rejoin is made when he hears the 'voices drop [...] rather queerly' as they steal from the dead bodies, but he fails to realise that they are 'stoical, ribald, good-natured and graceless, pilferers and heroes' (*RJ*, 281). His desertion is bound up in silence and ill communication, from his silencing in front of both officers and privates to his facility with French which enables him to pass undetected as a Frenchman for several years.

Desertion is surrounded by silence, a taboo subject within the army structure which enforces perseverance and uniformity. Ben Shephard asserts that for the Regular Army 'anyone neither sick, wounded, nor mad but nonetheless unwilling to or incapable of fighting was necessarily a coward, to be shot if necessary'.[41] In *Rough Justice* the topic can only be broached in an area which is secure, restricted to officers but with the potential for indiscretion, the callous and sadistic Captain Immals' tongue loosened by alcohol: 'Immals' second whisky was now at his right hand and the pride of knowingness leered from his face' (*RJ*, 317). Prior to the war the army was seen as the last refuge of the indigent and deficient, and the actions of Immals, the pre-war Regular Army officer, are undermined by his degenerate appearance: 'He was an ill-looking fellow; his face was well enough made, but foul in colour; it had the greenish pallor that some men show when thoroughly funked' (*RJ*, 316).[42] Auberon withholds information in response to Immals' recounting of Victor's details, 'bedevilled by [...] booze', a form of silent challenge to Immals' authority within the regulations (*RJ*, 320). The distaste for but subservience to superior officers is a result in part of Immals' violation of the sanctity of silence. Jaworski posits that 'the mention of a taboo topic, the breaking of silence, is socially more significant, observable or marked than the maintenance of a taboo itself'.[43] Zerubavel asserts that 'calling attention to what other group members make a special effort to avoid is an implicitly subversive act'.[44] In this particular case, the act is doubly subversive, in that it brings into the open the taboo of desertion, and this frankness also challenges the hierarchy, providing a rare instance of non-necessary information-sharing between superiors and lower ranks: 'social systems with particularly hierarchical structures (and thus more pronounced power differences) therefore make open discourse much less likely'.[45] However, Immals' drunken outburst is also an emphatic reassertion of authority. Auberon's subtle act of playing dumb, along with the attempts of Molly and Colin to rescue Victor, is contained by military justice. The danger of indiscipline is highlighted and the discomfort caused by Immals' broaching of the taboo subject of desertion in this small group reinforces his greater freedom to talk about it.

Even in the act of Victor's execution he is silenced by the military. The coincidences of dates relating to Victor are conspicuous: the news of his discovery is broken by Immals on the evening of 7 August 1918, the day before what Gary Sheffield calls 'truly a watershed battle, the turning point of the war', near Amiens.[46] Auberon is conscious from hearing about Victor's desertion that 'Nothing but a marvel of rushing victory and happy early peace could save what was left of Victor now' (*RJ*, 335–6) His execution is carried out on 27 September 1918, the day the Hindenburg line was pierced in the Cambrai attacks, and the day after the Bulgarians first requested a cessation of hostilities to negotiate an armistice (*RJ*, 347). Just two days before that, the first armistice treaty was granted.[47] In preparation for Victor's execution, his mouth is stuffed with cotton wool to silence him. Victor's end is verbally silent, but not kinetically silent: perhaps trying to speak, the frantic action of his face puts off the firing squad, which consequently only wounds him. For the first time in the war his own direct action has led to a desired outcome, but this hope is brutally extinguished by Immals. It is his duty to complete the execution, as he tells Auberon: 'Usual routine. March the men off. A.P.M. finishes prisoner. Revolver well into the mouth – muzzle turned slightly upwards. *I* didn't take long with the cur' (*RJ*, 348). Immals is the final representative of the army hierarchy to silence Victor: his mouth is filled first by the cotton wool and then by the gun, and Auberon envisages how 'the brains that had spun Victor's delicate fabrics of fancy and wit bespatter the wall of the slaughterer's yard' (*RJ*, 348). The delicate fabrics of fancy and wit are tacitly compared with Auberon's physicality even in wounding; the bullet into Victor's brain kills him, but the injury that removes Auberon from the war is the severing of his hand: 'when he looked down he saw a hand lying on the ground, with its raw end like a sheep's severed neck at a butcher's door' (*RJ*, 298). Auberon's physical vigour enables him to recover, even with such a serious injury. His physicality and enthusiasm allow him to endure where shallow intellectualism is unable to sustain life in wartime. Victor becomes a symbol of decay and of a lack of physical vigour, someone for whom there is no space in the post-war world. While Victor is 'the only man fit for [Molly] in the whole world' before the war (*RJ*, 178), Auberon is now the symbol of regeneration, prosthetically made whole after the war, able to start in business, literally building for the future by making bricks. Fortitude is important for Montague, particularly physical fortitude and recovery, which maps on to the social recovery of the nation.[48] Mosse comments that 'personal and national regeneration were often inseparable'.[49] Auberon's rebuilding of himself is the symbolic rebuilding of the country.

Disenchantment: After the war

Montague's writing about the war gives little sense of the war's end as a victory worthy of celebration; he explicitly links the Armistice with disenchantment. The traditionally English pre-war values embodied in the public school ethos are needed to facilitate post-war recovery, but are now irrecoverable; 'some mirage of the greater joys which we had forfeited [which] hung for a few moments over the sand' (*D*, 177). The joy which is brought by the Armistice, the 'last happy thrill of the war', is tempered by the cost at which it has come:

> What a victory it might have been – the real, the Winged Victory, chivalric, whole and unstained! The bride that our feckless wooing had sought and not won in the generous youth of the war had come to us now: an old woman, or dead, she no longer refused us. (*D*, 178)

Montague looks back to antiquity to represent the ideal victory which might have been won earlier and, as Ana Carden-Coyne argues, 'the classical body informed western identity, celebrating the beauty of muscularity as the exemplar of unity and wholeness'.[50] Ironically, the statue of Winged Victory (Nike of Samothrace) held by the Louvre is incomplete, missing its head and a wing: Montague's allusion highlights the inability of classical ideals of beauty to endure in modernity, and draws the parallel with Auberon's amputated hand. In the same month as *Disenchantment* was published the University of Manchester was considering a war memorial which featured a statue of a whole Winged Victory, but the proposal was rejected in favour of a less flamboyant mural plaque; to remember the war through restored bodily wholeness and as a victory was clearly inappropriate. Montague concludes the chapter 'Belated Boons' by quoting from Christina Rossetti's 'The Prince's Progress': 'The enchanted dove upon her branch / Died without a mate' (*D*, 179).[51] The death of the dove symbolises the ironic death of peace with the coming of the Armistice.

The post-war peace is in different ways as troubling as the war itself, particularly for its impact on those who volunteered to fight. Four years after the Armistice, Montague's narrator tells us that 'now the marred triumph would leave us jaded and disillusioned, divided, half bankrupt; sneerers at lofty endeavour, and yet not the men for the plodding of busy and orderly peace; bilious with faiths and enthusiasms gone sour in the stomach' (*D*, 176). Victory in the war came at an immense cost – financially, morally and physically – and the Armistice offered little relief. The souring of faith in the values of the public school ethos leads, for Montague, to a lack of drive for successful reconstruction, and an underlying sense that these deteriorations will lead to the failure of the peace. The unrest of the post-war world was partly a problem of the peace treaties.[52] The war is viewed throughout *Disenchantment* from a viewpoint rooted in the 'general post-war condition of apathy, callousness and lassitude', in which the 'common man' is 'sane in his disenchantment' (*D*, 66, 205). Paul Edwards argues that '*Disenchantment* is as much symptom as diagnosis, for it is itself disenchanted and resorts a little desperately to the values and culture Montague seems to know cannot be resurrected.'[53] The disenchantment of the post-war world extends from commemoration to the representation of the conflict which had come to define it. Montague's work suggests that silence is not an appropriate form of commemoration for a brutal and noisy war, writing in a peace which proved to be anything but; *Disenchantment* was instrumental in breaking the near-silence of former combatants about their discontent with some aspects of wartime experience, highlighting the dissatisfaction which so many felt, powerless in the political unrest of the post-war decade.

Notes

1 Michael North, *Reading 1922: A Return to the Scene of the Modern* (Oxford: Oxford University Press, 1999), 5; Janet Watson, *Fighting Different Wars: Experience, Memory, and the First World War in Britain* (Cambridge: Cambridge University Press, 2004), 190.

2 Nicky Losseff and Jenny Doctor, Introduction to *Silence, Music, Silent Music* (Aldershot: Ashgate, 2007), 1; Maria-Luisa Achino-Loeb, 'Silence and the Imperatives of Identity', in Maria-Luisa Achino-Loeb, ed., *Silence: The Currency of Power* (Oxford: Berghahn, 2006), 42.

3 John Cage, 'Experimental Music: Doctrine', in *Silence: Lectures and Writings* (London: Calder and Boyars, 1968), 13.

4 See John Potter, 'The Communicative Rest', in Losseff and Doctor, eds, *Silence, Music, Silent Music*, 155–68; and William O. Beeman, 'Silence in Music', in Achino-Loeb, ed., *Silence: The Currency of Power*, 23.

5 Adam Jaworski, Introduction to *Silence: Interdisciplinary Perspectives* (Berlin: Mouton de Gruyter, 1997), 3.

6 Adrian Gregory, *The Silence of Memory: Armistice Day 1919–1946* (Oxford: Berg, 1994), 13.

7 Aldous Huxley, *The Perennial Philosophy* (London: Chatto and Windus, 1946), 249.

8 C. E. Montague, *Disenchantment* (London: Chatto and Windus, 1922), 174. Subsequent references to this work are to this edition and are given in parentheses in the body of the text.

9 Pierre Sorlin, 'Cinema and the Memory of the Great War', in Michael Paris, ed., *The First World War and Popular Cinema: 1914 to the Present* (Edinburgh: Edinburgh University Press, 1999), 18.

10 Gregory, *Silence*, 18. See also Bohdan Szuchewycz, 'Silence in Ritual Communication', in Jaworski, ed., *Silence: Interdisciplinary Perspectives*, 239.

11 Jay Winter, 'Thinking about Silence', in Efrat Ben-Ze'ev, Ruth Ginio and Jay Winter, eds, *Shadows of War: A Social History of Silence in the Twentieth Century* (Cambridge: Cambridge University Press, 2010), 20.

12 James V. Wertsch, *Voices of Collective Remembering* (Cambridge: Cambridge University Press, 2002), 42.

13 Eviatar Zerubavel, *The Elephant in the Room: Silence and Denial in Everyday Life* (Oxford: Oxford University Press, 2006), 9, 56–7.

14 Gregory, *Silence*, 51–2, 54.

15 'Ex-Battery Commander', 'Our Debt of Honour: The Claim of Ex-Officers', *The Times* (4 February 1920), 10.

16 Samuel Hynes, *A War Imagined: The First World War and English Culture* (London: Pimlico, 1992), 311.
17 Niall Ferguson, *The Pity of War* (Harmondsworth: Penguin, 1999), xxix.
18 Hynes, *A War Imagined*, 308.
19 See Oliver Elton, *C. E. Montague: A Memoir* (London: Chatto and Windus, 1929), 8–21.
20 C. E. Montague, 'The Nerves of Parliament', *Manchester Guardian* (4 August 1914), 6. Montague kept cuttings books of his own leading articles, on which basis I identify his leaders. These books are in the C. E. Montague Papers in the archives of the John Rylands University Library of Manchester. There are 25 of these large books; CEM/1/1/1/22 covers 1914 and 1919–20.
21 See Adrian Gregory, 'British "War Enthusiasm" in 1914: a Reassessment', in Gail Braybon, ed., *Evidence, History and the Great War: Historians and the Impact of 1914–18* (Oxford: Berghahn, 2003), 67–85.
22 C. E. Montague, 'The Non-Combatant: What He Can Do', *Manchester Guardian* (7 August 1914), 4.
23 See, for example, C. E. Montague, 'The Rush to Enlist', *Manchester Guardian* (3 September 1914), 4.
24 Henry W. Nevinson, *Last Changes, Last Chances* (London: Nisbet, 1928), 139. See also H. G. Wells, *Experiment in Autobiography: Discoveries and Conclusions of a Very Ordinary Brain (Since 1866)* (London: Faber and Faber, 1984 [1934]), 682.
25 C. P. Scott to L. T. Hobhouse, 12 December 1914, quoted in Keith Grieves, 'C. E. Montague and the Making of Disenchantment, 1914–1921', *War in History*, 4, 1 (1997), 39. On Hobhouse, see Stefan Collini, *Liberalism and Sociology: L. T. Hobhouse and Political Argument in England, 1880–1914* (Cambridge: Cambridge University Press, 1979) and Vincent Sherry, *The Great War and the Language of Modernism* (Oxford: Oxford University Press, 2003), 23–7.
26 Grieves, 'C. E. Montague and the Making of Disenchantment', 39.
27 George Mosse, *Fallen Soldiers: Reshaping the Memory of the World Wars* (Oxford: Oxford University Press, 1990), 53.
28 Richard Holmes, *Tommy: the British Soldier on the Western Front 1914–1918* (London: HarperCollins, 2004), 277.
29 Mark Connelly, *The Great War, Memory and Ritual: Commemoration in the City and East London, 1916–1939* (Woodbridge: Royal Historical Society / Boydell Press, 2002), 83.
30 See Alan Kramer, *Dynamic of Destruction: Culture and Mass Killing in the First World War* (Oxford: Oxford University Press, 2007), 163–4.
31 Ernest Hemingway, *A Farewell to Arms* (London: Arrow, 1994 [1929]), 165.
32 See Sir Henry Newbolt, 'Vitaï Lampada', in *Collected Poems 1897–1907* (London: Nelson, n.d. [1908]), 131–3.
33 Oliver Goldsmith, *The Good Natured Man*, III.145–7, in *The Good Natured*

Man / She Stoops to Conquer, ed. A. S. Collins (London: University Tutorial Press, 1900), 39.

34 C. E. Montague, 'A Trade Report Only', in *Fiery Particles* (London: Chatto and Windus, 1923), 211. Subsequent references to this work are to this edition and are given in parentheses in the body of the text.

35 Zerubavel, *Elephant in the Room*, 74. See also Alina Kwiatkowska, 'Silence Across Modalities', in Jaworski, ed., *Silence: Interdisciplinary Perspectives*, 330.

36 Simon Jones, *World War I Gas Warfare: Tactics and Equipment* (Oxford: Osprey, 2007), 5–6.

37 Martin Gilbert, *First World War* (London: HarperCollins, 1994), 402–3.

38 Bullitt Lowry, *Armistice 1918* (Kent, OH: Kent State University Press, 1996), 11.

39 C. E. Montague, *Rough Justice* (London: Chatto and Windus, 1926), 194. Subsequent references to this work are to this edition and are given in parentheses in the body of the text.

40 Anthony Babington, *For the Sake of Example: Capital Courts-Martial 1914–1920* (London: Leo Cooper, 1983).

41 Ben Shephard, *A War of Nerves: Soldiers and Psychiatrists 1914–1994* (London: Jonathan Cape, 2000), 25.

42 On the pre-war army see Shephard, *War of Nerves*, 25.

43 Adam Jaworski, '"White and White": Metacommunicative and Metaphorical Silences', in Jaworski, ed., *Silence: Interdisciplinary Perspectives*, 392.

44 Zerubavel, *Elephant in the Room*, 78.

45 Eviatar Zerubavel, 'The Social Sound of Silence: Toward a Sociology of Denial', in Ben-Ze'ev et al., eds, *Shadows of War*, 38.

46 Gary Sheffield, *Forgotten Victory: The First World War: Myths and Realities* (London: Headline Review, 2002), 237.

47 Sir Frederick Maurice, *The Armistices of 1918* (Oxford: Oxford University Press, 1943), 14.

48 See Alexander Watson, *Enduring the Great War: Combat, Morale and Collapse in the German and British Armies, 1914–1918* (Cambridge: Cambridge University Press, 2008). See also Watson's chapter in this volume.

49 Mosse, *Fallen Soldiers*, 64.

50 Ana Carden-Coyne, *Reconstructing the Body: Classicism, Modernism and the First World War* (Oxford: Oxford University Press, 2009), 112.

51 Christina Rossetti, 'The Prince's Progress', in *The Complete Poems of Christina Rossetti: A Variorum Edition*, ed. R. W. Crump, 2 vols (Baton Rouge, LO: Louisiana State University Press, 1979), I, 108.

52 Sheffield, *Forgotten Victory*, 267.

53 Paul Edwards, 'British War Memoirs', in Vincent Sherry, ed., *The Cambridge Companion to the First World War* (Cambridge: Cambridge University Press, 2005), 17.

7

The *Bookman*, the *Times Literary Supplement* and the Armistice

Jane Potter

The works of novelists, poets and artists have regularly been invoked to give a picture of the world of 1914–18 and its aftermath, rather to the frustration of historians who see these literary and conceptual representations as obscuring or indeed hijacking the 'facts' of the First World War. Little attention has hitherto been paid to periodicals and reviews that interpreted and judged these works, but the journals give us particular insight into the issues at stake for many readers in the years immediately after the war. This chapter considers how two important review publications, the *Times Literary Supplement* and the *Bookman*, characterised, debated and recorded both the Armistice itself and its consequences into the 1920s and 1930s. I will explore what the editorials, advertisements and reviews featured in these journals tell us about the ways the silence of 11 November 1918 was communicated to and interpreted for a reading public. I will also ask how the hopes and disillusions of the peace were expressed in these journals and whether they bear out Eric Hobsbawm's later assertion that there was, in effect, a thirty-year war between 1914 and 1945.[1]

Certain themes recur in the books reviewed in the period after the Armistice: hope and disappointment, expectation and fear, the rise of fascism and socialism. There were many titles supporting the League of Nations in the years immediately following the Armistice, but alongside these were more censorious texts that questioned the terms of the peace settlement and the efficacy of the League. The *TLS* and the *Bookman* did not simply report on the books in question; in their critiques by various reviewers, the journals added their own voices to the debates. Both periodicals no doubt reflected the reading interests of their readers – but they also created those interests in the first place. This in turn has affected the ways in which war literature has been passed down over the generations. Books survive and are remembered not only for their intrinsic value, but partly because of the ways they are received and discussed at the time of publication.

Those who survived the First World War wanted variously to understand, to memorialise and also to forget the catastrophe in the inter-war period; the ways that books were marketed and promoted to them can tell us something about the mood of those years. The *TLS* and the *Bookman* are records of how publishers and booksellers responded to and profited from public interest in the Armistice and its consequences. More than this: the journals promoted a particular kind of response to the brokered peace that still dominates our perspective nearly 100 years on. The history of these journals is not widely known, so I begin with a brief outline of their origins and interests.

The *Bookman*

William Robertson Nicoll, editor of Hodder & Stoughton's highly influential periodical the *British Weekly*, believed there was a market for an exclusively literary monthly and so in 1891 he established the *Bookman*, with A. St John Adcock as assistant editor. The *Bookman* contained reviews, advertisements, editorials on book trade issues and articles on literary subjects. It was illustrated with pictures of books and portraits of authors, the latter a feature of each monthly cover.[2] In 1894 Nicoll was joined at the *Bookman* by Ernest Hodder Williams.[3] With strong connections to the Liberal government, Nicoll and Williams were 'exceptionally well informed about the progress of events'[4] during the First World War. (Nicoll and Williams were also in Paris when the Peace Treaty was signed in June 1919.) Thus they were uniquely placed to use their publications to support the war effort and regularly donated large sums of money to organisations such as the Red Cross from the profits from highly successful and lucrative publications such as *King Albert's Book* (1914). The firm was, moreover, a key contributor to the government's propaganda agency based at Wellington House, publishing over 130 pamphlets and books, and its shares in the New York firm of George H. Doran meant the partners were in an excellent position to influence American public opinion. A leading publisher of popular fiction, Hodder & Stoughton 'became increasingly identified with reading for entertainment',[5] and the literary aspirations of 'the active man' and indeed 'the active woman' were encouraged by the *Bookman* through its prize competitions. One recipient of the journal's commendation was Wilfred Owen. 'Song of Songs' was one of only five poems he saw published in his lifetime, and it received a special commendation with 'a book by way of consolation prize' in the lyric competition of May 1918.

In its advertisements for items such as bookcases, pens and bargain books, many of which used wartime associations to bolster their appeal, the *Bookman* shows how commodity culture was not diminished by the war; rather, commercial enterprises adapted to and exploited the new conditions. The *Bookman* featured advertisements for publishing firms and printers, as well as other periodicals. Here, the *Times Literary Supplement* was described as 'the surest guide to military and general literature'.[6]

The *Times Literary Supplement*

The *Times Literary Supplement* was founded in 1902, not, as legend has it, as a temporary review supplement to the *Times* newspaper, but as a 'permanent and distinguished' addition. Published weekly and known colloquially as *Lit Supp* until its rebranding as the *TLS* in 1969, it was from February 1914 issued separately from *The Times* and priced at one penny. Writers for the *TLS* ranged from novelists, poets and publishers to academics and politicians. Among the contributors during the war years and in the wake of the Armistice were Virginia Woolf, T. S. Eliot, John Middleton Murry, Edmund Gosse and Marie Belloc Lowndes, although articles were published anonymously.[7] Always marked by sharp, critical writing, intense debate and the occasional literary spat, and reviewing many of the important books of its time, the *TLS* tells us something about the social climate out of which those books were produced, not least during wartime. As Janet Watson has pointed out, 'publishing – and in turn reviewing – were generally on the increase, and literary criticism was considered by many to be as much a site for political and personal battles as for formal evaluation'.[8]

On the outbreak of war in August 1914, this 'purely literary journal' provided a long survey of 'Books on the Crisis' in its leading article (6 August), designed to 'help readers to understand the background' of the recent declaration.[9] Alongside it appeared a column advertisement for *The Times* Book Club's 'Books of Importance on the European Crisis'. 'Taking the lead from the August 6 issue, the publishers, almost to a man, concentrated on war books in their advertisements,' so that there was 'a steady stream of books, novels, and poems with a war interest'.[10] Moreover, Arthur Clutton-Brock, in his leader articles, frequently reflected on the 'moral conduct of the war', arguing that Britain was fighting a noble cause and thus should fight it nobly.[11] Clutton-Brock 'carried his firm moral note into the peace'.[12] In his leader of 14 November 1918, entitled 'The End and the Beginning', he wrote that Germany's 'task'

> now is to see herself as she is, to tell no more lies either to herself or to others [...]. This is no time for jeers or insolent triumph. If there were no nobler reason, we have suffered too much in our victory. If we are insolent in triumph now, we will be forgetting already that it is not we who have triumphed but the moral law that has made us its instruments.[13]

The nobility of Britain's cause was reiterated by both periodicals as they confronted the Armistice, yet although there was agreement about the goal of world peace, controversy raged about how this could be achieved. This 'exposed a gulf so profound in its breadth that the people on opposite sides seemed unable even to hear one another'[14] and was played out in the reviews of books that, like those issued on the outbreak of war in 1914, sought to explain and interpret events for the reading public.

The Armistice and after

The language of titles relating to the Armistice, Peace Treaty and the League of Nations is revealing. From the initial optimism sprang, sooner or later, a sense of pessimism. For many observers, the terms of the treaty were unworkable and unrealistic, and the League seemed doomed to fail. Its ability to settle disputes was questioned, its efficacy sometimes ridiculed. Reflections on what the war itself actually achieved were most notably played out in memoirs, novels and poetry of the second great flowering of war literature in the late 1920s and early 1930s – in works by Edmund Blunden, Robert Graves, Vera Brittain, Siegfried Sassoon, David Jones and Ford Madox Ford among others[15] – but they were also present in the handful of books examining the legacy of the peace. Works on the peace and on the League of Nations are small in number by comparison with war fiction and autobiography – itself an interesting fact. And the reviews of these texts are telling for what they reveal about attitudes to the international organisation that had begun with such hope.

Early on, in 1915, the *Bookman* canvassed the opinions of prominent writers about 'Life and Literature after the War'. Some authors responded that it was 'too early to tell', but generally commentators took the view expressed by Charles Garvice that 'there will be no great demand for the war element in fiction' after the war: 'Every novelist knows that the one thing he might not write about after the Boer War was – the Boer War.'[16] This was reiterated by David Hodge in the *Bookman* of 1919 when, in his article on Sapper, he notes that the

> public had become satiated with the War as a basis for reading matter of the imaginative order; weary of incomprehensible descriptions of gallant fights in the air; tired of the technicalities that shrouded the interest of what soldier-authors had to say; bored by the slang of the trenches and the officers' mess; and annoyed by the assumption of too many of the writers that a story, no matter how incompetently done, had claim to notice and serious consideration merely because it was the work of one who had been 'over there' and studied hell at first hand.[17]

Those who 'studied hell at first hand', however, were celebrated in the *Bookman*'s Christmas 1918 special number, which featured John Buchan, in a colonel's uniform, on the cover. The image presents a curious mix of the martial and the literary, for although denied active service due to ill health, Buchan, famous for his spy thrillers such as *The Thirty-Nine Steps*, was a key player in the intelligence service and in the dissemination of both official and unofficial propaganda.[18] Thus the cover is an intriguing marker of one of the main features of the issue, an article entitled 'Poets in Khaki' by A. St John Adcock. Accompanied by portraits mounted on heavy card of individuals such as Siegfried Sassoon, Herbert Asquith, American Alan Seeger, Canadian Robert W. Service and Australian Leon Gellert, this article considers the stylistic and thematic changes that poetry underwent over the course of four years of war. Reflections on the 'shining ideals' of the early days of the war were replaced by denunciations of 'the injustice, the madness, the tragic misery and indescribable beastliness of war'. While St John Adcock looks at a wide range of poets, including Robert Graves, Ivor Gurney, Julian Grenfell and John McCrae, he identifies Gilbert Frankau, Alec Waugh and Siegfried Sassoon as the poets who most represent the 'essentially modern attitude toward war'.[19]

Edwin Pugh declares in his review 'Three Anti-Climax Novels and One Other' in the *Bookman*'s November 1918 issue that he is exasperated with writers who used the war as a convenient dramatic backdrop:

> I believe I am expressing the opinion of countless novel readers when I say that I do wish authors would keep the war out of stories that have inherently nothing whatever to do with the war […]. [T]hose who are no more intimately familiar with any aspect of the war other than the obvious aspects

> that affect us all, would be better advised to leave it in the background [...]. For writers to seize upon the chances and the casualties of the battlefield as a means of disentangling the knots they have tied in the destinies of their created puppets is hardly fair, either to themselves or to their readers.[20]

New novels highlighted in this issue included *Where Your Treasure Is* by Beatrice Harraden, which Alice Sedgwick reviewed for the *TLS* and labelled 'an unfortunate outlet' for Harraden's eye-witness experience of working for the Committee for Relief in Belgium. Sedgwick asserts that

> our experience of contemporary fiction has frequently led us to wish that our novelists could have been kept ignorant of the fact that there was 'a war on', or else that they might have suspended their function 'for the duration'.[21]

Interrogations of war-themed texts turned quickly to considerations of what the Armistice meant for the future of nations. By Christmas 1918 the *TLS* was proclaiming that 'the turmoil has not yet subsided [...]. The peace we need for our peace of mind will not consist of what we can take from the Germans, but what we give to the world.'[22] This sense of moral optimism was invested, even before the Armistice, in President Wilson who, in the closing months of the war, was already seen as a highly influential figure. The October 1918 issue of the *Bookman* featured his portrait on the cover and contained the article 'President Wilson as a Man of Letters' by Frederic Whyte. Earlier, on 19 September 1918, James Wycliffe Headlam reviewed *President Wilson's Foreign Policy* for the *TLS*, declaring

> The personal will of President Wilson is at this moment one of the strongest forces in the world, the power which he wields arises not from any inherited position, not from military conquest [...] it is the outcome of his own personal character, and the position he holds is one in which he has been twice placed by the free and deliberate choice of the large majority of his fellow citizens.[23]

Yet for all the optimism Wilson may have generated, questions were raised almost immediately about the efficacy of the peace and the League of Nations, though both had their defenders. The *Bookman*'s review of Morris Jastrow's eerily prescient *The War and the Coming Peace* pointed out that

> peace must surely be 'more than a temporary patchwork settlement of the issues between the European nations that existed at the outbreak of the war'. He does not wish to see the next peace conference modelled on

> the pattern of that of Vienna in 1815, nor that of Paris in 1856, nor that of Berlin in 1878, because each of them contained the 'seeds of another war'.[24]

The *TLS* noted how W. T. S. Stallybrass's *A Society of States, or Sovereignty, Independence, and Equality in a League of Nations* asserts that the League's 'alleged interference with the individual sovereignty of its component nations' is overstated and that 'the doctrine of the absolute sovereignty and independence of States is not in conformity with fact, and therefore no longer serves a useful purpose'. The League, he argues, 'does not in fact involve so abrupt a departure from the practice in the matter of the recent past as is sometimes supposed'.[25]

That another war should be averted, if for no other reason than to recognise the debt owed to so many who fought and died, is explicit in the *TLS* leader of 30 January 1919, 'A Hamlet of War', a review of Arthur Graeme West's *The Diary of a Dead Officer*. The memoir is praised for helping the reading public 'see what [the war] meant to boys who might have been our own sons':

> We may be ardent patriots, we may be utterly sure that the war had to be fought out to a victorious end; but those of us who have lived through it without peril or hardship, or any bitter conflict of soul, will do well for the rest of our lives to remember what has been suffered by boys like West, some dead, some still living, but with years which ought to have been the happiest of their lives [...]. There never would be a war again if men, in peace time, could know what it meant. Even the Prussian Junker, if he had imagination enough to know that, would long for a league of peace.[26]

As if to bolster support, the *Bookman* prize competition offered a prize of three new books for 'the best motto from any British or American author for the proposed League of Nations'. The prize, announced in January 1919, was divided between Hubert H. Thomas of Wales, who suggested lines from Longfellow's *Hiawatha* ('All your strength is in your union, / All your danger is in discord; / Therefore be at peace henceforward, / And as brothers live together'), and Agnes Glynn of Ireland, who offered a quotation from Mr Dooley: 'Trust everybody – but cut the cards.' The editors noted, however, that although 'this competition has been gratifying in quantity' it was 'a little disappointing in quality'. They remarked that 'quite a large number of competitors sent Tennyson's "In Parliament of Man, the Federation of the World," which is a good description but no motto.'[27]

Another League of Nations competition, 'the best parable in not more than two hundred words dealing with the objections to the League of

Nations', was offered for May 1919. The winner, announced in June, was M. McDonnell of Lancaster who compared the League 'like unto a man who made a feast for his friends and, when the friends were sat down, each looked for his favourite dish and found it not'. When they embraced upon leaving the feast, 'how great was every man's surprise to feel a coat of mail beneath the festive robe of his neighbour – and that seemed stronger than his own [...]. And in the Netherlands there was laughing and gnashing of teeth.' As with the previous League-themed competition, the editors remarked, 'this competition has proved rather more difficult than usual, and the results are rather disappointing'; they did single out 'for honourable mention' a number of other contributors, though only six.[28]

Both competitions proved disappointing – a symbol perhaps of attitudes towards the League. Yet some found cause to celebrate the negotiations at Versailles, if for no other reason than to exploit the momentous events to sell their wares. Advertisements in the *Bookman* for Waterman's Ideal Fountain Pen (August 1919) proclaim that the brand was 'used in the signing of The Peace Treaty at Versailles'. It is 'the Pen with the International Reputation' and a testimony by Dr E. J. Dillon, 'the eminent writer', proclaims

> All that writing can accomplish to restore and maintain order and peace in the world was effected at Versailles on Saturday, 28th June. On that historic day the Peace Conference undertook to prove that good pens guided by far-seeing minds are mightier than swords and heavy guns. Pens which signed the Treaty for Great Britain, Italy, Japan, Poland, Belgium, Australia, Greece, Roumania, and Czecho-Slovakia, for they were mine and had been used by me in the service of truth and justice during the labours of the Conference. As for the quality of the statecraft whose decisions they recorded with time will bear witness to that. In the meanwhile the world must be content to wait and see.

While the actions of statesmen may be in doubt, the quality of this product is sound, perhaps sounder and more reliable than the decisions of statecraft. In April 1919 an advertisement entitled 'The fellowship of the Pen' states that the product which 'gratifies [the statesmen at Versailles] will gratify you – and your friends at home or on active service', reminding us that even after the Armistice, men and women were still on active duty throughout Europe.

Immediately after the Armistice, a new industry – battlefield tourism – began. Books such as the *Michelin Guide to the Battle Fields of France* played their part in this new commercial endeavour, and were advertised in both periodicals. The September 1920 issue of the *Bookman* notes how this book 'deals with the first battle of the Somme – telling the story of that Homeric conflict and describing the towns and villages through which it raged. Visitors to these battle scenes will find this an excellent and a thoroughly well informed guide.'[29] Nearly ten years later, tourists were addressed as pilgrims, and books such as *The Silent Cities*, 'an illustrated guide to every cemetery in France or Belgium in which more than forty British soldiers are buried', became memorials: 'at once a most useful guide and a book of remembrance'.[30] *Cenotaph: A Book of Remembrance in Poetry and Prose for November the Eleventh*, compiled and edited by Thomas Moult in 1923, was praised by the *Bookman* as 'a breviary of sacred recollections and enduring hope' that will 'bring consolation and light to those who walk still in the shadow of days that can never be forgotten'.[31]

Remembrance went hand-in-hand with recognition of the difficulties of peace and post-war problems. The *TLS* aimed 'at exerting its usual steadying influence' and 'gave constant support' to the League of Nations.[32] As the vanquished nation, Germany was still suspect, and the *TLS* review by John Edward Nutt Mackenzie of *The League of Nations: Way to the World's Peace* by Mathias Erzberger described the book as 'self-assertive, boastful', 'finished [...] last September, when it still seemed probable that, if Germany could not be victorious, she could not be defeated'. This, Mackenzie suggests, may account for the author's 'superior tone', giving insight into 'the claims that will be advanced by the German Delegates when they are admitted at the Peace Conference', for instance that Germany must have its colonies back. The implication here is that Germany will be as 'boastful' in peace as it was in war and its arrogance must be kept in check.[33] Yet for others, part of the peace was redefining the nations' image of the aggressor, now defeated. In *The New Germany* (1920), the *Bookman* reviewer declared that the author George Young aims 'to dispel the idea that the German nation is still obsessed with militarism' and show it instead 'as a completely stricken country, drifting with the apathy of despair farther and farther from a normal condition of society and affairs'. Young provides a warning similar to Jastrow's that 'the safety of Europe' rests on providing the 'moral and material assistance of its people back into the path of security and reason – a feat which their shattered condition does not enable them to perform of their own initiative'.[34] In a leader, 'Optimism after the War', the *TLS* admonished those who 'having been proved wrong in their expectations of our defeat in war, are revenging themselves by a confident assurance of our failure in peace'. It acknowledges that there is a hard road ahead, for although the Allies 'won the war [...] plainly, they have not yet won the peace'. The Peace Treaty 'is open to very serious criticism', but the path to peace must be met with 'a modest but unconquerable hope'.[35] Later, on 3 June 1920, the *TLS* further remarks that 'the virtue and working strength of the League, as we conceive it, is that its humanitarianism is constructive and articulate, resting on the perception that we can only become men in the universal sense after due realization of the successive particularities of our manhood'.[36]

In December 1920 Hutchinson's full-page advertisement in the Christmas supplement to the *Bookman*, 'Important Books with a World-wide Interest', demonstrates that books on the war were still profitable. These included Ludendorf's *The General Staff and its Problems* and *My War Memories*; *The War of the Future* by General von Bernhardi; *British Secret Service during the Great War* by Nicholas Everett; and *The Dover Patrol, 1915–1917* by Admiral Sir Reginald Bacon. Tellingly, *The Peace Conference* by E. J. Dillon is given less prominence although the review notes that 'It should be studied by every thinking reader who wishes to know what really happened at Paris during those fateful months when the peace of the world was being settled – we hope for all time.'[37] Rose Macaulay's 1922 novel *Mystery at Geneva* 'deftly envelops the League of Nations and Messieurs les Délégués',[38] while the need to educate the young was met by *Fight for Peace: Stories of the Work of the League of Nations* by Hebe Spaull. On 1 March 1923 the *TLS* asserted that the stories in this book 'are admirably told, and with a skilful use of local colour, are calculated to interest the child' with tales of many countries, including Switzerland, Albania, Poland, Japan and Samoa. 'The principal character in each case is, as is fitting, a child, and the story has nothing in it at first ostensibly to do with the League, but, as in a clever advertisement, the idea of the League and all it stands for is skilfully introduced in the end.' A foreword by Dr C. W. Kimmins 'testifies to the educational value of this little book as a school reader'.[39]

Gilbert Murray, chairman of the League of Nations Union, published what the *TLS* reviewer H. M. Stannard called 'a heartfelt book', *The Ordeal of this Generation*, in 1924. In it Murray argued that Britain 'should give a lead to public opinion in the matter of the League'.[40] Other titles reviewed in the *TLS* by Stannard were *They That Take the Sword: The Future of the League of Nations* by Douglas Jerrold (11 January 1936); *The League of Nations and the Rule of Law* by Alfred Zimmern (8 February 1936); under the collective heading 'Difficulties of Peace',

Collective Security, edited by Maurice Bourquin, *Peace in Our Time* by Lord Allen of Hurtwood and *Towards a New League* by H. N. Brailsford (5 September 1936); and under the heading 'Security on the Cheap: British Ideals and the League Covenant', *The Faith of an Englishman* by Sir Edward Grigg (31 October 1936).

On 8 September 1927, in an article entitled 'The Way of Peace', the *TLS* asserted that

> The League of Nations, though it has done good work, appears to inspire little confidence as an organization for guaranteeing peace. In short, if wars are to be avoided in the future, it seems that something more will be needed than leagues, conferences and agreements for the limitation of armaments. The essential problem, that is to say, can be solved neither by the soldier nor by the diplomatist.[41]

Lectures formed a large part of the dissemination of information about the League and prominent ones were published yearly, such as those delivered at the Geneva Institute of International Relations. Various publishers, including Humphrey Milford and Allen & Unwin, produced printed texts of each series entitled collectively *Problems of Peace*. In April 1928 the lectures were reviewed in the *TLS* alongside *The Protection of Minorities* under the heading 'League of Nations in Action', while in January 1934 Stannard reviewed the eighth series and commented that

> At a time when the status and even the existence of the League is imperilled it is good to study the crisis in League affairs from within [...] the Geneva Institute set itself the task which was really proper to it from the first of instructing the public upon the subject of international cooperation.[42]

More local considerations of the League and its role were noticed in the *Bookman* in its 'Literary Circle' section in December 1928. On 7 November in London, Mr Victor Evans 'spoke quietly, earnestly of the need to carry out the ideal for which the last War was fought, and find some way by which nations might settle their differences rationally and peacefully. He gave an admirably succinct idea of the object of the League of Nations, the work it had done and was doing, and held his audience intensely interested in the difficult subject which his manner of handling made easily understandable.'[43]

In an article considering *The Pathway of Peace* by R. McElroy, *The American Secretaries of State and their Diplomacy*, edited by Samuel Flagg Bemis, and *American Orations*, edited with an introduction by George Haven Putnam, the reviewer comments that:

> Respect for the sanctity of treaties, of course, though the corner-stone of peace, does not constitute its lasting foundation. A treaty may or may not remove the root causes of international antagonism; more often than not it does no more than effect a temporary accommodation; and general treaties, providing for definite action in circumstances which cannot be foreseen, are apt to cause more evils than they cure [...]. In short, to find the way of peace we must needs explore, and if possible clear, the jungle of national contradictions and antagonisms which are the causes of war.[44]

On 27 September 1928 the *TLS* carried an advertisement for Allen & Unwin's 'Important New Book', *The Origin, Structure, and Working of the League of Nations* by C. Howard-Ellis, touting it as 'by far the most thorough study of the League that has yet appeared, and should take its place as a standard work on the subject'.[45]

While it defends the League against the 'charge that it is based on an obsolete idea and therefore deserves the ironic gibes of those of wider vision', the *TLS* leader article of 17 November 1928 nevertheless bemoans the sententious and voluminous nature of most writing by and about it: 'humanity's first attempt at worldwide organization [...] has not thought it fit to commend itself as against the pressure of local interests by a compelling brevity of speech'. The contemporary reader and the historian of the future have a monumental task in trying to understand the origins and workings of the League and 'will surely be appalled to find', for example, 'that one American enthusiast's contribution to the preliminaries to the first draft of the Covenant runs to several hundred pages'.[46] On 29 November 1928 the *TLS* featured a one-column review of two books under the heading, 'Diplomatic Figures': *Diplomatic Europe Since the Treaty of Versailles* by Count Carlo Sforza and *Statesmen of the War: In Retrospect, 1918–1928* by William Martin, noting: 'It is always useful to have the observations on recent events by those who themselves have taken some part in them.'[47]

The turgid nature of many of the books about the League and the efforts to maintain the peace may be partly to blame for their obscurity in light of the more dramatic and considered literary texts emerging in the late 1920s and early 1930s. As the *Bookman* reviewer of H. M. Tomlinson's *All Our Yesterdays* observed in February 1930,

> the new War books were very different from the old; they were written with a more and more daringly naked realism of description and dialogue; all the filthy things seen and heard in and around the trenches were poured into their pages unreservedly, and those that were worst in this respect became

> the best of the best-sellers. Reading them, one after another, left you with an impression of almost unmitigated horror and bestiality.[48]

These 'best of the best-sellers' later became part of the canon of Great War literature; many are still in print today. These 'frank, sometimes disgustingly outspoken war books pouring from the press' did 'more to prevent another war than all the orthodox peace propaganda' in A. St John Adcock's view. He believed that

> if we are to be saved from more wars it is best that we should have the truth about them; if they were a filthy business let us go into the next – if we are so mad as to have another – with our eyes open and knowing it for the filthy business it is.[49]

If fiction writers and memoirists were expressing disillusion and anger, other veterans seemed to be lapsing into silence, at least according to H. E. Bates in his preface to R. H. Mottram's *Ten Years Ago* (1928): 'It has been a significant silence, like those two brief minutes on Armistice Day, and just as definitely it has meant "never again".'[50] Ernest Raymond, who reviewed Mottram's book in the *Bookman* in December 1928, took issue with Bates's rather negative view of this silence, arguing that the determination not to face another war is more powerful for being held quietly:

> That the Armistice Silence, speaking generally, is the expression of the world's subconsciousness, and that the dominant note of that subconsciousness is a wistful bewildered, rather blind, 'It must not happen again. It simply must not!' I at least am satisfied; and in the knowledge I find my only but sufficient comfort.[51]

Raymond goes on to argue how this non-vocal, undramatic view is characteristic of the soldiers who 'held the Ypres Salient', noting that 'the typical Englishman prefers his inarticulateness', but he is not 'the less or more potent for that'. This character 'without excitement, without *élan*, without mutiny, without despair, without hope almost, just stood obstinately still and proved unbeatable and won its way in the end'. Raymond declares that 'I am not so disturbed, as apparently Mr. Bates is, by the fact that we have all dropped into silence: I find my consolation [...] in the whole body of Mr. Mottram's essays' and he praises Mottram's quiet pacifist philosophy. In a review of *The Memoirs of Prince Max of Baden* entitled 'The End of the War', the *TLS* commented upon its 'firm moral note':

> And even though much has happened since which might seem little worthy of the motives and principles with which the War was fought, this country at least has the right to say that, where her influence and power prevail, she has not deserted the principles that she professed. She has not used her victory to reassert her power or to aim at world dominion. Freedom, for small as for large nations, ordered self-government and peace are what she has furthered. In the Dominions, in Ireland, in Egypt, in Palestine, in India, she is soberly working out the problems of the new order; and even for Germany herself a new future is opening.[52]

Yet as the problems of the 1930s increased, many people shared the view of Hugh Ross-Williamson in a 1933 leader article in the *Bookman* which asked 'Peace – for what?' In the wake of the First World War, 'peace, a mere cessation of hostilities, was desirable enough as an end in itself. Anyone who denied it, after the experience of those four years, would have been considered insane.'[53] But fourteen years after the Armistice, militarism was, worryingly, re-emerging with vigour in the proclamations of Hitler and Mussolini. Ross-Williamson goes on to argue that 'a desire for peace, which, ultimately, is based on a fear of death and whose advocates appeal emotionally to men's cowardice, will go down before the advance of the war-ideal of Fascism. And it will deserve to.'[54]

As Hitler's 'threat to peace in Europe' grew in the 1930s, 'a major preoccupation' of the *TLS* in these years was that 'Liberty must be defended – but how far and by what means?' Reviews of books on 'liberalism and socialism, and the state of affairs in Russia, Germany, Italy and Spain' abounded.[55] By 1939 the *TLS* had come full circle with its leader of 9 September, entitled 'Books for the Crisis', which was 'almost identical with that used at the outbreak of the 1914–1918 war'. The front-page advertisement for Hutchinson proclaimed that 'Every book in this list is of vital importance to every British citizen', with titles that included *Men Against Hitler*, *Modern Poland* and *The Defence of France*.[56]

On 12 February 1938 the *TLS* reviewed *The League at Lunch*, a book containing drawings 'originally made for the menus of the luncheons given by the International Press in Geneva'. These light-hearted, 'witty cartoons' depicting the 'busy activity' of the statesmen engaged in maintaining the fragile peace may also be said to be profound and disturbing metaphors: the politicians are shown 'swarming like Lilliputians about a colossal God of War, or adrift on a raft in perilous waters'.[57] Such representations visually depict what was continually articulated in the pages of the *TLS* and the *Bookman*. For every spirited defence of the League proclaimed in the reviews there was an equally pessimistic critique.

Moreover, books analysing the terms of the Versailles Treaty, the role of the League of Nations or the way forward in the prevention of future war are, in comparison to the vast numbers of other non-fiction and fiction titles, surprisingly few. Could it be that the peace was less popular, less intriguing than the war? The aftermath of the Armistice and the First World War were interpreted far more effectively in memoirs and fiction, and were therefore played out in literary rather than socio-political terms. And the idea of 'aftermath' was a potent one. Lieut.-Col. F. E. Whitton, the reviewer of the final volume of Winston Churchill's *The World Crisis*, argued in the *Bookman* in April 1929 that the meaning of the word had been skewed by the First World War:

> The essence of the real aftermath is that it is a gainful process, peacefully carried out – the second mowing of a perennial meadow, but nothing of that kind is intended when the word is used to connote the mucking out of the Augean stables after the War. We would much prefer the expression 'mopping up,' a real product of the War and a phrase the meaning of which might legitimately be extended to post-war problems [...] the price in blood had been paid. It remained to gather the results, to redraw the map of Europe, to pay the bill for the past, and to take what measures were possible to safeguard the future. This is 'consolation' with 'mopping up' included [...].[58]

The reviews featured in the *Bookman* and the *Times Literary Supplement* show that the silence of November 1918 brought much 'mopping up' but little consolation. As barometers of public interest and literary taste, more varied and more complex than hitherto has been acknowledged, both periodicals demonstrate that life in the inter-war period was, to some extent at least, 'lived and thought of in terms of world war, and even when the guns were silent and the bombs were not exploding', as Hobsbawn argues.[59] War was never far from public consciousness throughout the fragile decades of peace.

Notes

1 See Eric Hobsbawm, *Age of Extremes: The Short Twentieth Century, 1914–1991* (London: Michael Joseph, 1994).

2 In 1935 the *Bookman* merged with the *London Mercury*. The Editorial Notes for January 1935 'introduced' readers of the periodicals to each other, noting how 'the magazines have travelled far on their separate courses [...]. Now they have come to a broad space there their waters must mingle, in a region, let us hope, where Romanticism and Classicism may be reconciled.' Although

the brothers Hugh and Reginald Ross-Williamson 'brought [the *Bookman*] up-to-date with the literary thinking of the thirties', they were unable to compete 'in a world which could get advice about new books from so many new sources'. John Attenborough, *A Living Memory, Hodder & Stoughton Publishers, 1868–1975* (London: Hodder & Stoughton, 1978), 115. The *London Mercury* itself did not survive much longer, ceasing publication in April 1939.

3 The son of Matthew Henry Hodder's only daughter Frances and her husband John T. Williams, Ernest Hodder Williams adopted the surname Hodder-Williams in 1919 by deed poll. Throughout the war, however, his surname was Williams and he is therefore referred to as such in this chapter. Dorothy Windus Collin, 'Hodder, Matthew Henry (1830?–1911)', *ODNB*.

4 Attenborough, *A Living Memory*, 78.

5 Attenborough, *A Living Memory*, 78. See also Peter Buitenhuis, *Great War of Words: Literature as Propaganda 1914–18 and After* (London: Batsford, 1989) and Jane Potter, 'For Country, Conscience and Commerce: Publishers and Publishing 1914–1918', in Mary Hammond and Shafquat Towheed, eds, *Publishing and the First World War: Essays in Book History* (Basingstoke: Palgrave, 2007).

6 *The Bookman*, special Christmas number 1914.

7 It was only from January 1975 that contributions were attributed. Authors from the anonymous years can be traced by the digital index *The TLS Centenary Archive 1902–1990*.

8 Janet Watson, *Fighting Different Wars: Experience, Memory and the First World War in Britain* (Cambridge: Cambridge University Press, 2004), 187.

9 Derwent May, *Critical Times: The History of the Times Literary Supplement* (London: HarperCollins, 2001), 99.

10 *Advertising in the TLS: The Times Literary Supplement 1902–1972* (London: Times Newspapers Limited, 1973), 5.

11 May, *Critical Times*, 100, 101.

12 'Clutton-Brock had not been without his critics. In Cambridge and Bloomsbury, they were inclined to laugh at him.' May, *Critical Times*, 121. Among Clutton-Brock's critics were Goldsworthy Lowes Dickinson and E. M. Forster.

13 *TLS* (14 November 1918), 545.

14 Watson, *Fighting Different Wars*, 214.

15 Numerous studies of the literature of the First World War highlight both the well-known and lesser-known writings of the inter-war period. For example: Bernard Bergonzi, *Heroes' Twilight: A Study of the Literature of the Great War*, 3rd edn (Manchester: Carcanet, 1996); Samuel Hynes, *A War Imagined: The First World War and English Culture* (London: Bodley Head, 1990); Sharon Ouditt, *Fighting Forces, Writing Women: Identity and Ideology in the First World War* (London: Routledge, 1994); Trudi Tate, *Modernism,*

History and the First World War (Manchester: Manchester University Press, 1998).

16 *The Bookman* (April 1915), 11.

17 *The Bookman* (July 1919), 126.

18 Buchan's 24-volume *Nelson's History of the War* was published regularly from February 1915 to July 1915, and in addition to writing a series of books on the battles of Jutland and the Somme, he was also a correspondent for *The Times* and the *Daily News*. From 1916, when he became second lieutenant in the intelligence corps, Buchan drafted communiqués for the War and Foreign Offices and worked at the propaganda bureau at Wellington House under C. F. G. Masterman. In 1917 he was appointed director of the new Department of Information.

19 *The Bookman* (December 1918), 95.

20 *The Bookman* (November 1918), 64. *Beatrice Ashleigh* by F. E. Mills Young (Miss), 6s (H&S): 'the ghastly commonplace of the present world-conflict' – uses the war to 'dispose of [...] inconvenient characters'. *Perpetual Fires* by Eric Leadbitter, 6s (A&U): 'tumbles headlong into the same pitfall': 'the promise of a finer interpretation of the soul of an artist than I have read, even in French literature' is 'wrecked, and the whole plan defeated by the unutterably silly and unnecessary death of young Oliver Longways at the Front'. *Glenmornan* by Patrick MacGill, 6s (Herbert Jenkins): 'hardly to be described as a novel at all. It is rather a series of closely-studied impressions of a small, remote district of Ireland [...] always readable – until he blunders up against the usual tiresome anti-climax of the war.' *The Mirror and the Lamp* by W. B. Maxwell, 7s (Cassell): 'proves him to be perhaps our greatest living novelist'; 'the fineness and delicacy of this study'.

21 *TLS* (14 November 1918), 554.

22 *TLS* (26 December 1918), 649

23 *TLS* (19 September 1918), 435.

24 *The Bookman* (November 1918), 61.

25 *TLS* (12 December 1918), 631.

26 *TLS* (30 January 1919), 50.

27 *The Bookman* (January 1919), 132.

28 *The Bookman* (June 1919), 104.

29 *The Bookman* (September 1920), 187.

30 *The Bookman* (August 1929), 276.

31 *The Bookman* (December 1923), 181.

32 May, *Critical Times*, 180.

33 *TLS* (20 February 1919), 90.

34 *The Bookman* (May 1920), 93.

35 *TLS* (29 April 1920), 261.

36 *TLS* (3 June 1920), 342.

37 *The Bookman* (December 1920), 27.

38 *The Bookman* (Christmas 1922 Supplement), 100.
39 *TLS* (1 March 1923), 144.
40 May, *Critical Times*, 185. Harold M. Stannard was a regular contributor on the 'foreign political scene' especially interested in books on Russia, Italy and Germany, and his reviews of books specifically to do with the League are forthright and opinionated: 'He became the paper's leading voice in these years (20s and 30s) on both Communism and Fascism, and had a rather similar attitude to both.' Like many people not just in Britain, but across the world, he opted to give the rising dictators 'the benefit of the doubt': 'In many people's feelings, the First World War seemed only just to have ended, and the prospect of order rather than chaos on the continent of Europe had an undoubted attraction. Friendship towards the new regimes seemed like wisdom, and also to offer the best hope of curbing any unfortunate tendency in them to a new nationalism and a new militarism.' May, *Critical Times*, 183.
41 *TLS* (8 September 1927), 597.
42 *TLS* (25 January 1934), 51.
43 *The Bookman* (December 1928), 172.
44 *The Bookman* (December 1928), 597.
45 *TLS* (27 September 1928), 682.
46 *TLS* (17 November 1928), 967.
47 *TLS* (29 November 1928), 918.
48 *The Bookman* (February 1930), 299.
49 A. St. John Adcock, review of *Goodbye to All That*, *The Bookman* (January 1930), 238.
50 H. E. Bates, preface to R. H. Mottram, *Ten Years Ago: Armistice and Other Memories, Forming a Pendant to 'The Spanish Farm Trilogy'* (London:, Chatto and Windus, 1928), viii.
51 *The Bookman* (December 1928), 174.
52 *TLS* (4 October 1928), 694.
53 *The Bookman* (August 1933), 225.
54 *The Bookman* (August 1933), 226.
55 May, *Critical Times*, 227.
56 *Advertising in the TLS*, 13.
57 *TLS* (12 February 1938), 109.
58 *The Bookman* (April 1929), 8.
59 Hobsbawm, *Age of Extremes*, 12.

8

'Misunderstood … mainly because of my Jewishness': Arthur Schnitzler after the First World War

Max Haberich

In the first third of the twentieth century, Arthur Schnitzler was one of the most prominent literary figures in Europe. He was one of the first writers to make use of Freud's ideas, exploring his characters' psyches to understand their rational or irrational motives. He introduced the 'stream of consciousness' technique into German literature twenty years before *Ulysses*. His work was translated into English, French, Italian, Swedish, Russian and Japanese. MGM Studios used a novella of his for one of their early movies, *Daybreak* (1931).

Schnitzler spent his entire life in Vienna, from 1862 until 1931. He read medicine at the University of Vienna, and obtained his doctorate when he was twenty-three. He was one of the founding members of Young Vienna, a literary circle which included Hugo von Hofmannsthal, Felix Salten and Hermann Bahr. Schnitzler celebrated his first major success on the stage with *Liebelei* (*Flirtation*, 1895), and he was immediately recognised as being at the forefront of the Austrian literary avant-garde. He corresponded with many great German writers of the time: Thomas and Heinrich Mann, Hermann Hesse and Stefan Zweig.

He reached his prime at the Viennese Burgtheater with dramas such as *Das weite Land* (*The Open Land*, 1911) and *Professor Bernhardi* (1912). Throughout his literary career, he also produced a substantial number of short stories. Of these works, the two stream-of-consciousness novellas, *Leutnant Gustl* (1900), from the male perspective, and *Fräulein Else* (1924), from the female, are perhaps the most noteworthy. Schnitzler wrote two novels, the first of which, *Der Weg ins Freie* (*The Way into the Open*, 1908), is a social panorama of the assimilated Jewish middle and upper classes of Vienna. It is useful to any student of the period, as it provides a vivid reflection of the intellectual currents prevalent at the time, such as Zionism and socialism, against the background of rising anti-Semitism.

Although Schnitzler and Freud lived in the same city for years, they only began meeting regularly after Schnitzler's sixtieth birthday in 1922. In his congratulatory letter, Freud confesses to having avoided Schnitzler 'aus einer Art von Doppelgängerscheu' – out of anxiety of meeting his intellectual mirror-image. He also concedes that Schnitzler is a 'researcher into the deepest realms of psychology, as honestly objective and courageous as one can be'.[1] When Schnitzler and Freud finally did meet, they got along very well. Not only did they have their interest in psychology in common, but they also found themselves in a similar dilemma as independent-minded, assimilated Jews of the middle class.

His particular cultural background predisposed Schnitzler to be deeply sceptical of all things political. His pronounced aversion to nationalism meant that he was one of the very few European intellectuals to have opposed the First World War from the outset. While his friends Hermann Bahr and Hugo von Hofmannsthal allowed their literary talent to be conscripted into the service of the fatherland, Schnitzler refused to do so. At a time when other writers were profiting financially from the war, his resolute silence led to a substantial drop in his earnings, which his bank manager noted with some concern.[2] Fortunately for Schnitzler, his son Heinrich, born in 1902, was too young to serve in the army.

During the war, Schnitzler concentrated on plays and prose set in the era before 1914, such as the novella *Doktor Gräsler, Badearzt* (1917). Towards the end of the war he even turned to the eighteenth century, writing *Casanovas Heimfahrt* (*Casanova's Homeward Journey*, 1918) in prose, and *Die Schwestern oder Casanova in Spa* (*The Sisters*, 1920) for the stage. On a more personal level, during the first months of 1920 Schnitzler was reviewing his diaries from 1911, contrasting the period of his literary prime very favourably with the instability and perils of the present.[3] At the same time, he preferred reading Fontane to more contemporary authors.[4]

The war is, in fact, almost entirely absent from Schnitzler's literary work. The only real reference to it is to be found in the play *Komödie der Verführung* (*Comedy of Seduction*, 1924), in which Schnitzler refrains from the typical notation of 'Vienna, present'. Instead, he specifies that the three acts take place respectively on 1 May, mid-June and 1 August 1914. But apart from the occasional allusion to the deteriorating political situation, the war hardly features. There is a chance that the year was chosen to underline a certain decadence in the aristocratic setting for the three relationships on which the play centres. The inescapable descent into war is mirrored by the tragic heroine's fate. In act III, before her death, the declaration of war is pinned to the hotel notice board. But this is the only direct mention, and the outbreak of war does not impinge upon the plot. In the light of this, it would appear that Schnitzler's reviewers had a valid point in considering him 'the poet of a sunken world'. Furthermore, Schnitzler was very much repelled by Expressionism, protesting to his friends against the 'atmosphere of hate' in contemporary literature. Yet Schnitzler objected greatly to being classified as the writer of a bygone era. He wrote two pieces, *Fräulein Else* (1924) and *Traumnovelle* (*Dream Novella*, 1925), which are decidedly modern (or indeed modernist). Since Schnitzler knew this very well, why did he not emphasise his modernity publicly? As he was one of the most prominent authors in the German-speaking world, any major newspaper would have been only too eager to publish such a statement. One reason is that Schnitzler considered it safer to stand above the times rather than to go with them.[5] Another is his Jewish background, and his position in the highly diverse Jewish community of Vienna.

As Steven Beller argues, there was 'no particularly Jewish character to the culture the Jews in Vienna produced', and yet they were always treated as a group apart, a not fully assimilated ethnicity.[6] Sander L. Gilman points out that every stereotype has a positive and a negative element, which is especially true for anti-Semitic portrayals of the Jew.[7] As we will see later on, Jews were not only represented as exploitative capitalists but also, with respect to figures such as Marx and Viktor Adler, the founder of Austrian Social Democracy, as socialist revolutionaries.

Bryan Cheyette and Nadia Valman argue that anti-Semitism was a component of modernity just as much as nation-building. Within a people striving to unify, the Jews were perceived as a foreign element, and thus as an obstacle to ultimate unification. Jews supposedly had supranational ties and were suspected of disloyalty to the emerging nation.[8] With the advent of pseudo-scientific theories of race in the nineteenth century, the Jews found it increasingly difficult to assimilate into the nation-state. As a result of their 'race', they became the template against which some new nations such as Germany defined themselves, and thus permanent outsiders.[9] In Vienna, the Jewish community was in reality exceedingly heterogeneous, what Beller terms a 'community of individuals'[10] – staunch individualists such as Freud and Schnitzler.

Schnitzler's cultural identity was as particular as his approach to the

'Jewish Question' of the day. By the 1920s he had manoeuvred himself into a position whereby he was as much estranged from Zionists and orthodox Jews as he was from German nationalists and clerics. He remained at a critical distance from the Jewish religion throughout his life. One of the main reasons for his discomfort with the post-war world was the increasing intrusion of mass politics into society. Ever since his rise to fame, Schnitzler had maintained a strictly apolitical stance, and decidedly rejected any form of political commitment. This is crystallised in its clearest form in the play *Professor Bernhardi*.

Schnitzler was, above all, an individualist. His diary entries reflect not only his abhorrence of the ever-mounting clamour of political extremism, but also his fundamental distrust of the more moderate groups of the left and right. This was not only because anti-Semitism was shared by both the Christian Social and the Social Democrat parties. For Schnitzler, the fundamental nature of politics was dissimulation and insincerity. Just as he held that the Jewish dilemma could only be resolved on an individual, not a wider social basis, so it was his take on life to do what he considered right, irrespective of political bias in the press.

'Phrases of justice and peace' – Schnitzler's view of the Armistice 1918

> The Emperor's abdication. Hohenzollern and Habsburg within three days. – The awful, nonsensical terms of the armistice to Germany. The Entente is overstretching their bounds. Supposedly, the workers' and soldiers' councils are fraternising at the front.[11]

Thus runs Schnitzler's diary entry for 11 November 1918. Although Schnitzler had not made any political statements during the war, he was not impartial. In a letter to his publisher, Samuel Fischer, he defends the Austrian cause when Fischer claims that the Habsburg monarchy is not pulling its weight in the war effort. He mentions the 'readiness for sacrifice and the urge to help' among the Austrian population, and the army's military achievements.[12] This feeling arose more out of attachment to his native country, or *Heimat* – which Schnitzler distinguished from the political construct of the fatherland – than out of loyalty to the dynasty, or state. Two days before the proclamation of the republic, he notes laconically:

> About the upheavals. – I see no grounds for rejoicing yet. – Forms of state mean nothing, show me the one or several persons I can stake my hopes upon, – in Germany – or even in our country ... The same people who

> cheered the Emperor ... four years ago, and who shout today: Long live the republic. (10 November 1918)

When the republic is actually declared, Schnitzler remains true to his scepticism of politics. On that day he records shootings, provoked by the 'Red Guard', an effusion of news in the papers and by telephone, and concludes: 'A day, important for world history, is over. Up close, it doesn't seem that grand' (12 November 1918).

Like many Austrians, Schnitzler had little idea of what exactly the end of the war would bring. Much more important to him than the loss of the Habsburg territories was the lack of paper, which formed the main subject of his correspondence with Fischer throughout the later years of the war. His literary colleagues were in the same situation, and complained to Fischer as soon as someone else's book was published and not their own. Schnitzler, however, was one of the bestselling authors of the Fischer Verlag (along with Thomas Mann). In fact, his publisher valued Schnitzler so greatly that he founded a Viennese branch of his company late in 1918, which mainly published Schnitzler's works.[13] Thanks to this, and to his earnings in foreign currencies, Schnitzler doesn't appear to have suffered hunger. A more grave concern to him was the increasingly violent current of anti-Semitism.

In autumn 1918 alone Schnitzler records three pogroms: one in Lemberg, one in the German town of Posen and a terrifying one in Galicia.[14] On 13 October he heard from a friend, Leo Van-Jung, that houses were being marked for a pogrom in Vienna. A week later Schnitzler noted that he had 'the very worst expectations', and in early November that 'as a Jew, one must be ready for every eventuality'.[15] During these days the Schnitzler family packed several suitcases, so they would be ready to flee in case of a pogrom. Already in August, he had ordered a border pass.

Why had the situation deteriorated so greatly? There was a lack of everything in Vienna, as the British blockade remained in place into 1919.[16] Most pressing was the shortage of food, which the population was still suffering from in late 1919. Schnitzler records a visit to his brother-in-law's clinic, where the tracheotomy patients, unable to speak, were pleading for food with gestures – and all they received was a basic cheese from sheep's milk (28 November 1919). Christian Socialists and pan-German activists blamed the situation on supposed Jewish war profiteers. Likewise, Jews were blamed for the inflation of the immediate post-war years.[17] George Berkley points out that this was, in part, a result of the break-up of the Habsburg Empire. While the German Austrians were used to blaming their problems on the Jews, Czechs and Hungarians, now the Jews were the only scapegoats left. As such, they came to bear the full brunt of the frustration and desperation of the lost war.[18]

And yet, in 1914, the Jews of Vienna had hoped the war would bring an end to anti-Semitism. Here, at last, was an opportunity to prove that they could fight for their fatherland just as well as their Christian compatriots. The Austrian-Israelite Union was founded in 1886, the equivalent of the *Centralverein* in Germany. It represented the Jewish community of Vienna, advocating assimilation and loyalty to the state, while at the same time trying to sustain a unique Jewish identity, also in religious terms. In the early years of the war the Union issued a statement:

> With the blood of our children [...] we will prove to this state that we are its loyal citizens, as good as any other. [...] After this war, with all its terrors, there must be no more anti-Semitic harassment in Austria. [...] We will fight for our full, unlimited equality, for the unconditional acknowledgement of our rights as citizens.[19]

These aspirations were not fulfilled. Throughout the war, both in Germany and Austria, there was an unofficial understanding between the political parties known as the *Burgfriede*, evoking the image of peace within a beleaguered fortress. In the first months of the war this meant a provisional reduction in anti-Semitic abuse in the press. But in December 1914 Schnitzler had to defend himself against accusations in Russian propaganda that he had issued derogatory statements not only against Tolstoy, but also against Maeterlinck, Anatole France and Shakespeare. Schnitzler's public denial of this was taken by the anti-Semitic press as solidarity with the enemy, and interpreted as a lack of patriotism. The *Reichspost* lists Schnitzler together with the Zionist Max Nordau as an 'internal enemy' and as 'wolves in sheep's clothing'. The *Deutsche Tageszeitung* states that 'Schnitzler & Co.' are German only in the 'geographic-political sense'. The brief period of calm for the Jews of Vienna was over. By January 1915 Schnitzler is noting in his diary that the anti-Semitic allegations had returned in full force, and he remarks on the hollowness of the term *Burgfriede*.[20]

In the context of intensified post-war anti-Semitism, the refugees from Galicia constituted a major problem. Already before the war, the orthodox, Yiddish-speaking Jews from the east made for a visibly foreign presence in Vienna. They were considered less civilised than the assimilated western Jews, including Schnitzler, who distanced themselves from them. To cite his friend and literary colleague Jakob Wassermann: 'When I saw a Polish or Galician Jew, when I spoke to him … I felt sadness and pity, but there was no sense of brotherhood. He was entirely foreign to me … and when there was no individual sympathy, he even repelled me.'[21]

Since Galicia was the scene of repeated Russian invasions until 1917, Jewish refugees had been steadily streaming into Vienna since 1914. The Russian army occupied Galicia until late 1915, during which time the area was subject to extensive pogroms against Jewish people who were accused of spying for Austria. During this period alone 125,000 refugees fled to Vienna.[22] The increasing hostility against these miserable refugees was aggravated by the lack of food. The circumstances at the time were so serious that charitable collections were run as collections for Galician, not Jewish, refugees, although the terms were, in this case, synonymous. In a letter to the journalist Adolf Gelber, Schnitzler mentions that, according to the committee, the event must not be run as a collection for Jewish children 'out of consideration for the feeling and opinion in certain influential and official circles, which could endanger the success of the entire scheme'.[23]

Even after the war, Galicia remained the scene of bloody conflict, as Poland and Russia both claimed the border region. This meant that the refugees could not return. By 1923 the Jewish population of Vienna had reached a record high of 200,000, or 10 per cent of the population.[24] This increase was noticeable in the city, and fuelled the anxiety about a 'Jewish flood'. Anti-Semitic groups aggravated the situation by claiming there were between 500,000 and 600,000 Jewish refugees in Vienna, and by blaming them for the city's serious housing problem. Demagogues such as Walter Riehl, the founder of the Austrian Nazi Party, openly called for the expulsion of eastern Jews. The fact that anti-Semitic rallies managed to attract thousands of spectators led the *Ostdeutsche Rundschau* to comment that the citizens of Vienna were much more anti-Semitic now than they had been in the 1890s.[25]

It did not help the situation that the Social Democrats, considered by many to be a Jewish party, signed the Treaty of St Germain. Otto Bauer, a prominent Jewish party member and foreign minister in 1919, was one delegate to the conference in Versailles. He did, however, refuse to sign the treaty, since the Allies denied the option of Austria unifying with Germany. Thus, the humiliating document which sealed Austria's defeat was signed by the Chancellor, Karl Renner, who was a gentile.[26] In popular opinion, however, this counted for little. Too great was the humiliation and hardship of the lost war for fine distinctions such as this.

On 3 June 1919 Schnitzler records in his diary:

> The Entente's conditions of peace for us. – Words cannot express it. – Not what is happening here is the outrageous thing, in my opinion – a triumph is there to be exploited. But these phrases of justice and peace we keep hearing ... – they're new. Cruelty, power madness, crime and idiocy – these things repeat themselves in all 'great periods in history' ... but the Lie ... without purpose, jest, meaning or greatness, – we are experiencing for the first time.

Schnitzler is referring to the fact that Austria, as a defeated power, was exempted from US President Wilson's concept of national self-determination. Predominantly German-speaking lands in the east were given to Czechoslovakia and Yugoslavia, while South Tyrol, with 250,000 Austrians, was ceded to Italy.[27] Schnitzler was disgusted with what he considered the blatant injustice practised by the victorious powers in the name of peace, humanity and national self-determination.[28] Schnitzler felt that there was deception behind Wilson's ostentatious honesty (diary, 6 October 1918). He mentions his mendacity (12 February 1918) and his deceit (21 October 1918), suspicious of Wilson's pose as the liberator of suppressed ethnic groups and the broker of peace in Europe. Clemenceau's public statement that Austria deserved the miseries it was experiencing prompted the following response: 'The full shameless mendacity of the politician pur sang; the tremendous unscrupulousness of this breed shows itself in these official notes' (18 November 1919).

Many Austrians believed their mutilated rump state could not survive on its own economically. A month before the proclamation of the republic, Schnitzler takes note of the 'dismal situation of the world, especially Austria ... The federal state that no one wants' (18 October 1918). Less than a month later, on 12 November, the provisional national assembly voted for unification with Germany, with 164 out of 165 votes. The allies, however, expressly prohibited this act of union.[29]

Being attached to his Austrian *Heimat*, and strongly averse to pan-German nationalism, Schnitzler himself was not enthusiastic about the unification plans. On 6 January he writes of the 'folly of a union with Germany at this moment in time'. But only five days later, when pressed by an admirer for his view on the possible *Anschluß*, Schnitzler asks what Austria, 'that cannot support itself economically, should do, since ... the Czechs are irreconcilable in their hatred?' Then he mentions the possible 'Helvetisation' of Austria. If that should happen, he remarks, not without humour, Austria may well become a land of artists and waiters (11 January 1919). In spite of his serious concern with the threat of Bolshevism, not once did Schnitzler mention unification with Germany as a solution to this. As he knew well, Germany had its own problems in this respect, with Berlin becoming the stage for putsch attempts by the extreme left as well as the extreme right throughout the immediate post-war years.

More than once, Schnitzler registered a general rejection of the *Anschluß* idea: 'The Anschluß-question. Actually, the prevalent feeling is against it everywhere – even among those who advocate it for political reasons' (12 March 1919).[30] Finally he writes, with reference to the developments in Germany: 'Nationalism –?– Bolshevism? German Austria drawn into that –? End of the world –?' (20 May 1919). Although Schnitzler may have been indecisive in January, by May he seems to have felt that Austria was wiser to solve its problems on its own.

Jewish social democracy and fear of Bolshevism: The political left in Austria 1918–19

From the end of the war until well into 1921 Schnitzler was seriously concerned by the revolutionary threat of Bolshevism. Upon reading Bukharin's work on Bolshevism, the bible of the movement, he records: 'Beyond all discussion. What the idea was (if ever it was one) has been turned, by primitive enmity and lack of logic, into a bloodthirsty phrase' (29 March 1919). Hearing from acquaintances about the situation in Russia, he notes: 'Murder, misery, theft, hunger, – looting; – the leaders elegant, living well, each with a car ... hundreds of thousands killed, starved, the middle class almost eliminated.– ' (9 February 1919). In January and February 1919 he registers the possibility of a leftist putsch. There is the impending threat of a Bolshevist revolution in Vienna, which Schnitzler's friend and fellow writer Gustav Schwarzkopf considers 'inevitable' (13 February 1919). In March Schnitzler jots down: 'The terrible conditions, here and in the world in general. Bolshevism almost inescapable. Once again, we're getting ready for unrest, lootings, etc.' (1 March 1919). Already several months before there had been threats of looting in the wealthy district of Cottage. Schnitzler's friend Felix Salten was so intimidated that he moved to the inner city (7 November 1918).

Schnitzler also followed the revolution in neighbouring Hungary, and the subsequent violence unleashed by the socialist leader, Bela Kun, with concern.[31] With these developments just across the border, it seemed only a matter of time before the revolution spread to Austria. Schnitzler was anxious not only because he, with his solidly upper middle-class background, would be a primary target under the 'dictatorship of the proletariat'. He was also gravely concerned that in the lawless situation of revolution, what governmental checks there were against pogroms would be entirely removed, and the anti-Semitism simmering in the population would run rampant. This is what had happened in Poland and Russia in autumn 1918. Given the increasingly hostile atmosphere in Austria, why should things be different there?

In the end Vienna was spared revolution. The governing Social Democrat Party (SDAP) occupied a middle ground between socialism and anti-Semitism. Before long it was equated with Jewish financial interests. In order to pay for their ambitious social schemes, which included extensive housing projects, schools, sports facilities and so on, the Social Democrats levied considerable taxes on the middle and upper classes. This affected communication services, leisure activities and especially rents and property values. Since these and other new taxes were unavoidable in everyday life, and there was no longer the option for businesses to move to another major city of the monarchy, many Austrians, especially those owning property, were strongly critical of the governmental measures. Hugo Breitner, Vienna's finance director and the author of the new taxes, was Jewish, which only enhanced popular prejudice.[32] No wonder, then, that in the provinces, Schnitzler feared that 'the Viennese' were being identified with 'the Jews', because they voted for a socialist government (14 December 1919).

The SDAP was the only party in Austria that was not openly anti-Semitic, and the only real option for Jewish voters, even if the party's atheism was off-putting to orthodox Jews.[33] This is why Schnitzler, not a Social Democrat by any means, voted for the party in February 1919. His diary entry runs:

> We gave our vote to the Social Democratic candidate – as repellent as the workers' paper and the whole party is … But the main thing is to move as far away from the right as possible – moreover: to provide the Social Democrat Party with a sizeable majority, as unrest will be very likely otherwise. (16 February 1919)

In the Austrian election, the SDAP secured a landslide victory, and the excesses of violence, feared by many, were averted. But Schnitzler was not satisfied with the way the new government met its challenges. In early November he records that, by winter, the government would have collapsed into total anarchy. Two days later he mentions 'our miserable government ... the infamies of the workers' councils' (11 November 1919). The administration had considerable difficulty in dealing with the extremist agitation both from left and right, which is why Schnitzler felt 'entirely defenceless in the case of an uprising' (8 April 1919).

Another reason for Schnitzler's mistrust of the government was the Social Democrats' latent anti-Semitism, in spite of its being considered 'the party of the Jews'. A revealing incident was the strike at the Anker bread factory. In February 1920 one worker there refused to join the SDAP. The others called for his dismissal, and when their boss, Fritz Mendel, refused, they went on strike. The factory supplied 700,000 Viennese with bread, and given that the town was on the verge of hunger, the issue was particularly pressing.[34] The Social Democrat paper *Arbeiter-Zeitung* called for 'more anti-Semitism, sirs!', stressed the Jewish background of the factory owner, and repeatedly emphasised the link between Jews and the exploitations of capitalism.[35] Schnitzler was repelled by the party with their position of 'looking to anti-Semitism on the one, and to Bolshevism on the other side' (16 February 1919).

When Schnitzler met Hofmannsthal in January 1918, they had difficulty making conversation, which reflected a degree of estrangement between the two friends. Both were united, however, in 'nasty comments on some of the latest Expressionist fabrications' (11 January 1918). Similarly, when he met Thomas Mann, both writers shared in their rejection of the 'inner malevolence of the "Expressionists"' (9 January 1922). This may appear surprising at first, for did Schnitzler not belong to the literary avant-garde of his own youth in the 1890s? Was he himself not a critical author? Schnitzler not only criticised the rigid social conventions of his age, which made women from all walks of society firmly dependent on men, however irresponsible those men might be, but his work also caused numerous scandals for breaking social taboos: the double standards of society in *Das Märchen* (*The Fairy Tale*, 1893), duelling in *Freiwild* (*Fair Game*, 1897), the notion of military honour in *Leutnant Gustl* (1900), anti-Semitism in *Professor Bernhardi* (1912) and sexual mores in *Reigen* (*Round Dance*, 1920).

All this is true, but Schnitzler felt strongly that the overriding sentiment of the immediate post-war years was hate. Through Expressionism, this was translated into literature. After a conversation with Franz Werfel, he comments: 'Expressionism.– The element of hate in the latest art.– ' (11 April 1918). Werfel was one example of a political author.

After the war he was very interested in communism, while in later years he became more conservative and entertained Catholic sympathies. Schnitzler termed him a 'confused Communist' (9 February 1919). He commented on a conversation with him: 'Stroll with Werfel, who tried to explain Communism to me in his somewhat bewildering manner, without really being convinced himself' (22 December 1918).

For Schnitzler, Bolshevism and Expressionism shared an enthusiasm for revolutionary upheaval. In his eyes, Blei and Hasenclever were simply literary proponents of a political movement. Hence his almost interchangeable use of the term 'Bolshevists' for members of both movements. It speaks for Schnitzler's critical mind, however, that he was able to distinguish between the person and the artist, as in Werfel's case.

'Poet from a sunken world'

Schnitzler never refuted Expressionism in public, only privately, in his diaries and in conversation with his friends. Otherwise he would have reinforced yet another stereotype: the chronicler of a bygone era. In December 1924 Schnitzler wrote to Georg Brandes:

> Critics have found a new formula for me: That I describe a 'sunken world', which not a soul is interested in anymore. (One may only write plays of 1924 – did you know that?) Also, death and love are no longer suitable subjects – only border regulations, currency fluctuations, tax questions, theft, and hunger risings are of interest to the serious (especially the serious German) man.[36]

Given what we have seen of his strong opposition to Expressionist art, Schnitzler's contemporary critics seem to have a point. Towards the end of the war, he even turned to the life and times of Casanova. Another drama from this time, *Der Gang zum Weiher* (1931), is set in a pre-modern era and, like *Casanova in Spa*, written entirely in verse.

The fact is that, for all his scepticism of contemporary political developments, Schnitzler was more attached to the new era than his critics would have us believe. In spite of a strong aversion to Expressionism, Schnitzler defended himself against the allegation of being an out-dated author. He embraced the latest technological developments. He was greatly enthused by his first flight from Venice to Vienna. He was an avid cinema-goer, and was very interested in the artistic potential of film. In fact, throughout the 1920s he relied more and more heavily on his income from film rights, as his literary income dwindled.[37] *The Affairs of Anatol* was produced at Paramount by Cecil B. DeMille as early as 1921. *Der junge Medardus* was turned into a film in 1922. After a Danish production in 1914, *Liebelei* was filmed in 1927, *Freiwild* in 1928 and *Fräulein Else* in 1929. MGM Studios created *Daybreak* with Gloria Swanson in 1931.[38]

In spite of a certain scepticism about the art and politics of the new times, from today's perspective Schnitzler definitely belongs to the 'klassische Moderne'. The two most important arguments for this case, apart from his work on film scripts, are two prose works, *Fräulein Else* (1924) and *Traumnovelle* (1925). *Fräulein Else* is not only modern in theme and content, but also in form. Schnitzler describes a young woman of the new society, confident and sexually aware. Else's parents ask her to approach a wealthy acquaintance for a loan, who agrees on condition that he may see Else naked. This alone bears witness to the financial instability of the post-war period. Schnitzler traces every one of her thoughts and associations, using the modern technique of the interior monologue. In the end, Else sees no way out of her predicament but in an overdose of veronal. Although her family's financial quandary is not new in itself, Else as a female persona certainly is. The manner in which she reflects upon herself and her effect upon others is not that of a nineteenth-century woman. She dreams about lying unclothed on marble steps by the sea. Before getting dressed, she speaks admiringly to her image in the mirror about her own body. Such a relationship with one's own physique was not culturally acceptable, especially not for a woman, in the pre-war era. The narrative form of the novella, related to the 'stream of consciousness' taken up in English by Joyce, Woolf, Dorothy Richardson and others, is also thoroughly modern. *Fräulein Else* proved Schnitzler's mastery of the interior monologue yet again. In comparison with *Leutnant Gustl*, which is firmly rooted in late Habsburg society, the modernity of *Fräulein Else*, as a work of the post-war period, is evident.

The plot of *Traumnovelle*, published in the following year, is not as clearly tied to 1920s society, and could just as well be set in Habsburg Vienna. The total lack of reliability in the narrative voice, however, is a clear mark of literary modernism. Schnitzler plays with the credibility of the narrator's perspective, leaving the reader puzzled as to what is reality, what is a dream and what merely the imaginary product of the doctor's overwrought nerves. This lack of authority in the narrative voice reflects the disorientation of post-war society, its political and economic instability, and its social confusion. And yet the majority of contemporary critics were not prepared to recognise his modernity. Perhaps the most significant reason for this was his position as an Austrian-Jewish writer in a time of ever-increasing anti-Semitic hostility.

Professor Bernhardi is Schnitzler's most effective critique of institutional anti-Semitism. The play opens with a fatally ill patient in a stage of euphoria just before death. Bernhardi, the Jewish director of the clinic, forbids the priest from entering to perform the last rites, since he wants to ensure that his patient's final moments are free of distress. This occurrence, as soon as it becomes public, is blown up into a scandal and is vigorously debated in parliament. Eventually, intrigues among his colleagues lead to Bernhardi's voluntary resignation. Nevertheless, he is imprisoned for 'disturbing the practice of religion'. This is only possible because of anti-Semitic currents not only in Bernhardi's clinic, but also in the responsible governmental ministry and in the courts. Eventually, one of the witnesses confesses to having lied under oath at the trial. Bernhardi has the opportunity resume proceedings to avenge himself. Liberal journalists approach him, offering their help. He declines both options, however, stressing that the whole affair was an entirely personal, not a political matter. He only did what he felt was right, and he did so without compromise.

The play was banned in Austria in 1912, but successfully performed on the major German stages. With the abolition of censorship in the republic, the path was cleared for the Viennese premiere of the play. By November 1918 preparations to perform *Professor Bernhardi* at the Volkstheater under Alfred Bernau were in full swing. Although a police official had warned Schnitzler of potential demonstrations, the first Viennese performance on 21 December was a great success. Even the press reviews were, for the most part, favourable. By the end of May, Schnitzler's play had been shown more than 50 times.[39] It was one of Schnitzler's most lasting successes, and even brought him the renowned Volkstheater prize in 1920.[40] This is a clear indication that audiences in Germany and Austria were very well aware of what Schnitzler was driving at. They could not avoid noticing the increased anti-Semitic tendencies around them, and appreciated his stinging criticism of them. In spite of its pre-war setting, the play's attack on institutional anti-Semitism proved even more disconcertingly relevant during the post-war years, so much so, in fact, that the play formed the centrepiece of the memorial service for Schnitzler in October 1931.[41]

Professor Bernhardi was performed throughout Schnitzler's lifetime mostly without any public disturbance or political manifestation. At a show in Wiener Neustadt in Lower Austria, however, in early October 1919, things were very different. The following 'warning' appeared between 16 and 23 October in the 'Wiener Neustädter Nachrichten':

> If the directors intend to stage the play once more, the leaders of the anti-Semites refuse to take any responsibility ... No police force will be able to prevent the piece from getting the reception it deserves. The Jewish community should settle with the theatre directors whether it would like that or not. No one knows what wider consequences a Jewish theatre scandal can have. Our task is to warn publicly, just as we have warned in the theatre. The Christian population tolerated this crude offence once, – has seen what Jews are capable of – it must not happen a second time ...[42]

This note is openly threatening, not even trying to mask anti-Semitic sentiment with religious feeling, for example. On 23 October Christian Socialists and nationalists organised a protest. Students distributed anti-Semitic leaflets at the door, and hissed during the performance. The police arrested four students.[43] Two days later pupils of several local Gymnasia arranged a strike in protest against the play, which was supported by many of the teachers as well.[44] Evidently, anti-Semitic feeling had been intensified by the hardships of the war and the political instability of the peace. Schnitzler noted in his diary that these were the first scandals ever caused by *Professor Bernhardi*.[45]

'*Who* decides where I belong? I alone': Schnitzler's Jewish identity and post-war anti-Semitism

Why did Schnitzler not stress his modernism publicly, to counter the stereotype of the chronicler of a 'sunken world'? Because this would have placed him more firmly in the category of the modern, decadent, Jewish writer. The pace of everyday life had increased rapidly by the early twentieth century. Coupled with social and cultural tensions, this made for considerable anxiety among inhabitants of modern European cities. At the forefront of economic and industrial development, but also in the artistic and literary avant-garde – so journalists such as Adolf Bartels explained – stood the Jews. Conveniently, Jews could also be taken to represent the thoroughly modern movement of socialism by pointing to prominent representatives from Marx to Viktor Adler.

For Julius Langbehn, the notorious author of *Rembrandt als Erzieher* (1890), the Jew epitomised the restlessness, the cosmopolitanism, the liberalism and the general corruption of modern urban life. Langbehn turned against Naturalism, with its essentially destructive capital, Berlin.

Instead, he advocated a renewal of the German *Volksseele* through art tied to the provinces and the soil, free from the corrupting Jewish influence of urban modernism – *Heimatkunst*.[46] This term was coined by Adolf Bartels, who would subsequently become one of the most prominent philologists of the Third Reich. Taking a similar line as Langbehn, he explains:

> Since the decadents are here already, we cannot simply beat them to death, but we have no reason to treat them too kindly, either. We believe that our people are still healthy, or can become so again very soon; and we simply deny the diseased their right to national existence.[47]

Langbehn's and Bartels' ideas illustrate the fundamental anti-modernism of this branch of the anti-Semitic movement. In the words of Steven Aschheim, the 'Eastern Jews were too primitive, the Western Jews too modern'.[48] In addition to the stereotypes of the capitalist and the socialist Jew, this argument lent the anti-Semites another dual stereotype, that of the barbaric eastern Jew on the one hand, and the assimilated western Jew on the other, who represented all the corrupting influences of the modern age. The uniting factor in these paradoxical stereotypes was, of course, pseudo-scientific racism. Had Schnitzler emphasised his literary modernity – apart from the fact that he did not want to be identified with Expressionism – he would have become an even easier target for anti-Semitic journals than he already was.

It is important to stress Schnitzler's unique cultural identity in this context. The events of the war expanded this beyond the Austrian and Jewish dimensions to include his identification with the wider German-speaking world. Closely connected is Schnitzler's enlightened apolitical individualism, which kept him at a distance not only from political involvement but also from Zionism and religious orthodoxy. Schnitzler's manifest individualism estranged both the traditional Jewish community and journalists of all political denominations. His complex cultural identity, and his notion of doing what one is convinced to be right irrespective of slander in the press, set him above the political currents of the day. To his former wife, he wrote: 'To stand above the times is my line, not "to go with them" (in the pace of the journalists, politicians, and speculators).'[49] Elsewhere, he noted: 'Above all else, I am who I am, which is entirely sufficient for me.'[50]

There is a diary entry recording that Schnitzler rejected an invitation to contribute to the Zionist mouthpiece *Die Welt*.[51] Schnitzler also declined to give a speech on the tenth anniversary of Theodor Herzl's death in April 1914. His reason was 'that in my innermost conviction I never felt so close to Herzl as that, at an occasion such as this, I should be allowed to speak for him in public'.[52] Schnitzler acknowledged Herzl's efforts because he championed a cause with unwavering determination. But he would not let himself be harnessed to a political movement such as Zionism. Furthermore, Schnitzler disliked being considered a Jewish writer. A Jewish author wrote in Hebrew, he held, whereas a German one wrote in German.[53] In a letter to the Jüdischer National Fonds, which asked for support for the Zionist cause, Schnitzler clarifies: 'By no means do I consider myself a Jewish writer, but a German one, who, to the extent that this can be traced, belongs to the Jewish race.'[54]

Schnitzler was resistant to being classified as a Jewish author not only because this automatically reduced his capacity to be a genuinely Austrian writer, in the eyes of the contemporary press. Another reason was that he was opposed to certain orthodox Jewish rituals. During the war Schnitzler was requested to donate to provide Jewish prisoners of war with unleavened bread for Pesach. Instead of a donation, he sent a letter to the committee of the Israelitische Kultusgemeinde explaining that he considered this not only an outdated but also a dangerous idea. He maintains that the rabbis, rather than encouraging religious superstition, should work towards enlightening the Jews. Schnitzler also considers it imperative to change the Sabbath to Sunday. 'Even the most orthodox Jew,' he argues, 'will be persuaded by his rabbi that God, who … also tolerated the establishment of Christianity, is wholly indifferent to whether the Sabbath or Sunday is held holy.'[55] Schnitzler could not have stated his scepticism and disapproval of Jewish religious customs more openly.

Schnitzler was very much attached to Vienna, which he never left, except to travel, throughout his life. As noted earlier, Schnitzler was equally fond of German-speaking Austria, which he considered his native soil. Not the state but the country is the object of Schnitzler's affection. In a short, personal manifesto from 1904, he states: 'I do not love my fatherland because it is my fatherland, but because I think it is beautiful. I have *Heimatgefühl*, but no patriotism.'[56] *Heimatgefühl* is best translated as attachment to one's native region. He distinguishes between attachment to his *Heimat* and political allegiance.

If in more specific terms he identified with Austria, Schnitzler's wider sense of cultural identity was with the German-speaking world. He expresses this tripartite cultural allegiance in a letter to his sister-in-law, Lisl Steinrück, in the first months of the First World War:

> We Austrians are being treated like we Jews are. In relation to the rest of Europe, one could say: We Germans are being treated the same as we Austrians and Jews. *We* are being misunderstood. Strange that in these years, we have to feel ourselves as all these things at once. I am a Jew, Austrian, and German. I suppose it has to be that way. For I am offended in the name of Jews, Austrians, and Germans, when I hear slander against one of the three.[57]

Schnitzler's sense of German, Austrian and Jewish identity was fairly consistent. In a diary entry from 1918, he summarises his cultural identity in the phrase: 'I am an Austrian citizen of German culture, professing to the Jewish race' (1 November 1918). After discussing the blunders of the Jewish national council, constituted in November 1918, the 'spiteful comments from the anti-Semitic rabble', the Polish pogroms and the possibility of such an events in Austria, Schnitzler concludes: '*Who* decides where I belong? I alone' (27 November 1918).

This position brought him enemies on the clerical and nationalist side, as well as among Zionists and the orthodox Jewish community. The main grounds for his contemporaries' unwillingness to grasp the complexity of his cultural adherence lay, so Schnitzler felt, in his Jewish origin. The many other labels he saw himself confronted with were subsumed by that supreme stereotype, that of the Jew.

> Berlin reviews; on the whole a much more decent tone than here. ... But that I have no doubt whatsoever that – alone because of the continuous barking of the anti-Semitic riff-raff – since the invention of the printing press, no writer in the German language has been more frequently insulted than me. (31 December 1917)

This went both ways. In his statement on why he does not consider himself a Jewish author, he mentions that he has to struggle with 'Jewish-Zionist animosity' as much as with the 'absurdities and insolence of German nationalists'. He repeats this in his letter to the rabbis in 1915: 'I do not shy away from the allegation of overt assimilation on behalf of the Jews. Nor have the endeavours of the German nationalists, to deny my inextricable connection to German culture, ever succeeded in making me doubt my innermost character.'[58]

Who, then, was Schnitzler? He was an enlightened apolitical individual. Enlightened, because he rejected religious orthodoxy and those Jews, 'Renegaten', who converted to Catholicism. Schnitzler was profoundly sceptical of politics, and kept a distance from political movements throughout his entire life. And he was an individual because, like his literary alter ego Professor Bernhardi, he did what was in line with his personal convictions, irrespective of what his opponents might say. Schnitzler's approach to the 'Jewish Question' reflected this. In an interview with James Benvenisti for the *American Jewish and Hebrew Messenger* in 1924, he states: 'Each individual must find the solution to the Jewish problem for himself. There is no general solution.'[59] This idea can also be found as a side-note in Schnitzler's first novel, *Der Weg ins Freie*: 'For our time, there is no solution, that is quite clear. No general one, at least. Rather, there are a hundred thousand different solutions.'[60] Between these two formulations of Schnitzler's stance on the Jewish dilemma lies *Professor Bernhardi*. Although the professor never voices his opinion on the 'Jewish Question', it is clear that his individualism is very close to Schnitzler's own. The author had no qualms about identifying with the protagonist of *Professor Bernhardi*. Little wonder, then, that after re-reading the play, he notes: 'Nowhere am I more sympathetic to myself than in Bernhardi' (27 March 1918).

Schnitzler's sense of being misunderstood because of his Jewishness should not be reduced to mere frustration at anti-Semitic agitation. He had manoeuvred himself into an isolated position, where many Jews were estranged by his apolitical stance as well. The 'Renegaten', of course, used the outrage over Schnitzler's scandals to their advantage. Friends with strong Catholic leanings, such as Hermann Bahr and Hugo von Hofmannsthal, also distanced themselves from Schnitzler in later years. His *Heimatgefühl* estranged the Zionists, just as his religious scepticism put off the more orthodox Jews. Thus, Schnitzler's particular sense of Jewishness was a bar in both ways. That is the full implication of the following citation from his diary: 'All artists of a high standard are misunderstood, of course; – the degree – the emphasis – and the indifference of those "understanding" can be explained, to the largest extent, only with my Jewishness' (29 January 1919).

At this point, it is worthwhile to cast a glance at the conclusion of Freud's essay from 1925, 'Widerstände gegen die Psychoanalyse' ('Forms of Opposition to Psychoanalysis'):

> Finally, the author ventures the question, with all due restraint, if not his personality as a Jew, who never wanted to hide his Jewishness, contributed in some way to society's antipathy to psychoanalysis. An argument of this kind has hardly ever been voiced aloud. Unfortunately, we have become so suspicious that we cannot help but suspect that this circumstance was not entirely without effect. Perhaps it is more than just coincidence that the first representative of psychoanalysis was a Jew. To stand up for this new branch

> of knowledge required readiness to accept the lot of isolation and opposition; a fate which a Jew is more familiar with than others.[61]

This casts light on another parallel between Freud and Schnitzler, apart from the famous 'Doppelgänger' letter. Schnitzler felt that his work had been intentionally misrepresented as well, and he as an author deliberately misunderstood – because of his Jewish background. Freud never denied his Jewish origin either. He appears to have felt, likewise, that the wilful misunderstanding of psychoanalysis in its early years, and the vehement hostility he encountered, was due to his Jewish background. The above phrase, 'not entirely without effect', is a considerable understatement.

Why this particular argument was never expressed more openly at the time was due to the clandestine nature of anti-Semitism. *Professor Bernhardi*, but also Hermann Bahr's collection of interviews *Der Antisemitismus* (1893), prove that even rabid anti-Semites flatly denied their anti-Semitism, and instead justified it as anti-socialist or anti-capitalist views. One of the key features of anti-Semitism was that, for various reasons, it was not supposed to exist, and was therefore officially and repeatedly denied even by its most adamant proponents. This was especially true for Austria, where neutrality in questions of ethnicity and confession had been one of the ruling principles of the Habsburg dynasty.

Like Freud, Schnitzler faced serious adversity throughout his life because of his Jewish background. He felt misunderstood in his literary work and in his sense of cultural identity. The majority of reviewers did not, or did not want to, recognise his modernity during the 1920s. The nationalist and clerical anti-Semites objected loudly to his notion of being an Austrian author first and foremost, but one conscious of his Jewish origins. The Zionists and orthodox Jews, on the other hand, were alienated by his life-long scepticism of religious orthodoxy and his strict apolitical stance. His individualism was misread by the vast majority of his contemporaries, even by friends such as Hermann Bahr and Hugo von Hofmannsthal. More often than not, Schnitzler was correct in assuming that this misinterpretation was wilful. Those reviews which labelled *Professor Bernhardi* as out-dated, when it was performed in Austria after the war, testify to this. In a letter to his literary colleague Otto Schinnerer, Schnitzler wrote:

> The papers behaved as you would imagine: Depending on their political orientation, some said that the play is has only now reached its full contem-

> porary relevance. [...] Others declared it was from yesterday and even the day before, that all of those things no longer exist, and neither do the questions attached to them. The most radical papers claim that in this time of persecution of Christians, one should not perform a work glorifying Jews.[62]

Another obvious instance is the *Reigen* scandal, which Schnitzler himself called the 'biggest scandal in the history of the theatre' (20 February 1921). He was fully aware of the political implications of the affair, and that the whole scandal was not so much based on indecency as on anti-Semitism.[63] In this, his own Bernhardi affair, he remained the independently minded individual and playwright.

Notes

1 Cited in Konstanze Fliedl, *Arthur Schnitzler* (Stuttgart: Reclam, 2005), 61.
2 Edward Timms, *Karl Kraus, Apocalyptic Satirist: Culture and Catastrophe in Habsburg Vienna* (New Haven, CT: Yale University Press, 1989), 300.
3 Arthur Schnitzler, *Tagebuch 1920–1922* (Vienna: Verlag der Österreichischen Akademie der Wissenschaften, 1981–2000), 22 May 1920, 30 May 1920. Henceforth *TB*. References to individual diary entries are given by date in parentheses in the main body of the text.
4 Schnitzler, *TB 1920–1922*: *Stine* 21 February, *Poggenpuhls* 20 April, *Effi Briest* 25 April, *Kriegsgefangen* 4 June 1920.
5 Arthur Schnitzler, letter to Olga Schnitzler, 22 July 1928, *Briefe 1913–1931*, ed. Peter Braunwarth et al. (Frankfurt a.M.: Fischer Verlag, 1984), 561.
6 Steven Beller, *Vienna and the Jews 1867–1938. A Cultural History* (Cambridge: Cambridge University Press, 1989), 7.
7 Sander L. Gilman, *Jewish Self-Hatred* (Baltimore, MD: Johns Hopkins University Press, 1986), 4.
8 Bryan Cheyette and Nadia Valman, eds, *The Image of the Jew in European Liberal Culture, 1789–1914* (London: Vallentine Mitchell, 2004), 2–8.
9 Cheyette and Valman, *The Image of the Jew*, 22.
10 Beller, *Vienna and the Jews*, 109.
11 Unless otherwise indicated, all translations in this chapter are the author's.
12 Cited in Fliedl, *Arthur Schnitzler*, 55.
13 Renate Wagner, *Arthur Schnitzler – eine Biographie* (Vienna: Molden, 1981), 302–3.
14 *TB* 1917–1919, 27 November 1918, 18 November 1918, 31 December 1918.
15 *TB* 1917–1919, 13 October 1918, 21 October 1918, 3 November 1918.
16 *TB* 1917–1919, 8 March 1919.
17 Bruce Pauley, *From Prejudice to Persecution* (Chapel Hill, NC: University of North Carolina Press, 1992), 71, 80.
18 George Berkley, *Vienna and Its Jews* (Cambridge, MA: Abt Books, 1988), 149.

19 Cited in Bettina Riedmann, '*Ich bin Jude, Österreicher, Deutscher*': *Judentum in Arthur Schnitzlers Tagebüchern und Briefen* (Tübingen: Niemeyer, 2002), 40.
20 Riedmann, '*Ich bin Jude, Österreicher, Deutscher*', 41–3.
21 Jakob Wassermann, 'Mein Weg als Deutscher und Jude', in Dierk Rodewald, ed., *Jakob Wassermann - Deutscher und Jude* (Heidelberg: Schneider, 1984), 115.
22 Riedmann, '*Ich bin Jude, Österreicher, Deutscher*', 45.
23 22 December 1915, *Briefe 1913–1931*, 111.
24 Berkley, *Vienna and Its Jews*, 150.
25 Pauley, *From Prejudice to Persecution*, 80–1.
26 Pauley, *From Prejudice to Persecution*, 81–2.
27 Berkley, *Vienna and Its Jews*, 142–3.
28 *TB 1917–1919*, 4 November 1918, 3 June 1919, 11 June 1919, 25 June 1919.
29 Berkley, *Vienna and Its Jews*, 142–3.
30 See also *TB 1917–1919*, 24 April 1919.
31 *TB 1917–1919*, 11 June 1919, 14 June 1919.
32 Berkley, *Vienna and its Jews*, 151-2.
33 Berkley, *Vienna and its Jews*, 151–2.
34 Riedmann, '*Ich bin Jude, Österreicher, Deutscher*', 61.
35 Riedmann, '*Ich bin Jude, Österreicher, Deutscher*', 62–3.
36 Schnitzler, Letter to Georg Brandes, 14 December 1924, Folder B17a, Cambridge University Library (CUL).
37 Schnitzler, Letter to Dora Michaelis, 11 December 1920, *Briefe 1913–1931*, 217–18.
38 Renate Wagner, *Wie ein weites Land - Arthur Schnitzler und seine Zeit* (Vienna: Amalthea, 2006), 290–1.
39 Nikolaj Beier, '*Vor allem bin ich* ich…' - *Judentum, Akkulturation und Antisemitismus in Arthur Schnitzlers Leben und Werk* (Göttingen: Wallstein, 2008), 477.
40 Hartmut Scheible, *Schnitzler* (Reinbek bei Hamburg: Rowohlt, 1976), 141.
41 Hans-Peter Bayerdörfer, 'Österreichische Verhältnisse? Arthur Schnitzlers *Professor Bernhardi* auf Berliner Bühnen 1912–1931', in Mark Gelber and Hans O. Horch, eds, *Von Franzos zu Canetti - Jüdische Autoren aus Österreich* (Tübingen: Niemeyer, 1996), 224.
42 Cited in Beier, '*Vor allem bin ich* ich…', 480.
43 Beier, '*Vor allem bin ich* ich…', 480.
44 Riedmann, '*Ich bin Jude, Österreicher, Deutscher*', 298.
45 *TB 1917–19*, 25 October 1919, 15 November 1919.
46 Thomas Kraft, *Jakob Wassermann* (Munich: Deutscher Taschenbuch Verlag, 2008), 54–5.
47 Adolf Bartels, *Heimatkunst* (Leipzig: Müller Verlag, 1904), 18, cited in Kraft, *Jakob Wassermann*, 57.

48 Steven Aschheim, *Brothers and Strangers* (Madison, WI: University of Wisconsin Press, 1982), 76.
49 22 July 1928, *Briefe 1913–1931*, 561.
50 Schnitzler, Aphorismen, Folder A5, CUL.
51 *TB 1893–1902*, 18 December 1902.
52 11 April 1914, *Briefe 1913–1931*, 38.
53 Unabgesandte Briefe, Folder 124B, Nr. 5, CUL.
54 Unabgesandte Briefe, Nr. 3, CUL.
55 'An den Ausschuss zur rituellen Beköstigung der jüdischen Kriegsgefangenen und Zivilgefangenen an den Pessachfeiertagen', March 1915, Folder 60, Nr. 68–72, CUL.
56 Schnitzler, Aphorismen, Folder A5, CUL.
57 22 December 1914, *Briefe 1913–1931*, 68–9.
58 'An den Ausschuss'.
59 Cited in Beier, '*Vor allem bin ich* ich…', 209.
60 Arthur Schnitzler, *Der Weg ins Freie* (Frankfurt a.M.: Fischer Verlag, 1992), 236.
61 Sigmund Freud, *Die Widerstände gegen die Psychoanalyse*, in Anna Freud and Ilse Gumbrich-Simitis, eds, *Sigmund Freud – Werkausgabe in zwei Bänden* (Frankfurt a.M.: Fischer Verlag, 1978), II, 59.
62 Letter to Otto Schinnerer, 6 February 1930, *Briefe 1913–1931*, 661.
63 Letter to Konrad Maril, 7 November 1927, *Briefe 1913–1931*, 506.

9

Leaping over shadows: Ernst Krenek and post-war Vienna

Peter Tregear

Of all the cities in Europe where we might have expected the effects of the First World War to have found particular musical expression, Vienna seems an obvious choice. It is, after all, the self-styled City of Music, the wellspring of a musical tradition that became (and arguably remains) synonymous with the ideal of Western classical music. If that were not enough, by the early twentieth century Vienna had also become a 'testing laboratory for modernity', or as Karl Kraus more pungently put it, an 'experimental station for the end of the world', a place where many artists self-consciously grappled with the perceived contradictions and fissures of modern life, contradictions and fissures that by 1918 seemed to have played themselves out in the most dramatic and tragic of manners in the trenches of the Western Front.[1]

It is therefore remarkable that music scholars have, by and large, failed to engage with the First World War and its effects in Vienna in any sustained fashion over the years. This is a problem which has its origins a century or more earlier, when a 'Viennese School' of Mozart, Haydn, Beethoven and Schubert had codified the standard genres and forms – symphony, string quartet, piano trio, sonata and so on – that were adopted across the west as the quintessence of Western Art Music. Their ubiquity in turn helped secure a dominant historiography wherein canonical status was awarded to particular works to the degree to which they met the perceived intrinsic, purely 'musical' qualities that these forms epitomise – such as an adherence to principles of motivic unity and internal structural coherence. This obsession with the internal workings of a composition has helped saddle us with a post-First World War history of music that is little more than 'myth-making and cosmetics'.[2]

To understand better the history of music in Vienna in this period, however, we need a greater understanding of its context than is usually provided by musicologists.[3]

The First World War was instead to focus and amplify interest in (and a desire to express) the disillusioning and disenchanting aspects of modernity. However, composers who responded directly to this impetus have been marginalised by post-war music historians in defence of a narrowly conceived canon of Viennese modernist 'masterworks' of the post-war period. These works, or more correctly the criticism that surrounds them, eschew direct engagement with their place and time of origin and instead foreground their technical achievements, epitomised by the central place given to the rise of Schoenberg's so-called '12-tone technique' at the expense of what Malcolm Bradbury has described elsewhere as the 'chaos, contingency, and plurality' that characterises so much Weimar period art.[4] While there has been some significant scholarship in recent years that treats the impact of the war upon central European musical history as more than just a chronological marker, arguably we are still far from a properly inclusive rehabilitation of cultural memory of this time.[5] This is no mere historical oversight, since it is an attitude that, according to Peter Franklin, has helped to burden us 'in music more even than in other areas of artistic culture, with remarkably persistent, value-orientated oppositions' such as between 'high and low, serious and popular; between an ascetically noble autonomy and vulgar involvement with the market-place'.[6]

Vienna's war

While they had been some considerable distance from the fighting on either Front, the First World War had been particularly traumatic for the residents of Vienna. By the war's end the Austro-Hungarian Empire, of which it was the capital, had not just been defeated, it had been obliterated, and the political and cultural shock felt in its capital was perhaps greater than in any of the other defeated European states. Over the course of the long life of Emperor Franz Josef I (1830–1916), the population of Vienna itself had increased from around 300,000 to over 2 million. On 12 November 1918, however, German-speaking Austria was proclaimed a republic and Vienna went overnight from being the capital of a colourful and variegated empire of 54 million to being the 'oversized metropolis of an economically misshaped mountain country of 7 million'.[7] The population of the city itself went into decline as many of its residents returned to their ancestral homelands in Czechoslovakia, Hungary and elsewhere. The old economic certainties gone, '[e]veryone, from the state secretaries down to the last chimney sweep, believed firmly in the axiom [...] that Austria in its new shape could not survive'.[8] Vienna retained the physical trappings of the old regime, but with the breakdown of basic services and the shortages of food and fuel that accompanied the war's end, alongside the presence of decommissioned soldiers still in their uniforms for want of alternative clothing, the city itself quickly took on the appearance of a ruin.

More generally, the post-war period emerged as one of troubled relativism. The war had, as one contemporary distinctly put it,

> cancelled causality. It seemed to do so at the least, to the German people ... the people as a whole, regardless of their interest in politics, their state of education, or their profession and walk in life, realized the change quite clearly, long before it could be measured by historians or sociologists.[9]

Arguably, it had been the appearance of stability that had enabled an earlier generation to play the revolutionary to perfection.[10] As Adorno was later to write in *Minima Moralia*, '[o]ne must have tradition in oneself, to hate it properly'.[11] But now the wellspring of that tradition had disappeared almost overnight. Not just political but also cultural crisis followed in its wake.[12]

For the government of the new Austrian republic, the political situation was particularly fractious, with political debate frequently moving on to the streets in violent clashes between left- and right-wing paramilitary forces. If that were not enough to undermine confidence in the future, post-war Austria was soon to face the ravages of hyperinflation, which ended only with the decisive intervention of the League of Nations in 1922. It was not for nothing that Arnold Schoenberg, once certain of his status as a social outsider, now allowed himself to be styled as the leader of a 'Second Viennese School'.[13] For him, the collapse of the Habsburg Empire represented nothing less than 'the overturning of everything one had believed in' and the start of a 'war against all that is low and beastly'.[14] The new 'anything goes' attitude Schoenberg believed he saw in a new generation of composers he blamed directly on the outcome of the war. The new music must instead, he argued, arise out of 'something accepted and respectable, from first understanding the classics, from first acquiring *Kultur*'.[15] For Schoenberg, the avant-garde now had also to be an *arrière-garde*.

For many others, particularly the younger generation, however, the calamitous outcome of the war only pointed to the historical futility of the old ways of thinking and doing things.[16] Old traditions, if they continued, could only do so ironically, as representative of a failed historical enterprise. Paul Fussell has argued that the modern ironic attitude 'originates largely in the application of mind and memory to the event of the Great War'; if true, it could barely have a better breeding ground than in Vienna, an imperial city now without an empire.[17] If the contrast between the continuing presence of the physical form of Vienna's aristocratic past and its contemporary circumstances needed further underlining, less than six months after the end of the war the Viennese, exercising universal adult suffrage for the very first time, brought the Social Democratic Party into power, and with it the beginning of so-called 'Red Vienna'. On 3 April 1919 the Austrian nobility was officially abolished.[18] Austrians were now divided between those who exulted in the new-found freedoms and those who saw the collapse of the old systems of social order as a calamity of unparalleled proportions.[19]

Krenek's Vienna

There is hardly a better example of the impact these contradictory cultural forces had on post-war composition than that of Ernst Krenek. Born in Vienna in 1900, his childhood had been spent in a house that was in sight of the original burial place of Beethoven and Schubert. Yet he was to become internationally renowned as a musical iconoclast (his 'jazz' opera *Jonny spielt auf* had replaced the traditional New Year's Eve performance of *Die Fledermaus* in 1927), and then, as another world war approached, a disciple of Arnold Schoenberg's 12-tone technique.[20] Prolific as both a composer and essayist, he wrote a detailed memoir of these years, recently published in a German translation as *Im Atem der Zeit* (what follows, however, draws upon the yet-unpublished original English typescript).[21]

Krenek's parents had both been born in Caslav, in what was then Bohemia, and they had settled in Vienna in the fading years of the nineteenth century, no doubt expecting to remain loyal citizens of empire. Krenek senior was a captain in the commissary corps of the Imperial Austro-Hungarian Army, a representative of the army's success in incorporating elements of the approximately eleven distinct ethnic groups within and across its ranks. His son was brought up believing in the Habsburg ideal of a harmonious community of peoples in the Danube basin, but as this ideal faded Krenek's father could at least encourage his son to appreciate the Viennese enthusiasm, if not fanaticism, for the arts.[22] It did not matter that Krenek's parents were not practising musicians of any notable stature; he was as a matter of course exposed to music – and lots of it – from a very young age. And, as was befitting the son of a commissioned officer, Krenek took lessons on the piano and in music theory, and enrolled in a *Staatsgymnasium* on Klostergasse.[23] There his schooling also gave typically solid attention to the history and literature of classical antiquity, engendering in him a predilection to sense continuity in the broad sweep of Western history. From a young age, Krenek believed that he 'could see connections between the events of classical antiquity and the problems of today'.[24]

The onset of war in 1914 was to have little immediate impact on either Krenek's education or quality of life, though it did start to influence him politically and culturally. Krenek's father was given administrative duties and posted to Lemberg, far behind enemy lines, and Krenek continued to attend school as normal. There he was immersed in an aura of misplaced national self-assurance, one similar to that which had swept right across western Europe in 1914, but once the losses started to be reported, the contrast between image and reality helped feed a scepticism towards authority. Otherwise, piano and music theory lessons continued unabated and, although material living conditions in Vienna soon deteriorated, the war did not impede his musical progress. Indeed, across the city, musicians were playing a prominent and much more overt role in the effort to persuade people that everything was normal, and the populace responded warmly.[25] Krenek's father was one among many who rediscovered, for instance, a love for Viennese operetta at this time as a response to the grimness of the war and food and fuel shortages at home.[26]

Of the noted composition teachers of the day, Schoenberg had already been called up for military service. Franz Schreker, however, was continuing to teach in Vienna, and in 1916 Krenek sat the entrance examination of the Imperial and Royal Academy for Music and the Performing Arts where Schreker had been a lecturer since 1912. For the next two years Krenek attended his *Gymnasium* in the morning and classes in the academy in the evening. Quite the youngest in the class at this time, Krenek's contemporaries included Max Brand, Karol Rathaus, Wilhelm Grosz and Alois Hába, men who, like him, were to emerge as major musical figures in post-war Vienna, even if largely forgotten today.[27] Schreker's teaching was, as Krenek remembered it, 'vaguely delineated by the landmarks set up by Debussy, Max Reger, Richard Strauss, and perhaps Scriabin'.[28] The atonal adventurism of Schoenberg notwithstanding, this was the generally accepted image of pre-war Viennese modernism – one that fitted into the orthodox boundaries of musical progress, not overly shocking or absurd. Outside the classroom, indeed, Schreker was at the height of his fame as an opera composer. In 1909 the German music critic Paul Bekker had, in his *Musikdrama der Gegenwart*, urged opera composers to move beyond the historical costume drama and take up, in the manner of the modern novelist, themes of contemporary life.[29] Whether overtly or not, Schreker had taken up the challenge with gusto, and his most successful work, *Der ferne Klang*, drew upon features of pre-war suburban Viennese life: the café, the bordello, the bland middle-class house. Many critics found the blend of naturalism and romanticism evident in the libretto and the stylistic heterogeneity of the score unpalatable, but this was of no immediate concern for his pupils, as his teaching concentrated instead upon the practical discipline of traditional tonal counterpoint. All the same, Schreker's gregarious incorporation of musical and dramatic influences, his willingness – whether consciously theorised or not – to absorb the absurd, the ironic and the disruptive in his music dramas was something that many of his pupils, Krenek not least of them, found adaptable to their circumstances after the war.[30]

Outside the classroom, the situation was indeed becoming more ironic, absurd and disruptive, and it inevitably began to influence Krenek's reactions to what he was being taught inside it. Krenek recalls reading what became an infamous newspaper headline in August 1914, 'Lemberg noch in unserem Besitz' [Lemberg is still in our hands], and the electric effect it had on him. Here one of the empire's early military setbacks was conveyed as if it were the 'result of continued, if indefinite progress', but Krenek recalls that the general populace knew what it really meant.[31] The more the 'public mind during the war was fed with praise of straight-forward, simple and unproblematic heroism', the more he felt that the appropriate response was to develop a 'predilection for uncertainty, doubt, wavering'.[32]

The sense that all that had gone before was pretence was brought to a head with the death of Franz Joseph I, emperor since 1848, on 21 November 1916. As Krenek later observed:

> The war had become a tedious, sorrowful and gruesome business, a disquieting routine of blood, filth, misery and starvation, dragging on without

> sense and without hope. And now, the last living symbol which had connected a disappointed and harassed generation with a far distant past of greatness and glory, had faded away.[33]

Subsequently, the decline in the empire's military fortunes took on an air of dismal inevitability. Krenek was reluctantly called up for military duty early in 1918, but after completing basic officer training was given an administrative posting and was thus able to avoid frontline service. He was not directly exposed to the horrors of the battlefield, but his experience of army life was nonetheless enough to convey a strong impression of a 'gigantic, wasteful and gruesome bureaucratic enterprise of unheard-of dimensions and futility'.[34]

That same year Krenek also stumbled across a copy of Karl Kraus's satirical journal *Die Fackel*. Kraus had prominently and courageously opposed Vienna's uncritical endorsement of the war through the pages of the journal and elsewhere. But Kraus's means of protest extended far beyond merely lampooning the recklessness with the truth and journalistic excesses of the Viennese press. As early as 1914 the satirist had formulated an anti-war critique around his aesthetic thinking by prophesying that an abused language would avenge itself upon those who had perverted it.[35] Maintaining support for such a horrendous and perverse war had only been possible, he argued, because of a degrading of traditional literary values into propaganda and journalese. Kraus insisted instead upon the importance of maintaining a correspondence between form, content and idea, a principle which he applied not just to literature but to all works of art. This was an idea, essentially in line with Schoenberg's and the Viennese idea of classical music more generally, to which Krenek would struggle to reconcile himself in the face of the conflicting social and cultural forces of the immediate post-war years.

The self-questioning and reflection that marked the war's end for Krenek also marked the beginning of the end of his personal and artistic relationship with Schreker, whom he started to find 'disarmingly naïve' in the face of such ideas.[36] Instead he was attracted to Expressionism, a movement that had not attracted much attention before the war, but now seemed apt:

> It came to the fore after the catastrophe of 1918, as on the one hand the instinct of the public, disillusioned as it was and making all things past responsible for the present calamity, turned to whatever seemed 'modern', new, daring and progressive, and on the other hand the precarious uncertainty of post-revolutionary life opened the eyes of the public for the

> fantastic and unpredictable animation of the expressionist style. As far as the cause of progressive art is concerned, a complete collapse of political and social conditions is certainly a powerful promotional factor. Victorious countries are apt to emphasize a conservative attitude, since the powers that be have ostensibly justified their existence by accomplishing the victory so that there is little incentive for changing the cultural outlook. The vanquished, however, smarting under the defeat is psychologically ready to throw overboard what seems to remind him of the causes of his predicament, and is willing to open his mind to new ideas and styles.[37]

Another novel idea that appealed to him was that of communism, though he was quick to stress that this was 'animated by its organisational features rather than by its revolutionary aspects'.[38] Krenek was by his own admission quite immature in worldly affairs, but it nevertheless reflects his developing interest in the problem of the dialectical nature of both political and artistic freedom. In this respect, one anecdote that he recounts of daily life under the new Social Democrat regime is quite telling:

> The idea of freedom was further emphasized by removing the low fences that had surrounded the lawns in the public parks, because one had heard that in democratic countries like England and America people were allowed to walk on such lawns whenever they felt like it. The result was that soon little was left of the grass, without the general happiness having noticeably increased. The Social Democrats also declared that the working people had a 'right to the street', which meant that they could stage demonstrations on the streets whenever and wherever they pleased. One particular boulevard near the Ringstrasse being favoured by the champions of freedom for their exercises, it became a proverbial saying that 'revolution in Vienna is when tram number 2 does not run.' I was reactionary enough to believe that the street ought to serve the traffic and nothing else.[39]

It was, ironically, on the bookshelves of Schreker's teaching studio that Krenek found a compositional premise through which he could apply some sense of logic to his experiments in a quasi-Expressionist atonal style. The work was Ernst Kurth's *Grundlagen des Linearen Kontrapunkts* (1917). Principally a study of counterpoint in the music of J. S. Bach, the approach to counterpoint expressed therein seemed to offer a theoretical rigour which Krenek felt Schreker had neglected in favour of the 'poetic'.[40] Kurth's book presented a potent mix of technical precision and idealist philosophising, and although Kurth himself was no 'apostle of modernism',[41] his advocacy of linear autonomy made it almost inevitable that his theories would later be interpreted by Krenek and others as providing a basis by which modern music, wrested from its traditional tonal moorings, could be brought towards some new form of order. Without it, the enveloping musical disorder which followed in the wake of the collapse of tonality and the Expressionist movement could only mirror the political chaos that the end of the war had heralded.

Rather like the transition from empire to republic, there was, however, to be no easy replacing of one system of musical organisation with another. The very political and cultural openness of the early post-war years in Vienna also provided Krenek with his first taste of 'American entertainment music', which in turn sparked a desire to experiment with jazz.[42] This new music, which arrived on the back of two powerful post-war forces, American political and financial involvement in post-war reconstruction and the increasing presence of American commodities, seemed for many an ideal sonic representation of the emerging post-war world order, or as Paul Stefan was to describe it in 1925, 'a picture of the time … chaos, machine, noise, the highest intensification of experience'.[43] It also came to signify the perceived radical nature of the American metropolis. In contrast to central Europe, America was considered to be open to class and ethnic coexistence in radical new ways. For Krenek, it provided an unexpectedly new stream of musical thought that he felt he could not ignore; indeed he believed, at least to begin with, that 'great things were to be expected from this sort of music for the evolution of our own'.[44] If there were one thing that Krenek felt was certain for the direction of contemporary music in post-war Vienna, it was, indeed, that there were no longer any certainties.

Leaping over shadows: Vienna to Berlin and back again

The impetus to break free of the comparatively limited boundaries of Schreker's instruction became only more powerful when, early in 1920, Schreker was invited to become the director of the *Staatliche akademische Hochschule für Musik* in Berlin, and Krenek was invited to follow him there. His decision to accept the offer was not an easy one, not least because the political situation looked to be even more uncertain in Berlin. To his surprise, however, Krenek actually found Berlin free of many of the post-war insecurities of Vienna, though he was never to be happy during the three years he spent there. Berlin was a city on the make without the burden of past glories to slow it down, but as such it was a city that seemed to highlight all that Vienna had lost. In contrast to

Vienna, Berlin had undergone a frenzied period of urban expansion that had all but obliterated the character of the pre-modern city.

> As far as I knew, from my reading, especially from the books of the brilliant and fantastic E. T. A. Hoffmann, there must have been a sort of original culture of considerable charm in Berlin shortly before and after 1800. Yet, I was looking in vain for any traces of it [...]. With its former culture having become the victim of uninhibited industrial expansion [...] Berlin reflected very much the evolution of North America during the same period. Undoubtedly Berlin was the point at which the obvious process of the Americanization of Europe was most conspicuously going on and had reached an advanced stage.[45]

Even before the war, Berlin's perpetually novel character had been the cause for particular comment from both the right and left of politics. In his *Berlin: Ein Stadtschicksal* (*Berlin: The Destiny of a City*) (1910), Karl Scheffler commented that 'Berlin is condemned ever to becoming, never being'.[46] It was a fluid environment which seemed to demand a fluid state of consciousness. Similarly, for Siegfried Kracauer it seemed that 'whoever stays for any length of time in Berlin hardly knows in the end where he really came from'.[47] One easily got lost in the grid-based expanses of urban developments, or blinded by a multitude of flashing neon lights lining the great public boulevards, or indeed could dissolve among the waves of immigrants and tourists who flooded to the city to join in or simply marvel at its post-war recovery. Likewise, German cinema, which was centred around Berlin, had developed as an unashamedly commercial form of art, and was a medium which delighted in, rather than recoiled from, exploring the creative possibilities of montage and other forms of narrative disruption. On top of that, the city was also fermenting with new ideas about the social function of art, not least those emanating from post-revolutionary Moscow and Leningrad.

But this experience of freedom in the city was not received without anxiety, an anxiety Krenek shared at the very same time that he recognised its vitality. Alfred Polgar suggested in 1926 that the experience of living in Berlin was akin to living in a realised cinematic illusion. 'Confused by klieg [arc] lights,' he wrote, 'the stranger often has the impression that the true Berlin, at this moment, could very well be a film vision built out of cardboard, and that the real houses are only placed there in order to feign a little bit of "real city".'[48] The adoption of cinematic techniques such as montage and abrupt juxtapositions of scale and space seemed at the same time, however, well suited to approximate the visual experience of being in a city, namely 'a succession of different images and angles constructing a perception in strong contrast to the unifying and uniform perception of a village or a landscape'.[49]

Nevertheless, 'Berliners, unlike the natives of other German cities and other European capitals, seemed to be fascinated by the very idea of urbanism and technology', a fascination that had preceded the First World War and now seemed to make them best able to cope with its after-effects.[50] And here Krenek felt much more confident to experiment with the radical and the new, but also with new forms of musical organisation. His dissatisfaction with Schreker's teaching, which in comparison seemed to him to lack inner purpose, only grew. In the theatre music of Schreker, in particular, any pretence of wrestling with objective truth had, it seemed, given way to subjective intuition, illusion and deception; it was 'effect without cause'. Its aural chiaroscuro was inferred as also a moral and political one; Schreker's operas as a whole were 'rambling formations'.[51]

Krenek was only inspired to try to compose an opera himself after reading an essay on opera by Ferruccio Busoni published in 1921.[52] Busoni had argued that opera should not suggest an inner psychological drama but instead that the orchestral music should have its own formal and structural integrity, and the drama should be an allegory, 'sung pantomime'. Here, Krenek thought, was a way past Schreker's 'neurotic fancies' towards a form of drama that could offer a more explicit engagement with contemporary realities.[53] Busoni's essay also drew a connection by association between music and social organisation in that both share an urge to be free, an urge that we 'have never wholly comprehended, never realised to the full'.[54] This wish to find a new form of authentic community had become, after the end of the war, something of the 'characteristic emotional need of the Weimar period'.[55] Krenek felt the temper of the time and decided he would engage with it in the most direct way a musician at that time could, through the operatic stage. 'When the curtain goes up in the theatre,' he was to argue, 'we still see the formation of that communal body which is an essential part of any community.'[56]

His first work, a 'Scenic Cantata' – as Krenek liked to call it – entitled *Die Zwingburg* (*The Fortress of Compulsion*), Op. 14, was composed between 8 July and 15 September 1922, setting a libretto conceived by Fritz Demuth and later reworked by Franz Werfel. The libretto deals specifically with the problem of freedom. The fortress of the story is a giant factory where men and women toil for an unknown oppressor. They are given a chance to enjoy unbridled freedom, and so inspired they attempt a revolution. Its success, however, is foiled owing to the fact that in expressing their freedom they actually re-empower the old tyranny. In the opera, the force emanating from the factory is represented by the workings of an organ grinder, a character inspired in part by Busoni's recommendation that a composer should use characters with peculiarly musical attributes. But we are also reminded here of the last song of Schubert's 1828 *Winterreise* ('Der Leiermann') and its evocation of an outsider whose social status grants him access to some core truth that escapes the rest of us. So too, Dostoevsky's *Notes From Underground* (1864) describes the modern condition as one in which people 'are no more than a sort of piano keyboard or barrel organ cylinder'.[57] Adorno would later observe that the hand organ was symbolic of the modern transformation of subjectivity into an alienated mechanical form.[58] Whatever the allusions Krenek intended, the ideas in the work seem clear, warning his audience of the tendency for total freedom to collapse into terror, and thus the paradoxical requirement for freedom to be circumscribed by social obligation, and vice-versa. In this respect the work very much speaks of, and to, Krenek's experience of the end of the war in Vienna.

The character of the score itself also suggests, *a propos* the tension he felt between the post-war siren calls of musical Expressionism and American popular music, a wish to temper any dogmatic or doctrinaire incorporation of modernist musical language with a sensitivity to the practicalities of theatre, and the possibilities for a more direct engagement with the audience by means of tonal allusions. Two years later, in an address to the Congress of Music Aesthetics in Karlsruhe in 1925, Krenek explicitly criticised the overtly intellectual music of his contemporaries (Schoenberg in particular considered it a personal attack) in so far as it

> no longer addresses itself to those who share certain emotions, but rather to those who have reached the same stage of musical sophistication. It has become a game that is only interesting to those who know the rules. It has neither the capacity nor the inclination to address itself to the uninitiated community.[59]

Krenek reasserted his desire to engage directly with this new 'community', and the growing impact of these ideas is clear in his second opera *Der Sprung über den Schatten* (*The Leap Over the Shadow*), Op. 17 (1924). This time he produced his own libretto, but once again concentrating on the problem of freedom in a time of radical social change. In the opera a prince is deposed, and a president appointed – the nation tries to 'leap over its shadow', but instead the old tyranny reappears, merely repackaged. Along the way, Krenek constructs innumerable plot contrivances to satirise the fashions and inhibitions of modern life.

Once again making ironic reference to the situation in Austria and Germany after the war, *Der Sprung über den Schatten* suggests there may be a change in regime, but no one is better off; instead we just end up with a new variation of the same old problem. Apart from the fact that the work was a comedy, the striking difference from *Die Zwingburg* was the musical language:

> In the music to this opera I ventured for the first time into the field of contemporary entertainment music, putting in various numbers in the style of the then current versions of American dance tunes. Thus I created a sort of stylistic hodge-podge, since the basic idiom was still the aggressive atonal language that I had cultivated in the instrumental compositions of that period.[60]

We could consider *Der Sprung über den Schatten* perhaps an archetypal post-Armistice work, embedded as it is at the level of both plot and score with degrees of textural and musical irony. Curiously, it has its closest simile in some of the writing that emerged in the early years of the Bolshevik Revolution in Russia. For Kevin Platt, the literary works of Russia's periods of rapid transformation portray a similarly disorienting mix of otherwise irreconcilable material (especially mixtures of the traditional and the modern), creating what he describes as a 'revolutionary grotesque'.[61] Such works bring to the fore the tremendous ironies of historical acts such as war and revolution that might otherwise be proclaimed straightforwardly as moments of human triumph, emancipation and transcendence (and yet more often than not produce misery on a vast scale). Krenek never described his music in such terms but he did sense a connection between 'grotesque' literature, Expressionism and attempts to make sense of the horrors of war. He explicitly recognised an affinity between what he was doing and post-war surrealism, which he achieved principally by the 'juxtaposition of heterogeneous elements', and by indeed creating a 'stylistic hodge podge'.[62]

Der Sprung über den Schatten was in fact one of only a handful of contemporary western operas that were actually performed in the Soviet Union between the two world wars. Its Russian premiere performance took place on 21 May 1927 at the Maly Opera Theatre in Leningrad (*Jonny spielt auf* was to follow on 13 November 1928), and both operas also premiered in Moscow the following year. According to one reviewer, the original Leningrad staging was done

> with bare metal constructions, stressing mechanization, emphasising the grotesque. Point of view: social satire. Object: the modern bourgeois society. Purpose: an autopsy of the corpse. Methods: tearing off the cloaks, direct frontal lighting, abolishing of smoothing embellishments.[63]

The grotesque character of the work is evident from the very opening, where we are presented with a succession of pastiche forms derived from both traditional opera and operetta, and the latest dance sensations, especially the foxtrot. The jazz and popular elements of the score were not to be considered as some attempt at a 'jazz' opera per se. Krenek himself knew that '[t]he true jazz opera will be more than an opera with dance inserts and related musical forms'. Nevertheless he now felt that even the 'exaggerated instrumentation of unoriginal origin' [*outrierten und nicht originalen Instrumentation*] that stood for jazz in Europe still demonstrated an 'enormous suitability and relevance to the needs of people today'.[64] Krenek felt 'strongly attracted to the social sphere of which that music was an expression, as it seemed to hold promises in regard to the "real life" of which I was so eager to partake'.[65]

Staying with Russian interpretive theories for a moment longer, we could also incorporate the work's apparent stylistic freedom under Bahktin's formulation of the 'carnivalesque', which

> consecrates inventive freedom, to permit the combination of a variety of different elements and their rapprochement, to liberate from the prevailing point of view of the world, from conventions and established truths, from clichés, from all that is humdrum and universally accepted. This carnival spirit offers the chance to have a new outlook on the world, to realize the relative nature of all that exists, and to enter a completely new order of things.[66]

Whatever theoretical construct we might use, however, the underlying point is that the compositional approach in itself, and not just the plot, can be seen as responding directly to the conditions of the day. We might note that Bertold Brecht had also stressed the importance for modern, politically aware stage works not to ape the form of the *Gesamptkunstwerk*, that is, not to presume some kind of overarching organic unity; instead its various components should provide contrasting and mutually critical perspectives on each other.[67]

But, as Richard Stites notes, at a time of change the iconoclastic approach, and its concomitant delight in irony and satire, was also deeply troubling for many, as one 'could laugh out the old, but one could not laugh in the new. This is true of all religions, all culture-building movements, and thus of all modern revolutions.'[68] Outside of carnival was a world of hierarchical structure. Hierarchy demanded that forms of reverence, etiquette, even fear be taken seriously. But in carnival, according to Bakhtin, 'The laws, prohibitions, and restrictions that determine the structure and order of ordinary [...] life are suspended.'[69] In contrast, the solemn cloak of post-Wagnerian opera abhors laughter. Hence, by the time of the mid-1930s the new social orders in both Germany and Russia could no longer tolerate the kind of art that Krenek had produced.[70] As a result of the political and cultural shutdown that followed in both Germany and Russia, *Der Sprung uber dem Schatten* and its successor, the riotously successful *Jonny spielt auf* (1927), disappeared from the inter-war Austrian operatic stage altogether.

All the same, Krenek's play with styles and genres, his parodying of 'official' notions of not only what conventional opera should be, but also what contemporary opera should be, can be seen as not some kind of cynical disengagement from higher values in art, but rather as an attempt to engage with the very problem of value in a post-war world. True, Krenek's later operas are less and less infused with the ironic and the grotesque, in part because Krenek himself thought such artistic responses had become impotent in the face of the rise of fascism. But I think it is not too bold to say that the attempt to negotiate this dilemma of ambivalence distinguishes all of Krenek's subsequent operatic works.

Writing later in life, Krenek observed that 'composers like Beethoven and especially Wagner [...] were blessed with a sort of single-track mind' allowing them to 'proceed instinctively along a certain line which was relatively simple and clear to the minds of contemporaries'. By comparison, Krenek showed 'the world at large so bewildering a picture of my creative vein that the world at large eventually preferred not to pay any attention to it'.[71] What we can now recognise is that the kind of society that allows for such a 'single-track mind' was no longer in existence in Vienna by 1918. It is therefore much more difficult to impute that his musical approach was, prima facie, somehow less appropriate than others who more readily fit our canonical ideal. If anything, it is the traditional orthodoxy of the single-minded creative artist, and the music-historiography that sustains it, that now appears inappropriate. This conclusion seems especially true in view of the fragmentation of both musical style and academic discourse that has actually characterised Western music history since the latter half of the twentieth century.

From our perspective, Krenek's resulting penchant for self-doubt mixed with ceaseless exploration and experimentation in the years immediately following the First World War seems more to epitomise than to contradict the condition of the later twentieth-century artist.

As we have seen, the historical turning point for Krenek was the end of the First World War, which produced a deep sense of scepticism about the past and uncertainty about the future. Krenek mused that as a result he was someone who 'sympathized with weak, undecided, wavering characters in life and literature'. Cowardice 'was the only dignified human attitude, because it seemed to be the only sincere one', observing that this line of thought had been 'taken up later by literature in the great wave of pacifist novels and plays on World War I'.[72] In contrast, we might consider, by analogy, the musical 'call to order' that is implicit in the 12-tone technique as a technical apparatus for forgetting such history, instead proffering a critical resistance to reflection on the historical circumstances of its origins. If so, this became a more general act of amnesia in the West when serialism was accepted as high-modernist orthodoxy in the years following the Second World War.[73] In the end, however, it ultimately represents just one of many ways the First World War has influenced our collective music-historical imagination.

Notes

1 Carl Schorske, *Fin-de-Siècle Vienna: Politics and Culture* (Cambridge: Cambridge University Press, 1981), xviii; Karl Kraus, quoted in Edward Timms, *Karl Kraus: Apocalyptic Satirist: Culture and Catastrophe in Habsburg Vienna* (New Haven, CT: Yale University Press, 1986), 10. For Allan Janik, Vienna was a 'Silicon Valley of the mind'; quoted in Peter Berner, Emil Brix and Wolfgang Mantl, eds, *Wien um 1900: Aufbruch in die Moderne* (Vienna: Verlag für Geschichte und Politik, 1986), 14.

2 Richard Taruskin, 'Back to Whom? Neoclassicism as Ideology', *Nineteenth-Century Music*, 16, 3 (1993), 300. Taruskin singles out for criticism Alan Lessem's article 'Schoenberg, Stravinsky, and Neo-Classicism: The Issues Reexamined', *Musical Quarterly*, 68 (1982), 527–42.

3 See further Lawrence Kramer, 'The Strange Case of Beethoven's *Coriolan:* Romantic Aesthetics, Modern Subjectivity, and the Cult of Shakespeare', *Musical Quarterly*, 79, 2 (1995), 256.

4 Malcolm Bradbury, 'The Cities of Modernism', in Malcom Bradbury and James McFarlane, eds, *Modernism* (Harmondsworth: Penguin, 1976), 98–9. See also Christopher Hailey, 'Franz Schreker and the Pluralities of Modernism', *Tempo*, 219 (2002), 2–7.

5 See Glenn Watkins, *Proof through the Night: Music and the Great War* (Berkeley, CA: University of California Press, 2003).

6 Peter Franklin, 'Audiences, Critics and the Depurification of Music: Reflections on a 1920s Controversy', *Journal of the Royal Musical Association*, 114 (1989), 90.

7 Ernst Krenek, 'Memoirs', 232. Typescript in the possession of Gladys Krenek, Palm Springs. Quoted with permission.

8 Krenek, 'Memoirs', 233.

9 Albrecht Mendelssohn-Bartholdy, *The War and German Society: The Testament of a Liberal* (New Haven, CT: Yale University Press, 1937), 20.

10 See also William Johnston, *The Austrian Mind: An Intellectual and Social History 1848–1938* (Berkeley, CA: University of California Press, 1972), 66–73.

11 Theodor Adorno, *Minima Moralia: Reflections from Damaged Life*, trans. E. F. N. Jephcott (London: NLB, 1974), 52. Jacques Le Rider notes that men such as Freud, Hofmannsthal and their contemporaries 'felt shackled, almost exiled, by their life in Vienna, and never ceased to envy the cultural, intellectual and academic life of other great European cities. They would never have dreamed of vaunting their city as a centre of modernism. They would have been readier to describe it as a bastion of everything that was archaic.' See his *Modernity and Crises of Identity: Culture and Society in Fin-de-Siècle Vienna*, trans. Rosemary Morris (Cambridge: Polity Press, 1993), 15.

12 The most famous contemporary pronouncement on the state of 'crisis' was Oswald Spengler's widely read *Der Untergang des Ablendlandes: Umrisse einer Morphologie der Weltgeschichte* (Munich: Beck, 1923), the first volume of which first appeared in Munich in 1918. George Lukács considered Spengler's book the characteristic representative of the *Lebensphilosophie* of the post-war years. See *Die Zerstörung der Vernuft. Der Weg des Irrationalismus von Schelling zu Hitler* (Berlin, 1954), 364–8. See also the excellent discussion of the work in Paul Forman's book-length essay, 'Weimar Culture, Causality, and Quantum Theory, 1918–1927: Adaption by German Physicists and Mathematicians to a Hostile Intellectual Environment', *Historical Studies in the Physical Sciences*, 3 (1971), 58–63.

13 See Joseph Auner, 'The Second Viennese School as a Historical Concept', in Bryan R. Simms, ed., *Schoenberg, Berg and Webern: A Companion to the Second Viennese School* (Westport, CT: Greenwood Press, 1999).

14 Schoenberg to Kandinsky, 20 July 1922, in *Letters, Pictures and Documents: Arnold Schoenberg, Wassily Kandinsky*, ed. Jelena Hahl-Koch, trans. John C. Crawford (London: Faber and Faber, 1984), 74; Schoenberg to Fromaigeat, 22 July 1919, in *Arnold Schoenberg Letters*, ed. Erwin Stein, trans. Eithne Wilkins and Ernst Kaiser (London: Faber and Faber, 1964), 67. See also Peter Tregear, 'Schoenberg, Satire, and the *Zeitoper*', in Jennifer Shaw and

Joseph Auner, eds, *The Cambridge Companion to Schoenberg* (Cambridge: Cambridge University Press, 2010), 147.

15 Arnold Schoenberg, *Theory of Harmony*, trans. Roy E. Carter (London: Faber and Faber, 1978), 433.

16 Thomas Harrison, *1910: The Emancipation of Dissonance* (Berkeley, CA: University of California Press, 1996), 216.

17 Paul Fussell, *The Great War and Modern Memory* (Oxford: Oxford University Press, 1975), 35.

18 *Gesetz über die Aufhebung des Adels, der weltlichen Ritter- und Damenorden und gewisser Titel und Würden*, 3 April 1919 (StGBl. 211/1919).

19 See Alfred Diamant, *Austrian Catholics and the First Republic* (Princeton, NJ: Princeton University Press, 1960), 116–17.

20 For a description of the journey from *Jonny* to his 12-tone opera *Karl V*, see Peter Tregear, 'Musical Style and Political Allegory in Krenek's *Karl V*', *Cambridge Opera Journal*, 13 (1999), 55–88.

21 Ernst Krenek, *Im Atem der Zeit: Erinnerungen an die Moderne* (Hamburg: Hoffmann und Campe, 1998).

22 See the vivid descriptions of the intensity of pre-war Viennese cultural life in Stefan Zweig's autobiography *The World of Yesterday* (London: Cassell, 1943). See also Allan Janik and Stephen Toulmin, *Wittgenstein's Vienna* (New York: Simon and Schuster, 1973), 44.

23 John L. Stewart, *Ernst Krenek: The Man and His Music* (Berkeley, CA: University of California Press, 1991), 6–8.

24 Ernst Krenek, 'Why Pallas Athene Weeps', in *Exploring Music*, trans. Margaret Shenfield and Geoffrey Skelton (London: Calder and Boyars, 1958), 195.

25 See Kraus's satirical response to this state of affairs in his article '1916', *Die Fackel* (April 1916), 418–22; quoted in part in Frank Field, *The Last Days of Mankind: Karl Kraus and his Vienna* (London: Macmillan, 1967), 88.

26 Krenek, 'Memoirs', 137.

27 Krenek, 'Memoirs', 154–63. For a digest of student recollections of Schreker as a teacher, see Christopher Hailey, *Franz Schreker, 1878–1934: A Cultural Biography* (Cambridge: Cambridge University Press, 1993), ch. 3.

28 Ernst Krenek, 'Circling My Horizon', in *Horizons Circled: Reflections on My Music* (Berkeley, CA: University of California Press, 1974), 20.

29 Hailey, *Franz Schreker*, 37.

30 Hailey, 'Franz Schreker and the Pluralities of Modernism', 3.

31 Krenek, 'Memoirs', 124.

32 Krenek, 'Memoirs', 163–4.

33 Krenek, 'Memoirs', 139.

34 Krenek, 'Memoirs', 129.

35 'In dieser grossen Zeit', *Die Fackel* (December 1914), 1, quoted in Field, *The Last Days of Mankind*, 138. This moral attitude to the use of language was

to be mirrored in Heidegger's lectures on metaphysics at the University of Freiburg in 1935, in which he argued that 'words and language are not wrappings in which things are packed for the commerce of those whose write and speak. It is in words and language that things first come into being and are. For this reason the misuse of language in idle talk, in slogans and phrases, destroys our authentic relation to things.' *An Introduction to Metaphysics*, trans. Ralph Manheim (New Haven, CT: Yale University Press, 1959), 13–14. The impossibility of sustaining a 'pure' relationship to language was later to become the central theme of the composition of Schoenberg's opera *Moses und Aron*.

36 Krenek, 'Memoirs', 240.

37 Krenek, 'Memoirs', 210.

38 Krenek, 'Memoirs', 212.

39 Krenek, 'Memoirs', 235.

40 Krenek, 'Memoirs', 227, 224.

41 Krenek, letter to Lee A. Rothfarb, 10 September 1981, quoted in Lee A. Rothfarb, *Ernst Kurth as Theorist and Analyst* (Philadelphia: University of Pennsylvania Press, 1988), 225.

42 Krenek, 'Memoirs', 236.

43 Paul Stefan, 'Jazz?...', *Musikblätter des Anbruch*, 7 (1925), 187.

44 Krenek, 'Memoirs', 236.

45 Krenek, 'Memoirs', 261–2.

46 Karl Scheffler, *Berlin: Ein Stadtschicksal* (Berlin: E. Reiss, 1910), 267.

47 Quoted in Alexandra Richie, *Faust's Metropolis: A History of Berlin* (London: HarperCollins, 1998), 407.

48 Alfred Polgar, cited in Sabine Hake, *The Cinema's Third Machine: Writing on Film in Germany, 1907–1933* (Lincoln, NE: University of Nebraska Press, 1993), 126.

49 Michael Minden, 'The City in Early Cinema', in Edward Timms and David Kelly, eds, *Unreal City: Urban Experience in Modern European Literature and Art* (Manchester: Manchester University Press, 1985), 203.

50 Modris Eksteins, *Rites of Spring: The Great War and the Birth of the Modern Age* (Boston: Mariner Books, 1989), 75.

51 Krenek, 'Memoirs', 224.

52 The essay was presumably Ferruccio Busoni, 'Entwurf eines Vorwortes zur Partitur des *Doktor Faust* enthaltend einige Betrachtungen über die Möglichkeiten der Oper', *Faust* 1 (1921), 25–35. Soon thereafter Busoni's pupil and Krenek's exact contemporary Kurt Weill composed *Die Zaubernacht* (1922), a work inspired by his teacher's theories.

53 Krenek, 'Memoirs', 386.

54 Ferruccio Busoni, 'Sketch of a New Esthetic of Music' (1907), trans. Theodore Baker (New York: Schirmer, 1911); rpt in *Three Classics in the Aesthetic of Music: Monsieur Croche the Dilettante Hater, by Claude Debussy; Sketch of a*

New Esthetic of Music, by Ferruccio Busoni; Essays before a Sonata, by Charles E. Ives (New York: Dover, 1962), 77.

55 Forman, 'Weimar Culture, Causality, and Quantum Theory', 47.

56 Krenek, 'Music of Today', address to the Congress of Music Aesthetics in Karlsruhe, 19 October 1925; trans. in Susan C. Cook, *Opera for a New Republic: The* Zeitopern *of Krenek, Weill, and Hindemith* (Ann Arbor, MI: UMI, 1988), 201.

57 Fyodor Dostoyevsky, *Notes from Underground/The Double*, trans. Jessie Coulson (Harmondsworth: Penguin, 1972), 33.

58 Theodor Adorno, *Philosophy of Modern Music*, trans. Anne G. Mitchell and Wesley V. Bloomster (London: Sheed and Ward, 1973), 143–5.

59 Krenek, 'Music of Today', 196.

60 Krenek, 'Memoirs', 448–9.

61 Kevin M. F. Platt, *History in a Grotesque Key: Russian Literature and the Idea of Revolution* (Stanford, CA: Stanford University Press, 1997).

62 Krenek, 'Memoirs', 449. In the late 1950s Wolfgang Kayser offered his seminal analysis of the grotesque in art and literature as a fusion of elements that under normal circumstances are viewed as irreconcilable opposites: for example, the plants that end in human torsos or such-like in Renaissance ornamental stonework, or the combination of human and mechanical images in the works of the Surrealists. Wolfgang Kayser, *The Grotesque in Art and Literature*, trans. Ulrich Weisstein (New York: Columbia University Press, 1981), 29–47, 179–89. Originally published as *Das Groteske, seine Gestaltung in Malerei und Dichtung* (Oldenburg: G. Stalling, 1957).

63 N. V. Smolich, 'Krenek's Performance', in I. Glebov and S. Ginsburg, *The New Life* (Leningrad; Triton Publishers, 1927), II, 23.

64 Ernst Krenek, '"Materialbestimmtheit" der Oper', *Musikblätter des Anbruch*, 9 (1927), 48–52; rpt in Krenek, *Zur Sprache gebracht* (Munich: Albert Langen-George Müller, 1958), 25–30.

65 Krenek, 'Memoirs', 293.

66 Mikhail Bakhtin, *The Dialogical Imagination* (Austin, TX: University of Texas Press, 1981), 34.

67 Bertolt Brecht, *Werke: Große kommentierte Berliner und Frankfurter Ausgabe* (Berlin: Aufbau/Frankfurt: Suhrkamp, 1988ff.), vol. XXIV, 79.

68 Richard Stites, *Revolutionary Dreams: Utopian Vision and Experimental Life in the Russian Revolution* (New York: Oxford University Press, 1989), 98.

69 Mikhail Bakhtin, *Problems of Dostoevsky's Poetics*, ed. and trans. Caryl Emerson (Minneapolis, MN: University of Minnesota Press, 1984), 122–3.

70 The *Bol'shaia Sovetskaia Entsiklopedia*, 41 (Moscow, 1939) declared Krenek's 'many heterogeneous tendencies' to be a reflection of the 'ideological dead-end of European bourgeois culture' (563–64).

71 Krenek, 'Memoirs', 427.

72 Krenek, 'Memoirs', 246.

73 See Pierre Boulez's now infamous essay 'Schoenberg is Dead' (1951; trans. Stephen Walsh) in which he rejects the supposed decadent German romanticism of Schoenberg and Berg in favour of the 'formal purity' of Webern. In *Composers on Modern Musical Culture: An Anthology of Readings on Twentieth-Century Music*, ed. Bryan R. Simms (New York: G. Schirmer, 1999), 145–51.

10

Silence recalled in sound: British classical music and the Armistice

Kate Kennedy

The young composer Arthur Bliss served in the trenches from 1914 to 1918. He was injured at the battle of Boisselle on the Somme in July 1916, and invalided back to London. His brother Kennard, a clarinettist, also served, but was not as lucky as Arthur; he died of his injuries on the Somme in September 1916.[1] Soon after his brother's death, Arthur attended a concert. What he observed upset him greatly, and he wrote a forceful letter to the *Musical Times*:

> As one of those musicians who have fought German aggression in France, [...] It seems to me unseemly that a fine institution like the London Symphony Orchestra should have to put its financial security in front of its national feelings – if all had followed suit we should never have declared war. Moreover, by its choice of works it has missed a signal opportunity of showing its appreciation and gratitude to those of the profession who are fighting to maintain all the cherished institutions of this country.
>
> [...] I do not know whether as a class musicians have been less affected (except financially) than other professions, but when straight from being wounded on the Somme I went into a London concert hall and heard a public vociferously applauding a German soloist, it gives me furiously to think.

It seemed to Bliss that German music and German soloists were better treated in Britain than were British performers and composers. This in turn made him wonder what he and his generation had been fighting for, and how classical music was reflecting their sacrifices.

In the early years of the war there had been attempts to ban all German music.[2] However, these were quickly recognised as futile. Choral societies would be bereft of most of their repertoire. Wagner had been performed almost nightly in Covent Garden before the war; what would fill its place? Also, even those fighting the Germans did not necessarily feel the inclination to renounce German music. Bliss might have resented German performers, but he still found solace in Wagner's Ring Cycle during his sick leave in London in 1916–17. The conductor Sir Thomas Beecham instigated an English Music concert series, but it did not have the same attraction as Bach, Brahms and Mendelssohn.

The war had come at a time of transition for English composers. The older generation of Sir Hubert Parry, Sir Charles Villiers Stanford and Sir Edward Elgar was at the end of its reign, and a younger generation was being trained up, largely by the Royal College of Music under Parry and Stanford's tutelage. Ivor Gurney, Arthur Bliss, Herbert Howells and Eugene Goosens were all students in 1914. Ralph Vaughan Williams, approximately a decade older than the undergraduate composers, was slowly but surely finding his musical identity outside the academy, but interrupted his work to enlist. Frank Bridge had finished his studies and was pursuing a career as a chamber musician and conductor alongside his compositions. Although he was not personally involved in the fighting, he was profoundly influenced by the war. Of those composers who went to fight, George Butterworth, F. S. Kelly, William Denis Browne, Ernest Farrar, the Royal Academy's young star Willie Manson and the Scottish composer Cecil Coles did not return. Many instrumentalists were killed, too: Kennard Bliss and the viola player Francis Purcell Warren, a great friend of the younger generation of RCM students. Howells and Goosens did not fight. Ivor Gurney returned after fifteen months at the Front, having been shot and gassed. Ernest Moeran, composer of exquisite songs, returned with a drinking problem from his stint as a motorbike dispatch rider, and with a large piece of shrapnel in his head; and Vaughan Williams returned from his work with the Medical Corps saddened and traumatised by what he had experienced.

And yet this seemingly shattered generation was to prove the vanguard of a renaissance in British music in the post-war years. In 1921 Bliss could boast with some confidence that 'London is so primarily and clearly the hub of the world's musical wheel that going along the spokes to America, Holland, France, Italy, and Switzerland is like a prolonged provincial tour.'[3] The 1920s and 1930s were an emotionally turbulent but vibrant period in British music, dominated by the war generation. To look at how each of these composers wrote their wartime experiences into their music (or chose not to do so) is beyond the scope of this chapter. Instead, I'd like to suggest that, collectively, these composers made a lasting and profound contribution to the cultural legacy of the war through their music, as well as to the annual acts of remembrance on 11 November. Focusing on a now largely forgotten commemorative 'war symphony' by Bliss, entitled *Morning Heroes* (1930), I want to argue for classical music's important contribution to the shaping of the silence that was left by the war's end. Initially it was filled by the cacophony of sirens and cheers, then, as the years passed, by something more decorous – music.

Music and the First World War

When we think about the ways in which the arts helped to memorialise the war, we are likely to turn to literature and memoirs, and perhaps sculpture or visual art. Classical music has a far less prominent place in this cultural history. Even some musicologists have contributed to the neglect of First World War music. Writing in 1964, for example, Arnold Whittall commented that post-war England was 'a time for action, not recollection, and if little post-war music was inspired by bitterness [...] even less of it was commemorative'.[4] If this were indeed true, and classical music was the only art form uninterested in writing about the war, then why? One possible explanation for this assumption might be that, as the general musical language in England was noticeably more conservative at this time than on the continent, the specifically war-related pieces have been largely overlooked. Classical music, written in a diatonic, pastoral idiom, just didn't sound like war (although Vaughan Williams's *Pastoral Symphony* (1921) poses an obvious counter-example). There were few composers whose musical language could equal Wilfred Owen's and Siegfried Sassoon's poetry in expressing anger, bitterness and irony. The other explanation is that Whittall's claim is simply incorrect. Why, when all other art forms were engaging with the aftermath of the Armistice, as this book demonstrates, would music be any different? Whittall's assumption that commemorative works were obsolete is founded on a false reading of post-1918 society. It might have been true that some were intent on forgetting. However, other areas of society, and many artists and writers, were intent on remembering, and were involved in formulating how public remembrance might become an institution in the form of the Remembrance Day services, the Two Minutes' Silence and concerts.

Furthermore, there was plenty of music written that was commemorative. And some that was bitter. Whittall asserts that Bliss's *Morning*

Heroes is the 'first English work "about" the war'. The list given here, while not claiming to be definitive, shows how many other directly war-related pieces were written from the beginning of the conflict onwards. Far from being unique when it was completed in 1930, *Morning Heroes* entered into a small but very important tradition of music commemorating the First World War.

Timeline of war-related compositions between 1914 and 1933

1914

Sir Edward Elgar, *Carillon*, written to raise funds for wounded Belgian soldiers and first performed in October 1915.

1915

Sir Edward Elgar, *Polonia*, written as a fundraiser for Polish refugees; a 'symphonic prelude' that features melodies from Chopin and Paderewski.
Sir Edward Elgar, *Une Voix dans le Désert*, a theatre piece for speaker and orchestra, like *Carillon*, setting text by Belgian poet Cammaerts. Described in a review after its première: 'It is night when the curtain rises, showing the battered dwelling, standing alone in the desolate land, with the twinkling of camp fires along the Yser in the distance, and in the foreground the cloaked figure of a man, who soliloquises on the spectacle to Elgar's music. Then he ceases, and the voice of a peasant girl is heard coming from the cottage, singing a song of hope and trust in anticipation of the day the war shall be ended [...] The wayfarer stands transfixed as he listens to the girl's brave song, and then, as he comments again on her splendid courage and unconquerable soul, the curtain slowly falls.'
Sir Edward Elgar, *The Fringes of the Fleet*, setting texts by Kipling.
Cyril Rootham, *For The Fallen* (1914–15). Rootham was a Cambridge academic and too old to fight. He wrote *For the Fallen*, setting Laurence Binyon's text, unfortunately at the same time as Elgar set the same text in his *The Spirit of England*, and Rootham's work was overshadowed from the beginning.

1916

F. S. Kelly, *Elegy for Strings* (1915–16), dedicated 'in memoriam Rupert Brooke'.
Frank Bridge, *Lament,* for the victims of the *Lusitania.* It is dedicated to 'Catherine, aged 9', written for string orchestra, and is Bridge's most poignant work written during the war. Bridge was a committed pacifist,

and although his songs during and immediately after the war do not generally reflect his distress at the conflict, the musical vocabulary he developed during the early 1920s is seen as a response to the inadequacy of his previous language to articulate his response to the war.
Sir Hubert Parry, *The Chivalry of the Sea*, specially commissioned for a concert at the Queen's Hall on 12 December 1916 to commemorate the loss of the *Invincible* at Jutland. The text was by Robert Bridges.

1917
Sir Edward Elgar, *The Spirit of England* (1915–17), a cantata for soprano, choir and orchestra, the most famous of the works written during the war (although largely overlooked in comparison to Elgar's other great choral works). Like Rootham's work, it takes poems by Laurence Binyon from his collection *The Winnowing Fan* (1914). Dedicated to 'the memory of our glorious men, with a special thought for the Worcesters'. It was one of the most popular works for Remembrance Day concerts. It sets three poems: 'The Fourth of August', 'To Women' and 'For the Fallen'.

1918
Frank Bridge, *Blow out you Bugles*, a song setting for either piano or orchestra and tenor of Rupert Brooke's poem 'The Dead'. It has much in common with Parry and the pomp and circumstance of his ceremonial works such as *I Was Glad*, but has wistful moments away from the trumpets and bugle calls in which it contemplates the loss the dead youth have undergone, and their promise that would now never be fulfilled.

1919
Gustav Holst, *Ode to Death*, an elegiac work that has its roots in the requiem form, but sets texts by Whitman, and was a response to the loss of many young composer-friends, particularly Cecil Coles.
Ivor Gurney, *Ludlow and Teme*, a song cycle for tenor and piano quartet, setting texts by A. E. Housman. I have argued elsewhere for its inclusion in the canon of war compositions.[5] Gurney was drawn to Housman's poems while still in the trenches and recovering from a bullet wound in hospital, and the sounds of war are present in this troubled pastoral idyll. The music becomes highly disturbed as the texts contemplate the horrors of war and muse on the meaning of war service and premature death, struggling to find serenity by the end of the cycle.

1920

Ivor Gurney, *War Elegy*, an orchestral march written for Remembrance Day ceremonies, but probably not performed more than once, at the Royal College of Music.[6] It is still (2012) unpublished.

1921

Sir Charles Villiers Stanford, *At The Abbey Gate*, a short piece combining a funeral march with a setting of the description by Judge Darling of the arrival of the Unknown Warrior at Westminster Abbey.
Lilian Elkington, *Out of the Mist*, a short tone poem, 'the outcome of a poignant memory connected with the War [...] when the Unknown Warrior was brought home to his last resting place there was a thick mist over the Channel, out of which the warship slowly emerged as she drew near to Dover'.[7]
John Foulds, *A World Requiem* (1919–21) was written specifically for the Armistice concerts. Suggestively subtitled 'A Cenotaph in Sound', it requires enormous forces to perform, and controversially mixed a specially written libretto with the Mass of the Dead. It was forgotten for much of the twentieth century and is only now enjoying something of a revival.
Ralph Vaughan Williams, *A Pastoral Symphony*, with bugle calls in the second movement. Vaughan Williams had served with the RAMC in northern France. 'It is really wartime music, a great deal of it incubated when I used to go up night after night with the ambulance wagon at Ecoivres and we went up a steep hill and there was a wonderful Corot-like landscape in the sunset – it's not really lambkins frisking at all as most people take for granted.'[8]

1924

Frank Bridge, *Piano Sonata* (1921–4), an emotionally charged work of remembrance, which departed dramatically from his Edwardian-style chamber music with its roots firmly in the Romantic, German tradition. It is a shocking, troubling work and caused great controversy. It was dedicated to the young composer Ernest Bristow Farrar, who was killed in 1918. It is probably the first of the war-related works to use a modernist style, and represents a different sound-world to the works of Finzi and Vaughan Williams, the latter being still firmly rooted in the pastoral, nostalgic musical vocabulary of the pre-war during the 1920s.

1925

Ralph Vaughan Williams, *Sancta Civitas* (1923–5) is an oratorio for tenor and baritone soli, semi-chorus, distant chorus and orchestra.

Arthur Bliss, *Suite for Piano*. Bliss had already tried to write about the war in a piece he called *Battle Variations*, but abandoned the work. Instead, the slow movement of the *Suite for Piano* is dedicated 'F.K.B. Thiepval, 1916', to his brother Kennard who had not survived the fighting.

Gerald Finzi, *Requiem da Camera*, dedicated to the memory of his teacher, Ernest Farrar (Finzi had himself been too young to fight). It consists of an orchestral prelude, followed by settings of John Masefield's sonnet 'August 1914', Hardy's 'The Breaking of Nations' and 'Lament' by Wilfred Gibson. Sceptical of orthodox religion, Finzi expressed his own grief at the loss of friends and relatives through the sorrow of the poets he chose, and represented the progress of the war by his positioning of the three texts.

1929

Gordon Jacob, *Symphony no.* 1 (1928–9) is still unpublished, and was dedicated to his brother Anstey who was killed on the Somme. Jacob himself fought and was taken prisoner in April 1917.

1930

Frank Bridge, *Oration*, arguably Bridge's masterpiece, is a wordless requiem for cello and orchestra. It was intended as an 'outcry against the futility of war'.

Arthur Bliss, *Morning Heroes*, 'a symphony on war' for narrator, chorus and large orchestra, with an eclectic and carefully selected set of texts by poets including Li Tai Po, Walt Whitman and Wilfred Owen.

1936

Ralph Vaughan Williams, *Dona Nobis Pacem*, a cantata for soprano and baritone soli, chorus and orchestra. A work that looks ahead to the impending second conflict as much as it refers back to the first.

The need for 'war works' in music was identified before the war had ended. In 1917 the *Musical Times* published an article by a non-musician combatant, Robert Lorenz, describing in surprising detail a plan he had devised for a 'composer of genius' to write a Bugle-Call Symphony of the war. His modest 'genius' 'could write a work of real national importance by taking three or four of the most expressive [bugle] calls and enlarging symphonically on the meaning which they are supposed to convey.'[9]

- 'Retreat' (a fast movement following on a short slow introduction).
- 'Last Post' (the traditional slow symphonic movement).
- 'Battalion Orderly Room': A mighty colonel sees humble private (a scherzo in name only).
- 'Reveille' (the crowning movement, with probably a variety of tempi).[10]

The over-prescribed formula he offers would have been unlikely to have been taken on by any composer. However, he is not entirely off the mark on a number of points. Arthur Bliss, Ralph Vaughan Williams and Gordon Jacob, all combatants, were drawn to more symphonic expressions of their war experience. Both Vaughan Williams and Cyril Rootham were to use bugle calls, played on the trumpet, in their war-inspired works, the *Pastoral Symphony* (1921) and *To The Fallen* (1915). Bliss's 'symphony' *Morning Heroes* is a work whose emotional structure bears some similarity to the suggested Bugle-Call Symphony; both end with the weightiest movement, associated with the dawn.

In 1916, a year before Lorenz's article, Charles Villiers Stanford claimed that wartime music ought to provide a rallying cry, while acknowledging that this usually produced inferior compositions.[11] Stanford was too old to fight, but was a father-figure to the younger generation, many of whom were his pupils. The soldier Lorenz's simplistic suggestion is in fact more subtle than the older civilian Stanford's notion of music's wartime role. Lorenz's projected symphony is not a rallying cry, more a sentimental record of the musical sounds of war and an attempt to reflect something of the variety of emotions war engenders. He may not have devised the structure of a potential war masterpiece. What he did demonstrate, however, was that even before the Armistice, a need for classical music to respond had been identified, and the call was coming from the general public and soldiers, not the composers themselves. As the timeline suggests, few composers, combatant or civilian, responded to this demand during the conflict (those who were fighting had little opportunity to do so), but the Armistice was the beginning of a decade of compositions by Howells, Vaughan Williams, Bliss, Bridge and Gurney (among others) that mourned, commemorated and reflected upon the war.

As other chapters in this book have observed, the moment of the Armistice is remembered as a moment of profound silence, 'a stillness heard round the world' as Stanley Weintraub describes it.[12] It is the physical stillness marked on paper by the sound recording equipment of the US Army Signal Corps, measuring the sudden absence of gunfire on the Western Front.[13] The Armistice is, then, the negation of two of the quintessential elements that make up music: movement and sound. And yet it is to this very antithesis, to music, that culture turns to express the emotions that are felt in the wake of the war.

Art, literature and architecture all had their parts to play in shaping commemoration; the poetry and words used for formal remembrance services, or the design of cemeteries, quite literally sculpting and shaping remembrance, as Adrian Barlow argues elsewhere in this volume. Music's development had for centuries been bound up with collective expressions of emotion and ritualised occasions (the concert being one such ritual). It was natural that it would constitute part of any public recognition of loss, mourning ritual, or ceremonial commemoration. By 1918 the time for rallying calls had passed, and music had to resume a peacetime role and identity. But what kind of identity would that be? The BBC, ex-combatants, the composers themselves and the general public wishing to be part of some collective musical event all had an interest in how music might be used, and what form it might take as an act of remembrance.

Despite certain composers' alterations of style to reflect their experiences of the war (such as Frank Bridge, whose music became dramatically more dissonant and experimental), little was written during the actual course of the war that could be said to express the experience of combat, or speak for the soldiers themselves. This was primarily for the obvious reason that music during the war was mostly being composed by those not involved in it. Combatants' works came after the war: there are few musical equivalents during wartime to the war poets' immediate responses to the trauma of war. Indeed, it is amazing that any composition could take place in such inhospitable circumstances. Generally, the lack of manuscript paper and access to pianos, and the constant noise and disturbance worked against significant large-scale musical works being produced on active service. Some managed it, however. Cecil Coles began his orchestral suite *Behind the Lines* while in the trenches in 1918, but was killed before he could complete it, and the battle-scarred fragments have only recently been worked into a performable edition. Gurney wrote a handful of his most effective songs in France, 'By A Bierside', his most dramatic, indeed 'monumental', being written 'in a disused Trench Mortar emplacement'.[14]

The composing of commemorative works had for some a sense of great urgency. F. S. Kelly, sailing for Gallipoli in 1915, began his *Elegy* to Rupert Brooke while his friend actually lay dying next to him.[15] Herbert

Howells's *Elegy* for viola, string quartet and string orchestra, written in 1918, is dedicated to his friend Francis Purcell Warren, who had been killed at Mons a year before. The piece demonstrates Howells's understanding even before the end of the war of the need for a new musical expression of grief. His pupil, Alan Ridout, recalls a lecture Howells gave at the Royal College of Music:

> The lecture culminated in something like a testament; so far as I know, and simply by chance, only I fully understood it. He said that he was going to play a recording of a work – what it was, and who it was by, was of no consequence – which summed up all that could be stated in music about death. His exact words were: 'If there is a better expression of the music of mourning, I have yet to hear it.' I happened to know the recording and the work, though I did not let on, and thus became, from that moment, part of the conspiracy. It was his own Elegy.[16]

The fact that such an unlikely lecture was included in the college's programme is highly suggestive. Howells, as one of the generation faced with commemorating war, had consciously contributed to the development of a genre of mourning music that moved far beyond the traditional Requiem Mass.

Initially, the impulse had been to *celebrate* 11 November, rather than transform it into a memorial.[17] The dances and parties celebrating Armistice Day began to tail off in the late 1920s, leaving only the more solemn acts of remembrance such as the Two Minutes' Silence. The maverick composer John Foulds and his partner violinist Maud MacCarthy together wrote the music and libretto for *A World Requiem*, and coined the title 'Remembrance Festival' for their performance of it at the Albert Hall on 11 November 1923. The *Requiem* is a huge, unwieldy work, taking over 1,000 people to perform, and its text contained references to spiritualism that were difficult for some to stomach. Despite its difficulties, it is an intriguing and ambitious work. Foulds and MacCarthy hoped the piece, supported by the British Legion, would be performed throughout the country and become an annual fixture. However, the BBC had other ideas, choosing to ignore the Albert Hall Requiem premiere and instead mark Armistice Night with a broadcast of a far less controversial programme featuring Elgar. By 1927 the Remembrance Festivals had, against Foulds's and MacCarthy's wishes, been taken over by Lord Beaverbrook at the *Daily Express*, and the British Legion had withdrawn its support for the work.[18]

The victory balls and the celebrations of the first few Armistice Nights had served as a means of temporarily recreating the camaraderie of the war years, and to fulfil this need in ex-servicemen and women the *Express* devised the British Legion Festival of Remembrance for Armistice Day in 1927. In place of the ponderous and sombre *World Requiem*, it was an evening of community singing in the Royal Albert Hall, with an audience of ex-combatants, and featured a programme of popular and trench songs favoured by the armed forces. There were places for 10,000 to attend, and uniform was obligatory. H. V. Morton, an ex-soldier and journalist for the *Daily Express*, described the music's role in rekindling both memories and relationships:

> We did not realize until last night that the songs we sang in the Army were bits of history. In them is embalmed the comic fatalism which carried us through four years of hell. How easily we slipped back into it! Cynicism was blown clean out of us. We were young once more as we can never be again and we went deeper into our memories [...]. Thirteen years fell from us. We ceased to see the Albert Hall and the thousands of faces white in the arc lights; we looked into an abyss of memories where long columns passed and repassed over the dusty roads of France, where grotesque, unthinkable things happened day and night – the brief joys, the sharp sorrows of those days, the insane injustices of fate, and above it all the memory of the men we knew so well ... It seemed to me that we had caught the only decent thing in the war – the spirit of comradeship. We had come to the hall as individuals; we were now once more an army marching in our imagination to the old music.[19]

The concerts were hugely popular; the songs' mood of comic fatalism striking just the right note to recall the camaraderie of the war years (or at least a sentimentalised version of it). The concert's formula was repeated throughout the country. The London concert had been broadcast internationally since its inception, and is still an annual fixture, attended by the Royal Family. While it has now become a rather tame part of the tradition that grew up around the Armistice, in its early years it had the power of a musical séance, as Morton's (rather biased) account testifies. This summoning of the dead was powerful and often therapeutic for those who served, but could be threateningly exclusive for those who did not. Music needed to be mobilised through official channels for remembrance, and executive decisions needed to be made to reclaim music from the ex-combatants and find an inclusive musical language that would speak to civilian and combatant alike. By 1936 the BBC was denigrating the event privately in memoranda as a 'sing song', and calling for it to be followed by a suitably elegiac piece of music (to precede three Bible readings) which would 'wash out the taste of the super-sentimental orgy from the Albert Hall and reset the frame for these readings'.[20] The BBC, through a series of memos, meetings and draft programmes, consciously shaped a musical Remembrance Day that still informs the way in which Remembrance Sunday is presented to us now.[21]

A need was identified for a universally accessible music of remembrance for the post-war era that was not exclusively the property of ex-combatants. In something of a *volte face* (after all, Foulds's 'serious' work had been ousted by this 'sing song'), the Royal Albert Hall programmes were again altered to reflect a more classical, less socially divisive idiom. The January 1930 edition of the *Musical Times* includes an anonymous suggested programme for an Armistice Day concert, including Holst's *Ode to Death*, some Parry and some Elgar, which claimed to be a representation of 'the nobler aspects of Armistice Day commemorations':

1. Solo, Chorus and Orchestra – 'God Save the King', arr. Elgar
2. Chorus (unaccompanied) – 'Russian Kontakion for the Departed'
3. Orchestra – 'Mars, the Bringer of War', Holst
4. Solo, Chorus and Orchestra – 'For the Fallen', Elgar
5. Orchestra – 'Venus, the Bringer of Peace', Holst

Interval

6. Chorus and Orchestra – 'Ode to Death', Holst
7. Orchestra – Funeral March from 'Götterdämmerung', Wagner
8. Chorus (unaccompanied) – 'There is an old belief', Parry
9. Chorus and Orchestra – 'Jerusalem', Parry[22]

Through the BBC and Lord Reith's decision making, not only were individual pieces excluded from the canon, but the tone shifted from popular to highbrow, from celebratory to solemn. This process involved not only privileging Elgar above 'Goodbyee', but also excluding pieces specifically written for the purpose of commemorating the Armistice, if, like Foulds's unfortunate *Requiem*, they failed to find favour.

While the BBC drew largely on works that pre-dated the end of the war for its concert programmes for Remembrance Sunday, composers were themselves responding to the war, writing pieces directly or indirectly influenced by it. Some, like Foulds, wrote pieces specifically designed for commemoration; others dedicated works to dead friends.

Bliss's *Morning Heroes*

Literary historian Samuel Hynes suggests that 'one might argue that it is only after the passage of years that recollection can become an act of exorcism'.[23] In his music, Arthur Bliss struggled with the need to detach himself from traumatic loss while also engaging with it. Out of this struggle came the creative work; the work of mourning. Bliss initially attempted to memorialise his brother Kennard through *Battle Variations*, a piece reflecting his war experiences that he returned to repeatedly during the 1920s, but eventually abandoned. He then dedicated the slow movement of his *Suite for Piano* to Kennard in 1925, but this did not relieve him of the sense that he needed to write a large-scale monument for his dead.

Bliss believed that, with Kennard's death, the more promising sibling had been lost. 'As the years passed,' he wrote in his memoir, 'I came to realize more and more what a poignant loss to the family Kennard's death had been. Poet, painter, musician, he was the most gifted of us all.'[24] The decision to write *Morning Heroes* was taken while visiting his brother's grave in France, and the work is dedicated 'To the memory of my brother Francis Kennard Bliss and all other comrades killed in battle.' It is outwardly a celebration of heroism, but was also written to exorcise the composer's recurring post-war nightmare:

> Although the war had been over for more than ten years, I was still troubled by frequent nightmares; they all took the same form. I was still there in the trenches with a few men; we knew the armistice had been signed, but we had been forgotten; so had a section of the Germans opposite. It was a though we were both doomed to fight on till extinction. I used to wake with horror.[25]

Bliss was trapped with the dead and his memories around him, unable to make the transition from a present nightmare to a past, manageable memory. The nature of the dream suggests a curious tension between his view of his combatant self as insignificant and dispensable, and his association in music of his brother with heroism. It seems that his brother's death played a significant part in his post-war mental oppression. While the dead brother is memorialised and remembered, Bliss points to a fear that he, the survivor, has been forgotten; left behind in imagination by the war machine, and in reality by his brother. Bliss's wife later recalled:

> As the months went by it became clear to me what [*Morning Heroes*] was really about. Not so much about war, the emphasis was on courage, on the

> heroism of men and women in wars throughout the ages. Heroism, and waste, and sorrow. And musically *Morning Heroes* is a unity. Whether the words come from *The Iliad*, or Walt Whitman, or a Chinese poet writing twelve hundred years ago, Wilfred Owen or a friend of very long standing, Robert Nichols, all these poems are laced together by the music. By the ideal of heroism.[26]

Morning Heroes' eclectic selection of texts, and their strategic order, reflects the chronological progress of the war, from leave-taking and mass-mobilisation to battles and their aftermath. This is signalled by each of the five movements being given a title: I. Hector's Farewell to Andromache; II. The City Arming; III. Vigil; IV. Achilles Goes Forth Into Battle; and V. Now Trumpeter For Thy Close. The work begins with an extended orchestral prelude, which is subdued and elegiac. By introducing the orchestra before the text, Bliss sets the tone and texture of the work before any specific verbal images. Before the narration begins, the music has already communicated a sense of the 'waste and sorrow' that Lady Bliss describes. This orchestral passage is particularly important, as the text that follows, 'Hector's Farewell to Andromache' from Book VI of Homer's *Iliad*, is (very unusually) spoken by a narrator, necessitating the music to be kept in the background and to be unobtrusive enough not to detract from the spoken voice. The passage describes Hector's wife pleading with him not to go to battle, for the sake of her and their son:

> Nay, Hector, thou art to me father and lady mother, yea and brother, even as thou art my goodly husband. Come now, have pity and abide here upon the tower, lest thou make thy child an orphan, and thy wife a widow.

Hector replies that, as a hero, he must follow his destiny:[27]

> Then great Hector of the glancing helm answered her: 'Surely I take thought of all these things, my wife; but I have very sore shame of the Trojans and Trojan dames with trailing robes, if like a coward I shrink away from battle. Moreover mine own soul forbiddeth me, seeing I have learnt ever to be valiant and fight in the forefront of the Trojans, winning my father's great glory and mine own …

While Hector may indeed have had no choice, the passage raises ambivalent emotions. Hector, in all his glory and greatness, serves here only to frighten his little boy:

> So spake glorious Hector, and stretched out his arm to his boy. But the child shrunk crying to the bosom of his far-girdled nurse, dismayed at his

> dear father's aspect, and in dread at the bronze and horse-hair crest that he beheld nodding fiercely from the helmet's top.

The glorious regalia of war is, in reality, simply destructive and terrifying. Bliss writes that the scenario represents every leave-taking, of every war:

> I cannot as an artist express war except in a general (timeless) sense. Achilles is THE hero, whatever humbler name he may suggest in the minds of us who live now; the parting of Andromache and Hector is the last glimpse that ANY wife catches of her husband; Manhattan epitomizes ALL 'teeming and turbulent cities'.[28]

The texts serve a similar purpose to the Tomb of the Unknown Soldier in Westminster Abbey – every person parted from a loved one by war can use the work to mourn and remember. However, while great pains were taken to ensure the anonymity of the Unknown Soldier, Bliss's text is concerned with a specific couple, and a legendary one at that. Hector and Andromache's parting has been a well-known story since Euripides' *Andromache* and *The Trojan Women*, and has inspired numerous paintings (Jacques–Louis David's *Andromache Mourning Hector* [1783], for instance, and Racine's play *Andromaque* [1667]). In short, the story Bliss has chosen as the receptacle for individuals' emotions and personal histories is one that everyone knows ends tragically. The son, Astyanax, is thrown from the battlements, Andromache is made a concubine and Hector is killed by Achilles.

Despite his archetypal heroism, the heaviness of the funereal musical introduction and the pity Andromache commands cannot fail to call into question the necessity of Hector's actions and choices. While men's role is to kill, women and children must be left vulnerable, killed and enslaved.

> Go thou to thine house and see to thine own tasks, the loom and distaff, and bid thine handmaidens ply their work; but for war shall men provide and I in chief of all men that dwell in Ilios.

Andromache turns back to the house, 'oft looking back and letting fall big tears'.

There is no break between the first and second movement, the lower strings moving straight into a frenetic and bright G major, via a single, pivotal F#. This rush into '*allegro moderato* (with spirit and elation)' pre-empts the text. Walt Whitman's 'The City Arming', from *Drum-Taps* (1865) is a description of New York quickly mobilising itself during the American Civil War. Again, this stands for 'any city or country', and encapsulates the infectious mood of a powerful city united by one purpose. It is chaotic and energised, and the narration is given to the choir, who describe the crowds of civilians and large groups of newly armed soldiers. Through the collective voice of the choir the city speaks. The single voice of the narrator provided an intimacy that was appropriate to the subdued and personal first movement. Now, accompanying the more powerful chorus, the orchestra has free reign to establish its part in the action. Instruments and voices combine in the tumultuous rush to send off the troops. At figure 29, for instance:

> Our hive at daybreak pour'd out its myriads.
> From the houses then and the workshops,
> And through all the doorways,
> Leapt they tumultuous.

The lower instruments provide an urgent, staccato quaver *ostinato*, underpinning the upper strings' military, galloping rhythms, which rise in pitch as the war fever rises in the city. Over this, Bliss makes use of a choir's ability to sing different parts of the text at once, mirroring tenors and sopranos, but allowing the basses to anticipate the altos, adding to the impression of an undisciplined and excited crowd. Both orchestra and choir reach a point of frenzied hysteria on the shouts of 'War! War! An armed race is advancing!' with sopranos and tenors pushed to the absolute limits of their registers, screaming top B flats. This is accompanied by shivering, *tremolandi* strings, urgent triplet figures and *szforzandi* to emphasise the shouts of 'War!' However, the soldiers who have generated such a militaristic frenzy eventually pass on towards the Front, leaving the crowd subdued and absorbed in their own thoughts: 'how elate I watch'd you, where starting off you march'd'.

The divide between civilians and soldiers, women and men, has been established, and the *ppp* ending leads into the third section entitled 'Vigil', in which a translation of the eighth-century Chinese poet Li Tai Po's 'Vigil' is followed by Whitman's 'The Bivouac's Flame', again from *Drum-Taps*. Both are devoid of the frenzy of initial excitement that war can generate. Instead, this section concerns itself with loneliness and isolation. 'Vigil' describes the anxiety of a soldier's wife waiting for news from the Front, whereas Whitman imagines the army at camp, thinking of home. The divide between these feminine and masculine domains is illustrated by the choir, the 'Vigil' being scored for sopranos and altos, while the tenors and basses alone gaze into the 'bivouac's fitful flame'. Here the rhythm is tense, and the contemplations verging on paranoid:

'The shrubs and trees (as I lift my eyes they seem to be stealthily watching me;)' Foreboding turns to homesickness:

> While wind in procession thoughts, O tender and wondrous thoughts,
> Of life and death of home and the past and loved, and of those that are far away.

As the men contemplate the women they left behind, the sopranos and altos re-enter, with a ghostly and wordless descant sung to 'Ah'. Their imagined presence becomes an aural hallucination for the lonely soldier.

Movement IV, 'Achilles Goes Forth Into Battle', begins with an orchestral introduction marked *allegro con fuoco*, which calms down as the choir surveys Achilles ready for action, but resumes its speed and fieriness for an extended coda that lists the names of heroes. It is a roll call that is ambiguous as to whether it is of the living or the dead – the two categories become merged, and the final name, practically screamed by the choir, with a repetition nothing short of neurotic, is that of Hector, slain by Achilles. By moving from the entry into battle to the list of its casualties, Bliss omits the fighting itself, perhaps because of the impossibility of doing justice to the experience of battle in music. Musicologist Eric Blom observed that, rather than attempting to depict war itself, 'the realistic description of battle noises is the least of the composer's aims. It is the emotion engendered in those who come into contact with war, actively or passively, which urged him to write.'[29]

However, Bliss cannot entirely avoid the conflict itself. The first of the final two texts, Wilfred Owen's 'Spring Offensive' (1918), is a description of running into enemy fire. Combined with Robert Nichols's poem 'Dawn on the Somme' (1918), which follows, this final movement is the emotional crux of the work and coincides with Bliss's eventual homing-in on his, and Kennard's, experiences. Finally, Bliss is confronting his own war and his personal memories of the Somme, where he was wounded and his brother killed.

Excitement, glory and sorrow are all emotions that lend themselves to musical expression. However, the abject terror of an attack for the soldiers involved in the First World War is very difficult to convey in music. There is perhaps an established language in poetry, as in Sassoon's 'Attack' (1917):

> Lines of grey, muttering faces, masked with fear,
> They leave their trenches, going over the top,
> While time ticks blank and busy on their wrists,

And hope, with furtive eyes and grappling fists,
Flounders in mud.[30]

Bliss understands only too well the total disorientation that Sassoon describes. He translates it into music by dispensing altogether with pitch and harmony, two of music's ordering devices, and using only narrator and timpani to give Owen's 'Spring Offensive' a chilling immediacy. Even the timpani part, obviously reminiscent of gunfire, is notable for its sparseness and absence; much of the text is set to total silence – the negation of music. Owen's text itself denies the place of music, just as it denies any glory in war: 'No alarms / Of bugles, no high flags, no clamorous haste – '. This is a far cry from the exultant tumult of 'The City Arming'.

It is only as the men actually face the barrage of enemy fire that Bliss allows the timpani to break out from their distant *pianissimo* rumble, to two *forte* chords and a triplet, returning almost instantly to an ominous quiet again. As 'instantly the whole sky burned with fury against them' the timpani only smoulder; the memory is vivid, but Bliss avoids trite word-painting. The recollection of the barrage is eerily drained of sound, lending the episode something of the atmosphere of a silent film. Almost a decade earlier, in 1921, Bliss was asked to write some incidental music for a production of *The Tempest*. With the sounds of the Front fresh in his memory, Bliss used an enormous battery of percussion to illustrate the storm scene. The result was overpowering, shocking London audiences with its violence. But nine years later, when Owen's text called for the actual recreation of the sound-world of the war, he opted for an infinitely more subdued approach. This is partly, of course, to allow the spoken text to be heard. It is suggestive, though, of the internalised, almost subliminal memory, rehearsed and re-rehearsed in silence, long after the guns have ceased firing.

The final stanza, the nearest in the work to the actual description of warfare, is set to total silence:

And there out-fiending all its fiends and flames
With superhuman inhumanities,
Long-famous glories, immemorial shames –
And crawling slowly back, have by degrees
Regained cool peaceful air in wonder –

But the final line, 'why speak they not of comrades that went under?' is recited over a plaintive, compound-time string melody of fluid quavers as the orchestra is gently reintroduced for the final text, easing the listener out of this silent nightmare. Owen's impossible question concerns a silence that in itself communicates meaning. In writing *Morning Heroes*, Bliss is attempting to answer it. After twelve years of being haunted by those who 'went under', he dares now to set this question to music, after so long a silence.

In poetry, the war dead are frequently associated with silence and voicelessness; they are surrounded in our cultural memory with resonant phrases such as Charles Hamilton Sorley's 'millions of the mouthless dead'.[31] By writing a piece of music both for and about the silent soldiers and their dead, Bliss is giving them a voice. *Morning Heroes* is their tribute, and, in the first performances, it became quite literally the ex-soldiers' collective voice; so many were in the orchestra and choir that rehearsals broke down at one point, as they were moved to tears by the work.

Silence and noise, gunfire and its absence, are crucial aspects of the soundscape of war. One of the perversities of the Armistice was that it was experienced as a lack of sound – and frequently described in terms of death and the uncanny. The period immediately after 11 a.m. on 11 November was '*dead* silent', a silence so oppressive it almost became noise:

> The firing died away and an appalling silence prevailed.[32]
> An awesome hush ... The ear strains for the sound of [artillery] arrivals, the tattoo of a machine gun, the crack of a rifle. The lack of exploding missiles becomes oppressive.[33]

Bliss's setting of Owen and Nichols explores the interplay between sound and silence, through Owen's mute survivors, unable or unwilling to speak of dead comrades, and Nichols's silent 'morning heroes'. By giving these texts a musical treatment, Bliss is adding a dimension that is unattainable in poetry; music by definition is a medium that relies on a subtle relationship between sound and silence to convey emotion and meaning. 'Dawn on the Somme' is initially subdued, but builds as the sun rises to a triumphant climax as Nichols imagines the dead rising, ghostly like mist, and disappearing:

> Oh, is it mist, or are these companies
> Of morning heroes, who arise, arise
> Toward the risen god, upon whose brow
> Burns the gold laurel of all victories,
> Hero and heroes' god, th'invincible sun?

This resurrection has no hint of a Christian God. It is an image of exorcism, and Bliss is inscribing into his work his hopes for release from his own demons.

In a radio interview, Lady Bliss recalled:

> My husband had a fine command of the English language, but his use of words was not necessarily to express deep emotions. That was for poetry, that was for poets. He was a musician, and his innermost feelings were expressed as a composer. He had already, after a ravishing trip we made together to Sicily, he had combined poetry with his music to express great happiness. And when, very soon after, came this commission to write a work for the Norwich Festival in 1930 here was an opportunity to express great grief. So he chose the words of other men, and began a requiem for his brother. And this work was written, as he himself said, to sublimate the memories. That it did.[34]

Pieces written to memorialise tend to use text, rather than being absolute (i.e. wordless). This is particularly significant in Bliss's case, as he had been moving away from text-based music in the latter half of the 1920s; *Morning Heroes* marked a return to his earlier interests. Musicologist Andrew Burn suggests that Bliss's failure to represent both Kennard's loss and his own war experience in the aborted *Battle Variations* was because an adequate expression demanded the specificity and power of words and music combined.[35]

Morning Heroes is perhaps the most ambitious and insightful example of the rewriting of the requiem form, before Benjamin Britten's *War Requiem* of 1962. Britten set texts by Wilfred Owen, just as Bliss had done in the central movement of *Morning Heroes*. Britten acknowledged the substantial debt (which is rarely noted in discussion of the *War Requiem*)[36] in a letter to Bliss on his 75th birthday. Britten's strategy was to select poems by Owen that had some bearing or created an ironic commentary on the text of the Requiem Mass. The strategic placing of texts to make a particular point (a technique crucial to works such as the *Serenade for Tenor, Horn and Strings* and the *Nocturne*) was an idea he may well have taken from Bliss. By moving from the historically distant Greeks and Li Tai Po to narrow the focus on to the Somme, the actual location of Kennard's death, the emotional structure of *Morning Heroes* might be understood not only as a modernising of an established musical form, but as a framework specifically crafted to reflect the composer's own cathartic process. In other words, it is a rewriting of the requiem as an act of therapy, both personal and collective.

In his memoir, Bliss writes of his nightmares, and the decision to write *Morning Heroes*: 'I was now at last decisively to exorcise this fear. If sublimation, the externalising of an obsession, can be thought of as a cure, then in my case I have proved its efficacy.'[37] *Morning Heroes* covers the distance Bliss puts between himself and his loss in his writing. What Bliss struggles to articulate in words, he can approach in music. In his own notes to accompany a performance of the work, he writes:

> The finale brings with it the only reference to the Great War. … Only in my reference to the Somme do I describe the particular (particular to us at any rate) and so approach more nearly the memory of him for whom this requiem was chiefly written.[38]

Coda

Early in 1918 Siegfried Sassoon wrote 'Dead Musicians'. The poem reassesses his relationship to the war, his own losses and his uncertain future through an analysis of his changing relationship to music.

> I
> From you, Beethoven, Bach, Mozart,
> The substance of my dreams took fire.
> You built cathedrals in my heart,
> And lit my pinnacled desire.
> You were the ardour and the bright
> Procession of my thoughts toward prayer.
> You were the wrath of storm, the light
> On distant citadels aflare.
>
> II
> Great names, I cannot find you now
> In these loud years of youth that strives
> Through doom toward peace: upon my brow
> I wear a wreath of banished lives.
> You have no part with lads who fought
> And laughed and suffered at my side.
> Your fugues and symphonies have brought
> No memory of my friends who died.
>
> III
> For when my brain is on their track,
> In slangy speech I call them back.
> With fox-trot tunes their ghosts I charm.

"Another little drink won't do us any harm."
I think of ragtime; a bit of ragtime;
And see their faces crowding round
To the sound of the syncopated beat.
They've got such jolly things to tell,
Home from hell with a Blighty wound so neat...
...
And so the song breaks off; and I'm alone.
They're dead ... For God's sake stop that gramophone.

Music can, perhaps uniquely, capture something that has been lost, reawaken a lost sound-world, and offer a window into a past that is otherwise irretrievable. For Sassoon, who was to feel utterly lost after the Armistice, the experience is both torment and solace. The past that it reawakens is, more often than not, peopled by ghosts. In the bleak present, the ghosts and their music offer relief – a way of easing temporarily the grief of loss. In a strange twist of the anticipated silence of the Armistice, it is the silence after the song breaks off – the white noise of the still turning gramophone – that is unbearable.

Samuel Hynes writes: 'the heroic musical tradition would not be sufficient to express this war – [...] there would have to be a music of grief, too'.[39] Such a genre can be seen in the work of the younger generation of combatant and civilian composers, responding to their experiences in the aftermath of the war. It was a genre written out of trauma, with the ghosts of the dead dominating composers' minds. For some people, like Sassoon and Bliss, the silence of the Armistice was unbearable. It was a silence too resonant with loss, with the absence of musicians who should have been there to fill it. Through the writing of such works as *Morning Heroes*, the dead could be remembered and also laid to rest.

Notes

1 Arthur Bliss, *As I Remember* (London: Faber and Faber, 1970), 41.
2 See Jeremy Dibble, 'The Death of a Culture: Germany and British Music Before 1914', in Lewis Foreman, ed., *Oh My Horses! Elgar and the Great War* (Rickmansworth: Elgar Editions, 2001).
3 Arthur Bliss, 'What Modern Composition is Aiming At', a lecture given to the Society of Women Musicians on 2 July 1921, *Musical News and Herald* (23 July 1921), rpt. in *Bliss on Music: Selected Writings of Arthur Bliss 1920–1975*, ed. Gregory Roscow (Oxford: Oxford University Press, 1991), 15.
4 'The Great War: A Documentary', *Musical Times*, 105 (December 1964), 895.
5 Kate Kennedy, 'Ambivalent Englishness: Ivor Gurney's Ludlow and Teme',

First World War Studies, 2, 1 (2011), special issue on *Literature and Music of the First World War*, ed. Kate Kennedy and Trudi Tate, 41–64.

6 It has recently been recorded on CD: *The Spirit of England*, BBC Symphony Orchestra, Susan Gritton, Andrew Kennedy and David Lloyd Jones, Dutton, 2007.

7 Quoted in Lewis Foreman, ed., *Oh My Horses! Elgar and the Great War* (Rickmansworth: Elgar Editions, 2001), 126.

8 Letter of 4 October 1938, quoted in Ursula Vaughan Williams, *Ralph Vaughan Williams, A Biography* (Oxford: Oxford University Press, 1964), 121.

9 Robert Lorenz, 'Suggestions for a "Bugle-Call Symphony"', *Musical Times* (1 July 1917), 308–11.

10 *Musical Times* (1 July 1917), 309.

11 Quoted in Glen Watkins, *Proof Through the Night: Music and the Great War* (Berkeley, CA: University of California Press, 2002), 51.

12 Stanley Weintraub, *A Stillness Heard Round the World: The End of the Great War, November 1918* (London: Allen and Unwin, 1986).

13 Weintraub, *Stillness*, 202.

14 Letter from Ivor Gurney to Marion Scott, 16 August 1916, Gurney Archives, G.41.34.

15 Térèse Radic, ed., *Race Against Time: The Diaries of F. S. Kelly* (Canberra: National Library of Australia, 2004), 36.

16 Alan Ridout, *A Composer's Life* (London: Thames, 1995), 42–3.

17 Adrian Gregory, *The Silence of Memory: Armistice Day 1919–1946* (Oxford: Berg, 1994), ch. 1.

18 For more detail on the series of events that lead to the neglect of Foulds's *A World Requiem*, see James Mansell, 'Musical Modernity and Contested Commemoration at the Festival of Remembrance, 1923–1927', *The Historical Journal*, 52 (2009), 433–54.

19 H. V. Morton, *Daily Express* (12 November 1927), 2.

20 Gregory, *The Silence of Memory*, 84, quoting BBC memo ADM to Herbage and Reybould, 21 August 1936, R 34/227/2, BBC written Archives Centre, Caversham.

21 For a detailed analysis of the discussions within the BBC, see Rachel Cowgill, 'Canonising Remembrance: Music for Armistice Day at the BBC, 1922–27', *First World War Studies*, 2, 1 (2011), special issue on *Music and Literature of the First World War*, ed. Kate Kennedy and Trudi Tate, 75–107.

22 'Armistice Day Music', by 'Descant', Newcastle-upon-Tyne, *Musical Times* (1 January 1930), 58.

23 Samuel Hynes, *A War Imagined: The First World War and English Culture* (London: Pimlico, 1992), 425.

24 Bliss, *As I Remember*, 45.

25 Bliss, *As I Remember*, 96.

26 Lady Trudi Bliss, in an interview for a radio programme 'The Making of Morning Heroes', compiled and written by Malcolm Brown, 9 November 1985.

27 For a discussion of heroism in *Morning Heroes*, see Alison Hennegan, '"Fit for Heroes": Bliss, Britten and Requiems', *First World War Studies*, 2, 1 (2011), special issue on *Music and Literature of the First World War*, ed. Kate Kennedy and Trudi Tate, 109–19.

28 Arthur Bliss, *Monthly Musical Record*, LX, 718 (1 October 1930), 290, rpt. in *Selected Writings*, ed. Roscow, 60.

29 Eric Blom, notes to accompany a BBC broadcast of *Morning Heroes*, *The Music Teacher* (March 1931), 149.

30 Siegfried Sassoon, 'Attack', in *The War Poems*, ed. Rupert Hart-Davis (London: Faber and Faber, 1983), 95.

31 C. H. Sorley, Untitled ['When you see millions of the mouthless dead]' (1915), in Brian Gardner, ed., *Up the Line to Death: The War Poets 1914–1918* (London: Methuen, 1964), 45–6.

32 Quoted in Weintraub, *Stillness*, 198.

33 Captain Wendell Westover of the 4th Machine Gun Battalion, quoted in Weintraub, *Stillness*, 198–9.

34 Lady Bliss, interview, 1985, Sound Archive, British Library.

35 Andrew Burn, '"Now, Trumpeter for thy Close": The Symphony "Morning Heroes": Bliss' Requiem for his Brother', *Musical Times*, 126 (November 1985), 666–8.

36 But see Hennegan, '"Fit for Heroes"'.

37 Bliss, *As I Remember*, 96.

38 Bliss, 'Morning Heroes', in *Selected Writings*, ed. Roscow, 60.

39 Hynes, *A War Imagined*, 37–8.

11

Sacrifice defeated: The Armistice and depictions of victimhood in German women's art, 1918–24

Claudia Siebrecht

In October 1918 the German National Women's Association published a testimony on peace, 'Der Bund Deutscher Frauenvereine zum Frieden', that claimed to express the silent emotions of millions of German women. Contributing to the public debate on whether Germany should settle for peace or continue hostilities, the authors declared that:

> German women believe that it is a question of national integrity and duty to the dead who died for the honour of the fatherland, that the German nation will not bend to any measures that bear the character of 'punishment'. Lest the German nation accepts conditions that deny the memory of its dead [...], German women are prepared to mobilise their forces for a defensive battle until the very end.[1]

In the new spirit of world justice and international cooperation, the women insisted that it was dishonest to present peace measures that seemed to be designed purely to humiliate the defeated nation. It was impossible, moreover, to trust a League of Nations that was to be founded on 'shattered German honour'. For the authors, the war had been a necessary, defensive and existential conflict, selflessly supported by German women. Throughout the war years, husbands and sons had heroically sacrificed their lives while 'the cruelty of the means of extermination expanded and women and children were forced to endure the enemy's illegal blockade'. 'History has shown,' the authors concluded, 'that no other nation on earth has had to face such pressures of fighting for its mere existence and that no other nation has had to deliver greater sacrifices.'

The document gives us some idea of the ways in which the hopes and expectations of German women for a new and worthwhile post-war order were crushed by the prospects emerging from the peace negotiations. The wartime suffering and sacrifices endured by German women were supposed to be redeemed once the German forces had succeeded on the battlefield and many continued to see military victory as the only true redemption of their sacrifice.[2] The text also shows just how desperately the organised women's movement, which claimed to represent millions, clung to Germany's fading military strength in the final months of the war. In addition, it suggests that national honour was tied to sovereignty and power and seen as personal property, an attitude that heightened the emotive nature of the public debate on the meaning of defeat and peace.[3]

The Armistice was not simply a question of ending the war, but a particular way of ending the war, and German women, like the German population as a whole, were highly conflicted on the issue. Although public protests and left-wing anti-war activism, in which women played a prominent role, had intensified over the course of 1918,[4] for many Germans, the meaning of the war was intimately linked with the fate of those who fought and died in it. Members of the bourgeois women's movement were particularly hostile to the idea of abandoning the national cause they had passionately supported since August 1914, and found it difficult to accept the nature of the war's end.[5] Although not as uncompromising, women more generally, including women artists, also displayed ambiguous attitudes to the prospective peace as they contemplated in letters and diaries what defeat would mean for their wartime sacrifices. The images of hunger, homelessness and material hardship that prevail in the art that women produced between 1919 and 1924 constitute a striking shift from the key themes depicted during the war years. Although female artists had represented civilian sacrifice and suffering while the war was ongoing, the focus had been on the emotional pain and challenges experienced by bereaved women and not on the misery of those enduring quotidian hardship. Why then did female artists start portraying civilian economic destitution, and in particular female deprivation, once the war had ended?

Throughout the war years, mass death on the battlefield was somewhat mitigated in public discourse by the belief in a necessary defensive war, the anticipated victory and a new post-war order. Although the persuasive power of such connections was more limited on a private and emotional level, defeat nonetheless meant the collapse of a broader frame of reference in which painful and traumatic experiences had been located. It was not only the military deaths that now appeared futile;

women also found it difficult to reconcile ongoing civilian suffering with a lost war. Economic and military demobilisation brought additional hardship and, according to Greg Eghigian, produced a collective mentality of resentment as the German people translated their wartime losses and sacrifices into entitlements. As these were only partially met by the struggling new state, Eghigian argues, many Germans felt betrayed, saw their sense of national belonging undermined and became susceptible to radical politics.[6] Yet while female politicians, activists and artists were very much concerned with the suffering of their own sex and that of their children, the purpose of highlighting and depicting female deprivation was initially not, or not primarily, about claiming state benefits, but about coming to terms with the Armistice and coping with ongoing emotional and physical suffering.

Drawing on both visual and written sources, this chapter explores the context and prevalence of images of civilian material suffering in German women's art in the immediate aftermath of the war and considers examples from the *oeuvre* of Martha Schrag, Lotte Prechner, Käte Lassen and the most well-known German female artist of the period, Käthe Kollwitz. The highly evocative images produced by these artists reflect the way in which the economic and social displacement of the early post-war years became intertwined with the memory of wartime sacrifice. The apparently unnecessary cessation of hostilities deeply affected women's responses to the end of the war and transformed the ways in which women perceived their emotional and physical hardship.[7] No longer, it seems, were women prepared to suffer for a conflict that had ended and a state that was falling apart. The moral economy of sacrifice that had pertained during the war years had shifted as soldiers ceased to carry the burden of national defence and were no longer those who delivered the main sacrifice; this load had passed to the civilian men, women and children.

The images can be further understood as a response to the so-called *Dolchstosslegende*, the populist accusation that betrayal by various groups on the home front, supposedly including socialists, profiteers and Jews, had caused military defeat. This populist view also explicitly alleged that women's wartime hunger protests and inability to endure material shortages had undermined the morale and fighting spirit of the troops.[8] Portraying starving and homeless women and their children as suffering victims thus countered these accusations. Showing women passively suffering as innocent victims contradicted the stereotype of the disloyal and deceitful female. Contrary to the allegations, women from the middle classes had consented to and even voluntarily observed the officially maintained silence regarding civilian experiences of hardship during the war years.[9]

With the cessation of hostilities, and under the radically changed circumstances of the post-war world, however, the silent suffering of German civilians could no longer be rationalised as a (voluntary) contribution to the war effort. Now civilian hunger was reframed as a human catastrophe brought about by the harsh peace and the ongoing Allied naval blockade. The rationale for sacrifice had ceased with an Armistice that, for many, did not offer a redemptive context and was widely viewed as undeserved and unjust. In German women's art, this transformation is mirrored in a general sense of anxiety, dark atmosphere and a distinct absence of joy over peace. The most striking motif in these images is the repeated representation of skeletal women and children. Although civilian hunger had been a fact of German civilian life since at least 1916, the artists' focus on women's physical vulnerability, suffering and weakness after the Armistice was new. Women and children were now shown as the unambiguous victims of the war, a trope that continued to be regularly invoked until the mid-1920s.

Coming to terms with the Armistice

In 1914 the female cultural and political elite, and bourgeois women more generally, had been active and outspoken in their support for the war effort, had identified with German war aims and accepted the endurance of wartime sacrifice as their civic duty.[10] As the conflict wore on and the death tolls on the various battlefronts mounted, women's attitudes to the war became more conflicted as they struggled to reconcile their patriotism and loyalty to their male relations at the Front with bereavement and emotional trauma. This did not lead to an outright rejection of war or an embracing of pacifism, but it did give rise to ambivalent feelings about the conflict.[11] As the military prospects for the German armed forces began to look decidedly uncertain from the summer of 1918, these feelings increasingly included fear, disappointment, disbelief and confusion. Belinda Davis makes the case that German women at large vehemently rejected the war by 1918 and refers to correspondence in which women ask their men to leave the Front and return home. She also argues that women made public demands for an immediate cessation of the conflict from the beginning of 1918.[12] Yet the evidence suggests that during the final year of the war, women's attitudes regarding the conflict were more complex and ambiguous, and many women were uncertain about how to respond to the political and military situation that emerged in the late summer and autumn of 1918.

The correspondence of the Westphalian artist Ida Gerhardi shows, for example, that she continued to believe in and support German military action throughout the summer of 1918, expressing her faith in God's assistance and Hindenburg's ability.[13] Her refusal to even consider German defeat borders on denial, but also reflects the official information policy that sought to cover up the strategic failure of the German military on the Western Front.[14] Writing to her son Hans on 20 October 1918, the Berlin-based artist Käthe Kollwitz also confronted her own conflicted feelings regarding the impending peace, but appears to have been more realistic about the military outlook:

> It seems unbearable to accept the demands of the Entente and yet the thought of resistance to the very end seems even more unbearable. If this happens, then Germany will be dead and it should live. [...] These are truly hard times. Outside it is still war and it is not a victorious war. Inside we have epidemics and deprivation.[15]

Kollwitz's attitude to the war had been shaped by the loss of her son Peter in Flanders in September 1914. Having supported his wish to join the war effort and shared his idealism, the artist was deeply traumatised by his death. Yet despite, or perhaps because of, her bereavement and feelings of guilt, she found it very difficult to accept that the cause for which her son had given his life now appeared to be lost.

Other women writing in the final weeks of the war focus on the unjust nature of the impending peace. Although many women desperately wished for the war to end, they quite clearly desired a victorious peace, not a shameful military defeat and the territorial disintegration of the homeland. This sentiment was emphatically expressed in a declaration signed by over one thousand women, from a range of different social backgrounds, in Karlsruhe in mid-October 1918.[16] Free from the direct influence of any women's organisations or female professional associations, this declaration stated that German women truly desired the end of 'the murder', but faced with 'French and Slavic claims of German lands and British greed', which were understood to be behind the *Gewaltfrieden* (enforced peace), women were ready to act in self-defence. Just like German men, the signatories insisted, German women were prepared to continue making sacrifices for the homeland. The declaration, a copy of which was sent to the Chancellor, was held by at least one journalist to reflect a general mood among German women.[17] Such a claim is difficult to quantify, but, as with the BDF's 'testimony on peace', it indicates that a considerable number of German women found it difficult to accept the realities of defeat.

The uncertainty about precisely what the Armistice would lead to was compounded by the fear that a dishonourable peace would mean that wartime sacrifices had been made in vain. In early October 1918, Paula B., a war widow from Cologne, noted in her diary that after Germany had begun peace negotiations with US President Woodrow Wilson the nation wanted to end the war at all costs. She felt that it was disgraceful that the hardship experienced throughout the country had forced Germany to give in, as she believed that the situation at the Front was still tenable. She bemoaned the fact that it would drive one insane if 'all the precious blood was shed for nothing, and all the sacrifices were in vain'.[18] B. made these observations while recovering from a mental and physical breakdown in a sanatorium. Contemplating the end of the conflict brought her no relief, but instead evoked feelings of bitterness, anger and fear for the future.

Considering her wartime experiences, B.'s adamant rejection of the end of the war is quite striking. Widowed in 1914 after her husband died of typhoid on the Western Front, she struggled to care for her mother and three children. As her husband's army pension was insufficient to live on, she worked at a number of different jobs at the same time. The hardship of her daily life, the pain of her bereavement and the physical exhaustion and desperation of merely trying to make ends meet brought her to breaking point, and references to suicide appear at intervals in her writing. B. took in lodgers and recommenced training as a singer, hoping her voice would provide her with better-paid professional opportunities. She constantly sought to improve the financial situation of her family, which worsened after the end of the war when she lost the family house at a compulsory sale. The war had caused B. intense emotional pain and made her life one of constant hardship and struggle, and yet she did not welcome the Armistice.[19]

Gertrude P., wife of a Lutheran minister in the town of Stolpe in northern Germany, commented on the end of the war in her diary. Recalling the fate of her son and his experiences over the course of the summer of 1918, she writes: 'he predicted the collapse of Germany and when he was home on leave he spoke about this with much worry and sorrow, which we dismissed as pessimism. But he did not have to experience it [the collapse] in the end.' She describes how her son Wilhelm had tried to join the army from the outbreak of the war, but had been repeatedly rejected because he had only three fingers on his left hand. Given his sense of rejection – she recalls her son stating that he was 'not even worthy to die for his fatherland' – P. was pleased when he was finally allowed to enlist in the later stages of the war when recruits had become scarce. He was killed by a shell blast at the Front on 4 November 1918; the telegram announcing his death reached the family on 11 November.[20] The Armistice for this family thus came one week too late, but P. adopts a fairly neutral tone in her writing and is descriptive rather than emotional when talking about the loss of her son in the last week of the war. There is no obvious sense of bitterness, since her son had desperately wanted to be a soldier, but neither is there joy or relief about the end of the conflict.

The difficulty of coming to terms with the perceived undeserved peace is evident in many women's testimonies. The acute desire to see wartime sacrifices redeemed had been fuelled by the propaganda campaigns of the military authorities that deliberately targeted women's allegiance to the national cause during the war years. Such propaganda activities continued, and even intensified, after the military situation had become desperate for the German forces in the wake of the combined Allied attacks of August 1918 when the army on the Western Front had already begun to disintegrate.[21] On 1 September 1918, for example, the state of Württemberg in southern Germany celebrated 'Women's Sunday', an event initiated by the military authorities in Stuttgart that sought to strengthen women's morale and demonstrate how vital their continuing support was for 'the nation's final victory'.[22] In close cooperation with the local clergy, the propaganda officer of the Stuttgart headquarters, Heinrich Hermelink, veteran of the conflict and professor of theology at Marburg University, had organised sermons, speeches and activities that commended women of all classes for their contribution to the war effort. Pamphlets were distributed that appealed to women's duty to endure, as any 'weakness would undermine both the spirit and the strength of the soldiers who continued to defend the fatherland in the field'.[23] The authorities put significant moral pressure on women to remain a source of strength and support for the men in the trenches. Their influence on men's morale was highly valued and military officials hoped that women's encouragement would remobilise the spirit of the troops.[24] The idea that Germany was still fighting a defensive war was resurrected, and strengthened the unrealistic belief that a victorious military outcome was still possible. Women were thus deliberately made to share the responsibility for the outcome of the war. The evidence suggests that this was certainly something that some women struggled to come to terms with on a personal level.

After it had become clear that the military situation was indeed hopeless, the thought of yet more soldiers' deaths for an apparently 'lost cause' had, for some, become unbearable. This was the position adopted by Käthe Kollwitz after much reflection. Agitated after reading a public appeal by the poet Richard Dehmel in October 1918 demanding that all capable men should volunteer to mobilise for war and continue fighting whatever the cost,[25] she carefully formulated a public statement. In her *Response to Dehmel*, Kollwitz insists that continued human losses would hit Germany much harder than the loss of any territories, and offers a reinterpretation of 'national honour', which was commonly thought to be violated by the punitive peace conditions. She argues that Germany had to follow the example of Russia, a nation that had accepted a harsh peace in order to save its remaining strength for domestic reconstruction. Germany should proudly accept the 'forced peace' in the awareness that no honour was lost in bowing to forces of manifestly superior strength. She expresses her admiration for Dehmel, who at the age of 50 had volunteered in 1914 and again in 1918, but insists that 'it would be irresponsible to demand that thousands of youths sacrifice their unlived lives'. Evoking the words of Goethe over those of Dehmel she ends with the quotation, 'sowing seeds should not be milled'.[26]

Dehmel's appeal was published four years to the day after Kollwitz's son Peter had been killed in Flanders, a coincidence which affected her response. She had discussed her thoughts with a friend of Peter's, Hans Koch, who had volunteered with him in 1914, and his visit offered her great reassurance. She remarked in her diary how important it was to her that Koch remained unresponsive to Dehmel's appeal:

> Today it is the 22nd of October. Four years ago tonight. Hans Koch was here, he brought flowers for Peter. I spoke with him about Dehmel's appeal to fight to the end and read to him what I wrote about it. He said, and this was very important to me, that now he would no longer go to war voluntarily.[27]

Kollwitz's response was not immediately printed in the press, but was eventually published in several daily newspapers including the SPD organ *Vorwärts* and the liberal Berlin paper *Vossische Zeitung*. Her correspondence and diary entries from the period reveal the degree to which her attitude to war and peace evolved between October and November 1918. In her correspondence with her elder son, Hans, she regularly tries to clarify her own position and explains that she does not see herself as a pacifist, but feels that sacrifices could no longer be justified:

> I am not a politician and writing is not my thing. But I had to say something as things came to a head and I wrote about the idea of fighting until the very end. [...] What had to be in 1914 does not have to be now. Oh, I wish I could speak with angels' tongues now and prevent the final fight. What use could this possibly be? And what does it mean now, to die 'honourably'? The meaning of honour has changed.[28]

Despite the artist's opposition to the continuation of hostilities, she also writes quite openly about her dislike of radical anti-war socialists, though she admired them for the changes they were bringing about. She writes that she could see a resurfacing of the ideas that her son Peter had gone to war for.[29] The hopes for the renewal and cultural reform of Germany that so many artists and intellectuals had pinned on the war in 1914 were now, it seemed, pinned on the revolution.[30]

Over the course of the Armistice negotiations, Germany's political leadership was relieved of its duties. The Kaiser reluctantly abdicated and fled to the Netherlands and state affairs fell into the hands of councils that were formed in the various German states. These were comprised mostly of soldiers, sailors and workers, but artists and intellectuals also formed groups and councils and sought to play an active role in reshaping German politics and society.[31] Female left-wing political figures were actively involved in the revolutionary press, and women writers and artists sympathised with the idealism and promises of socialist rhetoric.[32] Some women also became involved in the artists' groups that emerged in the wake of the revolution. Female artists in the Berlin-based *Novembergruppe*, for example, included Dora Hitz, Katharina Heise, Margarete Kubicka and Ines Wetzel, while Irma Stern and Emmy Roeder were involved in the *Arbeitsrat für Kunst* (Workers' Council for Art). Other women, Hannah Höch being the most prominent example, were involved in the Berlin Dada group, which was perhaps the most radical and most political force in German post-war visual culture.[33] For some, including Kollwitz, the energy and idealism of these groups represented a glimmer of hope that their loved ones had not died in vain.[34] Kollwitz herself attended meetings of the *Arbeitsrat für Kunst* and the *Novembergruppe* and listened to speeches given by representatives of the Spartakus group, independent socialists and social democrats. She also approved of many points raised in the programme of the 'council of intellectual workers', and although she did not find a true political home, she viewed the revolution as an important achievement.

The poet and philosopher Ricarda Huch held a similar position. In a letter written in September 1918, she states that while the breakdown of such old great powers was somewhat tragic, 'one has to concede that they would not have collapsed if they had not already been in a state of decay and no longer alive and rooted in people's hearts. Their downfall thus leaves one generally cold.'[35] She goes on to assert that even before the war she had felt that German culture needed renewal, and closes by declaring her admiration for the intensity of the 'movement', and expressing her faith that after all the bitterness of the past years, 'new life' would finally emerge. As historian Klaus von Beyme has observed, however, most of the post-war artists' groups were revolutionary in terms of their rhetoric and in the manifestos they published, but this rarely translated into action, and many artists soon became disillusioned with their 'false idealism'.[36] Despite adapting revolutionary slogans such as 'liberty, fraternity and equality', the politicised art world was soon as fragmented as the world of politics with one revolutionary organisation accusing the other of not being revolutionary enough.[37]

Since the 'successful' Russian Revolution in 1917 and over the course of 1918, socialist ideas had found some resonance among female artists who were attracted by the utopian promise of a radical political alternative. Their engagement with these ideas is, to some degree, reflected in portraits of its fathers and figureheads. Artist Katharina Heise, for example, produced a woodcut of Karl Marx for the front page of the Expressionist journal *Die Aktion*, for an issue celebrating the centenary of Marx's birth in early 1918.[38] At around the same time, Wismar-based artist Sella Hasse created a linocut portrait of Gustav Landauer, a key figure in the revolution in Bavaria who was murdered by the *Freikorps* in 1919.[39] Käthe Kollwitz's drawings and woodcuts representing the murdered Karl Liebknecht also express respect for his ideas and spirit of commitment, and regret over his fate. Yet while these images are certainly significant, one must resist the temptation to read them as statements of political allegiance. As Kollwitz reflected in 1920 when contemplating a woodcut she had produced that depicted the workers saying their goodbyes to Liebknecht, she still felt confused politically. Indeed, she seems to have been ashamed of her own ambivalence:

> How cowardly is my attitude, how deep is my inner confusion. I cannot commit, not even to pacifism, and continue to flounder. If I am praised

> on occasion as revolutionary, I remain silent. My rejection of uniting with the young workers is partially rooted in my fear that my indecision will be recognised and I would be dropped.[40]

As an artist and as a woman, Kollwitz felt that she had the right to take in and portray the emotional content of events. She therefore reasoned that she should be able to depict the workers parting from Liebknecht without subscribing to Liebknecht's political views.[41] Despite some initial enthusiasm for the ideals of the revolution, the division, violence and radicalism of post-war politics were rejected by many German women. The world war was over, but peace by no means prevailed on what had been the home front, and daily life in Germany was widely characterised by hunger, hardship and homelessness.

Depicting victimhood

Weimar culture is generally perceived as an intense engagement with, sometimes even a radical confrontation of, the political and social circumstances that prevailed in Germany and urban life and modernity in general. Artists experimented with new media, new art forms and different styles, and the visual arts reflected and impacted upon the ways in which people saw the world and understood who they were.[42] The art of the 1920s is associated in particular with the formation of new gender identities, as Marsha Meskimmon has shown in her study of women artists in Weimar Germany. By offering challenging visual interpretations of women's roles that included the prostitute, the mother, the housewife, the new woman and the *garçonne*, women negotiated their place in society throughout the decade.[43] Although many of these images reflect social and political advancements for women, depict new professional careers and offer new perspectives on female sexuality, Meskimmon argues that just as women did not achieve social equality, so they did not succeed in gaining equality in Germany's cultural communities. In the immediate post-war period defeat and demobilisation caused identity battles of a different kind as artists dealt with the place of women in the wake of defeat.

The following images by Käte Lassen, Sella Hasse, Martha Schrag and Käthe Kollwitz provide examples of these artists' post-war work. They cover a range of different themes, from unemployment and displacement to harrowing images of hunger and famine. The artists are particularly concerned with the suffering of women and often portray mothers unable to provide food or shelter for their children. Men are largely absent from these images, as the artists portray the fatherless families that emerged over the course of the conflict. The high death toll at the Front impacted on demographics, and widowed mothers became a large and newly visible social group.[44] The only men that we see in these images are either disabled veterans or malnourished civilians, who, like the women, continue to endure hardship and suffer under the legacy of the conflict. Primarily, however, women artists focused on their own sex with dark, sad images that convey despair and anxiety in both style and aesthetics. The strong thematic and stylistic cohesion of these artworks, and in particular the recurring motifs of the skeletal mother and dying infant, powerfully express the artists' common concerns and anxieties. Although the nature of the art implies a social and moral commentary, the artists do not explicitly blame any guilty party. The experience of war on the home front and the manner in which the moral economy of the war affected civilians are key to both the artists' wartime and post-war work.

Northern German artist Käte Lassen produced a range of images of post-war life in her community. Much of her work is set at the seaside and shows individuals as well as groups of women and men outdoors, on the beach, in the dunes and by the sea. The strong presence of nature has a consoling force. These drawings and paintings contrast sharply with a series Lassen produced simultaneously that depict people, usually women, in urban environments, struggling with the routines of daily life in times of severe economic deprivation. In these scenes, groups of women or men assemble outside in the streets and on corners and, like the disabled veterans begging in the streets, become a very visible presence in daily life. Lassen's etching *Times of Need* (*Notzeit*) (fig. 11.1) depicts a group of women, some of whom gather at a corner while others walk aimlessly along the road. The women are all barefoot and their clothes appear simple and threadbare. Their faces are haggard and they all wear the same tired expression while their posture and body language mirror the burdensome nature of their lives and reflect the inertia and helplessness caused by poverty.

This sense of dislocation and disorientation as women struggle to cope with changing circumstances reappears in many of the images. Depictions of hardship, unemployment and homelessness express a general uncertainty, anxiety and bitterness, and address the fate of thousands of refugees, impoverished families and demobilised soldiers who fell victim to the severe housing shortage in Germany in the aftermath of the conflict.[45] The populations of German city centres had exploded in the nineteenth

11.1 Käte Lassen, *Times of Need* (*Notzeit*), around 1920. Pencil.

century and providing housing for the rising working population in the cities had already become a problem for municipal authorities in the decades before 1914. The outbreak of war interrupted urban planning and halted construction, so that by 1918 there was an estimated shortage of 800,000 dwellings.[46] Although the Weimar state would become known for its progressive housing developments, Bauhaus architecture and modern living, this development was prompted by a severe crisis that intensified with millions of refugees and forced migrants on the move in post-war central Europe.[47] Returning soldiers who had no place to go and fatherless families who were no longer able to pay rents further increased the number of homeless Germans. Many became dependent on the good will of neighbours and communities until state regulations were introduced and charity organisations were able to assist the needy.[48]

Cologne-base artist Lotte Prechner, whose post-war work is comprised almost exclusively of Expressionist-style woodcuts and linocuts, engaged intensely with the fate of refugees in her art and frequently depicted women and children walking towards an uncertain destination. The woodcut *Without Homeland* (*Heimatlos*) (fig. 11.2) was produced between 1918 and 1920. The image evokes a deep sense of disorientation and abandonment, showing a small family, a mother and two children, outdoors at night without shelter or protection. The mother is sitting down, tired and exhausted with a despairing facial expression while her children are looking to be comforted. The title of the piece is significant; the mother and her children are not simply homeless, but actually without a homeland. Prechner conveys the sense that people experienced different forms of displacement. Some were uprooted by losing their homes; others faced the disappearance, or complete reshaping, of their native states as a result of the collapsing empires and the redrawing of national borders in post-war Europe.

The most harrowing images produced by women artists in post-war Germany deal with the issue of hunger. The 1919 linocut *Famine* (*Hungersnot*) (fig. 11.3) by artist Sella Hasse shows an apocalyptic scene in which people appear to be losing the battle for survival. It portrays a group made up mostly of women and children, possibly a family, sitting close to each other in an open field. They have no shelter and appear worn out and weakened. The adults' faces are marked by deep lines and, again, despairing expressions. The artist captures the famished physicality of both adults and children with the raw medium of the linocut accentuating shape and form. The image presents death by starvation as an impending and inescapable fate. The inability of the mother on the left to feed her children carries a particular symbolic weight. A mother too weak and malnourished to breastfeed her infant presents a stark contrast to the traditional maternal role of carer and protector of her children. The child on the far left with its protruding ribcage and the weakened, crawling child in the foreground represent the hunger and suffering

11.2 Lotte B. Prechner, *Without Homeland* (*Heimatlos*), 1918–20. Woodcut.

of the innocent. The fields in the background are dotted with foraging people searching, apparently in vain, for remnants of the harvest, while the man in the middle of the group sustains a body posture that indicates helplessness, despair and possibly represents a form of prayer,

11.3 Sella Hasse, *Famine* (*Hungersnot*), 1919. Woodcut.

or acceptance of the inevitable. The entire sky is filled with black ravens, traditional heralds and symbols of death.[49] In this image they are part of a metamorphosis as people who have already died of hunger ascend to the sky and join the flock of birds. The figure playing the pipe on the right is evocative of the traditional cultural association with the otherworldly, the transient and with death, and symbolises the looming fate of the suffering people.[50]

Artist Martha Schrag produced a portfolio of lithographs inspired by the revolution. Entitled *Storms* (*Stürme*), her series presents the post-war phase as a moment of great uncertainty. In her series, the end of the war as a potential moment of hope and a new beginning is overshadowed by the severe hardship endured by vulnerable sections of the population. *The Dying* (*Das Sterben*) (fig. 11.4) depicts a mother holding an infant in her arms. Both appear haggard and close to starvation. Here Schrag focuses on the vulnerability of those suffering from hunger, rather than their physicality. The mother embracing an infant on her lap is reminiscent of a traditional *pietà* motif. Over the course of the conflict, some artists had begun to use Christian iconography in their work, and the

11.4 Martha Schrag, *The Dying* (*Das Sterben*), 1920. Lithograph.

pietà was employed not only to draw a link between the sacrifice of the soldier and that of Christ, but also to highlight the emotional pain and bereavement of mothers. In the aftermath of the conflict, the *pietà* was used on war memorials, showing mothers holding their dead soldier-sons. The civilian *pietà* depicted by Schrag thus present a strong counter-image, highlighting the sacrifice of innocents.

The very real social and economic difficulties that prevailed in Germany after the Armistice were, for many Germans, a direct result of the ongoing Allied naval blockade. Food shortages had affected Germany since the end of 1914 and the food policies of the war years had seen rationing, black-market trade, shortages and hunger protests. By the winter of 1916 the situation had become severe, and by 1917 the official food allocation was down to 1,000 calories per day, approximately half of the daily requirement.[51] This affected the civilian population most, as army food reserves were still largely intact. An estimated 300,000 extra civilian deaths were caused by food shortages during the war, with women affected most severely.[52] N. P. Howard argues that continuing the blockade after the Armistice was a deliberate strategy to prevent the resurgence of German military power. It contributed greatly to an increase in civilian mortality and the spread of disease, and brought famine conditions to central Europe.[53] Howard writes that conditions deteriorated severely in 1918, and that in October and November more than 3,500 people were dying each day of hunger and malnutrition. Deaths among women in all age groups were 25 per cent higher than in peacetime and the health of pregnant women was particularly at risk.[54]

Economic and material shortages had been endured by many in the context of the war when victory was still anticipated, but were not accepted as part of the peace. The injustice seemed obvious and was perceived as an atrocity, as the continuation of a war against innocents. The economic situation of the central powers was in extreme disarray, and many contemporary observers believed that the naval blockade was directly responsible for the plight of the population. Yet while the blockade contributed to the situation, it is difficult to quantify its actual effects.[55] Alan Kramer points out that, in 1914, Germany was still self-sufficient and imported only 10 per cent of its food. Like Jay Winter, he argues that the war economy and stretched resources for the duration of the conflict, combined with patterns of distribution and existing inequalities, were the main cause of the famine-like situation in Germany.[56]

In public discourse as well as in women's domestic and international politics, however, the ongoing naval blockade was held responsible for civilian suffering in Germany, and was for many a continuation of the war experience. The 'hunger blockade' was the key theme for female delegates in the new Weimar parliament, and a subject for their joint political action beyond party affiliations. The first motion jointly proposed by female delegates in February 1919 and passed by the parliament addressed the continuity and injustice of the *Hungerblockade*, which caused, the declaration states, a high number of deaths among young children, pregnant women and the weak, the old and the sick.[57] The war had ended, the declaration states, and yet this 'atrocious means of war' had not been stopped, but had instead become more severe. Appealing to 'humanity and justice', the declaration demanded the immediate suspension of the blockade, and also requested the prompt return of German prisoners of war.

Women's international peace politics also provided a context in which the peace regulations were criticised and feelings of victimhood were nurtured. At the women's peace conference in Zurich in 1919, delegates made conciliatory gestures to the Germans, and women from former belligerent countries cooperated in the name of world peace.[58] The first item on the agenda was the lifting of the economic blockade. The women denounced the 'man-made famine, epidemic disease and unemployment in central Europe as a disgrace to civilisation'. Some of these activists travelled through defeated countries to document the privations they believed were caused by the blockade; they also organised relief measures. The women of the International League for Peace and Freedom attacked the Versailles Treaty as an instrument which could only lead to future war. The punitive reparations and secret treaties caused women to protest to US President Wilson. The women's delegation, moreover, demanded a peace that specifically included women's rights in an international charter of human rights. In the aftermath of the conference, local chapters of the Women's International League for Peace and Freedom were held and summer schools were organised. A permanent delegation was set up to lobby the League of Nations for peace, disarmament and gender equality.[59] Yet even after the blockade was lifted at the Versailles conference, the economic destitution of women and children in Germany could not be resolved, and was now aggravated by inflation and economic breakdown.

The hardship of daily life and the burden carried by women provide the theme of the lithograph *The Yoke* (*Das Joch*) (fig. 11.5) by Martha Schrag from 1920. The word 'yoke' has a double meaning, suggesting both the agricultural tool and the physical plight of the people, and both

11.5 Martha Schrag, *Das Joch* (*The Yoke*), 1920. Lithograph.

meanings are present in this image. In the foreground we can see two women ploughing a field, literally carrying the yoke, while behind others lie weakly on the ground. The heavy physical labour stoically carried out by the two women can also be read as a commentary on the social and economic conditions in Germany. Produced after the Treaty of Versailles, which settled the questions of war guilt, reparations and territorial adjustments to the disappointment of the population, the image visualises the perception of a dictated peace that saw Germans under the yoke of the peace treaty.

Hardship and hunger remained key themes in women's art until the mid-1920s. The work of Käthe Kollwitz exemplifies the persisting moral force of such imagery. Kollwitz produced a number of images on the theme of starving children in 1919 and the early 1920s. Her troubled creative journey while working on a memorial to her son Peter remained a constant source of anguish and despair. Nonetheless, she completed a number of commissioned pieces which addressed current social issues, and felt encouraged by this work. She derived a great sense of achievement from the practical and meaningful use of her art.[60] In 1919, for example, she produced a cover illustration for a booklet entitled *Hunger: The Effects of Modern Methods of War*.[61] In 1920 she created a poster for the International Workers' Aid Organisation that addressed famine in Austria, and in 1923 she produced a poster for a charity to alleviate hunger in Russia.[62] In addition to the broader context of economic deprivation and malnutrition, Kollwitz also witnessed declining health within the circle of her own friends and family and, in her diary, noted illnesses, recorded deaths and commented on the effect of hunger on childbearing and breastfeeding.[63] In the same year Kollwitz composed a woodcut on behalf of the International Federation of Trade Unions (*Internationale Gewerkschaftsbund*). Entitled *The Survivors* (*Die Überlebenden*) (fig. 11.6), the image shows a war widow and several children surrounded by veterans. Five years after the end of the conflict, the legacy of the war was still cited as the main cause of severe social deprivation. It is also significant that the widow and children are represented side by side with the veterans, suggesting their joint victimhood. Two of the veterans are wearing eye-bandages, while the women and children have deep hollow eyes with dark circles. The group appear dishevelled and sad, and their abject need is expressed by the mothers' stern endurance as well as by the veteran's outstretched begging hand. The caption *The Survivors* refers not only to the veterans who managed to emerge alive from a very costly war, but also to the widow and children who managed to evade starvation. Survival in the image is portrayed not as joyful, but as burdensome and painful.

In 1924, on the tenth anniversary of the outbreak of war, Kollwitz published a lithograph entitled *Bread* (*Brot*) (fig. 11.7) for the International Workers' Organisation. It shows a mother with her two children tearing at her skirt, demanding, the title implies, to be fed. The clothing of the mother and children highlights their poverty. The mother's back is turned towards the viewer, avoiding their gaze as if she were ashamed of her misery and her inability to provide for her children. The caption 'Bread' is also highly symbolic, and has a clear biblical connotation. Bread was a staple in people's diets; a lack of it signifies severe privation. The year 1924 is seen as the year of anti-war art and the beginning of new artistic responses to the war.[64] Yet, by the mid-1920s, the war experience

11.6 Käthe Kollwitz, *The Survivors* (*Die Überlebenden*), 1923. Lithograph.

was viewed through the social, economic and political environment of that time, entailing new conflicts and ambiguities which affected people's memories of the conflict as well as the legacy of the Armistice. With the ongoing economic hardship resulting from massive inflation, it was impossible, it seems, to disentangle the memory of the war from suffering and hunger.

Conclusion

Once the conflict had ended, the context and concerns that had shaped women's wartime art changed. Most importantly, the mass killing in the various theatres of war had finally ended, and no further wartime sacrifice was demanded of German women. Yet the social realities of peace entailed economic hardship and malnutrition that affected the female population most severely and no doubt contributed to unresolved wartime trauma. Thus, the legacy and lingering pain of wartime sacrifice did not end with the Armistice. It was not the emotional but the material suffering of women and children that was more acute, and represented

11.7 Käthe Kollwitz, *Bread* (*Brot*), 1924. Lithograph.

a powerful platform from which to assert the suffering of innocents. The testimonial character of women's post-war images and their overpowering moral dimension served to highlight women's continuing suffering and sacrifice.

In many of the testimonies produced by women in response to the

Armistice, the nature of the peace is conditional. We see a strong connection between the sacrifices endured by German women over the course of more than four years of bloodshed and the perceived injustice of the *Gewaltfrieden* (enforced peace). Set against this is an emphasis on civilian suffering in women's politics and culture. Through victimhood, the shame of defeat and the now worthless sacrifice could be endured and even transformed. Hunger and civilian suffering became a post-war narrative that absorbed the legacy and continuing pain of wartime, the difficult peace, the perceived injustice of the blockade, and the disappointing revolutions. Depictions of civilian suffering established a continuity of sacrifice and served to establish an identity as victims that perhaps helped women to cope with the hardship and disappointments of the war and its aftermath. The material grievances were, to a degree, absorbed by the Weimar welfare state.[65] Yet even the tenth anniversary of the outbreak of the war revealed that bitterness and resentment, compounded by economic hardship and unresolved emotional wartime trauma, continued to have a very visible presence in Weimar culture and society.

Notes

1 'Der Bund Deutscher Frauenvereine zum Frieden', October 1918, Landesarchiv Berlin, HLA 187/1, 2742. Unless otherwise indicated, all translations in this chapter are the author's.

2 Wolfgang Schivelbusch, *Die Kultur der Niederlage* (Frankfurt a.M.: Fischer, 2003), 242–55.

3 Jost Dülffer, 'Frieden schließen nach einem Weltkrieg? Die mentale Verlängerung der Kriegssituation in den Friedensschluß', in Jost Dülffer and Gerd Krumeich, eds, *Der verlorene Frieden. Politik und Kriegskultur nach 1918* (Essen: Klartext, 2002), 30–5; Schivelbusch, *Die Kultur der Niederlage*, 227–49.

4 Belinda Davis, *Home Fires Burning: Food, Politics and Everyday Life in World War I Berlin* (Chapel Hill, NC: University of North Carolina Press, 2000), 219–36.

5 Raffael Scheck, 'Women against Versailles: Maternalism and Nationalism of Female Bourgeois Politicians in the Early Weimar Republic', *German Studies Review*, 22, 1 (1999), 21–42.

6 Greg Eghigian, 'Injury, Fate, Resentment, and Sacrifice in German Political Culture, 1914–1939', in Greg Eghigian and Matthew Paul Berg, eds, *Sacrifice and National Belonging in Twentieth-Century Germany* (Arlington, TX: Texas A&M University Press, 2002), 94.

7 On the construction and overcoming of silence, see Jay Winter, 'Thinking

about Silence', in Efrat Ben-Ze'ev, Ruth Ginio and Jay Winter, eds, *Shadows of War: A Social History of Silence in the Twentieth Century* (Cambridge: Cambridge University Press, 2010), 4–8.

8 Ute Daniel, 'Frauen', in Gerhard Hirschfeld, Gerd Krumeich and Irina Renz, eds, *Enzyklopädie Erster Weltkrieg* (Munich: Schönigh, 2004), 133; Karen Hagemann, 'Militär, Gewalt und Geschlechterverhältnisse im Zeitalter der Weltkriege', in Karen Hagemann and Stefanie Schüler-Springorum, eds, *Heimat-Front. Militär und Geschlechterverhältnisse im Zeitalter der Weltkriege* (Frankfurt a.M.: Campus, 2002), 23.

9 Kriegsarchiv Munich, Stv. Gen K. I. Armee Korps 1709, Richtlinien für die Presse, Propaganda; Zensurbestimmungen.

10 Claudia Siebrecht, 'Martial Spirit and Mobilisation Myths: Bourgeois Women and the "Ideas of 1914" in Germany', in Alison Fell and Ingrid Sharp, eds, *The Women's Movement in Wartime: International Perspectives, 1914–19* (Basingstoke: Palgrave, 2007), 38–52; see, for example, Dr Gertrud Bäumer, *Der Krieg und die Frau*, ed. Ernst Jäckh, vol. 15, *Der deutsche Krieg. Politische Flugschriften* (Stuttgart: Deutsche Verlags-Anstalt, 1914).

11 Claudia Siebrecht, 'Imagining the Absent Dead: Rituals of Bereavement and the Place of the War Dead in German Women's Art during the First World War', *German History*, 29, 2 (2011), 202–23.

12 Belinda Davis, 'Homefront: Food, Politics and Women's Everyday Life during the First World War', in Karen Hagemann and Stefanie Schüler-Springorum, eds, *Home/Front: The Military, War and Gender in Twentieth-Century Germany* (Oxford: Berg, 2002), 123.

13 Annegret Rittmann, *Ida Gerhardi, 1862–1927. Eine westfälische Malerin zwischen Paris und Berlin* (Münster: Ardey, 1993), 339–40.

14 Dülffer, 'Frieden schließen nach einem Weltkrieg?', 30.

15 Käthe Kollwitz to Hans Kollwitz, 20 October 1918, in Jutta Bohnke-Kollwitz, ed., *Käthe Kollwitz: Briefe an den Sohn, 1904–1945* (Berlin: Siedler, 1992), 176.

16 Hauptstaatsarchiv Stuttgart, Stellv. Gen-Kommando M 77/1; 482.

17 *Schwäbischer Merkur* (22 October 1918).

18 Paula B., diary, October 1918, 218, Deutsches Tagebucharchiv, Emmendingen [hereafter DTA] 63.

19 Paula B., diary, part 4: 1918–1935, 218, DTA 63.

20 Gertrud P., diary, October–November 1918, DTA 759/II.

21 Alexander Watson, *Enduring the Great War: Combat, Morale and Collapse in the German and British Armies, 1914–1918* (Cambridge: Cambridge University Press, 2008), 184–231. See also Watson's chapter in this volume.

22 Hauptstaatsarchiv Stuttgart, Stellv. Gen-Kommando M 77/1; 482.

23 Pamphlet, 'Den deutschen Frauen', Hauptstaatsarchiv Stuttgart, Stellv. Gen-Kommando M 77/1, 482.

24 Hauptstaatsarchiv Stuttgart, Stellv. Gen-Kommando M 77/1 482: 1918

Frauenaufklärung; Bayrisches Hauptstaatsarchiv, Kriegsarchiv Stv. GenKdo I AK 1724; 1729.

25 *Vorwärts* (22 October 1918).

26 Käthe Kollwitz to Hans Kollwitz, 27 October 1918, in Bohnke-Kollwitz, ed., *Käthe Kollwitz: Briefe an den Sohn*, 179.

27 Käthe Kollwitz, diary, 27 October 1918, *Die Tagebücher, 1908–1943*, ed. Jutta Bohnke-Kollwitz (Berlin: Siedler, 1999), 376.

28 Käthe Kollwitz to Hans Kollwitz, 25 October 1918, in Bohnke-Kollwitz, ed., *Käthe Kollwitz: Briefe an den Sohn*, 177–8.

29 Käthe Kollwitz, diary, 23 October 1918, *Die Tagebücher, 1908–1943*, 384.

30 Wolfgang J. Mommsen, 'German Artists, Writers and Intellectuals and the Meaning of War, 1914–1918', in John Horne, ed., *State, Society and Mobilisation in Europe during the First World War* (Cambridge: Cambridge University Press, 1997), 21–38. On the question of revolution, see Klaus Hofmann's chapter in this volume.

31 Ursula Büttner, *Weimar: Die überforderte Republik 1918–1933. Leistung und Versagen in Staat, Gesellschaft, Wirtschaft und Kultur* (Stuttgart: Klett-Cotta, 2008), 41.

32 'From Dada to the New Objectivity: Art and Politics', in Anton Kaes, Martin Jay and Edward Dimendberg, eds, *The Weimar Republic Sourcebook* (Berkeley, CA: University of California Press, 1994), 474–502.

33 Brigid Doherty, 'The Work of Art and the Problem of Politics in Berlin Dada', in Kathleen Canning, Kerstin Barndt and Kristin McGuire, eds, *Weimar Publics / Weimar Subjects: Rethinking the Political Culture of Germany in the 1920s* (Oxford: Berghahn Books, 2010), 42–65.

34 Käthe Kollwitz to Hans Kollwitz, 23 October 1918, in Bohnke-Kollwitz, ed., *Käthe Kollwitz: Briefe an den Sohn*, 176.

35 Ricarda Huch to Helene von Salis, 17 September 1918, in Peter Walther, ed., *Endzeit Europa. Ein kollektives Tagebuch deutschsprachiger Schriftsteller, Künstler and Gelehrter im Ersten Weltkrieg* (Göttingen: Wallstein Verlag, 2008), 320–1.

36 Klaus von Beyme, *Das Zeitalter der Avantgarden, 1905–1955* (Munich: Beck, 2005), 539–42.

37 For example, 'Offener Brief an die Novembergruppe', *Der Gegner*, II, 18–19 (1920–21), signed by the Opposition to the November Group, rpt. in Uwe M. Schneede, ed., *Die zwanziger Jahre. Manifeste und Dokumente deutscher Künstler* (Cologne: DuMont, 1979), 95–101.

38 The portrait is published under Heise's alias, K. L. Heinrich Salze, *Die Aktion*, 17/18 (1918).

39 Sella Hasse, *Bildnis Gustav Landauer*, 1918–19, linocut, rpt. in Staatliche Museen zu Berlin Kupferstichkabinett und Sammlung der Zeichnung Akademie der Künste der DDR, ed., *Selle Hasse zum 100. Geburtstag. Ausstellung in der National-Galerie* (Dresden: GGV Dresden, 1978), 148.

40 Käthe Kollwitz, diary, October 1918, *Die Tagebücher, 1908–1943*, 483.
41 Käthe Kollwitz, diary, October 1918.
42 Katharina von Ankum, ed., *Women in the Metropolis: Gender and Modernity in Weimar Culture* (Berkeley, CA: University of California Press, 1997); Gail Finney, ed., *Visual Culture in Twentieth-Century Germany* (Bloomington, IN: Indiana University Press, 2006).
43 Marsha Meskimmon, *We Weren't Modern Enough: Women Artists and the Limits of German Modernism* (London: I. B. Tauris, 1999).
44 Birthe Kundrus, *Kriegerfrauen, Familienpolitik und Geschlechterverhältnisse im Ersten und Zweiten Weltkrieg* (Hamburg: Christians, 1995); Robert Whalen, *Bitter Wounds: German Victims of the Great War, 1914–1939* (Ithaca, NY: Cornell University Press, 1984), 69–77.
45 Karl Christian Führer, 'Managing Scarcity: The German Housing Shortage and the Controlled Economy, 1914–1990', *German History*, 13, 3 (1995), 327–31.
46 Führer, 'Managing Scarcity', 327.
47 Peter Gatrell, 'Refugees and Forced Migrants during the First World War', *Immigrants and Minorities*, 26, 1–2 (2008), 83–7.
48 Richard Bessel, *Germany after the First World War* (Oxford: Clarendon Press, 1993), 69–90; Kundrus, *Kriegerfrauen*, 142–9; M. Schmidt-Behrmann, 'Wohnungsnot im Industriegebiet während der Nachkriegzeit', in Charlotte von Hadeln, ed., *Deutsche Frauen – Deutsche Treue 1914–1933. Ein Ehrenbuch der deutschen Frau* (Berlin: Traditionsverlag Rolf, 1935), 219–23.
49 Boria Sax, *Crow* (London: Reaktion Books, 2003).
50 Raymond Meylan, *Die Flöte. Grunzüge ihrer Entwicklung von der Urgeschichte bis zur Gegenwart*, 4th edn (Mainz: Schott Music, 1984); Philip Bate, *The Flute: A Study of its History, Development and Construction* (London: Benn, 1969).
51 Büttner, *Weimar: Die überforderte Republik*, 24.
52 Jay Winter, 'Some Paradoxes of the First World War', in Richard Wall and Jay Winter, eds, *The Upheaval of War: Family, Work and Welfare in Europe, 1914–1918* (Cambridge: Cambridge University Press, 1988), 30.
53 N. P. Howard, 'The Social and Political Consequences of the Allied Food Blockade of Germany, 1918–19', *German History*, 11, 2 (1993), 161–88.
54 Howard, 'The Social and Political Consequences', 166–8.
55 Alyson Jackson, 'Germany, The Home Front (2): Blockade, Government and Revolution', in Hugh Cecil and Peter Liddle, eds, *Facing Armageddon: The First World War Experienced* (Barnsley: Pen and Sword, 2003), 570–5.
56 Alan Kramer, 'Kriegsrecht und Kriegsverbrechen', in Hirschfeld et al., eds, *Enzyklopädie Erster Weltkrieg*, 285; Winter, 'Some Paradoxes', 38–41.
57 Motion no. 30: Frau Agnes u. Gen.: *Stenographische Berichte über die Verhandlungen des deutschen Reichstages* (VDR), vol. 335, 18th session, 410c.
58 Erika Kuhlman, 'The "Women's International League for Peace and Freedom"

and Reconciliation after the Great War', in Fell and Sharp, eds, *The Women's Movement in Wartime*, 227-43.

59 Ute Gerhard, *Frauenbewegung und Feminismus. Eine Geschichte seit 1789* (Munich: Beck, 2009), 90–3; Gisela Bock, *Frauen in der europäischen Geschichte* (Munich: Beck, 2000).

60 Käthe Kollwitz, diary, 4 December 1922, *Die Tagebücher, 1908–1943*, 542–3.

61 Max Rubmann, *Hunger! Wirkungen moderner Kriegsmethoden* (Berlin: Reimer, 1919).

62 'Wien stirbt! Rettet seine Kinder.'

63 Käthe Kollwitz, diary, April 1922, *Die Tagebücher, 1908–1943*, 527–8.

64 Annegret Jürgens-Kirchhoff, 'Kunst gegen den Krieg im Antikriegsjahr 1924', in Dülffer and Krumeich, eds, *Der verlorene Frieden*, 287–310.

65 David F. Crew, *Germans on Welfare: From Weimar to Hitler* (Oxford: Oxford University Press, 1998); Eghigian, 'Injury, Fate, Resentment', 90–117.

12

'Remembering, we forget': British art at the Armistice[1]

In memory of Marie

Michael Walsh

> at the end of a catastrophe to civilization, survivors map the ruins and locate the routes out, the new paths that lead to whatever it is that comes after such a war as this has been.[2]

As the dust settled on the debris around the cenotaph in Enniskillen on the morning of 8 November 1987, and as the dead and injured were removed to the Erne Hospital and others of the region, there emerged a widespread sense of outrage that what the IRA had done, this time, was unforgivable. It was not the first time civilians had died in 'The Troubles' in Northern Ireland and it was certainly not the greatest loss of life in any one event. It was, however, the violation of both the sanctity of time and place which was unprecedented and which triggered international disgust – a bomb, on Remembrance Sunday, at the war memorial, targeting those in the process of remembering the 'fallen' of two world wars and other conflicts. The bronze soldier of the First World War atop the memorial, his head bowed and rifle inverted, amid all the usual symbols of remembrance, was regarded as a potent symbol of 'Britishness' and so a *bona fide* target in the minds of those who had a new, or unfinished, struggle in mind. If John Terraine had observed on the eve of war in 1914 that 'The fate of nations appeared to hang upon the parish boundaries in the counties of Fermanagh and Tyrone',[3] these fissures had clearly not healed by November 1987 (fig. 12.1). By contrast, at the other end of Belmore Street (about 100 metres away) is the memorial to those Enniskillen men killed in the South African wars, less than two decades before the First World War. These are lives we *have* been allowed to forget, so much so that at the time of writing the

12.1 'The cost of remembering': Marie Wilson's funeral procession passes the Enniskillen war memorial.

memorial was actually being removed to facilitate road widening for a supermarket.

My interest, then, as a native of Enniskillen and as an historian of the art of the First World War, stems from two fundamental questions: What hold does the war still have over us that the desecration of its memory (more so than the murder of ten pensioners and a student nurse) should be the source of such widespread disgust? And what role might art and artists have played in the processes of creating this imagined, yet culturally ingrained, long-term community of mourners? This chapter explores some ethical, theoretical and practical considerations associated with the anticipation, and the creation, of memory in painting at the time of the Armistice in Britain, not the actual bureaucratic mechanisms of memory creation which have been well documented elsewhere.[4] Looking at issues of production and reception, I will explore the debates which surrounded post-war state patronage of the arts during this last great cultural mobilisation of the 1914–18 campaign. I will argue that two simultaneous debates had to develop hand-in-hand, and then become intertwined, to create a legacy loyal to both the integrity and continuity of British art, and to the memory of those lost in a terrible, but victorious, war.

British painting and the end of the First World War

During the war, officially employed artists had played an enormous role which the government had, in time, deemed a perfectly legitimate and valuable component of the overall war effort. Among them were some of the most notable names of the day, including George Clausen, Augustus John, Wyndham Lewis, the brothers Paul and John Nash, William Orpen and C. R. W. Nevinson. Emanating from London, and filtering to every shire, village and isle in the nation (and then to every corner of the empire and beyond), was the recognition that the nation had to make a serious commitment to struggle. British people would need grim determination to get through the difficult days ahead, yet were expected never to doubt that it would all be worth it when, inevitably, victory would come. In the post-war era (which Samuel Hynes suggests began in 1917)[5] art's mission had to change, however, to temper the realisation that the dead were not just dead for the duration of the war, and that the process of remembering, understanding, coming to terms with and evaluating loss came with the caveat that art had no power to heal.[6] There were, of course, those who thought this to be a quixotic enterprise from the outset, believing that painting, as a two-dimensional, static, mute and history-bound medium, largely irrelevant to the majority of the population and faced with what must have felt like an unattainable goal, had not the slightest chance of success. How, they argued, could a set of selected, edited and compressed experiences, reduced through symbols and codified response to the undepictable reality, really make the slightest impact on those engulfed in an enforced, and deeply subjective, mourning?[7] Could traditionally highbrow art even traverse old class divisions to attempt a homogeneous and relevant record of morality, justice, compassion and civilisation for the entire nation? Reginald Grundy had advised caution on this issue in 1916, saying that art and the institutions gearing up to lead the nation in remembering and mourning would need to include the rank and file (and so the grass roots of democracy), and not just in London either, if it was 'to seize the imaginations of posterity'.[8] Handled correctly, those to be depicted, perhaps nameless before and during the war and now 'known unto God', could yet become part of the very fabric of a great nation's history. Painting could offer a last, proud glimpse of a departed son, father or brother and afford him a status never enjoyed in life.

Others argued that it was precisely because of art's lofty status that the medium could be entrusted, not burdened, with the task of restoring decency and dignity to a war which had violated both. If handled correctly, art was surely the perfect vehicle for such an undertaking, because war destroys while art creates – implying that the very medium was the antithesis of the wholesale destruction of the previous four years. Ideally, art would reconstruct the memory of the war for a future society that would be the beneficiary of that war, and lead it confidently to a cultural sanity that could only have been brought about by the baptism of fire that was the war itself. Though it was as yet unclear how this was to be done, and what this investment might result in, it was certain that this was no time to demobilise the artists of the nation. Whether they were creating historical records of events, warning future generations, consoling those who were bereaved or highlighting the fruits of victory to those who had fought, they still had a vital role to play. In any case, if, as A. J. P. Taylor observed in relation to 1914, 'No man in the prime of his life knew what war was like',[9] then so too was the nation unprepared for remembering and historicising an event of such magnitude four years later.

Artists had been an important component of the war effort from the start, the images brought home being received eagerly by the public, and many a reputation made virtually overnight. There was no more dramatic a case than that of C. R. W. Nevinson.[10] Seeing this unharnessed resource, and comprehending its potential, the fledgling Department of Information under the command of C. F. G. Masterman at Wellington House brought in the artists, starting with Muirhead Bone and Francis Dodd. In time Eric Kennington, William Orpen, William Rothenstein, John Lavery and others were set to work for the nation in an official capacity. This, it was widely believed, would be a mutually beneficial relationship. If art was good for war, then so too war might be good for art. The *Daily Chronicle* critic Charles Lewis Hind, in a 1917 article entitled 'Art after the War', had no doubt about this, and referenced Ruskin's old idea that peace was fundamentally decadent and that through war a New Renaissance in art might even be possible. In such a cultural climate the artist would captain a civilisation made stronger and richer by the benefits of formative conflict, or rather the peace which followed it. It would be the artist who would 'flash the lyric upon our walls to restore our faith in the permanence of beauty, the consolation of nature, and the undying spirit of man who, after destruction, begins at once to reconstruct'.[11]

Charles Marriot of the *Evening Standard* supported this notion, arguing in 1917 that art was more persistent and durable than war and, far from being threatened by it, would probably benefit from its intensification of meaning and social relevance.[12] The military subject need not prevail, but the essence of what it had brought about would, via a Spartan rite of passage which would see off the impostor and the second rate. Robert C. Witt publicly condemned the irrelevance of any remaining introverted and elitist art and artists, urging them to work 'in public, [and] take a broader, less personal aspect, or public opinion will cry "A Plague on *all* your houses"'.[13] In other words, artists (both unruly rebels and conservative academicians) would have to sacrifice some of their selfish aims, just the way soldiers had done on the battlefields of Flanders and Picardy, in the name of unifying and harmonising the national interest after the guns fell silent.[14] And so it seemed appropriate to make memorial art, in technique at least, 'traditional' in order to spare culture one more fissure in addition to those already inflicted by the war.

Additionally, the subject was so powerful and so vital that it could not risk being obscured by an opaque method of delivery. But this was not the only balancing act and compromise to be considered. To commemorate war was to ask artists to depict the polarities of hatred and love simultaneously; to acknowledge loss, debt and triumph – not simply to lead a united front that wished only to sheathe the sword. War had been, at the same time, exhilarating and heartbreaking, noble yet tragic, and more than anything else, unendurably sad.[15] And so, even if the British painter of war was a painter of victory, could there be a place for military triumphalism when the horrors of the war on land, in the air and at sea were now so fully understood? Painting to remember would have to be respectful in both message and method, creating a precarious trade-off between mimetic and iconic, myth and fact, and simultaneously harmonising artistic innovation with political ideology and historical fact.

Art for whose sake? Mourning, memory and mythology

Art was truly at the heart of this lost, or at least disoriented, generation. These were the leaders of a cultured society, entrusted to take each mourning family and lead them forward as a nation in what Jay Winter calls 'the braiding together of family and national history'.[16] The artist was being asked by the nation to bridge the gulf between the living and the dead, the victorious and the defeated, the young and the old, those who had gone and those who had stayed at home. The artist's was the voice of reason, of mourning, of value and of permanence, acting as the chronicler for future generations. He or she was the interlocutor, the independent (yet patriotic) intellectual who sought an answer and might yet capture the vastness of the experience and its implications through his or her work. Painting was being asked to extract a seemingly illusive 'meaning' from the carnage from which most people still reeled, and offer a much-needed historical explanation for the loss that so many families had suffered. Returning soldiers too would, in time, need to understand what they had just been through and be reassured that it had been both worthwhile and appreciated.[17] And for those still fighting in Russia, the Ottoman Empire, Ireland, Palestine and elsewhere around the globe (and those whose consciences were troubled by the ongoing Allied blockade of Germany) the war, their war, was not over and needed continued support from a weary, though jubilant, nation.[18] But more than anything else art was brought into the service of those in grief, bereaved families and communities, starting out on their process of mourning and memory construction. Jay Winter places art (and other cultural schemes) at the heart of the process whereby 'Grief is a state of mind; bereavement a condition. Both are mediated by mourning, a set of acts and gestures through which survivors express grief and pass through stages of bereavement.'[19]

Through the application of paint to canvas, then, a cultural, historical and psychological responsibility descended upon the nationally commissioned artist whose task was to order memory, sanitise and Christianise it, then edit history and compress experience to view the living and the dead, and warn future generations, all at once. The artist knew that he or she had to create a memory of men who had been killed but who had never taken the life of another mother's son, 'the fallen' (not the butchered), the youth who had been sacrificed (yet who had not wilfully set out to slaughter), and those who were now 'sleeping' with comrades in a cosmetically tidied up version of history. Perhaps, the artist might have felt, the nation didn't want the truth anyway – the myth being easier to believe, to reiterate and perpetuate year after year. Was this not preferable, after four years of propaganda, deception and a cycle of nationalist lies, to the 'truth' which would surely be too sudden a shock or too grim a reality? The artist might also have wondered how to sidestep the bare fact that the aspiration of a warm summer's afternoon in 1914 had not led in a linear path from a set of clearly defined war aims to victory and the rightful spoils that had long been felt to be the justification for such a costly effort. Perhaps it was best not to refer to 1914 when painting in 1918.[20]

Additionally, as the Treaty of Versailles was being drafted it was clear to all but the most naive that 'the long weekend' had just begun and that the war mentality might yet be needed for another conflict in the not-so-distant future. It was perhaps not yet time to bury the hatchet, nor to consign European rivalries to history. In the meantime, the memory of horror would need to be replaced gradually with the decency of remembrance and the palatability of ritualistic commemoration for this most unfortunate generation who, in themselves, knew that their vivid memory, ironically, had to be blotted out. Henri Barbusse's protagonist in *Under Fire* anticipated in despair that 'The work of the future will be to wipe out the present, to wipe it out more than we can imagine, to wipe it out like something abominable and shameful. And yet – this present – it had to be, it had to be!' Another of the book's characters spoke for millions of men at arms when he declared 'We've seen too much to remember.'[21]

Committees, exhibitions and paintings: The conscious construction of memory

It would be a mistake, however, to think that post-war cultural production was left to the days following the Armistice. In fact, by 11 November 1918 many of the key images of remembrance had already been painted. Commissioned by the Ministry of Information (established in March 1918) under Lord Beaverbrook, the British effort followed the example set by the Canadian War Records Office in Ottawa and the Canadian War Memorials Fund, established in 1916. By 1918 the latter had 55 artists of Canadian, Belgian, Australian, Danish, Serbian and British nationality working towards clearly defined goals.

> A War Memorial of this kind, if it is to be of lasting value, if it is to teach lasting generations, to stir their imagination, to stimulate their patriotic feeling, must be a thrilling record of facts, based on personal experience.[22]

Indeed, some of Britain's finest artists – Wyndham Lewis, William Roberts, Frederick Etchells, Paul Nash, Edward Wadsworth, C. R. W. Nevinson and David Bomberg – were engaged in commemorating the Canadian war effort. Logically Beaverbrook turned his attention to a similar scheme for Britain and called the first meeting of the Imperial Permanent Memorials Committee (later to be called the British War Memorials Committee), which was attended on several consecutive days by C. F. G. Masterman, Arnold Bennett, Captain J. H. Jenkins (of the Canadian War Records Office), Robert Ross (advisor at the Imperial War Museum), Alfred Yockney and Thomas Derrick (both previously associated with the War Artists Scheme at Wellington House).[23] Later Muirhead Bone, P. G. Konody and Campbell Dodgson joined, while

Arnold Bennett (known to be pro-war and yet pro-individual) became perhaps the real driving force, though he played down his role as being 'on a committee which has charge of the task of having the war recorded in paint and marble. Great larks!'[24] Collectively, the committee, at the heart of which was the New English Art Club (NEAC) and the Slade School of Art, wanted future generations to judge them kindly for demonstrating not only 'the greatest artistic expression of the day, but the practical foresight of those responsible for such a legacy to posterity'.[25] If Masterman and Beaverbrook came across as superior and dismissive to both the War Office and the Treasury, they remained faithful and loyal to the heart of British cultural values. They had, after all, managed to get connoisseurs and artists into army jobs, and so driven a wedge between politics/the military and art, in the pursuit of higher intellectual aims. When completed, these astutely commissioned canvases would take pride of place together, in a wood-panelled room within a Hall of Remembrance, in the manner in which the Venetians had housed the works of Tintoretto and Tiepolo in the Scuola and Guild Rooms of Venice.[26] Accordingly, Ross suggested that a special building be constructed so that the images could be part of an overall architectural unity and coherence of memory, while Muirhead Bone felt that Richmond Hill would be a perfect location.

To do this effectively, it had to be made clear from the very beginning that there was a difference between using art for the noble cause of remembrance, and using it to cater for a booming industry in which it served merely to illustrate events and feed the propaganda machine. Likewise, some distinction had to be made between the priorities of the Imperial War Museum, which was busy creating a permanent record of war, and the Ministry (later the Pictorial Propaganda Committee), which was trying to memorialise it. Memorial art, both painted and sculpted, had to be modern, British and artistically significant, not reduced to mere depictions of events, people or places. This priority established, a framework of eight different categories of war effort was then decided upon and superimposed on to the contributions of some unsurprising names, such as Philip Wilson Steer and Walter Sickert (ironically born in Munich), who were selected to lead the field.[27] These were the 'old masters' of the nation who would shepherd the younger artists, who had actually fought in the war, to focus their compositions on 'physical force in relation to thought, labour, commerce, art, literature, faith, science, patriotism, domination, humanism'.[28]

Ideologically lofty in intent, each canvas would embody within it the reasons why the war had been fought, even if such 'meaning' might be viewed cynically by the average Tommy who had endured the trenches. The war would, in the fullness of time, be remembered not through a factual, sequential series of events, but via intensified (and perhaps fictionalised) social experiences that had benefited from, or at least been imperilled by, the war. If illustrative and technically conservative art had been good for Wellington House and the propaganda effort during the war, another vocabulary was now being created to commemorate it.

When the debates subsided and the balance of art and war was established, the myriad jobs were distributed by P. G. Konody to the who's who of British art. As their official task was to embrace the overall breadth of the effort, their subject matter covered a wide range including embarkation, training camps, the war council, German prisoners in Essex, shipbuilding, the Tube during a raid, women on the land, harbour works, flying schools, the work of the RAMC, camouflage and forestry in Scotland. The less palatable issues of filth, boredom, injury, mutiny, execution and so on were understandably not addressed. William Strang and George Lambert were asked to deal with 'The Channel Crossing' while William Nicholson, Philip Connard, Albert Rutherston, George Clausen, W. B. E. Ranken, James Pryde, D. Y. Cameron, Eric Kennington and Mark Gertler were asked to concentrate on scenes 'Behind the Front'. 'The Front' went to William Rothenstein, Paul Nash (Lieutenant), Rupert Lee (Lieutenant), Darsie Japp (Major, MC), C. R. W. Nevinson (Mons Star), William Roberts (Lieutenant), William Orpen, Alfred Munnings, C. J. Holmes, Henry Lamb (Captain, RAMC), Henry Tonks, Augustus John and Stanley Spencer (Private, RAMC). A further subdivision was drawn up to decide who would do the 'Pictures of the Largest Size', overseen by Tonks, Bone and Orpen in case the 'young ones' might yet abuse this lucrative commission and go off on one of their tangents so typical of the pre-war years.[29] Sue Malvern notes that 'Excluding Orpen, of the 29 artists who had received commissions from the Ministry of Information, the majority were under forty years of age in 1918.'[30] Individual exhibition galleries were also designated as follows: Gallery One – 'Scenes at the Front' (including the theatres of the Western Front, Macedonia, Palestine and Mesopotamia); Gallery Two – 'Home Front Subjects'; Galleries Three and Four – 'Naval and Air Subjects'; and Gallery Five – 'Other Smaller Scenes'.[31]

Next it was suggested that all artists should employ the same medium, and construct scenes and utilise characters within each painting which would relate to the next image. With the range of artists invited, and the disparity of their reputations and methods of working, this was going to be virtually impossible. Therefore, to put the canvases within a historical tradition of monumentality and the broader continuum of war art, Ross suggested that the scale for the major canvases should follow either Velazquez's *Surrender at Breda* (120 × 144 inches) or Uccello's *Battle of San Romano* (72 × 125 inches). Not everyone agreed, and Wyndham Lewis ridiculed the Uccello connection, saying

> Uccello's battle-piece is a magnificent still life, a pageant of armours, cloths etc., the trappings and wardrobe of War, but in the lines and spirit of it, as peaceable and bland as any tapestry representing a civic banquet could be. It does not borrow from the *fact* of War any emotion, and disturbing or dislocating violence, terror or compassion – any of the psychology that is proper to the events of War.[32]

The choice of Uccello and/or Velazquez carried with it, however, the distinct suggestion that the subject should dominate, but not obliterate, the method of delivery and, additionally, that war should not dominate the medium. This, if followed, would protect the scheme from accusations of vulgar militarism and ensure that the legacy of the painting would outlive the war and its immediate memory. It would also drive home the point that 'civilisation' was intact, and art a survivor of war, perhaps even invigorated by it and now healthier than ever. Lewis's interpretation was entirely different and he saw this kind of detachment, this coldness, as German, even Prussian, and far from the values that the British held so dear and had just fought a war for.

In June 1918, five months before the Armistice, a ruckus between Beaverbrook and his two art advisors, Konody and Ross, brought to light some other interesting facets of national memory creation. Bennett wrote to Beaverbrook to dissuade him from sacking the men, saying (about the Hungarian Konody) 'Moreover, he is not English … I should prefer him not to assist the Committee; but it is perfectly certain if you dismiss him now you will raise up a bitter and ingenious enemy for the Committee and for the Ministry.'[33] Ross, on the other hand, had always been a risky inclusion as 'his friendly relations with Oscar Wilde are well known; and Alfred Douglas is his declared enemy'.[34] Sexual orientation, almost as much as nationality, seemed an important issue when considering the creation of the memory of a heterosexual and masculine war. Before these debates were fully played out, however, Ross died, Beaverbrook resigned due to ill health and, to disrupt everything even more, the war finished, leading to the liquidation of the department and the termination of the period of planning.

Exhibiting in London

The first real post-war litmus test of relevance and gravitas came with the opening of *The Canadian War Memorial Exhibition* (January 1919) at Burlington House, where 400 paintings went on display to a crowd of two thousand, and where the Canadian prime minister, Sir Robert Borden, delivered the opening speech. Undoubtedly quick off the mark, the Canadians were in fact only the second nation to get their art on display in London, following the Australians in December 1918. But unlike the Australian paintings which had focused on 'the thing seen', the Canadians trod a fine line, encouraging 'diversity rather than uniformity, but diversity kept under control, with a definite end in view'.[35] The taste was intentionally catholic to include a variety of subjects, painted by a number of artists (both male and female), from countries other than, but including, Canada. In so doing, one reporter observed, the Canadians and the Royal Academy had let many 'Rebels in the Fortress'.[36] The key works shown included Major Richard Jack's *The Taking of Vimy Ridge* and *Second Battle of Ypres*, George Byam Shaw's *The Flag*, Laura Knight's *Physical Training (Boxing) Witley Camp*, Anna Airy's *Cook House at Witley Camp*, C. R. W. Nevinson's *War in the Air*, Wyndham Lewis's *Canadian Gun Pit* and Augustus John's *The Canadians Opposite Lens*, which was the pinnacle of the show. The prevalence of Slade and NEAC artists was unmistakable, and so Lewis issued a stern warning to the old avant-garde:

> Expressionism, Cubism, Vorticism, all these movements now have to set about construction and development, and evolve a new world of art out of the continent their enterprise has acquired.[37]

Sir Kenneth Clark, noting that London had been cut off from European influences since 1914, wrote admiringly:

> The canvases of Roberts and Wyndham Lewis had, on the few visitors who took them in, the same effect of liberating shock that the *Demoiselles d'Avignon* had produced in Paris ten years earlier.[38]

Most delighted, however, in the fact that Vorticism was dead and buried 'on the battlefields, and no one even knows where its decaying remains are'.[39] Likewise, the works of the 'older men seem meaningless,

12.2 John Singer Sargent, *Gassed*, 1919. Oil on canvas.

sentimental things, suitable for grocer's almanacs'.[40] For some people, the conservatism (and absenteeism) of the Royal Academy, the extremism (and incomprehensibility) of the pre-war ultra-modernists and the aesthetic disinterestedness (and perceived irresponsibility) of the Bloomsbury Group were irrelevant, and unwelcome, in the business of remembering the war. Looking back to Cézanne for a kind of moderate modernism, based on the post-Impressionism of 1912 in London, was seen as preferable. Interestingly, the Canadian show was actually criticised for not being modern enough, for being too descriptive and too much of a 'record of war'. Frank Rutter, frustrated, announced *nous avons vu tout ça devant la guerre.*[41] The *Nation* was equally unimpressed when its critic said 'More than ten million people, mainly men, have died violent deaths in Europe. Why? It is no use going to Burlington House to find out.'[42]

Sir Aston Webb, president of the Royal Academy, opened the Peace Academy in May 1919 in which the New Renaissance in English art, if there had been one, went on display. At the heart of this enormous show, in the Central Gallery, was John Singer Sargent's *Gassed* (fig. 12.2) in the location where Augustus John's *The Canadians Opposite Lens* had stolen the show only a few months earlier. Despite being an American, Sargent, it was felt, had balanced ethical value with visual truth on a sort of NEAC footing, and so conveyed something more than an event through the principles of design. It received some gushing reviews, which compared it in cultural significance to the Elgin Marbles, Piero della Francesca and even Stonehenge.[43] If pathos had been sought, combined with spiritualism, to relate the pity of war (as opposed to the jingoism and cheering crowds that characterised the summer of 1914) then here it was. And yet there were those who still felt that it did not go far enough, and that the artist here was 'merely a complicated camera'.[44] Laurence Binyon declared that Sargent had seen what he needed to see, then done nothing with the information, being satisfied with a realism that stultified creativity, sincerity and imagination.[45] Rutter jumped on board, saying that the outcome was all very hit and miss, this being a narrow miss. C. H. Collins Baker had no sympathy for the painting at all, believing that, far from residing on a monumental plane, it had resorted to being 'showy and sensuous' – the painterly equivalent of a musician reduced to making noise.[46] Others said it was good only for sentimental girls who would hang up a reproduction of it in their house in order to say 'Poor Fellows'.[47] Virginia Woolf acknowledged its 'moral significance', but concluded that this work had been the last straw in driving her out of Burlington House into Piccadilly. On the busy street at least was refuge from the new intellectual wounds inflicted by the 'brainless birds' in the 'parrot house' who 'shrieked and gibbered' about 'honour, patriotism, chastity, wealth, success, importance, position, patronage, power…'[48]

Overall, the critics were not being anything like as hostile to the young modernists as had been predicted, and, if anything, Orpen, John and Sargent (the backbone of the NEAC) had all been attacked for not being radical enough. By May 1919 it was an interesting lesson to have learned, and Wyndham Lewis was heartened to see that the advances of 1914 had survived the war after all. Next it was the turn of the British War Memorials Committee which had long fostered the idea of a memorial gallery and now needed to boost public interest in the project. Alfred Yockney, therefore, wrote to the president of the Royal Academy in January 1919 to ask if their current collection might be exhibited at Burlington House as a means of creating awareness. Permission was granted and so the collection, under the control of the Imperial War Museum, and without a gallery space anywhere else in London, was transferred to Piccadilly for one definitive show. The Selection and Hanging Committee (consisting of Yockney, Bone, Aitken, Dodd, Tonks, Sims, Sargent, Orpen and Holmes) tried to weed out 'illustrations' and give priority to the Ministry of Information collection (over the IWM) as they had been commissioned for entirely different reasons. This was an art exhibition, not an illustrated guide to the war, and so needed to be filtered through the appropriate channels. The exhibition would be both a record of war and art; it would patriotically honour those who had died without unwittingly endorsing the official mindset of the older generation that had caused so many deaths; it could not be a display of propaganda, nor could it be haughty. The exhibition

12.3 Sir George Clausen, *In the Gun Foundry at Woolwich Arsenal*, 1918. Oil on canvas.

12.4 Sir David Y. Cameron, *The Battlefield of Ypres*, 1919. Oil on canvas. 'English art, like England herself after the war, can never be the same again.'

opened in December 1919 and displayed over 900 paintings, sculptures and drawings from a total of 3,000 works by 176 artists. In the Central Gallery Sargent's *Gassed* appeared again, as did Clausen's *In the Gun Foundry at Woolwich Arsenal* (fig. 12.3), Tonks's *An Advanced Dressing Station in France*, D. Y. Cameron's *The Battlefield of Ypres* (fig. 12.4), William Roberts's *A Shell Dump, France*, Paul Nash's *The Menin Road*,

Stanley Spencer's *Travoys Arriving with Wounded at a Dressing Station at Smol, in Macedonia*, Colin Gill's *Heavy Artillery* and Henry Lamb's *Irish Troops in the Judean Hills Surprised by a Turkish Bombardment*. Gallery VI included Lewis's *A Battery Shelled* and Nevinson's *Harvest of Battle*. Michael Sadler spoke for many when he praised the government's support for the rights of art:

> Here is an official collection of pictures, bought by the Government with the nation's money ... [neither] conventional [nor] reckless [but] a very harvesting of the best that England can produce.'[49]

That such a collection could be commissioned, created and exhibited at a time like this was surely a victory that the nation could feel proud of, embodying as it did liberty, open-mindedness, democracy and all the other values the war had been fought for. Even if the world had not been made safe for democracy, it had certainly been made safe for art.

Ernest Renan observed 'suffering in common unites more than joy does. Where national memories are concerned, griefs are of more values than triumphs, for they impose duties, and require a common effort.'[50] Accordingly, not only were the young men being given the chance beside the old men, the nation was in fact turning to those who had fought the war to take the lead in remembering it. The *Daily Chronicle* didn't miss the point and wrote 'The New Men are here in full force and for good or ill, one thing is certain – English art, like England herself after the war, can never be the same again.'[51] For this writer, it was quite simply the art of the soldier versus that of the civilian. Who would paint with more passion or conviction than those who had been there? Youth had been made cruelly wise; in fact they now knew more than the elderly, who could produce well-painted images, but whose work was devoid of first-hand intensity. This was significance and stimulation channelled directly from the trenches. The art of youth would not be falsified, nor would it endorse the delusion of the absentee. Rather it was an act of bravery, a truth-telling that was wholly in keeping with the experience of war itself. And the consequences would be dramatic:

> Youth has rushed the gates and planted its standards in the very heart of the citadel. After this the Academy can no longer be its old dull self again. It must keep pace with the stride of the young battalions.[52]

Lewis's *A Battery Shelled* (fig. 12.5) was a fine example, leading traditionally hostile critics to enthuse:

12.5 Percy Wyndham Lewis, *A Battery Shelled*, 1919. Oil on canvas.

> It is like a symphonic poem, almost as free as music must be from imitation, and free also from musical pattern – whether you like it or not, you must confess you can almost see and hear the shells, so powerful an equivalent for their material force is given by those strange shapes across the sky.[53]

The nation, it seemed, was giving a seal of approval to the pre-war modernists who the Slade, it appeared in retrospect, had got ready just in time. Additionally, the war had provided the long-awaited substance which art had been crying out for as the same critic concluded: 'But the war, like Christianity long ago, has supplied a momentous theme.'[54] Was this then home-grown English Modernism at long last, cleansed of Paris and Berlin, and forged in war? Might this now be the first great movement in art since the Pre-Raphaelite Brotherhood, imbued with a Ruskinian appeal of truth to nature and social significance? Ruskin himself had talked of this phenomenon six decades before:

> I found, in brief, that all great nations learned their truth of word, and strength of thought, in war; that they were nourished in war, and wasted by peace; taught by war and deceived by peace; – in a word, that they were born in war, and expired in peace.[55]

It was as if the 'modern' vocabulary of 1910–12 had eventually found a suitable and worthy topic to make art relevant again and to bring it back into line with the public. 'Art for art's sake' had finally been buried with all its connotations of elitism and decorative aesthesis, while 'significant form' also looked to be on borrowed time. Frank Rutter wound it all up by saying 'Eccentricities and extravagancies, the dross of genuine feeling and legitimate ambition, were purified away in the fiery ordeal of modern battles.'[56] It was clear for most to see that, for all its horrors, the war had brought about the idea of virility, responsibility, the abnegation of self, the masculinity of discipline and the honour at the heart of all those who fought. Now art, as a universal, noble and sophisticated language, embodying within it a democratic core in which the public had a right to share, was bound to remember this honesty.

But not everyone was convinced, nor indeed optimistic, as could be seen when Muirhead Bone declared in 1919 'Beauty, always teaching, will then adorn our public places, instead of at present, in many instances, ornate ugliness.'[57] The Royal Academy, not pleased to be sidelined or spoken of so dismissively, made it known that it felt the show failed as both a record of war, and as a statement on the condition of British art. The RA may have lent its rooms for the show, but it certainly would not lend its unconditional support to those associated with Burlington, the NEAC, the Contemporary Art Society and the National Art Collections Fund who were currently, but only temporarily, at the helm. Clive Bell lamented that there was now only government sanctioned, second-rate art, devoid of all that had inspired English artists before the war. Worse, it was irritatingly proud, self-satisfied and philistine. The war had had nothing to do with art, he maintained, and neither could there be any link now with commemorating and mourning its dead. But Bell had not fought and so, in the view of some, was merely heckling from the sidelines.[58] Lewis saw his point though and maintained that Matisse and Vlaminck could have done no better had they been forced into the same strait-jacket English artists were wearing at this time. When Lewis tried to go it alone with Group X at the Mansard Gallery, fighting for his pre-war independence and attacking the RA, the Slade, the NEAC, the London Group and the 7&5 Society, he sank without trace. As 'before the war' had disappeared over the horizon into history during 1914–18, now 'during the war' was doing the same thing. 'Now' was rapidly becoming 'then', and the clock, it became clear, could not be wound back. Others wondered why, after such an effort and expense to collect this art, the exhibition only travelled to Manchester City Art Galleries and not to the countless regional cities, towns and villages which had also fought the war and paid a heavy price. The National Collection had been paid for by the people, and the Hall of Remembrance to house the National Collection would probably come out of the pockets of the people too. Again, this was not universally supported and so Sir Clement Kinloch-Cooke asked Sir Alfred Mond (director of the Imperial War Museum) in the House of Commons 'Is the Right Honourable Gentleman aware that £9,000 was spent on these freak pictures, and does he think that these freak pictures give a proper record of the War to future generations?'[59] In the end the Hall of Remembrance was never built and the collection of paintings was transferred to the Imperial War Museum.

Even if the name 'First World War' was coined before the war ended (in September 1918), implying clearly that this would not be the last, painters and gallery-goers still saw from the perspective of the here-and-now, and a painful chapter in history now firmly closed. Today we look at the First World War, and the paintings and other memory creation schemes associated with it, through the prism of the Second World War, the Cold War and a liberal democracy that is currently divided about conflict in Iraq and Afghanistan. Now, as then, we appreciate that the boundaries between informing and performing are porous indeed.[60] The war itself has become a lens through which we see the pre-war: the blissful summer of 1914 seems all the more blissful because we know what happened next. Looking at the paintings today, therefore, we are left with an increasingly long list of 'what-ifs' and open-ended questions which the benefit of hindsight affords us. For instance, one wonders what the path of memorial art, or art in general, would have been had Britain not been victorious. Or, in a globalised world, punch-drunk with electronic and mass-produced images, and in a post-imperial and now multicultural Britain, is there a risk that the gravitas and subtlety of these commissioned works is almost entirely lost on the modern viewer? Might he or she regard these paintings merely as mildly idiosyncratic illustrations of a distant war, functioning very much as backdrops might do at the theatre? And, though undoubtedly central to the mainstream of artistic production in 1919, might this loss of 'meaning' be exacerbated by their display in a war museum, far removed from the main currents of art criticism and appreciation so prevalent elsewhere in London?[61] One might wonder how, of the thousands of works that resulted from the Official War Artist scheme, so many important canvases have never seen the light of day to offer a new, perhaps forgotten, perspective on the events of 1914–18.[62]

The cynic might even suggest that if the idea of 'remembering' had been to inform, to warn and to prevent future generations from experiencing the same ghastly fate, then the history of the remainder of the

12.6 'Remembering, we forget'.

twentieth century and the opening years of the twenty-first has consistently mocked the failure of these lofty goals. It might also be suggested that in the absence of anyone who remembers the First World War at first hand, history should move in to replace this taught memory, allowing these iconic images to be retired – their work now done. The dead of the First World War, and the collective nationalised memory of them, was an important component in the construction of a new long-term political and social order in the United Kingdom, as the people of Enniskillen were to find out almost seven decades after the Armistice. With eleven new names inscribed on the base of their war memorial, a new process of remembering has begun (fig. 12.6).

Notes

1 A version of this article was published in 2008 in the *British Art Journal* to mark the 90th anniversary of the Armistice. The quotation is from Siegfried Sassoon, 'To One Who was with Me in the War', *Picture Show* (privately printed, 1919), 14.
2 Samuel Hynes, *A War Imagined: The First World War and English Culture* (London: Pimlico, 1990), 239.
3 Paul Fussell, *The Great War and Modern Memory* (Oxford: Oxford University Press, 1975), 25.
4 Sue Malvern, *Modern Art, Britain and the Great War* (New Haven, CT: Yale University Press, 2004); Sue Malvern, 'Art, Propaganda and Patronage: A History of the Employment of British War Artists 1916–1919' (unpublished PhD thesis, University of Reading, 1981); Melissa Hall, 'Modernism, Militarism and Masculinity' (unpublished PhD thesis, State University of New York at Binghamton, 1993).
5 Hynes, *A War Imagined*, 235.
6 For a different view, see James Fox, 'Art and World War I in Britain' (unpublished PhD thesis, University of Cambridge, 2010).
7 See Chapter 6 of J. M. Winter, *Sites of Memory, Sites of Mourning* (Cambridge: Cambridge University Press, 1995); Dan Todman, 'Introduction', *The Great War: Myth and Memory* (London: Hambledon Continuum, 1995).
8 Reginald Grundy, 'Local War Museums: A Suggestion', *Connoisseur* (November 1916), 168.
9 Cited in Fussell, *The Great War and Modern Memory*, 21.
10 Michael J. K. Walsh, *This Cult of Violence* (New Haven. CT: Yale University Press, 2002).
11 Charles Lewis Hind, 'Art after the War', *War Illustrated* (14 April 1917).
12 Charles Marriott, 'Art and War: A False Comparison', *Land and Water* (August 1917), 37.

13 Robert C. Witt, 'A Plea for Readjustment in the Art World', *The Nineteenth Century* (August 1917), 360.

14 James Fox, 'Fiddling while Rome is Burning: Hostility to Art during the First World War, 1914–18', *Visual Culture in Britain*, 11, 1 (2010), 49–65.

15 See Paul Gough, 'Introduction', *'A Terrible Beauty': British Artists in the First World War* (Bristol: Sansom, 2009).

16 Jay Winter, *Remembering War: The Great War between Memory and History in the Twentieth Century* (New Haven, CT: Yale University Press, 2006), 2.

17 Sharon Ouditt, 'Myths, Memories and Monuments: Re-imagining the Great War', in Vincent Sherry, ed., *The Cambridge Companion to The Literature of the First World War* (Cambridge: Cambridge University Press, 2005), 245–60.

18 Modris Eksteins, *Rites of Spring: The Great War and the Birth of the Modern Age* (London: Bantam, 1989), chs. 8 and 9.

19 Winter, *Remembering War*, 97.

20 For a fuller discussion on this see Malvern, *Modern Art*, ch. 6.

21 Henri Barbusse, *Under Fire* (1916), quoted in Geoffrey Dyer, *The Missing of the Somme* (London: Phoenix Press, 2001 [1994]), 17.

22 'The Canadian War Memorial Fund: Its History and Its Objects', *Canada in Khaki* (November 1917).

23 Memorandum of Proceedings of Preliminary Meeting of Imperial Memorials Committee, 16 March 1918 (IWM 460A/10).

24 Cited in J. Hepburn, ed., *Letters of Arnold Bennett*, Vol. III, *1916–1931* (Oxford: Oxford University Press, 1970), 53.

25 British War Memorials Committee Minutes, 21 March 1918 (IWM 460A/10).

26 Memorandum by Robert Ross, 8 April 1918 (IWM 460 A/10).

27 Hall, 'Modernism, Militarism and Masculinity', 668–71.

28 Ross to Bennett, Pictorial Propaganda Committee Minutes, 23 April 1918 (IWM 486/12).

29 From the Slade alone came Nevinson, the Nashes, Spencer, Adeney, Meninsky, Gill, Gertler, Roberts and Lewis. RAs were pretty much avoided, though some were admissible when they had a connection to the NEAC, such as Clausen, Orpen and Sargent. The NEAC was dominant with Orpen, John, Bone, Tonks, Lavery, Holmes, Strang, Rothenstein, Chowne, Connard, Airy, Pearce and McEvoy.

30 Malvern, 'Art, Propaganda and Patronage', 414.

31 British War Memorial Committee Minutes, 22 May 1918 (IWM 460/A 10).

32 P. W. Lewis, 'Foreword', *Guns* (exhibition catalogue), Goupil Gallery, February 1919.

33 Bennett to Beaverbrook, 12 June 1918. Cited in Malvern, *Modern Art*, 279.

34 Malvern, *Modern Art*, 279.

35 P. G. Konody, 'On War Memorials', in *Art and War: The Canadian War Memorials* (London: Colour, 1919), 15. The differentiation between the thing

'seen' and the thing 'witnessed' is explored further in Trudi Tate, *Modernism, History and the First World War* (Manchester: Manchester University Press, 1998).

36 *Daily Express* (3 January 1919).

37 P. W. Lewis, 'What Art Now?', *English Review* (April 1919).

38 New Metropole Centre, *War Artists Memorial Exhibition* (exhibition catalogue), Folkestone, August–September 1964.

39 John Cournos, *The Little Review* (June 1919), 48.

40 *Liverpool Echo* (12 December 1919).

41 Frank Rutter, 'Canadian War Memorials: Official Exhibition at the Academy', *Sunday Times* (5 January 1919).

42 'The Picture of the Sphinx', *Nation* (28 January 1919).

43 'The Royal Academy: Sargent's Great War Picture', *Morning Post* (3 May 1919).

44 P. G. Konody, 'Royal Academy: Pictures of the Year at Burlington House', *Observer* (4 May 1919).

45 Laurence Binyon, 'Art: The Royal Academy', *The New Statesman* (10 May 1919).

46 C. H. Collins Baker, 'The Royal Academy', *Saturday Review* (17 May 1919).

47 J. G., 'Fine Arts: The Royal Academy', *Athenaeum* (9 May 1919).

48 Virginia Woolf, 'The Royal Academy', *Athenaeum* (22 August 1919).

49 Michael Sadler, 'The Nation's War Pictures', *Westminster Gazette* (18 December 1919).

50 From a lecture entitled 'Qu'est-ce qu'une nation?' delivered at the Sorbonne on 11 March 1882.

51 A. M. B., 'Soldier Artists' War Pictures', *Daily Chronicle* (18 December 1919).

52 'The Nation's War Paintings: Youth at the Academy', *Liverpool Post* (12 December 1919).

53 Arthur Clutton-Brock, 'Art's Fresh Start', *The Times* (12 December 1919). He had at the start of the war emphasised how modernism and Prussianism could and should be compared.

54 Clutton-Brock, 'Art's Fresh Start'.

55 John Ruskin, 'War', in *The Crown of Wild Olives: Three Lectures on Work, Traffic and War* (London: Smith and Elder, 1866), 143.

56 Frank Rutter, 'The Influence of War on Art', in H. W. Wilson and J. A. Hammerton, eds, *The Great War: The Standard History of the All European Conflict*, vol. 12 (London: The Amalgamated Press, 1919), 161.

57 'Art and the People', *Daily Herald* (15 December 1919).

58 See Grace Brockington, *Above the Battlefield: Modernism and the Peace Movement in Britain, 1900–1918* (New Haven, CT: Yale University Press, 2010).

59 Hansard, *Proceedings in the House of Commons*, 24 February 1920.

60 Doris Sommer, *Proceed with Caution, When Engaged by Minority Writing in the Americas* (Cambridge, MA: Harvard University Press, 1999), 115.

61 The Imperial War Museum has an active education and learning programme within the art department. Also, as the Head of Art points out 'there is a balance which has always had to be struck between attracting visitors, meeting their expectations, and also perhaps challenging some of their preconceptions' (personal communication, 28 April 2011). For other student-related activities I recommend the following article: David A. Johnson and Nicole F. Gilbertson, 'Commemorations of Imperial Sacrifice at Home and Abroad: British Memorial of the Great War', *The History Teacher*, 43, 4 (2010), 563–85.

62 In a personal communication (28 April 2011), Kathleen Palmer, Head of Art at the Imperial War Museum, drew my attention to the display *From Crystal Palace to Lambeth Road* (curated by Richard Slocombe) which investigated the history of selection and brought to light how some paintings, such as Dodd's *The Interrogation*, iconic up until the 1920s, suddenly receded from public view.

13

Indecisive victory? German and British soldiers at the Armistice[1]

Alexander Watson

Hostilities cease at 11.00 today official.[2]

The Armistice of 11 November 1918 was a watershed in twentieth-century history. Although the Versailles Peace Treaty of June 1919 has received much closer scholarly attention, it was the November Armistice which halted the unprecedentedly bloody fighting of the First World War and played a crucial role in shaping both the form and reception of the final, ultimately flawed, peace agreement.[3] The failure of reconciliation in Europe had its roots not only in the divisions perpetuated by the Versailles demands. Reconciliation also failed because the conditions in which the Armistice was arranged led many in the 1920s and 1930s to reject the Allied victory as neither decisive nor final. Particularly for those on the German political right, the argument that capitulation had come about not through Allied military superiority but rather as the result of insidious British propaganda, Bolshevik agitation or the weakness and disloyalty of the home front provided a basis on which to assert that the peace conditions were unjust.[4] In some sections of the British populace during the 1930s the treaty also lost its legitimacy as doubts grew about the conflict's necessity, stories of German atrocities were dismissed as wartime fabrications and a resurgent, militarised Germany under the Nazis seemed to confirm that the victory of 1918 had been incomplete.[5]

The consequences of the failure to accept the decision of 1918 as final are well known. In Germany, the so-called 'stab in the back' theory shielded the army from disgrace and was exploited by the National Socialists to discredit Weimar democrats and prepare the people for a revanche. In Britain, doubts about the Versailles Treaty's justice and enforceability led to the Chamberlain government's maligned policy of appeasement, eroding the country's international credibility and resulting in opportunities to curtail Hitler's aggression being missed. Less clear, however, is the receptivity of the wider populace of both countries to such attitudes. In particular, historians have not investigated whether the Allied victory was already perceived as inconclusive in 1918 or if this construct was formed retrospectively in the inter-war years. Such considerations are important if the suitability of the Armistice as a basis for a stable peace is to be assessed and its role in the resumption of violence two decades later understood.

The purpose of this chapter is therefore to begin this process by examining how soldiers in the British and German armies – the section of the belligerent populations arguably best placed to assess the completeness of the Allied victory – responded to the Armistice in 1918. In order to assess reactions, the diaries and correspondence of forty combatants, divided equally between the German and British armies, have been analysed. The subjects served all along the Western Front in a variety of units, and held ranks ranging from private to colonel. Drawing on their personal testimonies and a range of other supporting material including censorship reports and recent secondary literature, the chapter will begin by briefly explaining the military and political considerations which prompted Germany to capitulate and then examining the expectations of peace among each army's personnel before the Armistice. The first section aims to show whether, before the onset of peace, combatants on either side anticipated an imminent end to hostilities. In the following section, the chapter will focus on British reactions to the Armistice announcement, investigating how soldiers responded to the ceasefire, analysing whether they considered the victory complete and questioning how far a sense of disappointment heralding the disillusionment of the 1930s was already present in November 1918. Finally, the third section will turn to the men and officers of the German army. It will study their comments on the war's termination, examine whether they accepted the capitulation and analyse the strategies they developed in order either to come to terms with or deny their defeat. Through providing a greater understanding of soldiers' responses to the onset of peace in 1918, the chapter aims to shed light on the role played by the Armistice in the failure of international reconciliation during the subsequent two decades.

The approach to the Armistice

On 29 September 1918 Field Marshal von Hindenburg and General Ludendorff, the leaders of Germany's armies, initiated the first moves towards peace by telling the Kaiser and his foreign secretary that the military required an immediate armistice. After more than four years of war, the nation and its forces were exhausted. The enormous, last-ditch offensive on the Western Front in the spring and early summer of 1918 had been a disastrous failure, costing the army almost one million soldiers killed, wounded and missing and dealing morale a hammer blow. Since mid-summer, the tired and much-depleted force had been in continuous retreat, as veteran British and French troops, supported by inexperienced but apparently limitless numbers of Americans, regained ground lost earlier in the year.[6] Germany's allies were also exhausted: the food supply in Austria-Hungary had collapsed and its army was worn out; the forces of the Ottoman Empire were in headlong retreat in the Middle East; and, in the Balkans, an Anglo-French offensive had shattered the Bulgarian army in the middle of September, prompting its troops to mutiny and turn on their own general headquarters.[7] By 29 September, as news came through of Bulgaria's armistice request and the British began their attack on Germany's last major fortified position in the west, the Hindenburg line, defeat appeared inevitable. Collapse on the Western Front seemed imminent unless immediate respite could be gained for Germany's troops.[8]

For soldiers on the ground, it was the unprecedented speed and scale of movement on the Western Front during the last three months of war that signalled a turn of fortunes, even before the onset of armistice negotiations. The five armies of the British Expeditionary Force (BEF), which bore the largest share of the Allied counter-offensive, advanced on average no less than eighty-four miles between their first attack at Amiens on 8 August and the Armistice.[9] This was a major achievement for an only partially mechanised army and its psychological impact on individual combatants was immense. For German troops, August and September were miserable and exhausting months of almost unceasing fighting and withdrawal. Konstantin Kramer, the observer of an anti-tank gun team in the Champagne, recorded 'days without rest and peace' spent in the front line, in which troops suffered under daily heavier artillery fire, were tortured by thirst, tension and sleep deprivation and fell ill through the influenza epidemic sweeping Europe.[10] The machine-gunner, Emil Bullinger, remembered the retreat similarly as a 'witches' Sabbath' characterised by 'the unceasing roll of artillery thunder, the hammer of machine guns, the drone of planes [and] the discharge of rockets'.[11] To men who had gone through the Germans' own offensives earlier in the year, the constant withdrawal over hard-won land was particularly depressing. Leutnant Friedrich Müller, an officer serving with Infantry Regiment No. 471, rued August as 'a difficult time for every patriotic man', as the hope that Germany might win the war evaporated.[12] Many soldiers developed what Vizefeldwebel Eugen Mortler described as a 'great longing for peace' under the intense strain; mass surrenders of exhausted troops became common, and by the end of the month the typical mood was characterised by the German Fifth Army's postal censor as comprising 'war weariness, moroseness and depression'.[13]

For British soldiers, the constant movement of the advance could be hardly less exhausting. By the Armistice men were complaining that they were 'ready to drop' and some even professed to be 'too knocked up [to] care' when they finally heard about peace.[14] Nonetheless, not only was the BEF in possession of more reserves than its enemy, and therefore able to rotate units to rest areas far more regularly, but advance could actually be experienced as exhilarating. For some British combatants, there was satisfaction that after coming so close to defeat earlier in the year, they were now clearly ascendant: 'Last spring we used to pull each other's legs about being good runners,' crowed the artilleryman, Charles Ramsdale, at the beginning of October, 'but it looks as if our friend the enemy is trying to break all previous records in that line!'[15] Others were jubilant at liberating French towns and villages long under German occupation. Colonel Stanley Brighten described 'the most wonderful receptions in the towns, the moment the Germans had gone, and we arrived, flags everywhere'.[16] In the ranks, George Barlow felt reaffirmed by this experience: 'One is mightily pleased and repaid, for all the hardships of active service, by the friendship and thanks and help of the people who have been newly liberated in Belgium from the detestable and execrable tyranny of the Boche,' he wrote.[17] Above all, however, the experience of advance was gratifying because men knew that it brought them closer to victory and therefore to home and their loved ones. Ramsdale's pleasure at the evidence of German athleticism, for example, lay principally in the calculation that, 'the faster and farther he runs[,] the sooner we can pack up and come home again'.[18] Already by the end of September, a few optimists were hoping for Christmas with their families, reasoning that 'the tables are turned & I think that Fritz must be beginning to realise it'.[19]

For soldiers under the constant pressure of battle, keeping up with political events was normally not a priority. Nonetheless, the news that the German government had sent America's President Wilson a peace note on 3 October aroused enormous interest on both sides. The postal censor of the Kaiser's Fifth Army, for example, noted the 'strong impression' which it had made on the troops and observed that 'almost every letter contains remarks about the offer'.[20] In the BEF, Barlow's unit 'was almost wild with excitement when the news of Germany's Peace Offer came through', while in the 13/Gloucesters, the men 'all nearly went mad' when they heard on 13 October that Germany had agreed to evacuate France and Belgium.[21] Despite the common interest, however, evidence from the letter and diary sample suggests that judgements on whether the negotiations would bring peace diverged greatly between the two sets of belligerents. In the British army, initial excitement was quickly tempered by caution, or even scepticism. Barlow, for example, also wrote that he thought the news 'too good to be true' and considered peace to be 'still far away'. By 22 October he had already dismissed the negotiations as 'a great disappointment to everybody' and ruled that only through the 'unconditional surrender of the enemy' could the war be ended.[22] While soldiers' diaries often indicate confidence in an eventual victory, few appear to have expected peace to be so imminent. Captain M. L. Walkinton, the acting adjutant of the 47th Machine Gun Battalion, was probably only marginally more pessimistic than the average in still estimating on 2 November that 'Easter should see the end of it all'.[23] Such conservatism was understandable. The German army was still almost everywhere occupying foreign soil, and although it had been forced out of its last prepared defensive positions, continued to inflict casualties on the BEF: 21,243 British officers and men were killed during October.[24] Past experience of disappointment at failed negotiations may also have prompted soldiers to regard the Germans' initiative with caution, and there is also some evidence that such an attitude was encouraged by British military authorities. Thus, for example, Lieutenant Colonel William Fraser, the commander of 1/Gordon Highlanders, viewed the peace note sceptically as 'the last effort of the Boche to make us slacken our efforts'. Worried about its effect on combat motivation, he ordered his troops to parade on 14 October and 'told them the Hun was not yet beaten and that we had got to go for him again'.[25]

German letters and diaries, by contrast, reveal a far greater inclination to accept that the negotiations heralded the end. Leutnant Müller, a highly patriotic officer, agreed on 13 October with his government's promise to withdraw from occupied territories, believing that although the army could still hold out for some time, further resistance would ultimately be futile; 'it is no disgrace to be overcome by so strong an opponent,' he reasoned.[26] Leutnant Hans Muhsal, fortunate to be serving in the comparatively quiet Alsace sector, also recognised that German defeat was inevitable. Following the negotiations in minute detail, he hoped first that Wilson's terms would be lenient, but even once it became clear that the Allies were using 'the uncompromising language of the victor to the defeated', he accepted that 'we will have no option other than to say yes'.[27] Among the rank and file, peace was not so much accepted as demanded once news of the negotiations became known. Gefreiter Bullinger recalled rumours circulating among the troops on 8 October that an armistice would come into effect the following morning and some soldiers did indeed surrender in the middle of the month, claiming that hostilities had ceased.[28] At the same time, the Fifth Army censor warned that peace at any price was being 'frantically demanded'.[29] This was hardly surprising given the state of the Kaiser's army. Many units were totally worn out through the months of continuous fighting, no rest and lack of replacement drafts: by the end of October, for example, Foot Guard Regiment No. 1, nominally 3,000 strong, comprised only one battalion of 250 soldiers, and its state was by no means exceptional.[30] With the prospect of an imminent end, discipline declined, particularly in the back areas: Eugen Mortler, travelling through the army's rear zone as a newly commissioned officer at the end of October, recorded that 'one hears and sees signs of the end, yes, even of collapse. Everything is in disorder.'[31] At the Front, combat motivation and fighting efficiency also plummeted further. As the line went back once more on 6 November, Leutnant Max Rütten, the adjutant of a machine-gun outfit, sadly yet accurately observed that 'the infantry is no longer holding. It is high time that an armistice came into effect – if not, there will be Bolshevik conditions.'[32]

Thus, when the Armistice was agreed on 11 November, it came as no surprise to the majority of German soldiers. In contrast, most of the sampled British personal papers reveal that their authors were generally unaware of peace's proximity until only a few days before the Armistice. Lieutenant Charles Bennet, fighting in the Royal Field Artillery, was earlier than most of his fellow officers in recognising on 6 November that he was 'in at the death' and that 'peace will be along in a few days'.[33] Most soldiers seem to have achieved a similar insight only once news that German envoys had crossed the lines had been disseminated, an event which sparked 'wild rumours' about imminent peace on 7 and 8 November.[34] Celebrations in some units began on the evening of 10 November, prematurely as the Armistice agreement was finally signed only at 5.20 on the following morning. News that hostilities were to cease reached many British soldiers at the Front only shortly before the deadline of 11 a.m. Lieutenant Colonel Fraser was informed of the peace just before his unit was due to move into positions to begin an attack on the enemy; official confirmation arrived at 8.30 a.m. Others further down the command chain were told even later. The infantryman, Robert Cude, who was actually in the firing line when the war ended, was 'staggered [at 9 a.m.] to read the news that, commencing at 11 a.m., today, an armistice will be in force, at Jerrys [*sic*] asking'. A. E. G. Garwood, an artilleryman, only heard about the Armistice at 10.30 a.m. and even then did not believe it, as his unit was still being shelled. Only when both sides ceased fire at 11.00 a.m. did the news become credible.[35]

Considerable variation thus existed between the expectations of peace held by combatants on either side in the months before the Armistice. Although British troops had known since August that they were winning, few anticipated that victory would be achieved in 1918. The German peace note of 3 October and the negotiations which followed made comparatively little impact on troops, many of whom treated the news with caution or even suspicion. In most cases, the realisation that peace was imminent seems to have dawned only once German delegates crossed the lines on 7 November. Even then, soldiers such as Cude and Garwood who were engaged in fighting and therefore unaware of recent diplomacy were flummoxed when suddenly ordered to cease fire on the morning of 11 November. For them, it could easily be foreseen that the victory might in retrospect have looked incomplete. For German soldiers, in contrast, Allied material superiority during the late summer and early autumn had already created intense despondency and exhaustion, resulting in precipitously declining combat motivation. News of the peace note in October inflamed expectations of peace and prompted a further drop in fighting efficiency and discipline. Already by the middle of the month, it was obvious to any soldier interested that the Allies' terms would not be easy: Muhsal was certainly aware of this and Mortler too was clear that Wilson demanded 'unconditional surrender for only an armistice'.[36] The final conditions would, as Unteroffizier Fritz Fritzsche warned his family from Berlin, be 'horrendous'.[37] Nonetheless, even many officers seem to have felt well before November that the military situation left little option but to accede. Once agreement with the Allies had been reached, the army's inability to transmit the correct time of the Armistice to its units provided combatants with a final, poignant illustration of its state of disintegration: soldiers' diaries tell of the ceasefire being ordered at 11.55, 11.45 or even 11.35 a.m., rather than correctly at noon (German time), with predictable confusion.[38] Ragged, disordered salvoes ended the war, and with it more than a month of expectation, for tired, demoralised and defeated German troops.

British reactions

As the previous section has demonstrated, the First World War finished very suddenly for British soldiers. Months of hectic advance were ended abruptly by the Armistice, although the enemy had been neither fully broken nor chased from Belgium, the aim with which Britain had officially entered the war. Under such conditions, the conflict's termination seemed anti-climactic to some combatants. Lieutenant Colonel Fraser was disappointed at the absence of 'the "great end" for which one has been keyed up all these years', while further down the hierarchy, Private Cude too complained that peace had been declared before Germany had undergone 'a decisive defeat'.[39] Sydney Fuller, a signaller serving with the 1/Cambridgeshires, wrote that when one of his comrades was woken up and told the news, he had simply 'grunted "Nice thing, waking a bloke up to tell him he's out of work," – turned over, and went to sleep again.'[40] Other men found themselves simply unable to adjust immediately to the abruptly altered circumstances. Two days after the Armistice, Captain Walkinton still found it 'curious being out here with no war', while Captain Jim Mackie admitted being unable to 'grasp the situation just yet – one still seems to have the idea that we shall be going back into the line in a few day's [*sic*] time'.[41] As Private Fuller himself remarked, after more than four long and bloody years of hostilities, the unexpectedly sudden peace could just seem 'too good to be true'.[42]

Reactions to news of the Armistice were, however, by no means all so low key. In many units, the first notification of the ceasefire sparked an enormous upsurge of relief and joy. Arthur Wrench described the 'absolute madness' set off by the premature announcement to the 4/Seaforth Highlanders on 10 November:

> What a racket. The Argylls['] band are out in force and even here we can hear them play. These drums are being beat as they never were beat before. I never dreamed the skins could stand such a 'walloping' nor the pipes to

> sound so wild and grand. What a great and glorious feeling it is. The war is over and we have won. Out in the yard there is a crazy bonfire of boxes of German rockets and star shells and they are spurting and fizzling dangerously in every direction and just like us, 'bursting' with enthusiasm at the glorious news.[43]

Mackie himself recorded that he and his fellow officers had cheered when they heard that the Armistice had been signed and recounted how in his unit too, the 2/4th Somerset Light Infantry, the band had played, flares and rockets had been launched and 'the men started firing their rifles in the air for pure joy'.[44] Discipline was dropped as men of all ranks rejoiced: Corporal A. H. Roberts of the 13/Gloucesters described how he had been caught by his celebrating officers, drenched twice with whisky and then danced with the party around the room.[45] Even the wounded and infirm gained a new lease of life on hearing the news: the neurologist, Foster Kennedy, described how the Armistice had been marked with bugles playing the ceasefire and the air-raid siren wailing the all-clear at his tent hospital south of Boulogne. 'The old "heads" in their beds cheered,' he wrote, 'and a boy, very ill of pneumonia, wheezed out [...] in a thin whisper, "that's the stuff to give them" and added, "Take them screens away – I'm not going to die now," and, by God, probably he won't!'[46]

Most accounts agree that this spontaneous sense of elation was fairly short-lived. By the following morning, Wrench recorded that 'we are more subdued than we were' and Mackie also confirmed that 'with the exception of a bit of dust on the first night, [news of the Armistice] was taken very quietly indeed'.[47] There is little evidence that this subsequent quiet reception was indicative of disappointment with the details of the Armistice agreement, however; indeed, soldiers were scarcely concerned with such matters. Rather, men seem to have needed a pause to take stock of their feelings and reflect on their own personal salvation after so much bloodshed. The medical orderly, H. Hulme, for example, found it 'strange to be alive' and recorded 'a feeling of shaking like a leaf', while Wrench thought that men were 'all pondering over the war that is past and the fact that we are among the survivors'.[48] Both Cude and Lieutenant Colonel Fraser commented on the good attendance at the voluntary church services held after the Armistice announcement.[49] Particularly common in soldiers' letters also is reflection on friends and comrades killed during the conflict. Mackie's thoughts at the Armistice very quickly turned to those deceased officers who had originally led his battalion during the war, while Lieutenant Savours remembered the men who had died in his company's last attack.[50] Possibly the most eloquent tribute was that of Private Cude, who described how, after bugles had sounded the 'Stand Fast':

> Our minds were taken back to our training days, so many years ago. With the thoughts of the past, come thoughts of those good chaps who were then with us, but have now departed for all time, having paid the Supreme Price, for the cause of Freedom. When I think of them, I have a keen sence [*sic*] of loneliness come over me, for in my 4 years out here almost, I have missed hundreds of the very best chaps that have ever breathed, and men, who ought to have been spared to take active part in the destiny of their Country.[51]

This sad reflection on lost comrades was, however, usually tempered by the fact that the war had ended in victory: as Savours told his family, 'we must remember that their sacrifice was not in vain'.[52] Given the unexpectedness of the Armistice and the difficulty many found in adjusting to the sudden absence of hostilities, it is striking that most other ranks appear to have accepted the victorious nature of the peace without question. This was certainly true of Wrench, and the men in Corporal Roberts's unit also clearly felt that the triumph was complete, for he reported on 13 November that the sole topic of conversation among them was demobilisation.[53] Officers' letters often contain more explicit consideration of the conflict's termination, but among them, too, there appears little sign that peace was considered premature. Major Saunders of the 24/London Regiment, for example, described the victory as an 'unconditional surrender' and celebrated 11 November as 'the most Historic Day of the Century'.[54] For Savours, the Armistice was 'as good as Peace'. Certain that the enemy's 'precarious position' would inhibit the resumption of hostilities, he concluded triumphantly that 'we are all very happy now we've beaten the Germans & are looking forward to the time when we get our discharge'.[55]

Key to British officers' satisfaction was the Armistice conditions themselves, which were effectively designed to neutralise the enemy's military might as well as provide a favourable basis for peace negotiations. Particularly important clauses included the immediate evacuation of the 'invaded countries', alongside which was significantly included Alsace-Lorraine,[56] withdrawal from the left bank of the Rhine and acceptance of Allied garrisons holding strategic bridgeheads on the right bank, the surrender of enormous amounts of war material, including 5,000 artillery pieces, 25,000 machine-guns, all submarines and a large portion of the surface fleet and the delivery of a large amount of railway rolling stock to the Allies.[57] Even to the most sceptical, these were impressive conditions. Captain Walkinton, for example, who at the beginning of November had still viewed the prospect of German capitulation pessimistically, declared himself 'quite convinced that we have won [the] war' when he saw them.[58] Moreover, although the outbreak of domestic revolution in November was acknowledged as limiting the Germans' options, the hectic advance of the previous months was sufficient to persuade officers such as Lieutenant Colonel G. S. Brighten that it was not 'internal troubles' but rather 'the military defeat which has forced and won the situation'.[59] The entry of Canadian troops into Mons on the morning of 11 November, the scene of the BEF's first battle against the Germans in August 1914, may also have encouraged this sense: the town's recapture was widely remarked upon in diaries, perhaps because with it the British had finally recovered through force of arms all of the land their army had lost since 1914.[60] Finally, even the most hardened doubters were won over by the fact that under the terms of the Armistice, British troops would enter Germany itself. Lieutenant Colonel Fraser, for example, whose reaction on 11 November had been decidedly muted, began to feel that the war effort had, after all, been vindicated as he marched with his battalion towards enemy territory two weeks later: 'The country came into [the war] to fight for the liberty of the World and *no other reason*,' he concluded with grim satisfaction. 'And this march marks the ultimate triumph of our cause after 4½ weary years.'[61]

In light of the fact that the Armistice came upon British soldiers so unexpectedly, their reactions were, perhaps, surprising. While combatants' letters and diaries do indicate that many experienced some difficulty in adjusting to the sudden fact of peace, the notion that the Germans had been decisively beaten was hardly questioned. Despite the fact that the enemy remained on French and Belgian soil and continued right up to the end of the war to inflict casualties on the BEF, hardly anybody seems to have thought peace premature. Of course, the principal reason for this was the Armistice itself, which was harsh enough to make further fighting superfluous. Officers, in particular, cited its conditions as the reason for their satisfaction; other ranks seem often inclined simply to have accepted the news of the capitulation. Probably, the crushing advance of the previous three months, which had indeed precipitated the victory, made questioning unnecessary. Certain that they had paid their debt to the dead and convinced that their triumph was total, the men of the BEF looked forward to demobilisation and the resumption of their civilian lives with a sense of satisfaction and vindication.

German reactions

Among German soldiers, demoralised and exhausted after the months of retreat, the initial reaction to the Armistice announcement was often simply relief at their own survival. The first act of Landwehrmann Johann Georg Schirmer on hearing of the Armistice, for example, was to head straight to church, 'in order to thank the Lord from the depths of my heart that I was allowed to see this hour in health'.[62] Leopold Wernicke, a battery clerk serving with the Bavarian Foot Artillery, marvelled at the 'calming feeling' of no longer seeing aeroplanes or hearing shooting.[63] Even officers expressed such sentiments: Leutnant Josef Schönfeld thanked God that he had escaped with a whole skin, while Walther Stölzl recorded that his comrades greeted news of the Armistice with cheering, chattering and laughter, many joking that their own personal war was won.[64] Such was the desire to be done with the fighting that some did not even wait for the ceasefire announcement to celebrate their salvation. Machine-gun officer Leutnant Paul Keppeler, for example, whose unit was withdrawn from what he termed the 'mess' and 'pigsty' of the Front, wrote home on 8 November confidently proclaiming that 'I have happily survived the war.'[65]

Many also greeted the Armistice primarily as the long-desired opportunity finally to return home. Soldiers in Leutnant Müller's unit gathered together after the ceasefire to sing *Heimatlieder* – songs about their homeland – and Leutnant Armin Schmitz of Infantry Regiment No. 130 went so far as to describe his men as 'extremely happy, for they can now go back home forever'.[66] Others also noticed that the mood was not universally depressed: Leutnant Wilhelm Lüthje, a supply column commander, recorded his soldiers' happiness at the ceasefire and Leutnant Rütten too heard men cheering when the news reached them.[67] So keen were many to return home that Mortler compared his troops to 'unleashed hounds' once the march back to Germany began.[68]

For other soldiers, however, the conditions in which peace was concluded prohibited any positive feelings. Any elation Rütten himself felt at surviving the war had been quickly dispelled by news of the Kaiser's and Crown Prince's abdications.[69] The outbreak of revolution in Germany, which had begun with the Kiel naval mutiny on 29 October and spread to Berlin by 9 November, left combatants still emotionally attached to the old regime deeply disturbed: Leutnant Herbert Sulzbach, serving with Field Artillery Regiment No. 63, felt that the country was 'at the bottom of the abyss', while Rütten wondered bitterly whether he 'had gadded about outside in the muck for four years in order now perhaps to die from the bullet [of a revolutionary] at "home"'.[70] The fact of military defeat was also heartbreaking. Hauptmann Helmuth Fuchs mourned that the Armistice conditions meant 'capitulation, wretched capitulation', while Muhsal considered them 'annihilating' and worried that the surrender of railway rolling stock might leave the country at risk of starvation.[71] The victory celebrations of the formerly submissive Belgian population, past whose flags the departing army had to march, simply underlined the Germans' humiliation.[72] In such grim circumstances, even men who had looked forward to the end of hostilities could change their minds: Keppeler, for example, abandoned his earlier relief at surviving the war and began to envy 'those who remained outside on the field of honour and do not have to see the weakness of our Fatherland'.[73]

For patriotic and conservative officers, not only the shame of national disaster but also the pain of personal humiliation made the Armistice period traumatic. The army was not completely isolated from the political turmoil at home, and during the transition to peace, officers suffered a loss of prestige and authority. Partly this was the result of orders issued by the high command, which, anxious to avoid any breakdown of discipline, instructed every unit to form a soldiers' council representing other ranks' interests. While the power possessed by these elected bodies was initially small and their demands often limited to better food, they could cause officers intense embarrassment. In Walther Stölzl's regiment, for example, the council unsuccessfully demanded that their commander be removed and another elected in his place.[74] Leutnant Muhsal's experience was even worse. From the day after the Armistice, he and his fellow officers were made to suffer an array of indignities. Epaulettes, the external marks of officers' authority, were removed by order of the regiment, horses were confiscated from company commanders and unpopular officers were gradually dismissed by the soldiers' council.[75] Moreover, once the Armistice had been announced, the insubordination witnessed in some units during the last weeks of war grew incrementally. Behaviour on the streets deteriorated and officers wrote of 'undisciplined hordes' in the rear areas.[76] Some contemporaries suggest that poorly trained line of communication troops were principally responsible for the disorder but other evidence indicates that combat units did not go entirely unaffected. Muhsal, for example, encountered young machine-gun crews who behaved 'quite atrociously' and all carried red flags, while Gefreiter Bullinger, himself a machine-gunner, condemned the behaviour of infantrymen, who 'pulled back to the homeland bawling and shouting, made themselves as difficult as possible [...] and incited disciplined troops to disobedience'.[77] For such soldiers, even violence against officers was no longer taboo: Mortler was held up by Bolshevik artillerymen, 'noisy, young boys without officers', who threatened him with bayonets and demanded his supply column's horses.[78]

As their world collapsed around them, some conservative officers sought comfort in denying the defeat. Hopeful rumours of mutiny in the British Royal Navy and revolution in France were seized upon by those reluctant to concede that the war was lost.[79] The performance of the Kaiser's army during the conflict was cited by others to prove that, at the very least, the moral victory belonged to Germany: Sulzbach, for example, declared that 'never before has a nation, a single army, had the whole world against it and stood its ground against such overwhelming odds [...]. We protected our homeland from her enemies – they never pushed as far as German territory.'[80] In contrast to the glum assessments of military potential issued while the fighting was still underway, such officers now actively sought evidence that the army remained in good shape. Rütten forgot his pre-Armistice lamentations about the state of the infantry and instead emphasised the troops' martial bearing, remarking on one regiment which marched by in good order under music that its complement 'didn't look very much like defeated men'. Sulzbach too ignored the evidence of disintegration and argued that the army was 'making its way home with perfect discipline'. Infantrymen whom he encountered on the march were, he reported, of 'splendid character' and 'convinced [...] that Germany will never be beaten' – a strange belief for men who were withdrawing from the battlefield as a defeated army.[81]

The army high command did its best to cultivate the notion that no military reverse had taken place and to attribute the defeat to revolutionaries at home. Crown Prince Wilhelm of Prussia, for example, issued an order on the day of the Armistice assuring his troops that 'the army group has not been defeated by force of arms!' and instead alluding to 'hunger and bitter need' as the factors forcing Germany to make peace.[82] Lower commanders also took up this theme: Müller wrote approvingly of a speech given by his regimental commander asserting that 'the German army is not defeated. The conditions and disunity at home have laid us low. The disorders were begun by people, sailors etc., who have spent the whole war in the rear.'[83] For the military high command, this was, of course, a face-saving exercise designed to divert blame from themselves and protect the army's prestige. It was attractive to some combatants, however, because they too had an emotional stake in rejecting the notion that the army was defeated and that their own hardships and sacrifices of the previous four years had been in vain. Moreover, wartime propaganda had conditioned troops to be receptive to such explanations: as historian Anne Lipp has pointed out, the dichotomy between strong, steadfast fighters and weak, perfidious civilians had been a staple of German military indoctrination throughout 1918, as the high command had sought to insulate the army from falling home morale.[84] Finally, the portrayal of the army as undefeated resonated partly because it was not totally divorced from troops' experiences. Not only had home revolution conveniently broken out before the Armistice but the victors' welcome received by soldiers as they arrived back in Germany and marched through 'narrow streets […] packed with civilians, who cheered us like anything' must have helped cloud the memory of the last three months' constant, awful retreat.[85]

Not all officers and men disappointed with the war's outcome found refuge in denial or the search for a scapegoat; it is important to recognise that more benign coping strategies were available, even to conservative soldiers still wedded to the old Imperial regime. Some found it more comfortable simply to accept the defeat and retreat into private life. Gefreiter Oswald Zetzsche, for example, decided when he heard of Germany's capitulation that 'there is actually nothing left for us now except a home full of love and contentment. A dear wife and child must replace everything.'[86] Leutnant Lüthje, a patriotic Jewish German, had similarly concluded by 9 November that 'one would do well to draw a line under the past and also to consider the peace conditions solely from the viewpoint that our future is safe, as we will anyway be in a position to rise once again economically'. Looking forward to the peace, he wrote, 'Just live until then! Then I want to work, for the Fatherland and for myself.'[87]

German soldiers' responses to the Armistice were by no means uniform. Both officers and men in many cases greeted the arrival of peace with relief, both as an end to the danger and a longed-for opportunity to return home. After four years of fighting many, particularly in the ranks, seem to have cared little about either the defeat or revolution; personal considerations outweighed everything. For others, however, particularly conservative officers whose identity was anchored in the old regime or army, the loss of the war and abdication of the Hohenzollerns was experienced with shame and horror. The 'stab in the back' explanation promulgated by the high command was attractive to these men because it emphasised the army's success in continuing to hold enemy territory 'undefeated' and absolved them from responsibility for the capitulation. Some officers absorbed it wholesale: Stölzl, for example, was vitriolic about the home front when he learned the Armistice conditions. 'They left us in the lurch,' he wrote. 'We are not defeated, we've never had the feeling of being defeated. It is shameless to have to capitulate as victors in the occupied land of the enemy.'[88] Nor, indeed, was such resentment limited to commissioned ranks. Konstantin Kramer, a 20-year-old, intensely patriotic anti-tank gunner, also insisted from his hospital bed at the war's end that 'only the front held on heroically until the last moment. Marxism smashed our Fatherland.'[89] How far this opinion was held throughout the army is impossible to establish, although its promotion by the authorities, superficial convincingness and appeal to the disappointed might suggest that at least a significant minority of German soldiers accepted it after the Armistice. While other coping strategies were available, even to conservative officers, the difficulty of writing off the years of sacrifice, the shame of capitulation and the uncertain situation at home provided an enormous impetus for many men quickly to forget the awful conditions and intense desire for peace in the summer and autumn, and instead emphasise in the safety of winter 1918 that there had been no military defeat.

Conclusion

A comparison of German and British soldiers' letters and diaries reveals considerable variations in how both groups of belligerents anticipated and interpreted the Armistice of November 1918. Until days before the cessation of hostilities, few men serving with the BEF had any idea that peace was imminent. Despite the rapid, morale-raising advance in the war's final three months, the enemy still appeared unbroken and continued to occupy French and Belgian soil. The expectations elicited by the opening of peace negotiations at the beginning of October therefore remained limited, and the Armistice came as an enormous, although welcome, surprise. German troops, in contrast, demoralised and exhausted by the failure of their own offensive in the first half of the year and the subsequent retreat under intense Allied pressure, regarded their government's peace note to President Wilson as a necessary admission of defeat. With the Armistice daily expected, discipline and combat motivation further declined: as one officer aptly observed, 'with the end now impending, no one wanted to let themselves be shot dead'.[90]

In light of these divergent expectations, combatants' subsequent interpretations of the Armistice are surprising. Despite its unexpectedness, British soldiers immediately welcomed the peace as a decisive victory. On the German side, reactions were more mixed. Certainly, many officers and men greeted the long-awaited ceasefire as a relief from danger and much-desired opportunity to return home to their families. A significant number, however, rejected the capitulation, even though in many cases they too had previously accepted its inevitability. The explanation for both sides' remarkable turnabout and polarisation rests both with circumstantial factors and human psychology. Cognitive psychologists have identified the so-called 'Confirmation Bias' heuristic, whereby people commonly seek information that supports their own preferred beliefs and dismiss conflicting evidence.[91] Confronted by the sudden cessation of hostilities, British troops therefore had little difficulty in accepting the attractive notion of a decisive victory by alluding to the harsh terms of the Armistice and the previous three months' dramatic advance. For those German soldiers devastated by the capitulation, the fact that their army still stood on foreign territory was probably not enough to deny the defeat. The outbreak of revolution at home just before the Armistice, however, added apparent veracity to the army high command's claim to have been stabbed in the back. Rather than come to terms with their own failure, those combatants so inclined could thus dismiss the significance of the military setbacks and instead blame Marxist treachery and civilian weakness.

The contribution of the Armistice towards a lasting peace in Europe was thus by no means wholly positive. Perhaps 'total war' demands 'total victory', in which, as at the end of the 1939–45 conflict, a firm decision can be achieved only with one army annihilated, its nation's capital occupied and its people prostrate. To argue, however, that the Allies should have rejected the German capitulation and continued fighting in 1918 would be absurd. While mistakes were made, most importantly the failure to insist on a top military representative as German signatory, the fact that the ceasefire not only satisfied British soldiers but was also accepted with relief by many exhausted and demoralised German troops suggests that it could have provided an adequate foundation for lasting reconciliation in Europe. Ultimately, it was not ambiguity in the war's conclusion that predestined the subsequent peace laid down at Versailles to remain merely an Armistice, a temporary break in hostilities which were to be resumed in a new and more terrible form twenty years later.

Notes

1 I am extremely grateful to Ms S. E. Glover, Mr J. H. F. Mackie, Ms R. Price and Mrs S. Woodrow for permission to cite from some of the British soldiers' private papers used in this research. In conformity with privacy laws, the surnames of all German archival sources have been replaced with pseudonyms. Every effort has been made to contact copyright holders and the author would be grateful for any information which might help to trace those whose identities or addresses are not currently known.

2 Imperial War Museum, Department of Documents, London [hereafter IWM], Misc 226 Item 3244: Urgent priority telegram announcing the armistice received by 87th Brigade, Royal Garrison Artillery at 7.55 a.m. on 11 November 1918.

3 For the Armistice, see particularly Bullitt Lowry, *Armistice 1918* (Kent, OH: Kent State University Press, 1996). For the Versailles peace treaty, see Alan Sharp, *The Versailles Settlement: Peacemaking in Paris, 1919* (Basingstoke: Macmillan, 1991) and Manfred F. Boemeke, Gerald D. Feldman and Elisabeth Glaser, eds, *The Treaty of Versailles: A Reassessment after 75 Years* (Cambridge: German Historical Institute and Cambridge University Press, 1998). For an excellent analysis of the final year of the war, see David Stevenson, *With Our Backs to the Wall: Victory and Defeat in 1918* (London: Allen Lane, 2011).

4 The archetypal example is Adolf Hitler, *Mein Kampf. Eine Abrechnung*, 2 vols. (Munich: Franz Eher Nachfolger, 1925, 1933), 1, especially 205, 214–15, 220, 225 and 367–8.

5 For a discussion of inter-war attitudes towards the Versailles treaty and the policy of appeasement, see Frank McDonough, *Neville Chamberlain, Appeasement and the British Road to War* (Manchester: Manchester University Press, 1998), especially 95–132.

6 See Alexander Watson, *Enduring the Great War: Combat, Morale and Collapse in the German and British Armies, 1914–1918* (Cambridge: Cambridge University Press), 184–231.

7 Holger H. Herwig, *The First World War: Germany and Austria-Hungary 1914–1918* (London: Arnold, 1997), 433–5; Maureen Healy, *Vienna and the Fall of the Habsburg Empire: Total War and Everyday Life in World War I* (Cambridge: Cambridge University Press, 2004), 305–8; Alan Palmer, *The Decline and Fall of the Ottoman Empire* (London: John Murray, 1992), 242; and R. J. Crampton, *Bulgaria 1878–1918. A History* (Boulder, CO: East European Monographs and Columbia University Press, 1983), 468.

8 For the circumstances surrounding Ludendorff's recognition that the war was lost and the meeting on 29 September, see Martin Kitchen, *The Silent Dictatorship: The Politics of the German High Command under Hindenburg and Ludendorff, 1916–1918* (London: Croom Helm, 1976), 253–7.

9 Paddy Griffith, 'The Extent of Tactical Reform in the British Army', in Paddy

Griffith, ed., *British Fighting Methods in the Great War* (London: Frank Cass, 1996), 18.

10 Deutsches Tagebucharchiv, Emmendingen [hereafter DTA], 506,1: K. Kramer, diary, 15 August 1918. Unless otherwise indicated, all translations in this chapter are mine.

11 DTA, 1083: E. Bullinger, memoir (possibly based on a diary) written in the 1920s, 206 (3 September 1918).

12 Staatsbibliothek zu Berlin, Preussischer Kulturbesitz, Handschriftabteilung, Berlin [hereafter Staatsbib. Berlin], MS. Germ. fol. 1651: C. F. Müller, diary, 30 August 1918.

13 DTA, 260: E. Mortler, diary, 26 July 1918 and Bundesarchiv-Militärarchiv Freiburg [hereafter BA-MA Freiburg], W-10/50794: Fifth Army censorship report, 31 August 1918. For the mass surrenders, see Niall Ferguson, 'Prisoner Taking and Prisoner Killing in the Age of Total War: Towards a Political Economy of Military Defeat', *War in History*, 11, 2 (2004), 156–7 and 160–3.

14 IWM, 85/51/1: A. E. Wrench, diary, 28 October 1918 and IWM, 92/3/1: A. E. G. Garwood, diary, 11 November 1918.

15 IWM, Con Shelf: C. W. Ramsdale, letter to mother and sister, 11 October 1918. Cf. IWM, 85/51/1: A. E. Wrench, diary, 21 October 1918.

16 IWM, 87/18/1: G. S. Brighten, letter to parents, 13 November 1918.

17 IWM, 86/40/1: G. R. Barlow, letter to 'Alice', 15 November 1918.

18 IWM, Con Shelf: C. W. Ramsdale, letter to mother and sister, 11 October 1918.

19 IWM, Cons Shelf and 84/58/1: W. J. Cotter, letter to mother, 30 September 1918.

20 BA-MA Freiburg, W-10/50794: Fifth Army censorship report, 17 October 1918.

21 IWM, 86/40/1: G. R. Barlow, letter to 'Alice', 8 October 1918 and IWM, 97/37/1: A. H. Roberts, diary, 13 October 1918.

22 IWM, 86/40/1: G. R. Barlow, letters to 'Alice', 8 and 22 October 1918. Cf. IWM, 97/37/1: A. H. Roberts, diary, 13 and 14 October 1918 and IWM, PP/MCR/172: A. H. Bowhill, diary, 13 October 1918.

23 IWM, DS/MISC/41: M. L. Walkinton, letter to female relatives, 2 November 1918. Cf. also the similar conclusions drawn from British soldiers' papers kept in the Liddle Collection, University of Leeds, in Peter Liddle, 'Britons Overseas', in Hugh Cecil and Peter Liddle, eds, *At the Eleventh Hour: Reflections, Hopes and Anxieties at the Closing of the Great War, 1918* (Barnsley: Leo Cooper, 1998), 53.

24 *Statistics of the Military Effort of the British Empire during the Great War. 1914–1920*, ed. War Office (London: HMSO, 1922), 270.

25 David Fraser, ed., *In Good Company. The First World War Letters and Diaries of the Hon. William Fraser, Gordon Highlanders* (Salisbury: Michael Russell, 1990), 314–5 (letter to father, 14 October 1918).

26 Staatsbib. Berlin, MS. Germ. fol. 1651: C.F. Müller, diary, 13 October 1918.

27 BA-MA Freiburg, MSg 1/ 3109: H. Muhsal, diary, 16 October 1918. For other entries concerning the negotiations, see 6, 7, 10, 13, 18, 21, 22 and 25 October.

28 DTA, 1083: E. Bullinger, memoir (possibly based on a diary) written in the 1920s, 215 (8 October 1918). For rumours and rumour-inspired surrenders, see Hauptstaatsarchiv Stuttgart, M30/ 1 Bü 337, Bl. 80: Order of Armee-Oberkommando 19 entitled 'Rumours of Armistice and Similar', 15 October 1918 and The National Archives, Kew, WO 157/ 199: Summary of Information, No. 296 (Fourth Army), 10 October 1918, 6.

29 BA-MA Freiburg, W-10/50794: Fifth Army censorship report, 17 October 1918, 106.

30 DTA, 141,3: M. Rütten, diary, 29 October 1918. For the much-reduced strength of the German army by the Armistice, see Wilhelm Deist, 'Verdeckter Militärstreik im Kriegsjahr 1918?', in Wolfram Wette, ed., *Der Krieg des kleinen Mannes: Eine Militärgeschichte von unten* (Munich: Piper, 1992, 1995), 159.

31 DTA, 260: E. Mortler, diary, 31 October 1918. For further evidence of rear-line indiscipline, in particular the plundering of supply trains, see DTA, 1083: E. Bullinger, memoir (possibly based on a diary) written in the 1920s, 217 and BA-MA Freiburg, MSg 1/ 2968: H. Fuchs, diary, 27 October and 7 November 1918.

32 DTA, 141,3: M. Rütten, diary, 6 November 1918. For further evidence of poor combat motivation, see also BA-MA Freiburg, MSg 1/ 565: Buchen, diary, 23 October 1918 and BA-MA Freiburg, W-10/ 50677: H. Reimers, notes (erroneously dated), 8 November 1918, 1534. Desertion also increased rapidly in the last weeks of the war. See Christoph Jahr, *Gewöhnliche Soldaten. Desertion und Deserteure im deutschen und britischen Heer 1914–1918* (Göttingen: Vandenhoeck & Ruprecht, 1998), 166–7.

33 IWM, 01/58/1: C. H. Bennet, letter to 'Mary', 6 November 1918.

34 IWM, PP/MCR/172: A. H. Bowhill, diary, 8 November 1918. Cf. IWM, 86/32/1: S. T. Fuller, 7 November 1918, IWM, 97/37/1: A. H. Roberts, diary, 7 and 8 November 1918 and IWM, PP/MCR/327: H. J. Savours, letter to family, 9 November 1918.

35 Fraser, ed., *In Good Company*, 331–2 (diary, 11 November 1918), IWM, Con Shelf: R. Cude, diary, 11 November 1918 and IWM, 92/3/1: A. E. G. Garwood, diary, 11 November 1918.

36 BA-MA Freiburg, MSg 1/ 3109: H. Muhsal, diary, 16 October 1918 and DTA, 260: E. Mortler, diary, 18 October 1918.

37 Author's collection: F. Fritzsche, letter to father, 31 October 1918.

38 See, for 11.55 a.m., BA-MA Freiburg, MSg 1/ 143: G. Leppin, diary, 11 November 1918 and BA-MA Freiburg, MSg 1/ 3109: H. Muhsal, diary, 11 November 1918. For 11.45 a.m., see Staatsbib. Berlin, MS. Germ. fol. 1651: C. F. Müller, diary, 11 November 1918, BA-MA Freiburg, MSg 1/ 1576: J.

Schönfeld, letter to family, 23 December 1918 and BA-MA Freiburg, W-10/ 50677: H. Reimers, notes (erroneously dated), 8 November 1918, 1535–6. For 11.35 a.m., see BA-MA Freiburg, W-10/ 50677: A. Schmitz, 11 November 1918.

39 Fraser, ed., *In Good Company*, 332 (diary, 11 November 1918) and IWM, Con Shelf: R. Cude, diary, 11 November 1918.

40 IWM, 86/32/1: S. T. Fuller, diary / memoir, 11 November 1918.

41 IWM, DS/MISC/41: M. L. Walkinton, letter to female relatives, 13 November 1918 and IWM, 02/16/1: J. R. Mackie, letter to parents, 13 November 1918. Cf. also IWM, 86/32/1: S. T. Fuller, diary / memoir, 12 November 1918 and IWM, Cons shelf and 84/58/1: W. J. Cotter, letter to mother, 19 November 1918. The letters of J. R. Mackie can be found in J. H. F. Mackie, ed., *Answering the Call: Letters from the Somerset Light Infantry 1914–1919* (Eggleston: Raby Books, 2002).

42 IWM, 86/32/1: S. T. Fuller, diary / memoir, 12 November 1918.

43 IWM, 85/51/1: A. E. Wrench, diary, 10 November 1918.

44 IWM, 02/16/1: J. R. Mackie, letter to parents, 13 November 1918. Cf. IWM, Con Shelf: L. W. Horner, letter to cousin, 13 November 1918.

45 IWM, 97/37/1: A. H. Roberts, diary, 11 November 1918. Cf. IWM, 02/16/1: J. R. Mackie, letter to parents, 13 November 1918.

46 Isabel Kennedy Butterfield, ed., *The Making of a Neurologist. The Letters of Foster Kennedy M.D., F.R.S.Edin. 1884–1952 to his Wife from Queen Square, London 1906–1910, New York City 1910–1912, British Expeditionary Force 1915–1918* (Hatfield: Stellar Press, 1981), 82 (letter to wife, 11 November 1918).

47 IWM, 85/51/1: A. E. Wrench, diary, 11 November 1918 and IWM, 02/16/1: J. R. Mackie, letter to parents, 24 November 1918. Cf. IWM, PP/MCR/138: E. R. Hepper, diary, 12 November 1918.

48 IWM, 01/60/1: H. Hulme, diary, 11 November 1918 and IWM, 85/51/1: A. E. Wrench, diary, 11 November 1918. Cf. IWM, 01/58/1: C.H. Bennet, letter to 'Mary', 13 November 1918.

49 See Fraser, ed., *In Good Company*, 332 (diary, 11 November 1918) and IWM, Con Shelf: R. Cude, diary, 11 November 1918.

50 IWM, 02/16/1: J. R. Mackie, letter to parents, 10 November 1918 and IWM, PP/MCR/327: H. J. Savours, letter to family, 11 November 1918.

51 IWM, Con Shelf: R. Cude, diary, 11 November 1918. For other examples, see IWM, 94/3/1: C. J. Saunders, letter to father, 11 November 1918 and IWM, DS/MISC/41: M. L. Walkinton, letter to female relatives, 13 November 1918.

52 IWM, PP/MCR/327: H. J. Savours, letter to family, 11 November 1918.

53 IWM, 85/51/1: A. E. Wrench, diary, 10 November 1918 and IWM, 97/37/1: A. H. Roberts, diary, 13 November 1918. For the widespread interest in demobilisation sparked by the Armistice, see also IWM, Con Shelf: L. W. Horner, letter to cousin, 13 November 1918 and, among officers, IWM, DS/ MISC/41: M. L. Walkinton, letter to female relatives, 13 November 1918.

54 IWM, 94/3/1: C. J. Saunders, letter to father, 11 November 1918.
55 IWM, PP/MCR/327: H. J. Savours, letter to family, 18 November 1918.
56 On Alsace, see Klaus Hofmann's chapter in this volume.
57 The Armistice conditions are reproduced in H. R. Rudin, *Armistice 1918* (New Haven, CT: Yale University Press, 1944), 426–32.
58 IWM, DS/MISC/41: M. L. Walkinton, letter to female relatives, 13 November 1918.
59 IWM, 87/18/1: G. S. Brighten, letter to parents, 13 November 1918.
60 IWM, 85/51/1: A. E. Wrench, diary, 10 November 1918. Cf. IWM, 97/37/1: A. H. Roberts, diary, 10 November 1918 and Kennedy Butterfield, ed., *Making of a Neurologist*, 82 (letter to wife, 11 November 1918).
61 Fraser, ed., *In Good Company*, 332 (diary, 24 November 1918).
62 DTA, 606: J. G. Schirmer, diary, 11 November 1918. Landwehr troops were middle-aged reservists.
63 DTA, 1040, II: L. Wernicke, diary, 12 November 1918.
64 BA-MA Freiburg, MSg 1/ 1576: J. Schönfeld, letter to family, 22 November 1918 and BA-MA Freiburg, MSg 1/ 854: W. Stölzl, notes on the Armistice written on 19 November 1918.
65 DTA, 758: P. Keppeler, letter to family, 8 November 1918.
66 Staatsbib. Berlin, MS. Germ. fol. 1651: C. F. Müller, diary, 11 November 1918 and BA-MA Freiburg, W-10/ 50677: A. Schmitz, notes, 11 November 1918, 1531–2.
67 BA-MA Freiburg, MSg 2/ 2797: W. Lüthje, diary, 11 November 1918 and DTA, 141,3: M. Rütten, diary, 11 November 1918. Cf. BA-MA Freiburg, W-10/ 50677: H. Reimers, notes (erroneously dated), 8 November 1918, 1535 and BA-MA Freiburg, MSg 1/ 2968: H. Fuchs, diary, 11 November 1918.
68 DTA, 260: E. Mortler, diary, 17 November 1918.
69 DTA, 141,3: M. Rütten, diary, 11 November 1918.
70 Herbert Sulzbach, *With the German Guns. Four Years on the Western Front 1914–1918* (London: Leo Cooper, 1973), 245 (diary, 9 November 1918) and DTA, 141,3: M. Rütten, diary, 11 November 1918.
71 BA-MA Freiburg, MSg 1/ 2968: H. Fuchs, diary, 11 November 1918 and BA-MA Freiburg, MSg 1/ 3109: H. Muhsal, diary, 12 November 1918.
72 See particularly DTA, 260: E. Mortler, diary, 16 November 1918. Also, DTA, 1040, II: L. Wernicke, diary, 11 November 1918 and BA-MA Freiburg, MSg 1/ 565: Buchen, diary, 11 November 1918.
73 DTA, 758: P. Keppeler, letter to family, 22 November 1918. Cf. BA-MA Freiburg, MSg 1/ 565: Buchen, diary, 11 November 1918.
74 BA-MA Freiburg, MSg 1/ 854: W. Stölzl, notes on the Armistice written on 19 November 1918.
75 BA-MA Freiburg, MSg 1/ 3109: H. Muhsal, diary, 12, 19 and 20 November and 1, 2 and 4 December 1918.

76 BA-MA Freiburg, MSg 1/ 565: Buchen, diary, 11 November 1918 and Sulzbach, *With the German Guns*, 249 (diary, 11 November 1918).

77 BA-MA Freiburg, MSg 1/ 3109: H. Muhsal, diary, 13 November 1918 and DTA, 1083: E. Bullinger, memoir (possibly based on a diary) written in the 1920s, 228 (13 November 1918).

78 DTA, 260: E. Mortler, diary, 14 November 1918. For evidence that conditions were worse among line of communication troops than in fighting units, see BA-MA Freiburg, MSg 1/ 565: Buchen, diary, 10 and 11 November 1918 and BA-MA Freiburg, MSg 1/ 2968: H. Fuchs, diary, 11 November 1918.

79 BA-MA Freiburg, MSg 1/ 565: Buchen, diary, 10 November 1918. Cf. DTA, 141,3: M. Rütten, diary, 16 November 1918.

80 Sulzbach, *With the German Guns*, 250–1 (diary, 13 November 1918).

81 DTA, 141,3: M. Rütten, diary, 16 November 1918 and Sulzbach, *With the German Guns*, 252 (diary, 17 November 1918).

82 BA-MA Freiburg, PH 5I/ 21: 'Order of the German Crown Prince after the Outbreak of the Revolution of 9.11.1918', 11 November 1918. Cf. also the order issued by the commander of the 18th Army, General von Hutier, partially reproduced in Sulzbach, *With the German Guns*, 248–9 (diary, 11 November 1918).

83 Staatsbib. Berlin, MS. Germ. fol. 1651: C. F. Müller, diary, 13 November 1918.

84 Anne Lipp, *Meinungslenkung im Krieg. Kriegserfahrungen deutscher Soldaten und ihre Deutung 1914–1918* (Göttingen: Vandenhoeck and Ruprecht, 2003), 311–14.

85 Sulzbach, *With the German Guns*, 254 (diary, 28 November 1918). For other similar accounts of the return, see BA-MA Freiburg, MSg 1/ 143: G. Leppin, letter to 'Erna', 22 November 1918, DTA, 1083: E. Bullinger, memoir (possibly based on a diary), 2 December 1918 and BA-MA Freiburg, MSg 1/ 3109: H. Muhsal, diary, 4 December 1918.

86 DTA, 1280,18: O. Zetzsche, letter to Steffi 'Doris' Meier, 13 November 1918.

87 BA-MA Freiburg, MSg 2/ 2797: W. Lüthje, diary, 9 November 1918.

88 BA-MA Freiburg, MSg 1/ 854: W. Stölzl, notes on the Armistice written on 19 November 1918.

89 DTA, 506,1: K. Kramer, diary, 9 November 1918.

90 BA-MA Freiburg, W-10/ 50677: H. Reimers, notes (erroneously dated), 8 November 1918, 1534.

91 See Willem A. Wagenaar, *Paradoxes of Gambling Behaviour* (Hove: Lawrence Erlbaum Associates, 1988), 108–9.

14

Mixing memory and desire: British and German war memorials after 1918

Adrian Barlow

The Armistice, bringing the fighting of the First World War to an end, allowed barely a pause before the next phase began: that of memorialising the events and the victims of the past four years. To memorialise is, according to the *Oxford English Dictionary*, 'to preserve the memory of; to be or supply a memorial of; to commemorate'. Memorialising is a way of giving significance to memory. It can be understood as the deliberate act of determining why someone or something should be commemorated, not forgotten. It is the action or process of creating a memorial, or of giving to something the status of a memorial. A mother's decision to erect a headstone over the burial place of her son, and to choose words to go on that headstone, is an act of memorialising. If she and her family later gather around the grave on the anniversary of her son's death, that is an act of commemoration. But when a parent, say, is unable to place a headstone because they have not been able literally to bury their son or daughter's body, then the desire for some substitute, some other way of figuratively enshrining the memory, 'Lest we forget', needs to be satisfied. As Catherine Moriarty has observed, 'The possibility of forgetting underlies the deeply felt need to create a memorial to posterity.'[1] Objects or places associated with the person may acquire memorial status; that is, they serve as a focus for memory and for commemoration.

For the individual mourners of the First World War, this substitute might have been no more than a photograph on the mantelpiece, a bundle of letters or (if they were lucky) the personal possessions of the soldier literally stripped from his body and returned to his family. Adrian Gregory has pointed out that

> The parents of those who were killed in the First World War suffered emotional stress to an unparalleled degree, victims of a transitional moment in the history of attitudes towards death. Their affective state was miserable, a combination of the worst of Victorian grief and modern sense of loss, but without access to the defensive strategies of either period.[2]

Vera Brittain gazed in horror at the blood-stained battledress jacket of her fiancé Roland, sent back to Buxton in a brown paper parcel;[3] Edward Thomas's pocket watch, stopped at the precise second he was killed by the blast from an exploding shell, came home to his family while Thomas himself was buried on the outskirts of Arras.[4] Today, thousands of people with no connection to the poet other than through his poetry (tourists, perhaps schoolchildren, on visits to the battlefields of the Western Front) visit Thomas's grave, which is located in a small cemetery now tucked away behind a suburban housing estate. The watch brings one closer to the poet than his gravestone, where even the name seems not quite right: no one ever called him P. E. Thomas.

Along with the need to bury an unprecedented number of fallen combatants and others caught up in the fighting, the First World War generated an equally urgent need to find ways of marking the significance of the events of the four years which ended on 11 November 1918; and then, on subsequent Armistice Days – now in Britain Remembrance Days – of giving public and private expression to such need. These acts of remembrance (commemorations) continue a century after the war began. War memorials and war cemeteries have themselves become historic monuments, the meaning of which is open to reinterpretation. This has been true both in Germany and in Britain, but in different ways. The following discussion will focus on these different ways, with a particular emphasis on the post-war creation first of cemeteries in Belgium and France and then, in England and Germany, of civic and local war memorials.

First World War cemeteries as war memorials

Within a year of the Armistice a battlefield tourist industry had got under way. Guidebooks such as Muirhead's *Blue Guide to Belgium and the Western Front*, complete with maps showing lines of advance and retreat and summaries of the military action associated with each location, appeared in 1919. Welfare organisations such as the Red Cross and the YMCA were actively involved in helping families to visit the graves of their dead sons and lovers, though this presupposed that the locations of such graves were already recorded and marked, and that they were accessible. The job of clearing the battlefields and making them safe was only just beginning and, indeed, to an extent is continuing to this day, as bodies continue to be uncovered and unexploded ordnance to be found and made safe. The latest British Commonwealth War Graves Commission cemetery to be established in France was opened as recently as 2010, at Fromelles.

That a new cemetery should be needed nearly a hundred years after the start of the First World War is remarkable enough; that it should be built in strict conformity to design principles established as early as 1917 is even more notable. Military cemeteries located outside the homeland of the fallen soldiers are both public and private spaces. Each individual burial is a focus for private memory, but collectively such a burial ground commemorates a historical moment. Indeed, the war cemetery serves several purposes. It might, for a start, assert the heroism or fortitude of the dead soldiers, transmuting such qualities into an ideal of sacrifice and thereby attempting to give meaning and value to what might otherwise seem meaningless. At the same time it will usually preserve national identity: with important exceptions, British soldiers lie in British cemeteries, Germans in German and French in French. More specifically, it may define regimental, and sometimes regional, allegiance (for example, the Devonshires' regimental cemetery at Mametz, where the actual trench which soldiers defended became their permanent burial site; the entrance bears this inscription: 'The Devonshires held this trench. They hold it still.')

On a practical level, a war cemetery is designed and organised in such a way as to enable relatives and other visitors readily to locate the exact burial place of the person they have come to find. On a philosophical level, the war cemeteries of the First World War raise questions about the political, historical or moral contingencies which led to death on such a scale. Educationally, they aspire today to offer a lesson to future generations: the German cemetery at Vladslo, Belgium, carries the following quotation from Albert Schweitzer: 'The soldiers' graves are the greatest preachers of peace.'

The desire to see the name of a fallen loved one or comrade inscribed in stone becomes paradoxically an almost irresistible substitute on the one hand for reclaiming the actual body of the fallen soldier, for closure, and on the other for declaring his continuing existence – if only in name. To remember (re-member) is, in the context of the First World War and the memorials created in its aftermath, a willed response to the biblical question, 'Can these bones live?' (Ezek. 37:3). One of the *OED* definitions of 'remember' is 'to have mind of and mention a person in prayer'.

The Armistice did not signal the moment remembrance could legitimately begin. It had begun almost as soon as the war itself. In England, Laurence Binyon's October 1914 poem 'For the Fallen' implies both immortality for those who die in battle, and an obligation on those 'who are left' – and are somehow diminished by not having themselves been killed in the war – to ensure these heroes are duly commemorated:

> They shall grow not old, as we that are left grow old:
> Age shall not weary them, nor the years condemn.
> At the going down of the sun and in the morning
> We will remember them.[5]

Rupert Brooke's 'The Soldier' (1914) needs to be read, I suggest, not as a soldier speaking to himself and mouthing patriotic platitudes, but as his advice to a mother, friend, wife, about ways to help them remember the individual who may not be coming home:

> If I should die, think only this of me:
> That there's some corner of a foreign field
> That is forever England.[6]

The poem is more about consoling the soon-to-be-bereaved than it is about delivering the poet's own elegy.

In Germany, too, the problem of finding fitting ways to remember began early. In October 1914 Peter Kollwitz, son of the Expressionist artist Käthe Kollwitz and her husband Paul, was killed in Belgium. His mother soon became preoccupied with the problem of what memorial would be most appropriate for her son. Her initial thoughts, persisting throughout the war, had revolved around the idea of a symbolic tableau, dedicated to the sacrifice of youth. However, it was not until after the Armistice that this most figurative of artists decided the exemplary form of memorial would be based on the dual figures of grieving parents (*Die Trauenden Eltern*) kneeling before the grave of their son, absorbed in their grief and seeking forgiveness from him for having encouraged his generation to take up arms on their behalf. Jay Winter has analysed Kollwitz's mourning in these terms:

> What gives Kollwitz's mourning an added dimension was her sense of guilt, of remorse over the responsibility the older generation had for the slaughter of the young. This feeling arose from her initial reaction to Peter's decision

> to volunteer. Her attitude was apprehensive but positive. Her vision was internationalist and hostile to the philistine arrogance of official Germany.[7]

Modelling the parents on herself and her husband, Kollwitz produced a more-than-lifesize double image at once deeply personal and recognisably universal. That the war and the loss of her son had turned her into a committed and active pacifist only added to the power and poignancy of her sculpture; it also helped to ensure she would be condemned in due course by the Nazis for her 'degenerate art' and prevented from exhibiting her work for the rest of her lifetime (she died in 1945).

Early cemeteries: The significance of St Symphorien

Physical memorials were, of course, erected from the moment the first soldiers were killed in 1914. Wooden crosses on which name, regiment and date of death could be recorded were manufactured in England and shipped across with other stores and supplies; cemeteries were created ad hoc; in some instances, mass graves too. Though attempts to accord fallen comrades some form of proper funeral were thought essential for morale, there was rarely time to construct and organise formal burial grounds. Nevertheless, one of the earliest cemeteries is also one of the most remarkable. Near Mons, the cemetery of St Symphorien contains the graves of both the first and the last known British soldiers to be killed in the First World War; more remarkably still, this was originally a German, not a British, cemetery. It was created on a site given by a local Belgian landowner, and work on laying it out began almost as soon as the battle of Mons (August 1914) was over.

Although the St Symphorien military cemetery was handed over after the war to the Imperial War Graves Commission (IWGC; now the Commonwealth War Graves Commission – CWGC), it had already been laid out in a manner decidedly not English. For a start it occupies a site that is both hilly and wooded. Secondly, the British and Commonwealth graves in it are not on the whole in the straight-line formation characteristic of most CWGC cemeteries. The German graves are marked by a variety of early First World War headstones – a reminder that the evolution of the design and development of military cemeteries took very different courses in Britain and in Germany. Thirdly, and most significantly, not only does St Symphorien now house large numbers of German and British graves adjacent to each other, but at its centre is a memorial obelisk, erected by the Germans after the First Battle of

Mons to commemorate the soldiers of the British army who fell in that battle. It carries the inscription, 'Here repose 46 English soldiers of the Royal Middlesex Regiment'. Elsewhere in St Symphorien are German memorials to two other British regiments: the Royal Irish Regiment and the Royal Fusiliers. The German memorial to the dead of the Middlesex Regiment is mistakenly dedicated to the *Royal* Middlesex Regiment but a visitor to the cemetery might well be reminded of the exclamation from Shakespeare's *Henry V*: 'Here was a royal fellowship of death.'[8] (The same quotation appears on the First World War memorial at Hyde Park Corner to the dead of the Royal Artillery.)

Then again, buried in the cemetery, close by each other, are two soldiers – one British, the other German – who won the Victoria Cross and the Iron Cross respectively. Lieutenant Maurice Dease was the first British soldier of the war to be awarded a posthumous VC, and Musketeer Oskar Niemeyer the first German to win the Iron Cross. Both were killed in the same action: the German forces were attempting to cross the canal at Mons and the British were attempting to prevent them. Lieutenant Dease (aged 24) took over a machine-gun position after all his men had been killed there, and, though wounded five times, managed to hold the advancing Germans at bay. His VC citation reads:

> On 23rd August 1914 at Mons, Belgium, Nimy Bridge was being defended by a single company of Royal Fusiliers and a machine gun section with Lieutenant Dease in command. The gunfire was intense, and the casualties were heavy, but the Lieutenant went on firing in spite of his wounds, until he was hit for the 5th time and was carried away to a place of safety where he died. A private (S F Godley) of the same Battalion who had been assisting the Lieutenant while he was still able to operate the guns, took over, and alone he used the gun to such a good effect that he covered the retreat of his comrades.[9]

In the same action Musketeer Niemeyer swam across the canal, under fire from the same machine-gun position, in order to operate the Nimy swing-bridge mechanism and enable his men to cross to the British side. He, too, died of his wounds that afternoon.

This, the first significant military action of the war, is thus memorialised both in official citations and in the memorials and layout of the St Symphorien cemetery. The bravery and achievements of individuals (both officers and other ranks) are singled out for record and reward by the authorities – military, executive and royal. The *London Gazette*, which officially announces all military awards and their accompanying citations, still carries the endorsement from its first edition in 1665: 'Published by Authority'.

By comparison with the later set-piece battles of the war, Mons, which lasted only two days (23 and 24 August), was a small-scale skirmish. St Symphorien military cemetery holds the graves of just 229 Commonwealth servicemen and 284 German soldiers – and these numbers include those killed near Mons up to the final hours of the war.[10] Today, overshadowed by the much larger concentration of cemeteries along the Western Front, St Symphorien is nevertheless particularly significant in memorialising war as a shared experience: the dead of both sides are interred together and the bravery of one side is commemorated by the other. Emblematically it foreshadows the famous closing lines from Wilfred Owen's poem, *Strange Meeting*:

> 'I am the enemy you killed, my friend.
> I knew you in this dark; for so you frowned
> Yesterday through me as you jabbed and killed.
> I parried; but my hands were loath and cold.
> Let us sleep now ...'[11]

Faith and doubt: The ambiguity of war memorial symbolism

Owen himself was killed just one week before the end of the war, also in an action that involved a canal – the same canal (though further south, and in France) – at Ors, on 4 November 1918. On this occasion the British were attempting to cross the canal in pursuit of the retreating German forces. Owen is buried, along with 62 other casualties of this action (two of whom posthumously received the VC) in an annexe to the communal cemetery of the village. The visitor approaches through the village cemetery with its bewildering variety of monuments laid out, as is characteristic of cemeteries across mainland Europe, between gravelled or shale-covered paths. One is struck at once by the contrast with the military annexe: it is a grass area (churchyards and cemeteries in England are almost invariably grass) enclosed by a symmetrical arrangement of low hedges, trimmed to be just higher than the headstones. One steps up towards the most prominent feature, a Cross of Sacrifice, with the headstones of the servicemen arranged with military precision in three ranks in the background.

In miniature, this military cemetery at Ors exemplifies several principles of the original IWGC cemetery design. The headstones are arranged communally, officers and other ranks being buried side by side. All headstones are of standard design and size: they contain the soldier's name, rank and regiment, and the regimental badge is prominent above the name. Below is (usually) a religious emblem – a plain cross or Star of David, for instance – and only at the very bottom may be found an inscription or quotation supplied at the request of the family. This design and sequence make it very clear that the dead man's military family (his regiment) and identity come first; often the family inscription is now almost hidden either by soil or plants. The inscription on Wilfred Owen's grave was chosen by his mother and is taken from his poem 'The End':

> Shall Life renew these bodies? Of a truth
> All death will he annul.[12]

Controversially, she left off the last three words and the final question mark of the second line. This should have read:

> All death will he annul, all tears assuage?

By this adjustment, Mrs Owen implied for her son a Christian confidence in life after death that Owen's own poem clearly refutes. The mother attributes to the dead son values that he did not share, just as the Cross of Sacrifice at the entrance to almost every IWGC cemetery and the stylised crosses on the headstones themselves suggest a universally Christian context which raises questions today just as uncomfortably as it did in the immediate aftermath of the war.

This ambiguity about Christian attitudes is clearly reflected in the controversies that dogged the design of the IWGC cemeteries and that – perhaps inevitably – created doubts about how, by whom, in what ways and, indeed, for what purpose the dead of the First World War should be commemorated. By its very name, the Cross of Sacrifice prioritises the idea of sacrifice ('Greater love hath no man, than that he lay down his life for his friend') over the idea of patriotism: the insistence that *all* soldiers dying in battle or on active service should be buried in, or as near as possible to, the place where they fell and alongside their comrades rather than back in Britain among their family and forefathers was one of the defining decisions taken by the British government in the aftermath of the Armistice.[13] The acts of bravery for which some of them were decorated were described in citations in terms of a heroic readiness to sacrifice their own lives to protect those of the soldiers around them ('reckless disregard of their own safety' etc.).

It is worth contrasting the emotions surrounding the creation of the St Symphorien cemetery in the first month of the war with the situation four years and three months later, when the Armistice was signed. In 1914 the dominant emotion was of respect by the soldiers of one side for their opponents on the other. The bloodiness of a fierce battle, in which mounted cavalry charges still played a part, was followed by a kind of modern chivalry. By 1918, on the other hand, Belgium (especially of course the area around Ypres) had seen many thousands of casualties on its soil, and the Belgian people were very reluctant to allow German graves to remain dotting the Belgian landscape. The idea at this moment that German, Allied and Commonwealth soldiers might be buried alongside each other was unthinkable. The IWGC was only now to begin the serious work of establishing the pattern of Commonwealth cemeteries that survive today across France and Germany. Germany itself had no equivalent of the IWGC: its nearest counterpart, the *Zentralnachweisamt*, was deprived of its role under the Treaty of Versailles (1919), which transferred the responsibility for German military cemeteries into the hands of the countries in which German soldiers were buried.

The Imperial War Graves Commission and the *Volksbund Deutsche Kriegsgräberfürsorge*

To understand the different attitudes to memorialisation exemplified today by the design of British and German military cemeteries in France and Flanders, one might trace the ways in which both countries, from 1914 onwards, set about the whole problem of recording their fallen. In England, an ex-colonial civil servant called Fabian Ware, who was attached at the start of the war to the Red Cross in France, quickly recognised that in the chaotic opening months of the war little thought had been given by anyone to the systematic recording of the dead and of the places where they were buried. He was able to persuade the War Office to allow him to set up a War Graves Registration Commission, which was given official standing in March 1915. Gavin Stamp, in *The Memorial to the Missing of the Somme* (2006), has summed up the way this single-minded, and at first almost single-handed, man set about establishing the principles by which the Imperial War Graves Commission would be defined:

> Ware realised that the task of creating proper graves and cemeteries would be immense, and that it would concern all the constituent parts of the British Empire. He also was concerned that proper policies be established

> for war graves, and that rich families were not able to erect more elaborate memorials or take bodies back to Britain for burial ... The Imperial War Graves Commission, as it was established by Royal Charter in April 1917, would achieve equality for all the dead – whether rich or poor, officers or private soldiers, titled or common.[14]

In Germany, after Versailles, it was also one man who took the initiative in creating an organisation that would undertake the tasks of registering the war dead and then negotiating and arranging their burial or reburial in properly established military cemeteries. Dr Siegfried Eulen, who had been in charge of military burials in Poland and later in Turkey, established a voluntary and non-governmental association of individuals concerned to look after the German fallen buried outside Germany. His scheme was based on the principle that there should be no political involvement or interference in the work of his association, which came to be known as the *Volksbund Deutsche Kriegsgräberfürsorge* (VDK – the People's Association for the care of German war graves). The first meeting of the VDK was held in Berlin in December 1919, and its aims suggest that it was attempting from the start to combine the roles of a body such as the IWGC (though without its official status or government funding) with those of voluntary organisations such as the Red Cross, the YMCA or the British Legion. Not only would the VDK be concerned with the creation and care of military cemeteries outside the newly redrawn boundaries of Germany, it would also look after the placing of wreaths, subsidise travel arrangements for families to visit their dead, provide support and information to relatives, and be the point of contact with authorities in countries where German military cemeteries were located. Controversially, the VDK also saw its mission as forward-looking: to provide a bridge to the future, to ensure that countries that had lately been enemies should develop ties of friendship that might prevent war from breaking out again in Europe.[15]

This last aim, no matter how aspirational, was important for two reasons. First, it showed that not all the VDK's focus was on the past and on the work of memorialisation; secondly, it implied that, with its emphasis on contributing towards the maintenance of peace in Europe, it was taking up a political position, even if it was not a political organisation – still less an official, government-sponsored one. This would have serious implications for its future standing in Germany once Hitler was in power, and this in turn would disrupt the completion of the work of reburying and remembering the German war dead.

Lutyens and the architecture of commemoration

In London, by contrast, the level of support given by Whitehall before the war was yet over meant that the IWGC could call on the director of the British Museum, Sir Frederick Kenyon, for guidance about the architectural design of cemeteries to be created once peace was restored. Kenyon recommended appointing Sir Edwin Lutyens, Sir Herbert Baker and Reginald Blomfield as the principal architects, and his choice was decisive: all three architects were established leaders of the movement away from Gothic Revival towards Renaissance precedents, in particular the English classicism of Wren. Lutyens and Baker were also already well known for their large-scale commissions on an imperial stage: Lutyens was the architect of New Delhi; Baker had been the chief architectural force in South Africa, responsible for the Kimberley Boer War Memorial and the Cecil Rhodes Memorial in Cape Town. Lutyens himself had designed the Rand Regiments Memorial in Johannesburg, which Gavin Stamp describes as 'a prophetic design in which he first explored the possibilities of the triumphal arch theme'.[16] It would, indeed, later be Lutyens's achievement, with the creation of the Thiepval Memorial to the Missing of the Somme, to reinterpret this theme architecturally, not as a triumphal but as a memorial statement.

At Kenyon's suggestion, Lutyens and Baker were sent to France in the summer of 1917. Lutyens, profoundly moved by what they saw, wrote to his wife on 12 July:

> What humanity can endure, suffer, is beyond belief. The battlefields – the obliteration of all human endeavour, achievement, and the human achievement of destruction, is bettered by the poppies and wild flowers – that are as friendly to an unexploded shell as they are to the leg of a garden seat in Surrey.[17]

From the start, Lutyens consciously recognised the symbolic power of the landscape itself, making connections with the English countryside and also with the garden design philosophy that he had learned in Surrey from his mentor and friend Gertrude Jekyll. He went on to describe to his wife the graveyards of the battlefields as:

> Haphazard from the needs of much to do and little time for thought – and then a ribbon of isolated graves like a milky way across miles of country, where men were tucked in where they fell – Ribbons of little crosses each touching each other across a cemetery – set in a wilderness of annuals, –

> and where one sort of flower has grown the effect is charming, easy, and oh so pathetic, that one thinks no other monument is needed.[18]

Lutyens's impressionistic writing here conveys powerfully his initial response to the battlefield burial plots, and highlights two features that would be central to his own concept for the IWGC cemeteries: the need to have gravestones placed close together, 'each touching each other' in close order, and the importance of flowers as integral to the overall design. The idea of the cemeteries as being in a sense like English gardens was only reinforced by Lutyens's choice of Gertrude Jekyll, doyenne of Edwardian garden designers, to advise on the choice of flowers and shrubs to be planted alongside the graves.

When ascribing general characteristics to British and German military cemeteries, it is worth noting two important facts. First, there was more than one IWGC architect: variations of style and symbolism within the overall design concept were accepted from the start. This was equally true of German cemeteries, with the added difference that many of them did not reach their final form until after (and sometimes well after) the Second World War. The British cemeteries were mostly completed before the end of the 1920s. This was in itself a formidable achievement: a decade after the Treaty of Versailles, nearly a thousand cemeteries had been 'architecturally constructed'[19] with as many Crosses of Sacrifice and 560 Stones of Remembrance.

The Cross of Sacrifice and the Stone of Remembrance

Lutyens did not have everything his own way. He would have preferred the cemeteries to be if anything pantheistic in spirit, and he was personally opposed to the imposition of the Cross of Sacrifice, designed by Sir Herbert Baker, with its bronze sword emblematically superimposed upon the shaft and crosspiece of every Portland stone cross. Nevertheless, in the face of pressure from the Church of England, the government insisted that there should be at least one cross in every cemetery, especially since the headstones themselves were not in the form of a cross. The introduction of the Cross of Sacrifice becomes in fact a key difference between British and German military cemeteries. The white cross, raised on an octagonal base, is always the most prominent object in a British cemetery, usually visible from some distance; in German cemeteries, by contrast, black crosses may be used as headstones (as at the largest German First World War cemetery, at Neuville-St-Vaast near Arras) or low, Teutonic basalt lava crosses may occasionally be placed in clusters of three to break the endless succession of flat square name stones ranked across the burial ground (as at Langemark). In the only German military cemetery on English soil – at Cannock Chase, Staffordshire, maintained by the VDK – the headstones are of Belgian granite, again reinforcing the sense of difference between British and German cemetery design. There are 2,143 German First World War soldiers in this cemetery, most of whom died in England while prisoners of war.[20]

For Lutyens himself, the Stone of Remembrance was meant to be the unifying symbol for the cemeteries: in effect an altar (though Lutyens was determined to avoid a word with religious connotations), its purpose was to provide for all but the smallest cemeteries a single point of focus monumental enough to embody all those commemorated in the cemetery. The biblical dedication chosen by Rudyard Kipling – 'Their Name Liveth for Evermore' – inscribed on every stone, coalesces all the individual names inscribed on the headstones or walls of the cemetery into a single 'name', an immortal memory; and all 560 stones, spread out across the battlefields of Europe and beyond, collectively define this 'name' in the phrase (again chosen by Kipling) inscribed on Lutyens's single most famous monument, the Cenotaph in London – 'Our Glorious Dead'.

It is hard to overstate the significance of what Siegfried Sassoon called 'the intolerably nameless names'[21] in the effort to memorialise the dead of war. Acclamations like 'Their Name Liveth for Evermore', with their biblical echoes (the phrase comes from the Apocryphal book of Ecclesiasticus), imply an action of religious dedication, one which is simultaneously an act of memory (looking back to recall the dead who are gone) and an expression of desire: that the memory attaching to every name individually and collectively will be retained by future generations so that it is never forgotten. As Daniel Sherman has noted:

> The names more than anything else constitute the monument as a place of mourning, inscribing it with the particularity of a place that the denomination of its inhabitants embodies. More than this, by virtue of their inscription the names constitute themselves as part of the signifying process that seeks to transcend memory and its limitations by assigning it, in its constructed 'collective' form, a historical role. In a manner both poignant and troubling, names as the irreducible synecdoche for monuments stake a community's claim to a place in history, representing its loss as its most essential link to the nation.[22]

The contrast in design and practice between British and German cemeteries is often striking. It was, for a start, a British principle that as far as possible cemeteries should be located on the site of temporary cemeteries along the Western Front, so that soldiers remained buried close to where they fought and fell. German military cemeteries, however, were fewer in number and often created by concentrating outlying graves and cemeteries into a small number of very large burial plots. One consequence of this was that whereas the aim in British cemeteries was to identify as many individual soldiers as possible by name and by a named headstone, German cemeteries house far larger numbers of the dead, often in multiple or mass graves. The dilemma for both British and German authorities, however, was in one respect the same: how to deal most appropriately with bodies that had no names, and names that had no bodies.

German cemeteries in Belgium: Langemark and Vladslo

The German cemeteries in Belgium, most particularly at Langemark, offer the starkest examples of this. Originally created in 1915, the Langemark 'collecting cemetery' some six kilometres north of Ypres has been repeatedly enlarged and redesigned, so that it now houses over 44,000 dead German soldiers, identified as well as unidentified.[23] By contrast, the nearby IWGC cemetery at Tyne Cot (the largest British military cemetery in the world) has 11,956 burials. This too, and unusually, was a 'collecting cemetery' bringing together British soldiers who had been buried in temporary cemeteries all around the Ypres Salient. At Langemark, the majority of German soldiers are buried under square flat stones listing up to eight soldiers per stone. Some of these will have name and rank; others are simply *unbekannten*. These stones are post-Second World War: before then, those soldiers buried at Langemark who could be identified were simply allowed their military number. More significantly still, the site houses a huge mass grave, the *Kameraden Grab*, holding 24,916 bodies. Originally unidentified, research has revealed the names of many of these soldiers, whose names are now inscribed on bronze tablets beside the grave; others have been carved on wooden panels in a chamber at the entrance to the cemetery. Significantly, and poignantly, a bronze wreath contains a text from the Lutheran Bible of 1912: *ICH HABE DICH / BEI DEINEN NAME GERUFEN / DU BIST MEIN* – a quotation from Isaiah: 'I have called thee by thy name, thou art mine.' This text underlines the desire to reunite the unidentifiable bodies with their names, and the unattributable names with their bodies: it does so by transferring the burden of remembrance to God, since no human individual or agency could succeed in identifying and naming each dead soldier.

The cemetery at Langemark is a large rectangular plot created on the site of some of the fiercest fighting in the early stages of the war. Indeed, the deaths of a large number of German student volunteers, killed in this area during October and November 1914, led to the first cemetery on this site being called the *Studenten Friedhof*. But Langemark memorialises both the dead and the place where they died: at its far corner a German blockhouse (pill box) is incorporated into the overall design. In this sense therefore the cemetery is both a memorial to the dead and a memorial to the field of battle itself. An identical architectural feature is literally built into the cemetery at Tyne Cot, where the Cross of Sacrifice has been constructed on top of another such blockhouse.

Langemark cemetery is set back from the road, from which it is divided by a walled ditch – as it were a dry moat. All around the perimeter, behind a low wall, tall oak trees form a giant pallisade separating the burial ground from the fields beyond. There is actually a sense in which the place appears to be shut off from the outside world; and this sense is reinforced by the architecture of the entrance: a low, wide building of red local stone, without windows and with only one doorway, narrow, dark, but very imposing. This doorway is constructed like an ancient trilithon: huge upright blocks of stone, rough hewn as they face the visitor, support a massive architrave almost a third of the width of the whole building. One has the sense of approaching a door into the dark: a place of the dead, a long barrow perhaps.

However, as one faces the doorway and looks through the dark chamber into the cemetery, one sees on the far side of the burial ground a group of four immobile figures. Like oneself, they appear to be about to enter but seem reluctant to do so. In fact, these figures are a row of four larger-than-lifesize bronze sculptures, the only figurative artwork to be seen anywhere at Langemark. Together with the sombre (even daunting) entrance doorway, their presence converts the whole cemetery into a dramatic tableau, enacting for the visitor the essence of what in itself it was designed to be: a place of the dead as well as a place of pilgrimage – created originally for grieving families, now for historians, scholars and curious tourists. Like all the First World War cemeteries along the Western Front, it is a site where the desire to acknowledge the past is mixed with the impossibility of conceiving what happened here and what each of the 44,000 individuals interred within this massive enclosure actually endured.

There is, however, one crucial difference between the British and German cemeteries. The former are essentially light, sometimes even sunny, places – low walls, open gateways, white headstones, flowers, the Cross of Sacrifice, the Stone of Remembrance. The classical idiom which Lutyens and his fellow architects chose is interpreted in a radically different way from the German cemeteries; at Sanctuary Wood, for example (south of Ypres) the entrance building – not dissimilar in footprint from that at Langemark – is so constructed to ensure that one can always see through and beyond it. The entrance does not puncture a solid massive wall as at Langemark. Instead, slender Tuscan columns, supporting an almost delicate architrave inscribed in Roman lettering with the name 'Sanctuary Wood Cemetery', give the building the sense of being a pavilion opening out into a garden, or a kind of antechapel leading into an open-air church. The Stone of Remembrance and the Cross of Sacrifice confront the visitor as it were from the far end of the central aisle.

Thus the British and German military cemeteries are designed to create atmospheres very different from each other. But just as there is consistency in the way British cemeteries conformed, from the outset, to the principles established by Lutyens, such too is the case with the German cemeteries, constructed and developed over a much longer period by the VDK. The *Soldaten Friedhof* at Vladslo for instance (further north of Ypres, and much more remote than Langemark) has a similar design of entrance chamber, again with the massive trilithon opening. Here, too, the site is completely enclosed – this time by high hedges and trees – and once more one looks through the doorway to see sculpture at the far end of the burial ground. This time, though, it is the monumental kneeling figures of Käthe Kollwitz's 'Grieving Parents' who are glimpsed in the distance. And if, having entered the cemetery, one turns back to face the entrance chamber, one sees this time a pair of squat, massive Doric columns supporting the architrave of a much wider opening than the trilithon entrance approached from the road. Such sculptural and architectural reference points each make their own statements. At Vladslo, a notice conveys this uncompromising message to the visitor: 'The dead of this cemetery admonish to peace.'

Local war memorials

Occasionally, when a formal cemetery was laid out after the war, the temporary wooden grave markers were returned to, or reclaimed by, the family of the dead soldier. The original memorial to Peter Kollwitz is now on display in the permanent Flanders Field exhibition in the restored Cloth Hall at Ypres. Sometimes one sees the standard British wooden cross displayed on the wall of an English church, rather like a trophy brought back from some distant war. One such cross can be seen at Mells, in Somerset. Mells, though a small village, is of particular significance both because of the people associated with the First World War buried there – they include Raymond Asquith, son of the wartime prime minister Herbert Asquith, and Siegfried Sassoon – and because of the artists and architects who worked there to provide memorials. Inside the church an equestrian statue by Sir Alfred Munnings, placed on a plinth designed by Lutyens, commemorates Lieutenant Edward Horner, killed at Cambrai in 1917. He was the son of the Horner family who lived in the adjacent Manor House; his sister had married Raymond Asquith, who is himself commemorated by a memorial inscription in the tower of Mells church, carved by Eric Gill. Gill was later commissioned to carve a further memorial plaque to Asquith, located on the south wall of Amiens Cathedral. Lutyens, meanwhile, had landscaped the south side of the churchyard at Mells, and designed the village war memorial. This stands at the entrance to the village and consists of a tall column supporting an image of St George slaying the dragon.[24]

It might be expected that St George would be a popular subject for English war memorials, but he is more often depicted in post-war stained glass windows donated in memory of particular individuals than on memorials dedicated collectively to local townsmen or villagers. There are, however, a few – as there are also in Germany. At Reiterswiesen in northern Bavaria, for instance, the memorial depicts St George on horseback, slaying the dragon. Raised on a substantial pillared plinth, this memorial is set in a specially landscaped corner of the parish churchyard. In Germany, as in Britain, war memorials may be found in or outside churches, or elsewhere in city, town or village: the civic centre, market place or village green, for instance.

German war memorials often depict soldiers helping their wounded or fallen comrades, a subject rarer in British iconography. More often, too, they explicitly depict the fallen: the *Kriegsdenkmal* in Munich has a lifesize stone figure of a German soldier, helmeted and wearing an army greatcoat, lying asleep with hands clasped and his head encircled by a great bronze wreath. The image is powerful: the sleeping soldier reminds one of a medieval knight carved in full armour on a chest tomb; the wreath is unmistakably intended to resemble a halo. The image is thus both romanticised and beatified: chivalry and Christianity combine.

This is perhaps more characteristic of Catholic southern Germany. Such imagery is less frequent further north. Nowhere is this seen more starkly than in the town memorial at Ettlingen, near Karlsruhe, where a powerful relief sculpture on the walls of the town *Schloss* depicts Death on horseback, shouldering his scythe and riding over the bodies of the dead soldiers who carpet the field of battle. It is an image at once medieval in its reference to the *Tötentanz* and modern in its Expressionistic idiom.

British First World War memorial sculpture and architecture rarely engaged with modernism. This was left to painters such as Nevinson, Nash, Bomberg and Spencer, who were official war artists but were rarely commissioned after the war to produce memorial art. The best-known exception is Stanley Spencer and the Sandham Memorial Chapel in Berkshire; but even this was a private, not a public, commission. Much less well known, but not less significant, is the war memorial created by Eric Gill at Trumpington village, outside Cambridge.

Eric Gill and the Stations of the Cross

Unlike the memorials at Mells, this war memorial was commissioned by the village itself, although the Pemberton family who owned Trumpington Hall had lost their son, Francis, in October 1914 and were the main donors to the village's war memorial fund. The memorial cross that Gill designed was unveiled in 1921 and stands outside the gates of the hall. This spot was the most prominent corner of the village, on the junction of the village street and the main road to Cambridge. Arguably it was Eric Gill's brother, MacDonald Gill, who had a greater influence on British war memorials than his more celebrated brother: he, after all, designed the lettering used on all IWGC headstones – a traditional, Roman font. Eric Gill's lettering on the Trumpington memorial is a less formal design, though still in a conventionally serif-based typeface. It is the four images carved in relief on panels at the base of the cross which are so striking.

Two of these represent religious subjects – St Michael triumphant in defeating the Devil, and the Madonna and Child (the parish church is dedicated to SS. Mary and Michael) – while the third depicts St George slaying the dragon. So far, so conventional. However, the fourth panel shows an exhausted soldier returning from the war, and this is one of the most profound, though least known, images of the experience of war to appear on any war memorial in Britain or Germany.

An infantry soldier turns his back on the battlefield. Behind him a signpost indicates E and W; he is heading westwards. Also in the background a shell explodes, highlighting the jagged stumps of two shattered trees. The soldier, whose dejected body fills the whole panel, wears a heavy greatcoat which trails almost to the ground while his arm and knees sag under the weight of an outsized pack and equally outsized rifle carried over his shoulder. Somehow, the image seems familiar but out of context – until one realises that the image, a man staggering under the weight of a wooden crosspiece carried over his shoulder, resembles one of the Stations of the Cross; the posture suggests Christ carrying his Cross. Indeed, shortly before undertaking this Trumpington commission, Gill had completed his first large-scale commission, the Stations of the Cross for Westminster Cathedral.[25] Instead of a crown of thorns, however, this figure wears a helmet; instead of a recognisable face, all the features of the soldier's face have been erased. This represents him at once as a universalised, not a particularised, combatant, the exact opposite indeed of the standard heroic, or at least stoical, naturalistic soldier usually displayed on war memorials – German as well as British.

This type of memorial is defined by its inclusivity. Other memorials are defined by the opposite. At Bedford, for instance, the decision was taken to create a very different kind of memorial, one with no names and an ambiguously symbolic figure of Justice, holding sword and scales, defeating the dragon of oppression and tyranny. Launching an appeal for £3,000 to commission and erect a memorial, the mayor of the town, Cllr Sowter, wrote to every householder:

> Bedford is worthy of a fine memorial [...] Next year, 1921, is the one thousandth anniversary of the defeat of the Danes by the English. This battle took place in the neighbourhood of Russell Park, not far from the site of the proposed memorial. Few towns have a history so ancient as that of Bedford, and it is hoped that the thousandth anniversary of this battle may be marked by the unveiling of this Memorial of the Great War.[26]

This appeal to civic self-esteem and local history appeared not to generate the response the mayor had wanted. Nine months later, when barely a third of the necessary funds had been raised, he sent a second letter with a more urgent tone:

> Don't let Bedford be behind. Bedford cannot and will not forget what her sons have done. A house to house collection is now being organised. Give what you can – Remember those who died gave their all.[27]

Eventually, the money was raised and the memorial unveiled – but not until 1922. The image of Justice, a Wagnerian figure of a woman with long plaited hair wearing a helmet and chain mail, seemed far removed – even symbolically – from the reality or memory of the war which was by then four years past. Today it is hard to see such a monument as a memorial to the First World War at all, still less as a tribute to the men who fought and died in it or as a reflection of the grief and pride of those who mourned for them. This is the more surprising since the artist commissioned to create the memorial, Charles Sargeant Jagger, was the sculptor responsible for some of the most humane representations of soldiers to be found on memorials anywhere in Britain; the Great Western Railway memorial at Paddington Station of an off-duty soldier reading a book and the exhausted artillerymen standing guard over the body of a dead comrade at Hyde Park Corner are among the most telling sculptural images produced in Britain after the Armistice.

Over time, war memorials created in response to the ending of the war have come to acquire new meanings and to ask difficult questions about the old meanings. Both in Germany and in Britain, changed political and historical contexts have produced different perspectives: it is hard to imagine today that a Cenotaph in Whitehall would be inscribed with the words 'Our Glorious Dead'. Indeed, the erection in 2005 of a new memorial higher up Whitehall shows how far attitudes have moved. This monument, far from being to the dead or the missing, is to all 'The Women of World War II'; in contrast to the stark white Portland stone of Lutyens's Cenotaph, it is made of unburnished bronze. Instead of the formal iconography of wreaths and flags associated with the Cenotaph and its rituals of commemoration, here the women and their various contributions to the war are represented by their uniforms and caps casually hanging from coat hooks.

This almost light-hearted symbolism, however, remains ambiguous in a way that the symbolism of First World War memorials generally is not. Do the uniforms metonymically bring the women who wore them back into mind, if not into view? Or do they imply that, the war being long over, the women who once occupied these clothes have disappeared so far from memory that they need to be recovered? Might they alternatively suggest that, as soon as they could, the women whom the memorial acknowledges sloughed off their wartime temporary outfits and went back to resume their peacetime lives? In fact, the memorial is not so much a monument to the women of the Second World War, collectively or as individuals, as to the roles they undertook and the contribution they made in support of a war effort conducted and dominated by men.

This recent memorial to the Second World War reminds us that nearly all the names of the First World War fallen recorded on headstones, gravestones and war memorials, and all the names of the missing inscribed on monuments such as the Thiepval Memorial on the Somme or the New Menin Gate at Ypres, are of men. By contrast with Australia, New Zealand and America, in Britain there are very few memorials acknowledging the contribution of women to the war effort (munitions workers, nurses, ambulance drivers) in the First World War. By the same token there are very few British civic memorials acknowledging the fact of women as chief mourners after the war. The most moving exception is in Birmingham, where a larger than lifesize bronze statue of a young woman placing a wreath takes its place outside the city's Hall of Memory alongside three idealised sculptures representing the Army, Navy and Royal Flying Corps. An American architectural historian, Kirk Savage, asks in a 2010 essay, 'The War Memorial as Elegy', 'Whose name deserves to be graven in stone?' The question is overdue. Savage concludes:

> Public monuments ultimately do have to justify their own existence. In one way or the other today's monuments must still offer up some self-explanation, stated or unstated, that allows us to understand why we placed them in public space in the first place, and why we continue to care for and about them.[28]

Historians such as Savage argue that 'the burden of the public monument is no longer to help its own citizens to confirm the righteousness of the state over and over again'.[29] This perspective might have applied to post-First World War memorials in Britain, but ignores the *Unruhe* with which national and local communities – to say nothing of families and individuals – in Germany came to terms with the reality of defeat in the wake first of the Armistice and then of the Treaty of Versailles. Even before November 1918, so absolute a concept as the righteousness of the state was challenged by artists such as Käthe Kollwitz. In her journal for 19 March 1918, she reminded herself that in 1914 there had been

> the conviction that Germany was in the right and had the duty to defend herself. At the beginning it would have been wholly impossible for me to conceive of letting the boys go as parents *must* let their boys go now, without inwardly affirming it – letting them go simply to the slaughterhouse. That is what changes everything. The feeling that we were betrayed then, at the beginning. And perhaps Peter would still be living had it not been for this terrible betrayal. Peter and millions, many millions of other boys all betrayed.[30]

With hindsight it is possible to see that Kollwitz's unflinching image of the grieving parents, kneeling to ask forgiveness before the grave of their son, provided the most articulate of all possible responses to the question of how to memorialise the First World War. In so doing she became in effect the artistic conscience of Germany. Today her work (and indeed her own commitment to pacifism) embodies the conviction that in any war the fallen and the bereaved, the named and the missing on every side – and even the survivors – are all victims.

In 1993 the government of the newly reunified Germany reopened the *Neue Wache* (the 'New Guardhouse') on Unter den Linden in Berlin. Formerly, under East German control, this had been designated a memorial to 'victims of fascism and militarism'. Now renamed the *Zentrale Gedenkstätte der Bundesrepublik Deutschland für die Opfer von Krieg und Gewaltherrschaft* (the 'Central Memorial of the Federal Republic of Germany to the Victims of War and Tyranny') the building, an austere eighteenth-century classical pavilion by the architect Schinkel, is silent and empty inside except for a single sculpture in the centre of the space. It is a *Pietà*, a mother with her dead son, and the artist is Käthe Kollwitz.

Notes

1 Catherine Moriarty, 'Private Grief and Public Remembrance', in Martin Evans and Ken Lunn, eds, *War and Memory in the Twentieth Century* (Oxford: Berg, 1997), 125.

2 Adrian Gregory, *The Silence of Memory: Armistice Day, 1919–1946* (Oxford: Berg, 1994), 22.

3 Vera Brittain, *Testament of Youth* (London: Virago, 2004 [1933]), 225.

4 Matthew Hollis, *Now All Roads Lead to France: The Last Years of Edward Thomas* (London: Faber and Faber, 2011), 332–3.

5 Laurence Binyon, 'For the Fallen', in *Poems of To-day* (London: Sidgwick and Jackson, 1915), 26. This bestselling anthology, published for the English Association in August 1915 and designed for use in schools, was highly influential in establishing the canon of First World War poetry. It was the earliest anthology to include Rupert Brooke's 'The Soldier', printed immediately before 'For the Fallen'.

6 Edward Marsh, ed., *The Collected Poems of Rupert Brooke: With a Memoir* (London: Sidgwick and Jackson, 1918), 9.

7 J. M. Winter, *Sites of Memory, Sites of Mourning: The Great War in European Cultural History* (Cambridge: Cambridge University Press, 1995), 108–9, 111.

8 Shakespeare, *Henry V*, IV.viii.101.

9 Supplement to the *London Gazette*, Issue 28976 (16 November 1914), 9374.
10 Statistical data from Commonwealth War Graves Commission (CWGC): www.cwgc.org/search/cemetery_details.aspx?cemetery=90801&mode=1 (accessed 10 May 2011).
11 Wilfred Owen, 'Strange Meeting', in *Wilfred Owen: The War Poems*, ed. Jon Stallworthy (London: Chatto and Windus, 1994), 36. In an earlier draft of the poem, Owen had written 'I was a German conscript and your friend'.
12 Stallworthy, ed., *Wilfred Owen: The War Poems*, 46.
13 Gavin Stamp, *The Memorial to the Missing of the Somme* (London: Profile Books, 2010), 87.
14 Stamp, *Memorial*, 73–4.
15 See Volksbund Deutsche Kriegsgräbefürsorge e.V., *Deutsche Kriegsgräberstätten Belgien* (Kassel: VDK, 2008), 24.
16 Stamp, *Memorial*, 38.
17 Colin Amery, Margaret Richardson and Gavin Stamp, *Lutyens: The Work of the English Architect Sir Edwin Lutyens (1869–1944)* (London: Arts Council of Great Britain, 1981), 150.
18 Amery et al., *Lutyens*, 150.
19 Stamp, *Memorial*, 99.
20 Volksbund Deutsche Kriegsgräbefürsorge e.V. *Deutsche Kriegsgräberstätten Cannock Chase* (Kassel: VDK, 2008), 5.
21 Siegfried Sassoon, 'On Passing the New Menin Gate', in Dominic Hibberd and John Onions, eds, *The Winter of the World: Poems of the Great War* (London: Constable, 2007), 312.
22 Daniel Sherman, 'Art, Commerce and the Production of Memory in France after World War I', in John Gillis, ed., *Commemorations, and the Politics of National Identity* (Princeton, NJ: Princeton University Press, 1994), 206–7.
23 Volksbund Deutsche Kriegsgräbefürsorge e.V., *Deutsche Kriegsgräberstätten Belgien*.
24 For a detailed discussion of the First World War memorials at Mells, see Kate Tiller, *Remembrance and Community: War Memorials and Local History* (Ashbourne: BALH, 2013), 36–40.
25 For an account of Gill's designs for these Stations of the Cross, see Patrick Rogers, 'Stations of the Cross', *Oremus* (London: Westminster Cathedral, 2005).
26 Letter dated 9 November 1920 (private collection).
27 Letter dated 1 July 1921 (private collection).
28 Kirk Savage, 'The War Memorial as Elegy', in Karen Weisman, ed., *The Oxford Handbook of the Elegy* (Oxford: Oxford University Press 2010), 656.
29 Savage, 'The War Memorial', 656.
30 Käthe Kollwitz, journal, 19 March 1918, quoted in Victor Miesel, *Voices of German Expressionism* (London: Tate Publishing, 2003), 167.

Select bibliography

Achino-Loeb, Maria-Luisa, ed. *Silence: The Currency of Power* (Oxford: Berghahn, 2006)

Alexander, Sally. 'Men's Fears and Women's Work: Responses to Unemployment in London Between the Wars', *Gender and History*, 12, 2 (July 2000), 401–25

Barham, Peter. *Forgotten Lunatics of the Great War* (New Haven, CT: Yale University Press, 2004)

Barlow, Adrian. *The Great War in British Literature* (Cambridge: Cambridge University Press, 2000)

Barr, Niall. *The Lion and the Poppy: British Veterans, Politics, and Society, 1921–1939* (Westport, CT: Praeger, 2005)

Ben-Ze'ev, Efrat, Ruth Ginio and Jay Winter, eds. *Shadows of War: A Social History of Silence in the Twentieth Century* (Cambridge: Cambridge University Press, 2010)

Berger, Maurice. *Germany after the Armistice: A Report, Based on the Personal Testimony of Representative Germans, Concerning the Conditions Existing in 1919* (New York: G. P. Putnam's Sons, 1920)

Bessel, Richard. *Germany after the First World War* (Oxford: Clarendon Press, 1993)

Bessel, Richard. 'The Great War in German Memory: The Soldiers of the First World War, Demobilization, and Weimar Political Culture', *German History*, 6, 1 (1988), 20–34

Best, Nicholas. *The Greatest Day in History: How the Great War Really Ended* (London: Weidenfeld and Nicolson, 2008)

Boemeke, Manfred F., Gerald D. Feldman and Elisabeth Glaser, eds. *The Treaty of Versailles: A Reassessment after 75 Years* (Cambridge: German Historical Institute and Cambridge University Press, 1998)

Borg, Alan. *War Memorials: from Antiquity to the Present* (London: Leo Cooper, 1991)

Braybon, Gail, ed. *Evidence, History and the Great War: Historians and the Impact of 1914–18* (New York: Berghahn, 2003)

Brockington, Grace. *Above the Battlefield: Modernism and the Peace Movement in Britain, 1900–1918* (New Haven, CT: Yale University Press, 2011)

Brockington, Grace, ed. *Internationalism and the Arts in Britain and Europe at the Fin de Siècle* (Oxford: Peter Lang, 2009)

Brüstle, Christa, Guido Heldt and Eckhard Weber, eds. *Von Grenzen und Ländern, Zentren und Rändern: Der Erste Weltkrieg und die Verschiebungen in der musikalischen Geographie Europas* (Schliengen: Edition Argus, 2006)

Bryder, Linda. 'Healthy or Hungry? The First World War', *History Workshop Journal*, 24, 1 (1987), 141–57

Buitenhuis, Peter. *The Great War of Words: Literature as Propaganda 1914–18 and After* (London: Batsford, 1989)

Cage, John. *Silence: Lectures and Writings* (London: Calder and Boyars, 1968)

Carden-Coyne, Ana. *Reconstructing the Body: Classicism, Modernism and the First World War* (Oxford: Oxford University Press, 2009)

Carsten, F. L. *War against War: British and German Radical Movements in the First World War* (London: Batsford, 1982)

Cecil, Hugh, and Peter Liddle, eds. *At the Eleventh Hour: Reflections, Hopes and Anxieties at the Closing of the Great War, 1918* (Barnsley: Pen and Sword Books, 1998

Cecil, Hugh, and Peter Liddle, eds. *Facing Armageddon: The First World War Experienced* (London: Leo Cooper, 1996)

Cohen, Deborah. *The War Come Home: Disabled Veterans in Britain and Germany 1914–1939* (Berkeley, CA: University of California Press, 2001)

Connelly, Mark. *The Great War, Memory and Ritual: Commemoration in the City and East London, 1916–1939* (Woodbridge: Royal Historical Society/Boydell Press, 2002)

Cork, Richard. *A Bitter Truth: Avant-Garde Art and the First World War* (New Haven, CT: Yale University Press, 1994)

Cross, Robin. *In Memoriam: Remembering the Great War* (London: Ebury, 2008)

Cross, Tim, ed. *Lost Voices of the First World War: An International Anthology of Writers, Poets and Playwrights* (London: Bloomsbury, 1988)

Crouthamel, Jason. *The Great War and German Memory: Society, Politics and Psychological Trauma, 1914–1945* (Exeter: University of Exeter Press, 2009)

Das, Santanu. *Touch and Intimacy in First World War Literature* (Cambridge: Cambridge University Press, 2005)

Das, Santanu, ed. *Race, Empire and First World War Writing* (Cambridge: Cambridge University Press, 2011)

Davis, Belinda. *Home Fires Burning: Food, Politics and Everyday Life in World War I Berlin* (Chapel Hill, NC: University of North Carolina Press, 2000)

DeGroot, Gerard. *Blighty: British Society in the Era of the Great War* (London: Longman, 1996)

Diehl, James and Stephen Ward, eds. *The War Generation: Veterans of the First World War* (Port Washington, NY: Kennikat Press, 1975)

Dülffer, Jost, and Gerd Krumeich, eds. *Der verlorene Frieden. Politik und Kriegskultur nach 1918* (Essen: Klartext, 2002)

Eksteins, Modris. *Rites of Spring: The Great War and the Birth of the Modern Age* (London: Bantam, 1989)

Evans, Martin, and Ken Lunn, eds. *War and Memory in the Twentieth Century* (Oxford: Berg, 1997)

Fell, Alison, and Ingrid Sharp, eds. *The Women's Movement in Wartime: International Perspectives, 1914–19* (Basingstoke: Palgrave, 2007)

Freud, Sigmund. 'Thoughts for the Time on War and Death' (1915), in *Civilization, Society and Religion*, Penguin Freud Library, 12 (Harmondsworth: Penguin, 1985)

Garrett, Richard. *The Final Betrayal: The Armistice 1918 and Afterwards* (Southampton: Buchan and Enright, 1989)

Gilbert, Martin. *First World War* (London: HarperCollins, 1994)

Gilbert, Martin. *The Routledge Atlas of the First World War*, 2nd edn (London: Routledge, 1994)

Gillis, John. *Commemorations: The Politics of National Identity* (Princeton, NJ: Princeton University Press, 1994)

Goebel, Stefan. *The Great War and Medieval Memory: War, Remembrance and Medievalism in Britain and Germany, 1914–1940* (Cambridge: Cambridge University Press, 2007)

Goemans, H. E. *War and Punishment: The Causes of War Termination and the First World War* (Princeton, NJ: Princeton University Press, 2000)

Gregory, Adrian. *The Last Great War: British Society and the First World War* (Cambridge: Cambridge University Press, 2008)

Gregory, Adrian. *The Silence of Memory: Armistice Day 1919–1946* (Oxford: Berg, 1994)

Hammond, Mary, and Shafquat Towheed, eds. *Publishing and the First World War: Essays in Book History* (Basingstoke: Palgrave, 2007)

Hart, Peter. *1918: A Very British Victory* (London: Weidenfeld and Nicolson, 2008)

Herwig, Holger. *The First World War: Germany and Austria-Hungary, 1914–1918* (London: Arnold, 1997)

Hibberd, Dominic, and John Onions, eds. *The Winter of the World: Poems of the Great War* (London: Constable, 2007)

Higonnet, Margaret. 'Authenticity and Art in Trauma Narratives of World War I', *Modernism/Modernity*, 9, 1 (January 2002), 91–107

Hobsbawm, Eric. *Age of Extremes: The Short Twentieth Century, 1914–1991* (London: Michael Joseph, 1994)

Horne, John, ed. *A Companion to World War I* (Oxford: Wiley-Blackwell, 2009)

Horne, John, ed. *State, Society and Mobilisation in Europe during the First World War* (Cambridge: Cambridge University Press, 1997)

Howard, N. P. 'The Social and Political Consequences of the Allied Food Blockade of Germany, 1918–19', *German History* 2, 2 (1993), 161–87

Hüppauf, Bernd. 'Langemarck, Verdun and the Myth of a *New Man* in Germany After the First World War', *War and Society*, 6, 2 (1988), 70–104

Hynes, Samuel. *A War Imagined: The First World War and English Culture* (London: Bodley Head, 1990)

Jaworski, Adam, ed. *Silence: Interdisciplinary Perspectives* (Berlin: Mouton de Gruyter, 1997)

Keene, Jennifer, and Michael Neiberg, eds. *Finding Common Ground: New Directions in First World War Studies* (Leiden: Brill, 2010)

Kendall, Tim. *Modern English War Poetry* (Oxford: Oxford University Press, 2009)

Kennedy, Kate, and Trudi Tate, eds. *First World Studies*, 2, 1 (March 2011), special issue on *Literature and Music of the First World War*

Keynes, John Maynard. *The Economic Consequences of the Peace* (London: Macmillan, 1919)

King, Alex. *Memorials of the Great War in Britain: the Symbolism and Politics of Remembrance* (Oxford: Berg, 1998)

Kitchen, James, Alisa Miller and Laura Rowe, eds. *Other Combatants, Other Fronts: Competing Histories of the First World War* (Newcastle upon Tyne: Cambridge Scholars Press, 2011)

Kramer, Alan. *Dynamic of Destruction: Culture and Mass Killing in the First World War* (Oxford: Oxford University Press, 2007)

Kramer, Lawrence. *Musical Meaning: Toward a Critical History* (New York: Garland, 2000)

Lambert, Constant. *Music Ho! A Study of Music in Decline* (London: Faber and Faber, 1934)

Lawson, Tom. '"The Free-Masonry of Sorrow?" English National Identities and the Memorialization of the Great War in Britain, 1919–1931', *History and Memory*, 20, 1 (Spring/Summer 2008), 89–120

Leed, Eric. *No Man's Land: Combat and Identity in World War I* (Cambridge: Cambridge University Press, 1979)

Lees, Peter. *Shell Shock: Traumatic Neurosis and the British Soldiers of the First World War* (Basingstoke: Palgrave, 2002)

Leichtentritt, Hugo. 'German Music of the Last Decade', *The Musical Quarterly* 10, 2 (April 1924), 193–218

Lerner, Paul. *Hysterical Men: War, Psychiatry and the Politics of Trauma in Germany, 1890–1930* (Ithaca, NY: Cornell University Press, 2003)

Losseff, Nicky, and Jenny Doctor, eds. *Silence, Music, Silent Music* (Aldershot: Ashgate, 2007)

Lowry, Bullitt. *Armistice 1918* (Kent, OH: Kent State University Press, 1997)

McCarthy, Helen. 'The League of Nations, Public Ritual and National Identity in Britain, c. 1919–56', *History Workshop Journal*, 70 (Autumn 2010), 108–32

Malvern, Sue. *Modern Art, Britain and the Great War* (New Haven, CT: Yale University Press, 2004)

Marwick, Arthur. *The Deluge: British Society and the First World War*, 2nd edn (Basingstoke: Macmillan, 1991)

Maurice, Frederick. *The Armistices of 1918* (Oxford: Oxford University Press, 1943)

Meyer, Jessica. *Men of War: Masculinity and the First World War in Britain* (Basingstoke: Palgrave Macmillan, 2008)

Millman, Brock. *Managing Domestic Dissent in First World War Britain* (London: Frank Cass, 2000)

Mosse, George L. *Fallen Soldiers: Reshaping the Memory of the World Wars* (Oxford: Oxford University Press, 1990)

Mottram, R. H. *Ten Years Ago: Armistice and Other Memories, Forming a Pendant to 'The Spanish Farm Trilogy'* (London: Chatto and Windus, 1928)

Moult, Thomas, ed. *Cenotaph: A Book of Remembrance in Poetry and Praise for November the Eleventh* (London: Jonathan Cape, 1923)

Natter, Wolfgang. *Literature at War, 1914–1940: Representing the Time of Greatness in Germany* (New Haven, CT: Yale University Press, 1999)

Noakes, Vivien, ed. *Voices of Silence: The Alternative Book of First World War Poetry* (Stroud: Sutton Publishing, 2007)

Ouditt, Sharon. *Fighting Forces, Writing Women: Identity and Ideology in the First World War* (London: Routledge, 1994)

Ouditt, Sharon. *Women Writers of the First World War: An Annotated Bibliography* (London: Routledge, 2000)

Painter, Karen. *Symphonic Aspirations: German Music and Politics, 1900–1945* (Cambridge, MA: Harvard University Press, 2007)

Parfitt, George. *Fiction of the First World War* (London: Faber and Faber, 1988)

Paris, Michael, ed. *The First World War and Popular Culture, 1914 to the Present* (Edinburgh: Edinburgh University Press, 1999)

Pick, Daniel. *War Machine: The Rationalisation of Slaughter in the Modern Age* (New Haven, CT: Yale University Press, 1996)

Potter, Jane. *Boys in Khaki, Girls in Print: Women's Literary Responses to the Great War 1914–1918* (Oxford: Oxford University Press, 2005)

Pugh, Martin. *We Danced All Night: A Social History of Britain Between the Wars* (London: Bodley Head, 2009)

Raitt, Suzanne, and Trudi Tate, eds. *Women's Fiction and the Great War* (Oxford: Clarendon Press, 1997)

Rhodes, P. J. *Cultures of Commemoration: War Memorials, Ancient and Modern* (Oxford: Oxford University Press/British Academy, 2010)

Roper, Michael. *The Secret Battle: Emotional Survival in the Great War* (Manchester: Manchester University Press, 2009)

Rudin, Harry. *Armistice 1918* (New Haven, CT: Yale University Press, 1944)

Saleeby, C. W. *The Whole Armour of Man: Preventative Essays for Victory in the Great Campaigns of Peace to Come* (London: Grant Richards, 1919)

Savage, Kirk. 'The War Memorial as Elegy', in *The Oxford Handbook of the Elegy*, ed. Karen Weisman (Oxford: Oxford University Press 2010)

Scutts, Joanna. 'Battlefield Cemeteries, Pilgrimage, and Literature after the First World War: The Burial of the Dead', *English Literature in Transition*, 52, 4 (2009), 387–416

Schneider, Uwe and Andreas Schumann, eds. *Krieg der Geister: Erster Weltkrieg und Literarische Moderne* (Würzburg: Königshausen and Neumann, 2000)

Sharp, Alan. *The Versailles Settlement: Peacemaking in Paris, 1919* (Basingstoke: Macmillan, 1991)

Sheffield, Gary. *Forgotten Victory: The First World War, Myths and Realities* (London: Headline Review, 2002)

Shephard, Ben. *A War of Nerves: Soldiers and Psychiatrists 1914–1994* (London: Jonathan Cape, 2000)

Siebrecht, Claudia. *The Aesthetics of Loss: German Women's Art of the First World War* (Oxford: Oxford University Press, 2013)

Simmonds, Alan. *Britain and World War I* (London: Routledge, 2011)

Smith, Angela K. *Suffrage Discourse in Britain During the First World War* (Aldershot: Ashgate, 2005)

Stallworthy, Jon. *Anthem for Doomed Youth* (London: Constable, 2005)

Stallworthy, Jon. *Survivors' Songs: From Maldon to the Somme* (Cambridge: Cambridge University Press, 2008)

Stevenson, David. *With Our Backs to the Wall: Victory and Defeat in 1918* (London: Allen Lane, 2011)

Strachan, Hew. *The First World War* (London: Simon and Schuster, 2003)

Strachan, Hew. 'The First World War as a Global War', *First World War Studies*, 1, 1 (March 2010), 3–14

Strachan, Hew, ed. *The Oxford Illustrated History of the First World War* (Oxford: Oxford University Press, 1998)

Summers, Julie, and Brian Harris. *Remembered: The History of the Commonwealth War Graves Commission* (London: Merrell Publishers, 2007)

Swenarton, Mark. *Homes Fit for Heroes: The Politics and Architecture of Early State Housing in Britain* (London: Heinemann, 1981)

Tate, Trudi. 'The First World War: British Writing', in *The Cambridge Companion to War Writing*, ed. Kate McLaughlin (Cambridge: Cambridge University Press, 2009)

Tate, Trudi. *Modernism, History and the First World War* (Manchester: Manchester Unversity Press, 1998)

Tate, Trudi, ed. *Women, Men and the Great War: An Anthology of Stories* (Manchester: Manchester University Press, 1995)

Tatum, James. *The Mourner's Song: War and Remembrance from the Iliad to Vietnam* (Chicago: University of Chicago Press, 2003)

Todman, Dan. *The Great War: Myth and Memory* (London: Hambledon Continuum, 2005)

Turner, Ian, ed. *Britain and the First World War* (London: Unwin Hyman, 1988)

Tylee, Claire. *The Great War and Women's Consciousness* (Basingstoke: Macmillan, 1990)

Wall, Richard, and J. M. Winter, eds. *The Upheaval of War: Family, Work and Welfare in Europe, 1914–1918* (Cambridge: Cambridge University Press, 1988)

Walther, Peter, ed. *Endzeit Europa. Ein kollektives Tagebuch deutschsprachiger Schriftsteller, Künstler and Gelehrter im Ersten Weltkrieg* (Göttingen: Wallstein Verlag, 2008)

Watkins, Glen. *Proof Through the Night: Music and the Great War* (Berkeley, CA: University of California Press, 2002)

Watson, Alexander. *Enduring the Great War: Combat, Morale and Collapse in the German and British Armies, 1914–1918* (Cambridge: Cambridge University Press, 2008)

Watson, Janet. *Fighting Different Wars: Experience, Memory and the First World War in Britain* (Cambridge: Cambridge University Press, 2004)

Weinstein, Joan. *The End of Expressionism: Art and the November Revolution in Germany, 1918–1919* (Chicago: University of Chicago Press, 1990)

Weintraub, Stanley. *A Stillness Heard Round the World: The End of the Great War, November 1918* (London: Allen and Unwin, 1986)

Wilson, Trevor. *Myriad Faces of War: Britain and the Great War, 1914–1918* (Cambridge: Polity, 1986)

Winter, J. M. *The Great War and the British People* (Basingstoke: Macmillan, 1985)

Winter, J. M. *Remembering War: The Great War between Memory and History in the Twentieth Century* (New Haven, CT: Yale University Press, 2006)

Winter, J. M. *Sites of Memory, Sites of Mourning: The Great War in European Cultural History* (Cambridge: Cambridge University Press, 1995)

Winter, J. M., ed. *The Legacy of the Great War: Ninety Years On* (Columbia, MO: University of Missouri Press, 2009)

Winter, J. M., and Antoine Prost, eds. *The Great War in History: Debates and Controversies, 1914 to the Present* (Cambridge: Cambridge University Press, 2005)

Winter, J. M., and Jean-Louis Robert, eds. *Capital Cities at War: Paris, London, Berlin, 1914–1919* (Cambridge, Cambridge University Press, 1997)

Zerubavel, Eviatar. *The Elephant in the Room: Silence and Denial in Everyday Life* (Oxford: Oxford University Press, 2006)

Ziemann, Benjamin. *War Experiences in Rural Germany, 1914–1923*, trans. Alex Skinner (Oxford: Berg, 2007)

Index

CPSIA information can be obtained at www.ICGtesting.com
Printed in the USA
BVOW08s0935220116

433764BV00003B/11/P

9 781784 99116